The Welfare of the Child

The principle and the law

A study of the meaning, role and functions of the principle as it has evolved within the family law of England and Wales

KERRY O'HALLORAN

Ashgate
ARENA
Aldershot • Brookfield USA • Singapore • Sydney

Published by
Ashgate Publishing Ltd
Gower House
Croft Road
Aldershot
Hants GU11 3HR
England

Ashgate Publishing Company
Old Post Road
Brookfield
Vermont 05036
USA

Ashgate website: http://www.ashgate.com

British Library Cataloguing in Publication Data
O'Halloran, Kerry
The welfare of the child : the principle and the law
1. Children - Legal status, laws, etc. - England 2. Children - Legal status, laws, etc. - Wales 3. Child welfare - Law and legislation - England 4. Child welfare - Law and legislation - Wales
I. Title
344.4'20327

Library of Congress Catalog Card Number: 99-76362

ISBN 1 85742 290 2 (HBK)
ISBN 1 85742 291 0 (PBK)
Printed and bound in Great Britain by MPG Books Ltd, Bodmin, Cornwall

Contents

PART 3
PUBLIC FAMILY LAW

PART 4
PRIVATE FAMILY LAW

PART 5
THE FUTURE ROLE OF THE WELFARE PRINCIPLE: AN INTERNATIONAL PERSPECTIVE

Acknowledgements

This book derives from my longstanding interest in the law as it relates to children. As social worker, lawyer and now academic, I have over the past two decades learned much from the many professionals it has been my privilege to work with. As father to Neil and Connor I continue to learn more.

While it is not feasible to render a full account of the debt owed to the many individuals who contributed in various ways to this study, it would be very wrong not to acknowledge the support and influence of the following. The colleagues, families and children with whom I worked in Causeway H&SS Trust taught me more than I then realised about respect for children. The judiciary of the High Court (FD) and the staff of the Courts Service for Northern Ireland have, over many years, provided opportunities for me to learn from their professionalism. Writers such as J Eekelaar, S Cretney, J Fortin, M Freeman and R Mnookin and others have been a particular source of inspiration. I must also record my gratitude to D Fisher whose thesis *The Concept of the Welfare of the Child*, though read many years ago, first prompted an analytical approach to this subject. My colleagues in the Centre for Voluntary Action Studies at the University of Ulster have been most helpful throughout the prolonged gestation period of this study. My thanks to Arthur Williamson, Nick Acheson, Derek Bacon and John Offer for their friendship and support.

Lastly, in this endeavour as in others, I owe a huge debt of gratitude to my wife Elizabeth.

Kerry O'Halloran
Whitepark Bay
Co Antrim

May 1999.

Introduction

The Welfare of the Child: the Principle and the Law

A Study of the Meaning, Role and Functions of the Principle as it has Evolved Within the Family Law of England & Wales.

The modern dilemma for family law is to strike an appropriate balance between those principles which bind and those which loosen the ties between family members. This conflict has implications as profound and uncertain for the future structure of the courts and the continued viability of some of its oldest jurisdictions as for the future of those who become the subject of family proceedings. Arguments for both camps have rested their case on the welfare of the child.

This book takes an analytical look at the meaning given to the welfare principle, the reasons for the controversy it now attracts and the growing legal significance attached to it. By tracing the principle's evolution over the centuries this book provides a record of the milestones which have shaped its development. By analysing the content of the principle the essence of what has been termed 'the golden thread running through the common law' is disclosed. By considering the ways in which the legal system has shaped and been shaped by the principle it becomes possible to appreciate its structural influence. By identifying and assessing the significance of its present operational role and functions it provides a measure of the impact of this principle on the coherence of modern family law. Finally, by drawing from recent international legislative and judicial developments this book demonstrates the extent to which a common law principle forged in medieval England, having informed the law relating to children in some of the most developed western societies, is now being refracted through such developments to challenge the future shape of family law in the UK.

Part 1 examines the beginnings of the legal relationship between state, child and parents. It traces the emergence of several fundamental age-old social policy dilemmas. How best to set the grounds on which the right of parents to manage the upbringing of their children should give way to a public concern that they do so in a manner which does not endanger a child's welfare? When and how to give an appropriate weighting to the welfare of a child in the context of such other competing considerations as those of justice? What types of conduct, circumstances or materials are so inherently harmful to children that they should be legislatively proscribed? When is a parent entitled to what form of assistance from the state in support of their parenting responsibilities? What are the different responsibilities of first and third parties for safeguarding the welfare of a child? These and other such issues, the integrity and challenge of which have endured across many centuries, are explored in the following three chapters.

This Part identifies and traces the development of key elements in the law's earliest concern for children. It provides a chronological overview of the process whereby the welfare principle came to be established in the law of the UK. It analyses the basis for the distinction made between the public and private dimensions of that principle; as recognised first by the judiciary and then by the legislators. It considers the role and weighting of welfare in relation to other important principles. Finally, it provides an historical record of the emergence of the three legislative strands – private family law, public law and general social welfare law – in which the welfare principle has since evolved. In so doing it outlines the context and sets the parameters for the remainder of the book.

Part 1 leaves the reader with an historical outline of the principle's legal development, a clear picture of its component parts and an understanding of the different rules and proceedings through which the law gives effect to it. By identifying and differentiating between the various elements comprising the legal definition of child welfare, this Part sets the agenda for the book's following thematic approach.

Part 2 acknowledges a major development in the role played by the welfare principle in the modern law as it relates to children. Part 1 charted the principle's evolution from judicial genesis in the courts of Chancery to eventual incorporation in legislation. The principle then functioned largely as a brake to constrain an irresponsible exercise of rights by parent, guardian or stranger and as a litmus test to identify and legislatively proscribe those circumstances, conduct and materials judged to be harmful to children. Part 2 sees the principle grow from a role as determinant of the subject matter for legal processes to its present position of also governing, to some extent, the means whereby the law relates to children. This Part acknowledges that the principle functions not only as a factor or objective in proceedings, but is now so infused within the legal system that it shapes the appropriate structures, governing principles and particular statutory duties common to both public and private law.

Part 2 consists of four chapters which examine the content and structural role of the welfare principle. It begins with a chapter that takes stock of what is meant by the welfare of the child; it identifies and assesses its primary ingredients as disclosed by caselaw. The next chapter considers the ways in which the principle affects the legal system as it now relates to children under the Children Act 1989; the jurisdiction and operation of the courts, access and the governing rules and principles. The final two chapters focus on the ways in which the legal system gives effect to the principle by providing for the identification and representation, respectively, of matters having a bearing on a child's welfare interests; attention is given to the role of the child, other parties and the range of professionals now engaged in bringing welfare interests before the court.

This Part thereby lays a foundation for Parts 3 and 4 which examine the distinctive operational features of public and private family law in some detail.

Part 3 examines the role and functions given to the welfare principle in public law, as represented almost exclusively the Children Act 1989, which governs coercive and consensual intervention by the state in matters affecting the upbringing of a child. The objective is to explore the way in which the law defines the content of the principle in this context and provides mechanisms for applying it. Attention is give to identifying the degree of discretion available to court and local authority in their respective management of the disposal options available to give effect to the welfare interests of particular children. It also pursues themes about the balance between the welfare principle and other principles and considerations. For example, it considers the right of a parent to determine how best to rear their child and their entitlement to state support while doing so. It also considers the interface between the principles of justice and welfare and the realities of welfare in criminal and child protection proceedings.

Part 3 consists of four chapters which deal in turn with each of the previously identified hallmarks of the principle in a public law context (care, control, protection, prevention and promotion). It examines them in the light of governing legislative provisions, the specific powers and duties involved and actual judicial and professional practice. In relation to each it identifies and assesses the different thresholds for coercive and ameliorative intervention by the state in relation to welfare matters, the rights and discretionary powers of the parties to define what constitutes such matters, and the indicators of success/failure in respect of intervention. It considers the type of authority (prescriptive, discretionary etc), the weighting (first consideration, paramount etc) and the priority (objective of, or a factor in, proceedings) relied upon to give effect to the principle. It identifies and assesses the representation of a child's welfare interests and rights in the context of coercive proceedings and when 'in care'. It considers the outcomes of the different proceedings in terms of their capacity to benefit the child concerned.

Part 4 identifies the formal place and role given to the principle in a private family law context, on matters affecting the upbringing of a child and examines the functions it performs. For most purposes, this involves considering specific provisions of the Children Act 1989 and the powers, duties and areas of discretion which it provides to govern the choices available to the court, the parties and the children concerned. It takes each of the relevant previously identified hallmarks of the principle (direct care responsibility, contact, maintenance etc), considers the governing legislative provisions and assesses how they are applied in actual judicial and professional practice. This Part examines the changing legal balance between child welfare and parental rights with particular attention to the growth in rights of a 'mature minor' and an unmarried father and to the rights now available to a carer, sibling, grandparent etc. Particular attention is given to the *locus standi* of the child in private family law, their right to initiate or participate in proceedings and the significance of his or her consent in relation to decisions affecting their interests. An assessment is made of the differential application of the welfare principle as the basis for state intervention in private law proceedings.

Part 4 consists of three chapters dealing with parenting arrangements in contested and uncontested proceedings and in adoption. It explores modern developments in the balance traditionally struck between child welfare and parental rights, with particular reference to the current selective application of the paramountcy principle. The difficulties inherent in ensuring that intervention is welfare related and that outcomes are compatible with welfare are examined. It analyses the change of emphasis from an adjudicative to an adjustive judicial function and relates this and the growth in influence of mediatory professions to the central problem of whether welfare factors are amenable to 'objectification' and 'once-off' decision-making processes. It raises the question as to whether judicial process is giving way to administration.

Part 5, by way of conclusion, considers the implications for the future role and functions of the welfare principle within the family law of the UK arising from recent developments originating outside the jurisdiction. It draws from a growing body of international material, as contrasted with indigenous legislation and caselaw, to establish the main precepts upon which the principle now rests and to identify the resulting issues facing family law in the UK. It considers, in particular, the extent to which the principle's paramountcy weighting has threatened the foundations upon which family law has been constructed. It suggests that this development may have distanced the child welfare orientation of family law in the UK from the concern to sustain family unity which is more characteristic of the European Conventions. It considers the inherent complexities and, to some extent, the contradictions involved in the tensions between the legal rights of children and their welfare interests.

Part 5 consists of two chapters one dealing with the international influences which shaped and continue to have a bearing upon the modern role of welfare interests in UK law and the other considering its future role within that law. A record is compiled of the considerable range of sources of international influence. An analysis is provided of their influence on welfare interests in both the public and private family law of the UK. An assessment is then made of the content, role and weighting of welfare interests. Consideration is given to how the latter relate to other interests and how the welfare interests of children compare with their rights. Finally, this Part and the book conclude with a brief examination of the arguments for a family court as a means of bringing more integration and coherence to the law as it relates to the welfare interests of children.

Part 1: The Legal Origins of Child Welfare

Introduction to Part 1

Prior to the Judicature Act 1873 the courts of equity assumed a paternalistic jurisdiction as guardian in respect of children and others with legal incapacity. Afterwards, following the statutory fusion of the courts of equity and common law, the *parens patriae* power of the former became available to the judiciary of all superior courts. The welfare of the child was thereafter a matter to be judicially addressed, in accordance with principles established through centuries of caselaw in the courts of equity, whether the child was before the court on foot of proceedings of a statutory, common law or of an equitable nature.

In the decades following the introduction of the 1873 Act many of the rules established by common law and equity were displaced or augmented by statutes regulating parental conduct and defining the grounds on which the state could intervene in parenting matters. Three separate and distinct strands of legislation developed in which the welfare principle was explicitly represented: private family law, mostly concerned with proceedings for custody, guardianship and adoption; public family law, concerning criminal proceedings and care, protection and control issues; and general national health, safety and social care law. The mode of state intervention in family life then established and regulated by statute was either coercive or consensual. These alternative approaches and their accompanying legal characteristics continued thereafter to provide the hallmarks of contemporary legislation as it related to the welfare interests of a child.

1 State Recognition of Child Welfare: Feudalism; the Common Law; and the Poor Laws

Introduction

The history of the principle of the welfare of the child predates the present formal division of family law into its public and private sectors. This chapter traces the principle's origins back to an era characterised by the fusion of both sectors in the law of feudal England. Then, as in modern totalitarian states, any significant re-ordering of family property or adjustment to inter-family allegiances was a 'public' matter requiring endorsement by the ruling authority. Where the interests of a child became entangled with the rights of an adult to property or with the latter's duty to provide services to lord or king, the royal courts could readily be persuaded to take an interest in that child. During that era certain basic hallmarks of the principle emerged and its formulation within the legal construct of guardianship became established.

Subsequently, parental death, absence, incapacity or destitution prompted the common law and the poor laws to lay the foundations for the role of the state as guardian/parent of last resort. From a developing common law jurisprudence concerning the grounds justifying a voluntary or compulsory transfer of child welfare responsibilities from family to state grew a body of caselaw and eventually of statute law dealing more particularly with the grounds for compulsory transfer within the family, most usually between a child's parents.

The modern sophisticated legislative framework, regulating and differentiating the role of the welfare principle in public and private transfers of responsibility for the care of a child, has its origins in ancient caselaw concepts and constructs. This chapter sets out to identify and examine those early beginnings.

Feudal England: wards and their guardians

The feudal system being predicated on territory, entailing the loyalty and knight service of the major landowners, gave particular attention to the protection of infant successors. Maintaining the *status quo* in terms of territorial power and knight fealty was central to the rigid hierarchical social structure and institutions of the feudal system. During the middle ages a child in England, without an interest in land, was scarcely recognised by the law. Where property was involved, however, then the law extended protection to the interests of children almost exclusively through the constructs of wardship and guardianship. The earliest forms of guardianship, known as guardian in chivalry and guardian in socage, derived directly from the carefully regimented structure of social relationships that comprised the feudal system.[1]

Guardians in chivalry and socage

The protection of a young heir's right to inherit property, and with it the protection of his inherited duty of fealty to his lord, were initially the main purposes of guardianship. Until the abolition of the military tenures and the Court of Wards and Liveries in 1660, this was achieved through guardianship in chivalry; where land was held in knight service. So, when land was inherited by an unmarried male heir under 21, or ward, the lord's duty to provide for his maintenance was balanced by his right to custody of the ward's person and land until the latter reached the age of majority. Wardship was thus a property right in the hands of the lord; it was transmissible and saleable; custody moreover could be delegated to a third person. Guardianship in socage was conceptually similar; where the next-of-kin was guardian of an infant who held land by socage tenure. But the common law courts had no power to appoint guardians. Testamentary guardians also were largely unrecognised by the common law.

There were differences between guardianship in chivalry and guardianship in socage: they terminated at different ages (chivalry at 21, socage at 14); the office of guardian in socage was not so freely transmissible as that of guardian in chivalry. The latter difference is particularly significant. Although guardians in chivalry and in socage were liable to protect, maintain and educate their ward, the guardian in chivalry seems to have been concerned largely if not entirely with his own interest in the office. On the other hand, the law of guardianship in socage "was settled at any early period with some regard for the welfare of the ward himself". Guardianship in socage was "admitted to be a personal trust wholly for the infant's benefit..." This form of guardianship had no opportunity to influence the development of the law until guardianship in chivalry (which tended to benefit the lords not the wards) faded with the abolitition of military tenures and the Court of Wards and Liveries in 1660.

Guardians by nature and by nurture

Prior to the 18th century, the welfare doctrine took the form of a duty placed upon parents/guardians and enforced by the feudal institutions recognised by the law. This duty was rooted in the feudal inter-relationship between concepts of seisin and property. From this conceptual context, where a child was seen almost as an item of property,[2] evolved the beginnings of guardianship. The political and social institutions of the feudal system provided not only for the protection of the property of children but also for the care and protection of the individual child. The medieval concept of guardianship was as much concerned with the child's person, and hence his welfare, as with his property. However, the rules governing guardianship by nature only applied to children who were heirs apparent to the family estate, almost always the elder surviving legitimate male child and lasted until he reached the age of 21. This restriction seems to have been prompted by a concern for ensuring an orderly succession to land and gave the guardian the duty to protect the interest of the deceased by rules which provided for guardianship directions regarding arrangements for the marriage of the heir apparent. The powers of guardians were basically directed towards limiting the lord's interest in the child's inheritance.

All other children fell under the only other type of guardianship known to the common law: guardianship by nurture. This concept was founded upon a parental duty to care for their children rather than any desire to secure a child's inheritance. It was restricted unambiguously to "government of the person". As explained by Bowen LJ in *In re Agar-Ellis*:[3]

> The strict common law gave to the father the guardianship of his children during the age of nurture and until the age of discretion. The limit was fixed at fourteen years in the case of a boy and sixteen years in the case of a girl, but beyond this ....the father had no actual guardianship except only in the case of the heir apparent, in which case he was guardian by nature till twenty one.

In certain circumstances it was also available to the child's mother. If the father had appointed testamentary guardians the mother had no right to interfere with them. If, however, no such guardian had been appointed by the father then the mother became guardian by nature and nurture. If the child was illegitimate then the mother had a *prima facie* right, though not absolute, to custody until the child reached the age of fourteen; enforceable against all other persons, including the putative father.

By the middle ages the law relating to children was conceived almost entirely in terms of guardianship or wardship. Not until the Tenures Abolition Act 1660 did statute law make reference to guardianship. It then provided that a guardian should have responsibility for the custody and tuition of the child in question and should:

> ...take into [their] ...custody to the use of such child...the profits of all lands, tenements and hereditaments of such child...and also the custody, tuition, management of the goods, chattels and personal estate of the child...and [could] bring such action in relation thereto as by law a guardian in common socage might do.

Following the abolition of military tenures and the Court of Wards and Liveries in 1660, the more child-biased rules of guardianship in socage, by nature and by nurture, became the means whereby the law could outreach its feudal origins. This development is evident in such earlier authorities as *Frederick v Frederick* [4] and *Duke of Beaufort v Berty* [5] where the idea of a guardian as a trustee for the benefit of the child seems to be the underpinning principle. In the words of West LC in 1724:

> At common law, before the statute...by which the Court of Wards and Liveries was erected, the Lord Chancellor was the sole judge of wardships; but with this difference, that where they were lucrative to the Crown, there the Lord Treasurer acted, who had a concurrent jurisdiction with the Chancellor; but where wardships were not lucrative to the Crown, but only for the benefit of the ward, then the Chancellor alone had the disposition and management of the ward; therefore as the law now stands, the *onera feudorum* being extinct, and the Court of Wards abolished, and all the old tenures being turned into free and Common Socage, all wardships which are beneficial for the wards must return to this court as to the original fountain.

Thus the benefit of the ward lay first in the ward's relationship with the guardian, the 'private trust'; and secondly in the supervisory jurisdiction of the Chancellor over the guardian, the 'public trust'.

The whole ethos of the equitable jurisdiction in England may well be founded upon a 'public trust' idea: the acceptance of a public responsibility for the well-being of children. This notion of public responsibility, albeit limited in nature, scope and application, appears to have been one of the foundations upon which the later structure of the law, both common law and equitable, was erected.

The Common Law: parental rights, duties and child welfare

The common law respect for paternal authority was itself a legacy from Roman times founded on the doctrine of *patria potestas*. The edict of Emperor Justinian in 560 AD had abolished the doctrine and the legal concept of an autonomous patriarchical family unit, but in Britain its hallmarks lived on to underpin feudal society and to become absorbed into the common law. Some of the more characteristic features of this doctrine included: the private autonomous household ruled by the father, the actual or virtual ownership of children, the blood tie, filial piety, the power and limits of corporal punishment, the expectation of maintenance and the diminished relationship between child and state. Parents were guardians of their children as of right, a right which included a custodial authority based on a ownership of the child. After Justinian's edict, parents were left with the right, and perhaps the duty, to control a wayward child by chastisement but more serious transgressions were a public rather than private matter and the state would intervene to bring the child before the courts. Parents were also left with the duty to maintain their children.

The common law, like that of ancient Rome, was essentially grounded on the rights and duties of the individual. There was no sense of collective legal interests, no provision made for class or community actions; the law consisted of categories of causes actionable by or against individuals. It did recognise, and placed great importance upon, legal status. In the context of the family, this meant that it focussed on the individual with rights, the father, and then on the legal status if any of the others involved. The recognition given to the father with marital status was all important. The *locus standi* of this individual in common law was very powerful, that of others involved as members of his marital family were given recognition but those without status (as mistress or non-marital child) were denied any. The common law gave no recognition to an illegitimate child. The marital family unit was also denied any collective *locus standi*. Any actionable rights, in relation to the members of his autonomous marital family unit, belonged to the father. Thus, for example, for centuries he had the right to sue a third party for the loss of services to which he was entitled as father or spouse.

The common law courts enforced parental authority, subject to very few limitations. Parental rights underpinned the jurisdictions of both equity and the King's Bench. Disqualification from those rights rested, in varying degrees, on grounds provided by the welfare principle; albeit a negative interpretation of welfare.

Doctrine of paternal rights

By the middle of the 19th century the doctrine of paternal rights was firmly established. The judiciary had moved away from the earlier principle of guardianship, parental or otherwise, as being rooted in a concept of 'trust' or 'office'. Instead this had been displaced by a concept of paternal authority. The evolution of guardianship from a concern with nature and nurture to something approximating an 'office of parenthood' had by Blackstone's time reverted to something similar to the doctrine of *patria potestas*. This was an important change of direction; the welfare of a child was no longer viewed as entrusted as a duty to parent or guardian but as an inherently vested aspect of paternal authority.

At common law the *prima facie* right of a father to the control and custody of his legitimate children, subject to an absence of abuse,[6] was virtually impregnable. It was absolute as against the mother.[7] The approach of the common law was reflected clearly by the judgment of Lord Ellenborough for the Court of King's Bench in *De Manneville v De Manneville*:[8]

> We draw no inference to the disadvantage of the father. But he is the person by law entitled to the custody of his child. If he abuses that right to the detriment of the child, the court will protect the child. But there is no pretence that the child has been injured from want of nurture or in any other respect. Thus he having a legal right to the custody of his child and not having abused that right is entitled to have it restored to him.

The rationale for judicial insistence on vesting over-riding authority in fathers in respect of matters affecting the upbringing of their children was later articulated by Cotton LJ in *In re Agar-Ellis; Agar-Ellis v Lascelles*:[9]

> This Court holds the principle that when by birth a child is subject to a father, it is for the general interest of families, and for the general interest of children, and really for the interest of the particular infant, that the Court should not, except in very extreme cases, interfere with the discretion of a father, but leave to him the responsibility of exercising that power which nature has given him by birth of the child.

A view endorsed by James LJ when, on delivering the decision of the Court of Appeal, added:

> The right of the father to the custody and control of his children is one of the most sacred rights.

In this judgment, which treated paternal authority as almost absolute in the absence of any misconduct, the high water mark was reached for paternal rights. Paternal authority had evolved in consequence of the inadequacies of the feudal common law. Its principal characteristics concerned the paternal right to custody of a child and the accompanying rights to determine religious upbringing and education.

The strength of the paternal right to custody[10] applied only to legitimate children. The Court of King's Bench became involved only if an attempt were made to enforce that right.[11] Until 1839 the custody of a legitimate child vested automatically and exclusively in the father. As head of the family he had the right to administer reasonable chastisement to his child.[12] His status was also the basis of the action for enticement.[13] Kidnapping a child was viewed essentially as an infringement of the paternal right to custody.[14] Such was the stringent judicial approach to the legal standing of the father that the courts would not permit a father to avoid his parental responsibilities by voluntarily giving up his right to custody and control.[15] No separation agreement - purporting to regulate the future care, custody, education and maintenance of his children - would be enforced by the court against a father as this was viewed as an attempt "to fetter and abandon his parental power" and "repugnant entirely to his parental duty".[16] Where the welfare of a child was referred to as a factor in the judicial determination of such cases, it was only to justify judicial control of the father.

The resolve with which the courts defended the doctrine of paternal rights, created in relation to custody, was also evident in issues relating to the religion of a child.[17] A father had the right to determine questions relating to the religious upbringing of his child[18] who had to be brought up in his religion even though, if deceased, had left no directions to that effect.[19] In *In re Scanlan, Infants* [20] Stirling J decided that the 1886 Act made no difference to the father's right to decide in his lifetime the appropriate religious upbringing for his children or to the guardian's duty after his death to ensure that the children were trained in the father's religion. Only evidence of paternal abuse or neglect would result in judicial refusal to enforce a father's right to determine religious upbringing,[21] where the court refused to allow a father, unfit to have custody, the right to determine religious upbringing. However, parental control of the child's religion - which could possibly restrict judicial endorsement of the welfare approach - failed to survive the 1925 Act.[22] Indeed, in *In re JM Carroll (An Infant)*[23] the court ruled that s 1 of the 1925 Act required that in an inter-parental dispute priority should be given to the welfare interests of the child at the expense, if necessary, of either parent's views on religion.

The duty to educate was overshadowed by the paternal right to decide on the child's religious education. Any interference with the right of the father to control his child's education met with consistent judicial approbation.[24] So strong was this right that the cases only record issues arising in relation to the religious education of children whose fathers were dead. In *Hawkesworth v Hawkesworth*[25] the court held that it had no alternative but to give effect to the

Protestant father's stated wishes regarding his child's religious education, even though he had died 8 years earlier, leaving no specific directions, and the child had since been brought up by her Catholic mother. In *Andrews v Salt*[26] Mellish J considered that unless the father had disqualified himself in some way, the court was obliged to give effect to his wishes.

Habeas corpus proceedings, a common law remedy, became one of the principal methods for enforcing the evolving paternal power. However, *habeas corpus* could not be used to assist a father to regain custody of a child (ie person below the age of 21) who had reached the "age of discretion" (14 for boys, 16 for girls) against the latter's will.

Parental duties

The relationship between parents, their children and criminal activity was relatively uncomplicated under common law. A child would be held responsible and accountable for his or her criminal behaviour and like an adult could be sentenced to prison, flogging, transportation or hanging. A parent was not responsible for their child's crimes, unless as an accomplice or under the usual rules of principal and agent.

In addition, however, the common law recognised a specific duty particular to the parental relationship: the duty to provide for a child. As Sir W Blackstone stated:[27]

> The duty of parents to provide for the maintenance of their children is a principle of natural law; an obligation ....laid on them not only by nature herself, but by their own proper act, in bringing them into the world....

This duty was underpinned by the criminal law. The common law evolved a number of criminal offences particular to children and their parents. They were focussed not on the welfare of a child but on the abuse of a parental right; welfare was legally recognised only in an obverse relationship to parental right. A conviction would ensure court removal not just of custody but of all parental rights in respect of the child. These offences share the common feature of providing only for a negative recognition of the principle of the welfare of the child; not until it was irretrievably breached did the courts acknowledge the relevance of welfare. The common law was never prepared to concede that a positive welfare advantage to the child would in itself provide grounds for displacing the parental right. Parental culpability alone set the threshold for state intervention on behalf of child welfare.

Firstly, the criminal law recognised that offences of assault, neglect, murder or manslaughter could be committed against children, by parents or third parties. The common law charge of assault was used by prosecutors. Thus putting a child in a bag and leaving it suspended on palings[28] or exposing a child in inclement weather[29] were treated as assault. Any person failing to implement the duty upon them to supply the child with food and clothing so that the child died could well be guilty of murder or manslaughter.[30] The same conduct would subsequently be prosecuted as an offence of neglect under the 1933 Act, even where death resulted.

Secondly, the criminal law was used to prosecute for the offence of cruel and unnatural treatment. In practice there was a fairly close affinity between the common law offences of cruel and unnatural treatment and neglect. The latter, however, was then and remains now a fairly flexible and indeterminate offence. Cruel and unnatural treatment is a more definite concept, although it too is broad in application. There are several common law cases featuring children being beaten, left out in the cold, cold water poured over them etc.

Thirdly, there was the criminal offence of endangering a child. There would seem to be little doubt that it was and remains an offence at common law for a child to be treated in such a way that his or her life is endangered. Mere possibility of injury has long been sufficient. For example, in *HMA v Jane Thom*[31] the mother allegedly threw the child from a railway carriage in motion. The charge was endangering the child's life and assault to the danger of life. The court decided that actual injury was unnecessary to establish danger to life. Such an offence clearly had the effect of protecting the physical welfare of the child. The genesis of the modern law relating to child protection, particularly the concept of 'likelihood of significant harm' can be traced to this common law offence and the resulting caselaw.

Finally, the last common law offence which directly protected welfare was the charge of confining and imprisoning a child. The classic instance is *HMA v Fairweather*[32] where a child was kept for three weeks in a purpose built wooden cage in an unheated outhouse. The child's life was endangered and she was reduced to almost total idiocy. These circumstances constituted confinement or imprisonment; also elements of cruel and unnatural treatment, endangering life and neglect.

The flexibility and inter-changeability of the common law charges are evident in the above illustrations. As has been pointed out:

> The common law is not a system of rigid rules, but of principles, whose application may alter over time, and which themselves may be modified. It may, and should, be renewed by succeeding generations of judges, and so meet the needs of a society that is itself subject to change.[33]

The Poor Laws: the state as guardian of last resort

Pinchbeck, maintained that:[34]

> ...the 20th century conception of the duty of the state towards the child has its origins, not in the reforming movement of the 19th century, but in the paternalistic policy of the Tudor state.

He considered that by the 16th century Parliament had established principles to govern the relationship between the state and the child similar to those currently applicable. In particular he identified two such principles which seem to be embodied by the Poor Laws:[35]

> The children of vagrant and demoralised parents were to be removed from parental control and placed in a new environment to secure their welfare. And finally, the state accepted in principle the responsibility for securing the proper treatment and training of the children thus brought into community care.

From 1572 a system of parish relief had been available for the destitute. This was extended by the Elizabethan legislation of 1597-1601which provided for the appointment of parish overseers to work with local churchwardens and raise the funds necessary to assist all classes of destitute persons. The modern concern of the state for the welfare of children, as vulnerable citizens as opposed to young heirs, was legislatively introduced in England at the beginning of the seventeenth century with the Act for the Relief of the Poor 1601. This was adjusted by subsequent legislation and ultimately regulated by the Poor Law Commissioners under powers vested in them by the Poor Law Amendment Act 1834.

State intervention in standards of parental care

This new public concern for children, evidenced in the Poor Laws, stemmed from a state interest in avoiding bearing the cost for their upbringing. The primary characteristics of these early beginnings in state intervention on child welfare grounds were a focus on parental responsibility, a negative interpretation of child welfare and a reliance on the good offices of voluntary organisations.

One of the more explicit purposes of the Poor Law legislation was to enforce, wherever possible, parental responsibility for the care and maintenance of children. Parents, with the means, were required to provide for their children. Otherwise parents were left to determine a child's welfare as they saw fit; unless they transgressed the criminal law by, for example, willfully neglecting to provide adequate food, clothing, medical aid or lodging for them or t them as thieves. Parenting standards that breached the criminal law always make the future care arrangements of children a matter warranting coercive state intervention (see above).

The Poor Laws significantly extended the state interest in parenting standards by making the fact of child need itself, rather than its cause, a sufficient threshold for voluntary state intervention. Parental culpability was not a necessary prerequisite for the transfer of a child from private to public responsibility. Parents unable or unwilling to continue caring could voluntarily place their children with the Poor Law authorities. Once in care, parental rights could be assumed by the authorities under s 1(1) of the Poor Law Act 1889,[36] subject to subsequent judicial confirmation.

Poverty was most often the root cause of parental failure necessitating coercive state intervention, by Poor Law guardians, to remove children from parental care and commit them to the care of the state. The destitution of whole communities resulted in a high infant mortality rate and very many parents being unable to provide adequately for their children. The welfare of a child, often the life of a child, was itself the criteria for state intervention and state assumption of care responsibility; parental failure was not necessarily associated with parental fault or culpable default in care standards; the transfer of parental responsibility to the state was often voluntary. But, as in the criminal law, not until a child's welfare had been impaired did the state initiate intervention and future care arrangements then become a matter of public rather than private law.

The influence of various philanthropic societies during the period governed by the Poor Laws laid the foundation for the development of their modern role in relation to child welfare. Most charities and other voluntary and religious organisations, particularly the Quakers, provided alms, accommodation or distributed food to the destitute without any particular regard for the separate and distinct needs of children. Not until the end of the nineteenth century did child welfare voluntary organisations make an appearance. Organisations such as Dr Barnardo's and the NSPCC began their current specialist services for children by developing a 'child rescue' approach to those who were abandoned, impoverished or ill-treated in the era of the Poor Laws. Their intervention, being on a voluntary rather than a coercive basis, was probably more acceptable than that of the state to the families concerned.

State intervention on 'child rescue' grounds often had to be followed up by a state assumption of care responsibility for the children concerned. The Poor Laws era introduced the formal role of the state as public guardian of child welfare. A role evidenced by the beginnings of statutory criteria for the state to formally acquire care responsibility for children, schemes for boarding-out orphans and the children of destitute mothers and the provision of residential homes for children permanently separated from their parents.

Conclusion

The common law of England grew out of proprietary concepts. From beginnings rooted in guardianship of the heir's interest in inherited property it gradually expanded to include a concern for the child's person. It emphasised the rights of the individual – providing for paternal rather than familial rights – and it shaped the basic law applied in the wardship jurisdiction. The constructs which came to underpin the statute law relating to child protection such as neglect, abandonment, exposure and ill-treatment had their origins in the common law. The approach of objectively proscribing conduct and circumstances judged to be detrimental to a child's welfare interests, setting thresholds for state intervention and determination by adjudication without recourse to discretion were all characteristics of the common law before they became assimilated into statute law.

Many of the indices of welfare interests and their parameters are also clearly traceable to the same origins. The significance of age groups, the separateness of criminal responsibility and the 'blood-tie' person were established in the early days of the common law as were provision of home and maintenance, education, religious upbringing, chastisement and custody of the person. Again, the importance attached to the status of the parties first emerged in a common law context as did the obverse legal relationship between parental rights and child welfare and legal recognition of welfare as a negative rather than positive concept; only justifying action after the child concerned had suffered harm.

A rudimentary differentiation between public and private responsibilities in respect of child welfare was clearly established at common law. Respect for the privacy of the family was embedded in the doctrine of paternal rights. The concept of the state as guardian of last resort, accessed by voluntary parental relinquishment of children and given effect by residential care or boarding out was statutorily introduced by the Poor Laws. The association between community poverty, the welfare of the child and public care has endured for centuries in England and Wales, as elsewhere.

Notes

1 See *Morgan v Dillon* (1724) 9 Modern 135 at p 141 per West LC.

2 See, for example, *Lecone v Sheires* (1686) 1 Vernon 442 where the father granted the guardianship of his child in security for a debt).

3 (1878) 10 Ch D.

4 (1721) 1 Peere Williams 711.

5 1 Peere Williams 703 at p 139.
6 See *Re Thomasset* [1894] 300.
7 See *Ex parte Skinner*, 9 Moo 278; Simpson on Infants, 2 nd ed {1908), p 115.
8 1804, 10 Vessey Junior 52.
9 (1878) 10 Ch D 49 (CA), at p 334).
10 See *De Mannerville v De Mannerville, op cit.*
11 See *R v Greenhill* (1836) 4 Adolphus and Ellis 624.
12 See *Gardner v Bygrave* [1889] 6 TLR 23 DC, *Mansell v Griffin* [1908] 1 KB, 160, *obiter*, *R v Hopley* [1860] 2F and F 160.
13 See *Lough v Ward* [1954] 2 All ER 338; this remained the case until abolished by s 5 of the Law Reform (Miscl Prov) Act 1970.
14 See, for example, *R v Hale* [1974] 1 All ER 1107 it was alleged that the accused had "unlawfully secreted ...a girl aged 13 years, against the life of her parents and lawful guardians."
15 See *St John v St John* (1805) 11 Vessey 530 and *Vansittart v Vansittart* (1858) 2 De Gex and Jones 249 at p 256; *Hamilton v Hector* (1872) LR 13 Equity 511.
16 See *Van v Van* p 259, per Turner LJ.
17 See *Re Bessant* (1879) 11 Ch D 508 and *In re Grey* [1902] 2 IR 684 at p 691.
18 See *Re Browne, a minor* [1852], 2 ICR 151 and *Hawkesworth v Hawkesworth* LR 6 Ch 542 and *In re O'Hara* [1900] 2 IR 684 and *F v F* [1902], 1 Ch 688 and *Re Agar-Ellis* op cit.
19 See *Talbot v Shrewsbury*, 4 My and Cr 672; *Re Montague* 28 Ch D 82.
20 (1888) LR 40 Ch D 200.
21 See *Re Newton (Infants)* [1896] 1 Ch 740.
22 See *Re Collins (An Infant)* [1950] Ch 498.
23 [1931] 1 KB 317.
24 See *Re Agar-Ellis* [1883] 24 Ch D 317, *In re May: Eggar v May* [1917] 2 Ch 126 and also *Hawkesworth v Hawkesworth* (1871) LR 6 Ch App 539.
25 *Op cit.*
26 (1873) LR 8 Ch App 622.
27 See *Commentaries on the Laws of England*, Oxford, Clarendon Press,1765.
28 See *R v March* (1844) 1 Carrington and Kirwan 496.
29 See *R v Ridley* (1811) 2 Campbell 650.
30 See, for example, *R v Bubb; R v Hook* (1850) 4 Cox CC 455.
31 (1876) 3 Couper 332.
32 (1842) 1 Brown 309.
33 See Laws J in *C (A Minor) v DPP* [1994] 3 WLR 888 at pp 897-898.
34 See *The State and the Child in 16th Century England -II* (1957) at p 72.
35 *Op cit* at p 59.
36 Continued by s 52 of the Poor Law Act 1930 and subsequently by s 2 of the Children Act 1948. This power was regarded by the Curtis Committee as a "very important provision" (para 19) and in 1945 about 16% of children in the care of poor law authorities had been the subject of a s 52 resolution (*ibid* para 29). This was later echoed by the Houghton Committee (para 153).

2 Judicial Acknowledgement of Guardianship Duties: the Jurisdiction of Equity

Introduction

The welfare interests of a child, as a factor in proceedings concerning his or her upbringing, rested from the outset on judicial rather than legislative initiative.

This chapter examines particular judicial initiatives to recognise and further the development of the welfare principle occurring during the period framed by two statutes which, in this context, proved to be of exceptional importance: the Tenures Abolition Act 1660 and the Judicature Act 1873. The role of the Court of Chancery in relation to guardian, parent and child, where their interests are in conflict, lies at the heart of this chapter. It considers the period when the courts of common law and of equity developed separately. Particular attention is given to the degree of commonality in the principles applied by the judiciary towards guardians and parents taken in guardianship and custody proceedings respectively. It examines also the link between welfare interests and the duty of care owed to a child by parent or guardian. The rise and entrenchment of the countervailing doctrine of parental rights, or more accurately of paternal rights, is also considered.

Equity and the Tenures Abolition Act 1660

The Tenures Abolition Act 1660 abolished military and similar tenures and the Court of Wards and Liveries. This statute formally marked the end of the feudal system. Its demise opened up the Court of Chancery enabling it to entertain wardship applications in respect of children other than the young male heirs whose property rights had been so important to the maintenance of the rigid hierarchical social relationships that characterised feudalism. Until then, the jurisdiction of the Chancellor had been largely ineffective. In the opinion of Pollock and Maitland, the common law of guardianship was "disjointed and incomplete". The law, they indicated,

> ...had been thinking almost exclusively in terms of infant heirs, and had left other infants to shift for themselves...The law had not even been careful to give the father a right to the custody of his children....[1]

After 1660 the way was clear for equitable principles to have a dramatic impact upon the legal position of children.[2] The legislative intent, underpinning s 8 of the Tenures Abolition Act 1660, was to give firm endorsement to the authority of a father in respect of the children of his marriage. It conferred wide powers on fathers but, significantly, did not refer to the powers in terms of wardship or guardianship. That section empowered a father 'to dispose of the custody and tuition of such child or children (those under 21)' with the effect that

> ...such disposition ...shall be good and effective against all and every person or persons claiming the custody or tuition of such child or children as guardian in socage or otherwise.

This provision, as noted by Lord Penzance,[3] authorised the father to "dispose of the custody of the child as he thinks fit." The year 1660 thus saw not only the end of the feudal concept of wardship but also the emerging importance of paternal rights particularly the right to custody.

Chancery

According to Holdsworth, the generally accepted view is that the Chancellor's powers were based

> ...not on any inherent jurisdiction, but upon a special delegation by the Crown of its prerogative right, as *parens patriae*, of looking after their (infant's) interests.[4]

The modern duty of the state to extend protection to those incapable of protecting their own interests evolved from the ancient duty of the Crown to protect the person and the property interests of a subject who not being fully *sui juris* lacked the legal capacity of other subjects. In practice this was due to their being mentally handicapped or a child. The King was regarded as the natural protector of those without kin;[5] apparently this had a statutory foundation. Royal protection was, in particular, given to young heirs, usually orphans, during their childhood. From this prerogative right of the Crown, tied to direct knight service[6] derived the inherent jurisdiction of the court to make a child a ward of court.

This duty in practice rested on the Lord Chancellor who initially delegated it to the Court of Wards and Liveries until 1660 when it passed to the Court of Chancery.[7] As was stated by Lord Cranworth LC in *Hope v Hope*:[8]

> It is the interest of the State and of the Sovereign that children should be properly brought up and educated; and according to the principle of our law, the Sovereign, as *parens patriae*, is bound to look to the maintenance and education (as far as it has the means of judging) of all his subjects.

The Court of Chancery, exercising the *parens patriae* jurisdiction, conferred the protection of wardship on its young charges and appointed a guardian to bear day-to-day care and protection responsibilities. From the outset wardship was concerned with protecting the person as well as the property of its wards. After the 1660 statute, however, the exercise of this jurisdiction for welfare purposes became increasingly, less dependant upon whether or not a ward had rights to property. The primary object of the wardship jurisdiction has always been to protect those who owe allegiance to the Crown. Hence, historically, the jurisdiction to entertain wardship applications has been based on the "allegiance" of the child.[9]

The Court of Chancery appears to have conferred upon itself a very wide interpretational discretion in determining the grounds for intervention. Chancery judges were more inclined to intervene than were their common law counterparts. Once having intervened, the availability of prerogative powers and control of court officers enabled the judiciary to exercise direct hands-on management of a child's circumstances in a manner not achievable under the common law. The issue of a wardship order vested in the court the parental duty to maintain, protect and educate a child and was exercisable on behalf of the court by its appointed guardian. The emphasis was on preserving the *status quo* in relation to such aspects of upbringing until the infant heir attained the age of majority. This was the essence of the wardship jurisdiction over orphans. It was established as such during the era of feudalism and laid the foundation for the modern welfare approach.

Chancery also brought the added dimension of continuity. Because the responsibility of Chancery for its wards was a continuing one, so the welfare of a child was not simply a matter for adjudication but one that required continual re-appraisal and on-going management. The welfare of the child remained the principal if not the sole concern of the Court of Chancery in all circumstances where, for one reason or another, parental rights were irrelevant, secondary or unimportant.

Chancery and guardians

Chancery had from time immemorial supervised the conduct of guardians in relation to their wards.[10] From the principle of trust underpinning 'guardianship in socage' and that of a parental duty to care which grounded 'guardianship by nurture', Chancery developed firm expectations that a guardian would use his position of trust for the benefit of a child. Guardianship rested on parental duties rather than rights. The parent/guardian was held to be vested with the powers necessary to give effect to his or her duties. Concern for the child and his property was the basis of the guardianship concept. Prior to the 18th century the welfare principle took the form of a duty placed upon parents/guardians and enforced by the feudal institutions recognised by the law.[11]

The feudal concept of guardianship, founded on a sense of *loco parentis* duties and fiduciary responsibilities, can be seen as a form of public office. This accords with the role of the Court of Chancery which always had available to it not only the power of appointment of guardians but also their control and supervision: the sanction being forfeiture of office. In *Morgan v Dillon*,[12] for example, the issue facing the court was the power to remove a testamentary guardian. In the eyes of Chancery any abuse of trust, such as had occurred in that case, amounting to:

> ..any misbehaviour or ill-usage of the person of the ward,

and then,

> ...this Court could remove the person out of his custody.

West LC decided that guardianships were intrinsically the same. The differences were not created by the method of appointing or nominating a guardian. Therefore there was no reason why testamentary guardians should not subject to equitable control. This view in effect overruled the earlier approach of Lord Nottingham LC in *Foster v Denny*[13] where he decided that equitable intervention related only to common law guardianship and therefore "...here being a Guardian by Act of Parliament, I cannot remove him or her...".

Significantly, West LC added the caveat that when the interest enforceable by the wardship was "lucrative" to the guardian rather than "for the benefit" of the child (reflecting the distinctive purposes of guardianship in chivalry and socage) the court could not intervene. This suggests that the equitable intervention of the Chancellor was designed, at least partly, to protect the interests of the child. This was probably limited to guardianships which acknowledged the child as the beneficiary of the trust created by the wardship.

Once military tenures had been abolished in 1660, such equitable intervention extended to all guardianships.

The intervention of Chancery in relation to guardians rather than parents was significant in two respects. Firstly, while the child's welfare was not itself a ground for intervention, where there was the least suspicion of a child's interests being detrimentally affected by the guardian's conduct then Chancery would intervene. Secondly, while recognising that the jurisdiction was exercisable for the benefit of the child, the Chancery judges at the same time were prepared to accord some weight to the views of the parents.

Chancery, parents and the common law concept of custody

The concept of guardianship initially provided the basis on which the Court of Chancery intervened in matters affecting the upbringing of a child, including conflicts of interest between guardian and child. The principles gradually worked out in the context of a third party's duties towards a ward eventually came to be extended to the parent/child relationship. The eventual extension of this jurisdiction to include the conduct of parents was thus natural and one to which Chancery were able to bring a ready formed body of principle. The concept of guardianship had been, and even throughout the 18th century remained, the cornerstone of the law. Until the intervention of equity in the 18th century, custody of the child's person, as opposed to issues of guardianship, played a very minor role. Custody then emerged out of guardianship.

Parents and the 'office' of guardian

The principal characteristic of the medieval common law had been its application of rigid rules. This, arguably, is the antithesis of the current approach. Entitlement to office, extent of the fiduciary powers and duties of the guardian, forfeiture of office: each was closely regulated. The courts limited their role to deciding on the guardian's fitness for office, establishing the grounds warranting disqualification and the vesting of responsibilities in another. This retrospective and negative approach was to become a hallmark of future judicial intervention.

By the early eighteenth century caselaw begins to demonstrate the judicial transfer of principles forged to govern the office of a guardian to govern equally the responsibilities of a parent. In *ex parte Hopkins*,[14] for example, the link between parental rights and a father's duties as a guardian was alluded to by King LC

> The father is entitled to the custody of his own children during their infancy, not only as guardian by nurture, but by nature...

A century later the Court of Chancery had made the further step of determining that a father, like a guardian, could be deprived of his position of trust in relation to a child if found guilty of abusing that trust. As Lord Eldon LC declared in *Lyons v Blenkin*:[15]

> It is certain that the court will interfere against the acts of a guardian, if acting in a manner inconsistent with his duty; and it is equally clear that the court will control a parent if acting in a manner in which he should not.

The duties of parents were being viewed by the judiciary as an extension of their position as guardians. The welfare interests of the child, at least in a negative sense of preventing abuse, came to provide the justification for ultimate judicial control of the father as it had done in respect of the guardian.

Thus the Court of Chancery in the 18th and early 19th centuries, before the era of statutory reforms, can be seen to have developed a jurisprudence in which both a guardian and a father were viewed as holders of an office of trust in relation to a child. Common grounds of disqualification for abuse of this office were slowly forged by Chancery. Those grounds were adopted also by judiciary applying the common law jurisdiction and within it the writ of *habeas corpus*. During this period, of the two jurisdictions, the equitable jurisdiction was the one most frequently invoked. By the end of the nineteenth century it was the caselaw of equity rather the common law which had established the welfare interests of the child as a benchmark against which continued entitlement to exercise paternal rights would be measured.[16] The judiciary in the Court of Chancery provided the foundations for the future evolution of the welfare principle: a guardian, even if a parent, held a position of trust in relation to a child; the exercise of rights inherent in such a position was conditional upon first fulfilling a basic duty of care owed by a 'guardian' to a 'ward'; failure to fulfill the duties of a guardian would justify removal of the rights even from a parent.

Custody

Custody proceedings, like those for guardianship, have always been matters of private civil law. In guardianship proceedings the Court of Chancery had been concerned mostly about the methods and purposes of intervention in the parent/child relationship. In custody proceedings, however, the focus was firmly on the grounds for intervention. A parent was deemed entitled to custody and this presumption of parental care had to be displaced before authority could be exercised by others. This common law right of a father to the custody and control of his legitimate child was subject to the constraints of the criminal law (see chapter 1) and, eventually, to the paramount consideration of the child's welfare.[17]

The authority of the father[18] was, as noted by Lord O'Hagan LC in *re Meades (Minors)*[19] "..a very sacred thing bestowed by the Almighty, and to be sustained to the uttermost by human law", but he then went on to add the qualifying condition that it was: "..a trust and not a power, and the abuse of it will justify its restraint". The courts demonstrated their reluctance to interfere with paternal authority by refusing to withdraw a father's right to custody in cases concerning cruel discipline,[20] comparative destitution[21] or 'mere incontinence or habits of intemperance'.[22] The sort of abuses justifying, at common law, the removal of a parental right to custody were '..grave moral turpitude',[23] '..abdication of paternal authority',[24] grievous physical abuse of wife,[25] expressing anti-religious views which were 'pernicious, noxious to society, adverse to civilisation',[26] committing an unnatural crime (homosexuality) which might cause him to 'morally contaminate' his children or cause others to 'shun their society'[27] and being a labouring man who deserted his wife.[28] According to Macpherson, the removal of the parental right to custody was permissible in two situations: failure to provide adequate maintenance (probably including desertion) and failure to provide proper education. But, also, the Court of King's Bench would refuse to enforce a parent's *prima facie* right to custody by issuing a writ of *habeas corpus* "when the enforcement of (the father's right) would be attended with danger to the child; and it has declined to deliver the child to him, when there was an apprehension of cruelty, or of contamination, by some exhibition of gross profligacy".[29] This reflected the view of parental power as a concession to parents merely to enable them to implement their duties. In this sense the legal imposition of duties and the powers needed to give them effect were logically dependent aspects of the same concept. The grounds for removing the power were simply failures to comply with the correlative duties. Macpherson identified one further ground for intervention:

> ...where his character is such that they will be in danger of personal ill-treatment or of moral contamination if they reside with him, the court has not hesitated to take the children from him, and to place them in safe custody....[30]

Although Chancery allowed itself to be used to remedy deficiencies in the common law capacity to focus on parental duties, it was ineffective in enforcing its judgments. This was noted by Lord Eldon LC in *Wellesley v Beaufort*:[31]

> The courts of law can enforce the rights of the father, but they are not equal to the office of enforcing the duties of the father. Those duties have been acknowledged in this his Majesty's Court for centuries past.

Developing a legal role for the welfare interests of a child

The courts were initially interested in the circumstances whereby a father could be held to have forfeited his rights by particularly reprehensible behaviour. That is to say, the courts were concerned more with applying sanctions against a father, in order to defend socially approved standards of behaviour, rather than with protecting or promoting the welfare of his child in pursuance of any recognition of the latter's separate legal interests. The emergence and consolidation of the common law concept of custody as the main parental right was accompanied by the corollary that a child's welfare was, in a sense, only taken into account by the judiciary *in absentia*. Not until welfare interests had been seriously infringed did they come into play as a factor capable of disentitling parent or guardian from their office of trust in respect of that child. The role played by the welfare principle was thus both negative and secondary in the context of custody proceedings. Having determined that the father's behaviour was in breach of the law, the courts turned to examine the effect of that behaviour on the child and it only then went on to consider arrangements which might safeguard the child's future welfare. The first step was court recognition that a fixed objective threshold had been breached by the father. This breach licensed the second step by which judicial discretion was exercised to take into account the welfare interests of the child concerned when disposing of the proceedings.

This profoundly negative interpretation of welfare, existing only as a measure of an abuse of rights, defined and confined the legal role initially assigned to the welfare interests of a child. But it was from this judicial approach that eventually a more positive affirmation of the separate legal interests of a child was to grow. In time the Court of Chancery expanded its supervisory role, not only to protect children but also, to some extent, to play a positive role in promoting their welfare. In doing so Chancery felt bound to pay some attention to the wishes of parents as well as those of child of a certain age. This created a new approach: the exercise of an administrative discretion. This is probably the essence of the later statutory system.

Equity and the Judicature Act 1873

In England, during the eighteenth and nineteenth centuries, a dual judicial system existed to deal with matters affecting the welfare of a child. Such matters might be determined by judges in the common law courts applying precedents drawn from a jurisprudence based upon the rights of the individual, adjudicating on a breach of statutorily prescribed duties and enforcing their judgments by use of habeas corpus. Alternatively, they could be judicially determined in the courts of equity which would employ a more flexible and discretionary approach in which judgment would conform with the dictates of the welfare principle and, if necessary, be enforced by use of the prerogative powers. The records clearly show that in the mid-19th century the majority of issues concerning the upbringing of a child were being determined in the common law courts rather than those of equity.

The background to the Judicature Act 1873

In 1839, Parliament introduced legislation designed to strengthen the position of a non-adulterous mother, relative to that of an irresponsible father, in respect of the right to custody of their child. Section 1 of the 1839 Act (Talfourd's Act) enabled a judge in equity "if he should see fit" to make an access or custody order in the circumstances prescribed, where the infant was in the sole custody or control of the father. The judge was also enabled to attach to the access order any temporal or other regulations "as he shall deem convenient and just". There was no direct reference to the welfare of the child; this was incidental to the interests of the mother. These provisions conferred wide discretionary powers on the judiciary.

The courts, however, continued their defence of paternal rights and failed to implement the provisions in the spirit of the legislation. Only where a father could be proven to be in absolute dereliction of his duties, could a judicial challenge to his rights arise. *In re Fynn*[32] was a case where a grandmother sought appointment as guardian in the place of the father who was alive and seeking his parental rights. Knight Bruce V-C explained:

> Before this jurisdiction can be called into action between them it must be satisfied, not only that it has the means of acting safely and efficiently, but also that the father has so conducted himself or has shown himself to be a person of such a description, or is placed in such a position, as to render it not merely better for the children, but essential to their safety or to their welfare, in some very serious and important respect, that his rights should be treated as lost or suspended - should be superseded or interfered with. If the word "essential" is too strong an expression, it is not much too strong (pp 474-5).

The father's conduct - to his late wife and towards the children - made him unfit to care for the children but did not render it essential that his right should be removed.

In *Re Halliday's Estate: Ex parte Woodward*[33] Turner LJ was of the view that the purpose of the 1839 Act was to control the father's exclusive right to custody but in so doing the court should consider the father's marital duty to his wife and the interests of the children. Jessel MR in *In re Taylor, an infant*[34] considered that in deciding whether a father was to be deprived of his right to custody, "there was to be kept in mind, first of all, the paternal right; secondly, the marital duty; and, thirdly, the interests of the children". Where the plaintiff was an unmarried mother or a non-adulterous mother, and the subject a young child, judicial recognition was more readily given to the welfare of the child. As Romilly MR stated in *Austin v Austin*:[35]

> The welfare of the child is so intimately connected with its being under the care of the mother that no extent of kindness on the part of any other person can supply that place. It is the notorious observation of mankind that the loss of a mother is irreparable to her children and particularly so if young (p 263).

The Judicature Act 1873

Section 25 of the Judicature Act 1873 provided that:

> ....in questions relating to the custody and education of infants, the rules of equity shall prevail.

This provision consolidated within judicial practice the equitable principle that the welfare of the child should be given priority in all legal issues affecting his or her upbringing.[36] The effect of this statute was summarised by Fitzgibbon LJ in his judgment in *In re O'Hara*.[37] He then reiterated the principles stated in *The Queen v Gyngall*:[38]

> (i) At Common Law, the parent has an absolute right to the custody of a child of tender years, unless he or she has forfeited it by certain sorts of misconduct;
> (ii) Chancery, when a separate tribunal, possessed a jurisdiction different from that of the Queen's Bench, and essentially parental, in the exercise of which the main consideration was the welfare of the child, and the court did what, on consideration of all the circumstances, it was judicially satisfied that a wise parent, acting for the true interests of the child, would or ought to do, even though the natural parent desired and had the common law right to do otherwise, and had not been guilty of misconduct;
> (iii) the Judicature Act has made it the duty of every Division of the High Court to exercise the Chancery jurisdiction;
> (iv) in exercising the jurisdiction to control or ignore the parental right the Court must act cautiously, not as if it were a private person acting with regard to his own child, and acting in opposition to the parent only when judicially satisfied that the welfare of the child requires that the parental right should be suspended or superseded.

In theory, the fusion of equity and the common law placed the High Court in a position to give a new and consistent priority to identifying and securing the welfare of a child when the latter's interests had been impaired by a parent. The overriding authority of equity was demonstrated in cases[39] where use of the common law writ of *habeas corpus* to enforce the paternal right to custody were quashed by recourse to equity when such an enforcement would be contrary to a child's welfare interests. The responsibility for safeguarding a child's welfare had been clearly vested in the state, to be discharged in accordance with the principles of equity rather than of parental rights. In practice, however, for most of the 19th century the judiciary proved to be either unable or unwilling to employ and enforce equitable principles.

The 1873 Act and *Re Agar-Ellis*

The continuing impasse reached its nadir with the ruling in *Re Agar-Ellis.*[40] The judicial rationale then presented to assert the doctrine of parental rights, demonstrated the resilience of the common law approach to matters affecting the upbringing of a child. James LJ stated:

> The right of the father to the custody and control of his children is one of the most sacred of rights.

In his view, custody, was simply the vehicle for giving effect to paternal duties, of which one clearly was the "education of his children". Education included bringing up the child in accordance with the father's wishes on religion. Cotton LJ went on to declare:

> But this Court holds this principle - that when by birth a child is subject to a father, it is for the general interest of families, and for the general interest of children, and really for the interest of the particular infant, that the court should not, except in very extreme cases, interfere with the discretion of the father, but leave to him the responsibility of exercising that power which nature has given him by the birth of the child (p 334).

This ruling in particular finally convinced Parliament that further legislation would be needed to require the courts to take into account matters other than paternal rights in cases where the welfare of a child was at issue.

Conclusion

The Judicature Act 1873 was a landmark piece of legislation. It closed the book, in theory, on centuries of divided judicial practice in cases where the welfare of a child was at issue. In providing for the fusion of equity and common law, it provided also for the continuation of the *parens patriae* doctrine, its transference to all superior courts and for its eventual bearing on modern child care law. By the late 19th century the legal cohesion and autonomy of the patriarchical marital family unit emerged as the central pillar of family law.

From an initial interest in the property rights of young beneficiaries the court developed its present concern to protect the welfare of a child and the power to displace a parent who abuses that welfare. The doctrine originated in the courts of equity and remained rooted there. This has allowed equity rather than statute law to lead the evolving jurisprudence based on the principle of the welfare of the child.

Notes

1 See Pollock F., and Maitland F.W., *The History of English Law*, London, 2nd ed 1968, pp 443 and 444.

2 See Holdsworth, *History of English Law*, vol 5, p 315; vol 6, p 648.

3 See *In the goods of Thomas Parnell* (1872) LR 2PandD 379, at p 381.

4 See vol 6, p 648.

5 See Holdsworth, vol 2, p 99.

6 See Holdsworth, vol 10, p 356.

7 Thereafter this duty fell to be exercised as follows: in 1875 it passed to the Chancery Division of the High Court; in 1971 it was transferred to the Family Division; and in 1989 it became exercisable by the family proceedings court.

8 (1854) 4 De GM and G 328, 345.

9 See, for example, *Hope; Re Willoughby* (1885) 30 Ch D 324; *Harben v Harben* [1957] 1 WLR 261; *Re P (GE)* [1965] Ch 568).

10 See the Latey Report, 1967, Cmnd 3342, para 192.

11 The first statutory description of a guardian's powers was given in the Tenures Abolition Act, 1660, where it was stated that a guardian, being granted the custody and tuition of a child, was also to:

> …take into [their] custody to the use of such child….the profits of all lands, tenements and hereditaments of such child…and also the custody, tuition, management of the goods, chattels and personal estate of such child…and [could] bring such action in relation thereunto as by law a guardian in common socage might do.

12 (1724) 9 Modern 135.

13 (1677) 2 Chancery Cases 237 at p 238.

14 [1732], 3 Peere Williams 152 at p 153.

15 (1821), Jacob 245 at p 253.

16 See *Re Agar-Ellis* (1883) 24 Ch D 317, CA.

17 See *Re Thomasset* [1894] 300.

18 See J Eekelaar *Family Law and Social Policy*, (1984), at p 156:

> The absolute power of parents over their children was integral to the social structure. The normal protective reach of the criminal law would stop at the family's threshold. No compelling social interest existed to justify, let alone compel, its intrusion.

19 [1871] IR 5 Eq 98.

20 See *Blake v Wallscourt* (1846).

21 See *Ex parte Pulbrook* (1847).

22 See *Re Goldsworthy* (1876) 2 QBD 75.

23 See *Re Agar-Ellis* (1883) 23 Ch D 317.

24 See *Wellesley v Wellesley* [1828] 2 BI, NS 124.

25 See *Warde v Warde* (1849) 2 Phillips 786.

26 See *Thomas v Roberts* (1850).
27 See *Anon* (1851).
28 See *Re Halliday's Estate ex parte Woodward* (1852) 17 Jurist 56.
29 Macpherson, pp 157 and 158.
30 p 142.
31 [1827] 2 Russell 1 at p 23.
32 (1848) 2 De Gex and Smale 457. See, also, *Hope v Hope* (1854) 4 De Gex, Macnaghten and Gordon 328 and *In re Curtis* (1859) 28 LJ Ch 458.
33 (1852) 17 Jurist 56.
34 (1876) 4 Ch D 157 p 160.
35 (1865) 34 Beavan 257.
36 See *Re Ethel Brown* (1884) 13 QBD 614 at p 617, per Lindley LJ.
37 [1900], 2 IR 232.
38 [1893], 2 QB 232.
39 See *Rv Barnardo, Jones's Case* [1891] 1 QB 194, 210 CA; also, see, *Andrews v Salt* (1873) 8 Ch App 622.
40 (1883) 23 Ch D 317, pp 71-2.

3 Legislative Endorsement of Child Welfare: Statutory Law Defines and Extends the Principle's Role, Function and Weighting

Introduction

A mixture of judicial obduracy and ineffectiveness characterised the role of the courts in relation to paternal rights throughout the first half of the 19th century. While the judgments given in the courts of Chancery continued to be flexible and balanced in their recognition of interests other than those of a father, the judiciary was ineffective in enforcing them. The judgments in the courts of the King's Bench were readily enforced but were mainly concerned with defending paternal rights. The Judicature Act 1873 brought together the courts of equity and the common law, giving primacy to the former. However, the principles and precedents underpinning each continued to be evident. By the latter half of the nineteenth century Parliament was forced to legislate to enforce recognition of the interests of mothers and children and to curb the dominance of paternal rights.

This chapter examines the forming and evolution of three separate legislative strands; private family law, public law and general public welfare and social care law. It does in a descriptive manner by presenting an essentially historical account of developments. Beginning with private family law, the chapter deals with the statutory endeavour to curb judicial enthusiasm for parental rights, particularly paternal rights. It then considers the broadening of the public family law remit in relation to child welfare, with special regard for the steady growth in authority of the criminal law relative to the doctrine of parental rights. The third strand, the developing role of general public health and social care provision, is then outlined. The latter is considered only insofar as is necessary to trace the assimilation of certain welfare related responsibilities into the public family law domain. This approach enables the chapter to identify the legacy which the modern welfare principle owes to legislative initiatives of the late 19th century.

The three legislative strands

The doctrine of paternal rights owed a great deal to the common law emphasis on the rights and duties of the individual and had become evident in the proprietary frame of reference, centred on parental status, which shaped the growth of a body of private family law legislation. At the same time, the public law jurisprudence concerning child welfare was formed primarily by statutory extensions of the criminal law, itself derived from the common law. In addition and in piecemeal fashion, the broad range of civil public law was gradually extended by health and social care legislation. The latter development coalesced towards the middle of the twentieth century to form the basis of the modern 'welfare state', in which child welfare considerations were also prominent. As the general public welfare remit consolidated, the parameters of modern family law became more distinct, defining and confining the subsequent legal development of the principle of the welfare of the child. But, initially this third strand provided a natural context for statutorily addressing the public interest in child welfare and, as it contributed to forming the role and content of the principle, it is outlined for background purposes in this part of the book.

At first legislative intervention on behalf of children's welfare interests was concerned with conditioning the exercise of paternal/parental rights but ultimately the public interest provided the rationale for a broad framework of interventionist social care legislation in which the welfare principle was implicitly or explicitly incorporated. The Judicature Act 1873 was only the beginning, and in many ways a false start, on the road leading to the Children Act 1989.

Private family law

The court of Chancery, in cases such as *Mytton v Mytton*[1] where a mother was granted custody of her five children, demonstrated its willingness to break with the doctrine of paternal rights in circumstances where not to do so would cause an injustice to the interests of other family members. The court of King's Bench would also occasionally refuse to use the powers of *habeas corpus* to enforce a father's rights where to do so would endanger the welfare of a child. As was then stated by Lord Denman CJ in *R v Greenhill:*[2]

> The court, it is true, has intimated that the right of the father would not be acted upon where the enforcement of it would be attended with danger to the child; as where there was an apprehension of cruelty, or by contamination of some gross profligacy.

But at best, until legislative initiative demanded a more robust response, the welfare of a child continued to operate only negatively, as a judicial brake on an irresponsible exercise of paternal rights. (See, further, Chap 2). Legislative intent to interpose other considerations into judicial decision-making began to take effect towards the mid-nineteenth century in marital proceedings, custody and separation contests, guardianship, wardship and adoption.

Matrimonial proceedings

The starting point for any consideration of the law relating to child welfare in the context of marital proceedings is the Custody of Infants Act 1839 which was introduced while the matrimonial jurisdiction was still the responsibility of the Ecclesiastical Court. The court's traditional defence of paternal rights was maintained as evidenced in its rigorous enforcement of the statute's provision that maternal fault would disqualify any right to custody:

> s.4...no order shall be made by virtue of this Act whereby any mother against whom adultery shall be established by judgment in an action for criminal conversation or by sentence of an ecclesiastical court shall have the custody of or access to any infant...

The Matrimonial Causes Act 1857, however, abolished the matrimonial jurisdiction of the Ecclesiastical Court and transferred it to the newly constituted Divorce Court. Under s 35 the court was authorised in the appropriate context to make provision 'with respect to the custody, maintenance and education' of the relevant children 'as it may deem just and proper'.[3] The two principal factors influencing the exercise of this custodial provision were the rules of common law and the concept of matrimonial fault which underpinned the jurisdiction.

The common law approach, based on the rights of the individual and the grounds for disqualifying an individual from exercising his or her rights, immediately asserted itself. It was apparent in the ruling of Ordinary J in *Cartlidge v Cartlidge* [4] when he said of the discretionary power under s 35:

> ....but I think I ought to exercise that power with reference to the *prima facie* right of the father, and the petitioner must establish a case beyond the mere natural desire of a mother to have the custody of her infant child

He decided that, there being no good reason in the interests either of the mother or of the child to do otherwise, effect should be given to the paternal right. Again, in *Chetwynd v Chetwynd* [5] Lord Penzance held the paternal right to custody to be forfeited because "the common home has been broken up by the conduct of the father" but the mother would only succeed if she "has been free from blame". He determined that the mother was not without blame so custody of the children was awarded to an aunt and uncle. A mother found guilty of adultery would forfeit any right to custody and access.[6] Indeed, any parent responsible for the breakup of the family home would similarly be rejected for custody.[7] These cases gave rise to the so-called 'doctrine of the unimpeachable parent' the influence of which continued to be brought to bear on judicial decision-making into the second half of the twentieth century. Matrimonial fault was the basis for forfeiture of parental rights; parental fault was beside the point. The courts were more concerned with matrimonial conduct than child welfare.

After the introduction of the Custody of Infants Act 1873, the court in *D'Alton v D'Alton*[8] felt able to reject parental claims and instead appoint a guardian. Hannen J in the court of first instance was required to choose between parents each of whom were seeking custody in order to determine a different religious upbringing for their children. He posed the question "...what is most for the benefit of their offspring, whose interests are of paramount importance upon this application?" On appeal it was decided that neither parent should have custody; instead this was awarded to the head of the children's boarding school. However, it was not until the Report of the Morton Commission in 1956[9] that the welfare interests of children were positively asserted as an appropriate factor to be statutorily provided for in marital proceedings. The report concluded that the most suitable arrangements were not always being made for children.[10] The principal reason identified was that nobody was 'specifically charged to look after the child's interests'.[11] The Morton Report also recommended that the courts should have the power to require a local authority to receive children into care where, in the course of matrimonial proceedings, it appeared to a court that neither spouse was an acceptable parent and no other relatives were available, willing or suitable to undertake care responsibility. The provision for mandatory assessment of child welfare interests was reviewed in 1968 (the Hall Report)[12] and found to be to some extent unsatisfactory; it has since been subject to minor amendments; until legislatively repealed.

Eventually the extent of judicial compliance with legislative intent became evident in cases such as *Cammell v Cammell* [13] where the court was concerned with the basis of its jurisdiction to grant ancillary relief under s 26 of the Matrimonial Causes Act 1950. Scarman J based his decision to some extent on the following proposition:

> In my view, however, the court in construing the statute should have regard [not only to...but also] to the policy of the law that, where in any proceeding before any court the custody or upbringing of an infant is in question, the court, in deciding that question, shall regard the welfare of the infant as the first and paramount consideration.

The Divorce Reform Act 1969 (later consolidated in the Matrimonial Causes Act 1973) in theory abolished the fault based grounds for divorce and replaced them with the single ground of 'irretrievable breakdown'. In practice as that ground could only be established by proof of one or more of five facts, three of which were fault based and were frequently relied upon because proceedings were then shorter, the change was not as substantive as had been intended. Section 41 of the 1973 Act, in keeping with the Morton Report recommendations, made the granting of a decree of divorce, or nullity being conditional upon court satisfaction that arrangements compatible with the best interests of any children of the marriage had been made. Given that such children formed a large proportion of all those appearing in proceedings requiring judicial determination of matters concerning their welfare, this condition was an important manifestation of the welfare principle (see, further, Chap 12).

The Family Law Reform Act 1987, for most purposes, removed the distinction between legitimate and illegitimate children; it also sought to substitute less stigmatising terminology.

Consideration of welfare interests in the context of custody and separation agreements must also begin with the Custody of Infants Act 1839 (Talfourd's Act). This gave a non-adulterous mother a right to apply to the court for access to her infant, or for custody, where the child was less than 7 years of age. It amounted to no more than a discretionary judicial power to intervene in a father's rights in favour of the mother. It did not imply any specific legislative recognition of a child's welfare interests. The Custody of Infants Act 1873 repealed Talfourd's Act but otherwise did no more than extend the application of the 1839 Act to include custody and access orders in relation to children under 16. Whereas previously the courts would not enforce a separation agreement, to the presumed disadvantage of the father, under s 2 of the 1873 Act they could enforce it. The judiciary, however, continued to use their discretion to largely ignore the potential opportunities provided by both statutes to improve the relative weighting given to the welfare interests of a child when taking decisions regarding custody arrangements.

Guardianship

The Guardianship of Infants Act 1886 made the first specific statutory reference to the welfare of the child and the modern judicial approach to children can be dated from that Act. Thereafter, in the words of Jessel MR in *In re Taylor, an infant*[14] when deciding whether a father was to be deprived of his right to custody "there was to be kept in mind, first of all, the paternal right; secondly, the marital duty; and, thirdly, the interests of the children". This rank ordering of judicial priorities was subsequently evident in cases such as *In re A and B (Infants)*[15] where Rigby J failed to acknowledge the welfare of the child as even a secondary objective of the Act. As Lord MacDermott later remarked in *J v C* [16] the Acts of 1839 and 1873 together with those of 1886 and 1891 "record an increasing qualification of common law rights and the growing acceptance of the welfare of the child as a criterion."

Guardianship, like wardship, had its origins in the duty to protect, maintain and generally care for the child (see, Chap 2). Custody, in the sense of personal control over the child, was only incidental. During the 19th century this changed as custody came to be regarded as the hallmark of paternal rights and a cornerstone in judicial espousal of the related doctrine. Not until the Guardianship of Infants Act 1886 did statute law begin to redress the balance and restore the duty to respect a child's welfare interests.

Section 5 of the 1886 Act directed the court to have regard 'to the welfare of the infant, and to the conduct of the parents, and to the wishes as well of the mother as of the father'. This did not give a mother parity of parental rights with a father. The one substantive right created was that of a surviving mother's right to guardianship either alone or along with any guardian appointed by the father (s 2). In s 3(2) she was given a power to provisionally appoint a guardian to act with the child's father after her death and the court was authorised to confirm that appointment 'if it be shown to the satisfaction of the court that the father is for any reason unfitted to be the sole guardian of his children'. Parental unfitness could thus deprive a father of his guardianship.

The Guardianship of Infants Act 1925 represents a landmark in the development of the law's capacity to protect the legal interests of children. This Act introduced some fundamental changes: equality of parental right to custody or upbringing (s 1); equality of parental right to apply to court on any matter affecting their child (s 2); specific right of mother to apply for custody, even if still resident in the matrimonial home (s 3); equality of right of surviving parent to guardianship and to appoint a testamentary guardian (s 4 and s 5). Not until the 1925 Act did the legislative intent to assert the legitimacy of the welfare principle become unequivocally stamped on the statute books.

The Guardianship of Infants Acts of 1886 and 1925 were consolidated in the Guardianship of Minors Act 1971which embodied the paramountcy principle, and which was amended in the Guardianship Act 1973. The principle related to matters affecting a child's custody or upbringing and property or income. It declared:

> Where in any proceedings before any court....the custody or upbringing of a (child) is in question, the court, in deciding that question, shall regard the welfare of the (child) as the first and paramount consideration, and shall not take into consideration, whether from any other point of view, the claim of the father in respect of such custody, upbringing....is superior to that of the mother, or the claim of the mother is superior to that of the father.

This particular statutory framing of the welfare principle represented a substantive increase in its legal role and weighting. The references to 'upbringing' and to 'court' indicated that the principle was in future to be applied in legal, equitable and statutory proceedings in relation not only to issues of custody and access but also to ancillary matters. Equality of parental rights was introduced by s 1(1) of the Guardianship Act 1973. Section 1(3) gave a parent a power to apply for a direction from the court in the event of any disagreement on a question affecting a child's welfare other than a matter of custody or access. The court was given a discretionary power to settle such disagreements 'as it may think proper'. When so doing it was directed to regard the child's welfare as the factor of paramount importance.

Wardship

Wardship was never a creature of statute. Although a species of guardianship, it has always been a distinct legal concept.[17] The revival of wardship did not really begin until after 1948 - partly in response to the increased powers of official authorities as statutory guardians of children. The simplified procedures introduced by s 4 of the Law Reform (Miscl Provisions) Act 1949 made it even more attractive. It then grew in popularity as a means of solving disputes between parents and potential adopters, parents and foster-parents and even inter-parental disputes. Because it rested on unfettered judicial discretion, at least in relation to matters not already specifically addressed by statute, it permitted considerable creativity in decision-making relating to the welfare, upbringing and property of children. For the next three or four decades, until the Children Act 1989 finally barred the door on wardship as an alternative to statutory jurisdiction, exercises of judicial discretion in wardship were to play a pivotal role in developing the law as it relates to the welfare principle.

Adoption

This, the most recent addition to private family law legislation, has provided the proceedings which have proved to be least conducive to the evolution of the welfare principle.

The practice of adoption has a long history.[18] It was known to the courts long before Parliament introduced the first adoption legislation in 1926. Where the responsibility for an illegitimate, abandoned or orphaned child could be assumed within the care arrangements of a private family, instead of becoming an additional burden on public rates and the resources of the Poorhouse, the courts did not interfere. The informal process whereby a natural parent voluntarily relinquished all future responsibility for the care and upbringing of a child to a third party was countenanced by the courts in circumstances where such action could not be construed as the avoidance of paternal duties. In effect this confined the practice to the relinquishment of illegitimate children by their unmarried mothers. The sympathetic approach of the judiciary was illustrated by Fitz-Gibbon LJ in *In re O'Hara*[19] who expressed the view that:

> ...the surrender of a child to an adopted parent, as an act of prudence or of necessity, under the pressure of present inability to maintain it, being an act done in the interests of the child, cannot be regarded as abandonment or desertion, or even as unmindfullness of parental duty within the meaning of the Act.

Following publication of the Hopkinson Report,[20] the Adoption Act 1926 permitted, for the first time in these islands, a formal legal procedure for the adoption of children. Since then the Hurst Committee in 1954[21] has suggested that the 'primary object ...in the arrangement of adoptions is the welfare of the child' and the Houghton Committee in 1972[22] recommended that 'the long-term welfare of the child should be the first and paramount consideration'. Though legislative intent has subsequently and consistently made clear that the paramountcy principle does not have a role in adoption law, the Children Act 1975 introduced a new part for welfare to play in the adoption process. Section 3 stated:

> In reaching any decision relating to the adoption of a child, a court or adoption agency shall have regard to all the circumstances, first considerations being given to the need to safeguard and promote the welfare of the child through his childhood; and shall so far as practicable ascertain the wishes and feelings of the child regarding the decision and give due consideration to them, having regard to his age and understanding.

This indicated that welfare was to be considered in all decisions, not just the decision to make an adoption order. The Adoption Act 1976, which came into effect in 1988 and remains the governing legislation, incorporated s 3 of the 1975 Act but stopped short of making adoption contingent on the agreement of the child concerned.

Public family law

The period from 1850-1930/40 was one of conflict between courts and Parliament: the courts trying to enforce as far as possible the parental rights doctrine and Parliament seeking to extend the role of the law in relation to children's matters. It was a period which witnessed the beginnings of a more sustained public concern for the welfare of children. This was particularly evident in the statutory reform of private family law introduced by the Guardianship of Infants Act 1886, the Custody of Children Act 1891 and the Guardianship of Infants Act 1925. It was evident also in the legislation dealing with public family law. The criminal law relating to the punishment of parents for child abuse or neglect was gradually supplemented by civil legislation dealing with parental duties in relation to the care and protection of their children, the duties of state authorities to support families and to provide alternative child care arrangements when required to do so by parent or court. It is important to note that accountability for child abuse or neglect under the criminal law was not restricted to parents; any third party in a *loco parentis* relationship would be held responsible for criminal harm incurred by the child in their care.[23]

Criminal law

The criminal law relating to child abuse was first comprehensively addressed in the Offences Against the Persons Act 1861 in the context of general assault charges, whether committed against adult or child. Many of these offences continued to underpin the basic civic duty regarding child welfare – the responsibility to respect his or her physical integrity – throughout the twentieth century and into the post 1989 era. Child neglect was specifically addressed by s 37 of the Poor Law Amendment Act 1868 which made it a criminal offence for a parent wilfully to neglect to provide adequate food, clothing, medical aid or lodging for his children, being under 14 and in his custody, so that their health should have been likely to be seriously injured. This provision formed the basis for s 1(1) of the 1933 Act which embedded significant protection for the welfare of children, from acts of neglect by both parents and third party carers, in the criminal law:

> If any person who has attained the age of 16 years and has custody, charge, or care of any child or young person under that age, wilfully assaults, ill-treats, neglects, abandons or exposes him, or causes or procures him to be assaulted, ill-treated, neglected, abandoned or exposed, in a manner likely to cause unnecessary suffering or injury to health (including injury to or loss of sight, or hearing, or limb, or organ of that body, and any mental derangement), that person shall be guilty of a misdemeanour.

To secure a conviction under this provision it was essential to prove 'likely to cause' unnecessary suffering or injury to health in addition to proof of exposure or abandonment.[24] This reference to likelihood of harm has resonances with the prospective welfare considerations in the 1989 Act. Subsection 2(a) treats certain behaviour as neglect; e.g. by failing 'to provide adequate food, clothing, medical aid or lodging'. These provisions list and proscribe a comprehensive range of specific types of conduct deemed to be prejudicial to the physical welfare of the child and warranting prosecution. The legislative focus was on identifying types of proscribed conduct by adults rather than the constituent elements of child welfare. The consequences of the conduct were are all important; whether resulting from wilful intent, neglect or recklessness, if the conduct was intended then responsibility for the consequences was unavoidable. For example, it was held that a considered parental refusal to consent to an operation amounted to neglect contrary to s 1 of the 1933 Act;[25] again providing resonances with modern law. The law sets out the welfare interests of children only in relation to certain stated sources of identifiable risk. The real underpinning focus of the criminal law was on parental rights which formed the reference points for proscribed conduct. Sometimes this linkage was quite explicit as in the offence of child-stealing. This was first proscribed by Parliament in 1814; then by sections 55 and 56 of the Offences Against the Person Act 1861 and sections 19(1) and 20(1) of the Sexual Offences Act 1950. By proscribing the removal of a child from her parents for non-sexual as well as sexual purposes these provisions enforced parents rights and thereby also afforded protection for the welfare of a child. The various offences of kidnapping, abduction and child stealing all seemed to be founded on a parental rights approach; the retention and continuity of the parental relationship being presumed to be in a child's best interests.

Care and protection

The civil law relating to the care and protection of children emerged in the latter half of the nineteenth century following a number of reported cases where the Society for the Prevention of Cruelty to Animals had turned its attention to the rescue of children from abusing adults. This was a period of well-publicised philanthropic 'child rescue' initiatives which saw orphanages and special schools established.[26] The views of writers such as Macpherson[27] proved very influential. In 1884, the London Society for the Prevention of Cruelty to Children was formed. The introduction of the Prevention of Cruelty to Children Act 1889 was largely due to effective lobbying by this precursor of the NSPCC. The current law may be traced through s 1 of the Prevention of Cruelty and Protection of Children Act 1889, s 1 of the Prevention of Cruelty to Children Act 1894, s 1 of the Prevention of Cruelty Act to Children Act 1904 and s 12 of the Children Act 1908.[28] The legislative intent was considered in a number of important cases at the turn of the century. For example, in *R v Senior*[29] the father of a child who died was charged with wilful neglect by failing to provide medical aid and medicine for the child contrary to the Prevention of Cruelty to Children Act 1894. Russell LJ then considered the effect of s 1(2)(a) of that Act:

> ...a parent or other person legally liable to maintain a child or young person shall be deemed to have neglected him or her in a manner likely to cause injury to his health if he has failed to provide adequate food, clothing, medical aid or lodging for him, or if, having been otherwise unable to provide such food, clothing, medical aid or lodging, he has failed to take steps to procure it to be provided under the enactments applicable in that behalf.

He held that the offence of neglect was committed by "the omission of such steps as a reasonable parent would take". In *R v Connor*[30] the judiciary had the opportunity to examine the statutory paternal duty to provide care and protection. This case concerned an allegation that the father had departed leaving the mother with insufficient money to feed the children. The evidence was that the children were clean but poorly clad and fed. The father was found guilty of wilful neglect under s 1(1) of the Prevention of Cruelty to Children Act 1904. In this case Lord Alverstone CJ referred to:

> ...the intention of the legislature as early as 1868 (Poor Law Amendment Act 1868) to make a parent who neglected to provide adequate food for his children in his custody amenable to the criminal law...

as an aid to interpreting section 1 of the Prevention of Cruelty to Children Act 1904. The Children Act 1908 followed the example set by the 1889 Act. Parliament in establishing the juvenile courts provided, for the first time, the authority to remove an abused or neglected child from culpable parents to a place of safety. Subsequent legislation refined the state's coercive interventionist responsibilities; differentiating between functions of care, protection and control. This trend towards increased coercive intervention culminated in the Children Act 1975. Since then developments have witnessed a narrowing of the grounds for coercive intervention and an emphasis on consensual state intervention duties; giving effect to functions of prevention[31] and promotion.

Carers

The civil law relating to children was also concerned with those whose care had been assumed by persons other than their parents. The child care responsibilities assumed by third parties, with or without parental consent, was a defining issue for family law at least a century ago. English cities in the throes of the industrial revolution, particularly London, harboured many homeless and begging children abandoned by parents when they were young and needing care and maintenance but reclaimed when they were old enough to earn a wage. Charitable organisations which had been providing care sought to retain the children within a rehabilitative environment despite the proprietary demands of parents. The Custody of Children Act 1891 was introduced to provide a civil remedy for third party carers where their provision for destitute children was opposed by fathers demanding restitution of their custody rights. The rationale for the 1891 Act, was explained in the course of the preceding House of Commons debates:

> ...the Bill is intended to deal with...children who have been thrown helpless on the streets, and wickedly deserted by their parents, and who are taken by the hand by benevolent persons or by charitable institutions...

Its purpose was to provide a civil remedy to protect abandoned children from their neglectful parents by not enforcing parental rights. As such it was the first piece of legislation to offer protection for children from their parents and to others acting in *loco parentis*. A third party (e.g a foster parent, voluntary agency or whoever had care of the child) could thereafter rely on a statutory 'right' created by the legislation to resist a parental claim to custody. A parent could only recover their right by proving 'fitness'. It provided an important benchmark for the respective rights of parents and third parties in relation to the welfare interests of children, anticipating both the rationale for compulsory care orders and the concept of 'custodianship' in the Children Act 1975.[32]

This was also the era of 'baby farming'. The Infant Life Protection Act 1872 had sought to extend legal protection not only to the vulnerable young residents of workhouses but also to all those whose care was entrusted by their unmarried mothers to child minders who would then often arrange for their informal adoption. This statute, the precursor of contemporary child-minding legislation, required all such care arrangements to be registered with the local authorities and inspected by them and all deaths to be reported to the coroner. It was deficient in that its protective provisions applied only to care arrangements in respect of children aged less than one year. This was remedied by the Children Act 1908 which raised the age to seven years and introduced the concept of state responsibility for supervising the arrangements made for all children, from poor or wealthy parents, who were placed in the care of third parties.

Abandonment

Public responsibility for abandoned and destitute children had been a social problem long before the mid-nineteenth century. The response of Parliament had included measures such as the provision of training facilities. The Parish Apprentices Act 1698 (9 & 10 Will 111 c 14), for example, had by 1780 evolved into three types of apprenticeships: the binding of the child to a master for a fee; the allotment of children to parish rate-payers; and the binding of children to manufacturers for work in factories. Parliament also sought to simply prohibit vagrancy. The Vagrancy Act 1824 was specifically introduced for that purpose but proved to be an ineffective legislative response to the growing numbers of children abandoned by poor parents and left to fend for themselves by begging and stealing unless rescued by charitable organisations. Many such rescued children were sent overseas or for adoption by those organisations. Abandonment was subsequently addressed in a number of statutes relating to children.[33] It eventually became a threshold requirement enabling a local authority to assume parental rights under s 2 of the 1948 Act.

In the Children and Young Persons Act 1933, the criminal law and the law relating to child protection were consolidated.[34] The implementation of this legislation was examined in the Curtis Report[35] which gave rise to the Children Act 1948. The latter established specialist children departments under the control of local authorities and gave the latter such duties as: to receive children into care; to pass a resolution vesting in itself all parental rights in respect of a child voluntarily admitted; to provide comprehensive care arrangements for children whose parents could not do so; to give preference to boarding-out rather than residential care; to promote the development of children in care; and to provide expenses for education and training on discharge from care. In many important respects, the provisions of this legislation foreshadowed that of the 1989 Act.

Juvenile justice

Juvenile justice also had its origins in the public family law initiatives of the mid-nineteenth century. Although the first 'reform school' was established in 1806 in Bermondsey, with several others set up in the period 1810-1830, relevant legislation was not introduced until the Industrial Schools Act 1866 (preceded by the Industrial Schools Act 1861) and the Reformatory Schools Act 1866 (preceded by the Youthful Offenders Act 1854). Reformatory schools were established for the correction of offenders while industrial schools offered training for young vagrants in 'moral danger'. As with child abandonment, the legislative response to child offenders owed much to the initiative of voluntary organisations. The Society for the Suppression of Juvenile Vagrancy (later called the Children's Friendly Society) had been established in 1830 and the work of liberal activists such as Mary Carpenter[36] were influential in generating an awareness of the problems associated with juvenile delinquency. Again, many such children were destined to be sent overseas. The early legislative provisions were subsequently consolidated in the Children Act 1908. This deserves to be remembered as a landmark statute in the evolution of role of the welfare principle, if for no other reason, because it abolished the death penalty for children,[37] at least for those aged less than 16. It also introduced Borstal institutions which succeeded the industrial and reformatory schools as providers of residential training facilities for criminal or delinquent children. The 1908 Act was subsequently amended and consolidated by the Children and Young Persons Act 1933 which continued the established approach of treating children brought before the courts exhibiting welfare needs differently from those exhibiting criminal deeds for whom trial and punishment was appropriate. Not until the Criminal Justice Act 1948 were penal servitude, hard labour and whipping abolished in relation to children and not until the Children and Young Persons Act 1969 did statute law give the courts the power to provide welfare oriented disposal options for children found guilty of offences.[38]

The 1969 Act, as a matter of policy, sought to assimilate court disposal options in respect of children guilty of an offence[39] and children who were victims of parental inadequacy.[40] This extension of the welfare principle to bridge the care and justice jurisdictions was to prove highly controversial until the separation of both categories was formally restored at the end of the twentieth century with the former being re-assigned to the Children Act legislation and the latter to Criminal Justice. The vulnerability of the welfare principle to manipulation by ideology based policy developments was to attract comment in other contexts in the late twentieth century.

General public welfare and social care legislation

Parliament, from at least the time of the Poor Law 1601, had made a distinction between public and private responsibilities in relation to children and sought to ensure that the onus to safeguard the latter's welfare rested on parents rather than the state. Where family care was not possible - in circumstances of parental death, absence or criminal abuse - then Parliament had used the Poor Laws to place responsibility on public authorities for the provision of residential child care facilities. This responsibility can be seen as derived from the feudal concept of *parens patriae* (see, Chap 1). The duties of the person or body 'standing in the shoes of the parent' included responsibilities for the nurture, safety and education of the child. In legal terms this simply amounted to the state assuming all first party parental responsibilities for the child concerned.

By the nineteenth century, Parliament had begun to extend the principle of public responsibility in circumstances of family failure to include also a level of responsibility in circumstances where family care remained intact. The duties of public authorities in respect of children, whether in the nature of direct service provision or the setting and monitoring of standards, were no longer assumed by the state acting solely *in absentia* of the parents. The nurture, safety and education of children were not to be left exclusively to first party parental discretion. The state would also assume some third party responsibilities in respect of all children in relation to such matters. This application of the *parens patriae* concept, to vest a level of responsibility for aspects of child development in the state, laid the foundations for the evolution of the modern comprehensive public welfare and social care legislative framework. This evolutionary process may be traced in relation to three distinct areas of general public welfare and social care as they affect the welfare interests of children: working conditions; education; and health and social care.

Employment

From the times of the Roman Empire, through the Middle Ages and the industrial revolution, until the beginning of this century, children of 6-8 years of age worked on farms, in shops, factories and professions; girls of 8-10 were servants in the households of other families, boys were apprenticed. The dangerous and arduous working conditions suffered by young children in the factories, mines and mills during the early years of the industrial revolution in Britain are well documented. By 1830 there were an estimated 26,000 children under the age of 14 working in factories.[41]

But this new machine age was also an era of opportunity for the many families which benefited from the labour of their children. Sending children out to work for long hours in dangerous environments was, for some, no more than a natural extension of the paternal rights doctrine. The prevailing attitude towards paternal authority and the autonomous marital family unit was reflected in the opinion of a writer who stated:[42]

> I would far rather see even a higher rate of infant mortality than has ever yet been proved against the factory district or elsewhere...than intrude one iota further on the sanctity of the domestic hearth and the decent seclusion of private life...

A view which a more modern writer believes to be not unrepresentative of the values of that time. Fox Harding suggests that there was considerable opposition to laws restricting child labour and introducing compulsory education because these were seen as constituting an unwarranted state interference with parental authority.[43] Parliament, however, viewed the private exploitation of small children as a matter of public concern and reformers, such as Lord Shaftesbury, worked to safeguard children from exploitation by factory owners. In a series of paternalistic statutes Parliament prohibited the employment of children as chimney sweeps and set standards for publicly acceptable working conditions for children.[44] Eventually, the Education Act 1918 prohibited the employment of children aged 12-14 in factories.

Education

The history of the development of education in England is one in which the separate provision made by Church and the wealthy initially prevailed at the expense of a national system. Public secular education for young children in England was not universally available until the latter half of the nineteenth century. Private education had been available to those who could afford it at least a century earlier and a patchy system of schooling for poor children was provided by the churches. For most of the nineteenth century, state intervention took the form of grant aiding education provision made by Church based and nonconformist schools. The 'public school' system, providing education for the children of a wealthy elite, was established during this period and consolidated in the early decades of the twentieth century.

In 1856 a Dept of Education was established and eventually the first legislation was introduced when the Education Act 1870 laid the foundations for a system of mandatory primary education which was to be secular and freely available to poor children. The Education Act 1902 provided for the abolition of school boards, which had become obstructive in their protection of the Church's vested interest in controlling education, allowed for state assimilation of voluntary schools and required local government funding to be made available for Church based schooling. The Education Act 1918 raised the school leaving age to fourteen and made education freely available for all children. However, not until the Education Act 1944 were the basic components of a modern national education system put in place. This legislation made provision for: free secondary education, free meals, milk and transport; standard examinations, notably the 11+ were introduced; grants were made available to assist entry to university; and the school leaving age was raised to fifteen (to sixteen in 1972). The extension of this national approach to higher and further education was undertaken in the 1960s.

Health

Health and social care initiatives, relating to the welfare interests of children, also owed a good deal to the work of voluntary organisations and children's charities which played a significant role in providing initial care and treatment facilities for poor children in need. The Thomas Coram Hospital for foundling children, for example, was established in 1739. The Infant Life Protection Society, founded in 1870, provided such support as was then available for the protection of newly born babies in workhouses and campaigned for the introduction of the Infant Life Protection Act 1872. But for the most part the health and welfare of poor children depended upon the rudimentary state care system provided by the Poor Laws through the workhouses which remained in effect until 1929 when the local authorities were established. This limited recognition of a level of state responsibility for children within the

Poor Law system was in time extended to an acknowledgement of broad responsibilities towards all children within the welfare state system. Certain contemporary services, child health care practices and welfare benefits originated with the Poor Laws.

During the nineteenth century the Poor Law authorities initiated boarding-out schemes. These enabled children to be placed, where possible and for a fee, with families in country areas. By boarding-out children the authorities increased their likelihood of survival; many otherwise died in the appalling conditions that prevailed in most workhouses. The current practice of giving preference to family based rather than institutional care, as provided by foster parents, had its origins in the Poor Law era.

The Poor Law Act of 1834 had placed new responsibilities on workhouse inspectors to prevent or control the spread of infectious diseases. But it was not until the Public Health Act 1848 that this approach was extended nationally to become underpinned by specific duties in the Acts of 1871 and 1875 and in the Sanitation Act 1866. It was this legislation which gave rise to public health care duties and the responsibilities of health visitors which were to be consolidated within a comprehensive National Health Service in 1948.

Welfare benefits

Arguably, the single most important factor in raising physical standards of child care was the introduction of a scheme of financial benefits payable to mothers and enabling them to buy the essentials necessary to ensure the welfare of their children. The Royal Commission on the Poor Laws was set up in 1832 and its findings formed the basis for the Poor Law 1834 which made provision for a financial benefit to be paid to an unmarried mother in her own right. This was amended in 1844 to place the responsibility on such a mother to take affiliation proceedings against the putative father and secure maintenance payments from him. The financial difficulties faced by single mothers led to an increase in the rates of infanticide and abandonment. In 1918 the National Council for the Unmarried Mother and her Child was formed and maintenance payments were at first increased and then doubled in 1923. But not until financial support was addressed on a centralised basis, linked to schemes of national insurance, assistance and family allowances, were single mothers placed on a more secure financial footing to provide for the welfare of their children.[45]

Conclusion

The balance between the three legislative strands changed significantly during the period under review in this chapter. Intervention in family affairs, coercive and consensual, on matters relating to the welfare interests of the child, became increasingly more prevalent under the headings of public law and general social welfare. As private family law was legislatively prised open, despite judicial defence of the doctrine of paternal rights, responsibilities in respect of child welfare were steadily extended to other parties. In particular, as the process began of demarcating those areas of responsibility such as education, health and benefits to be met by national service provision and form the foundations for the welfare state, so the parameters were established for private and public family law.

In private family law, paternal rights slowly gave way to parental rights and duties. Custody, which had been viewed as the hallmark of paternal rights, directly and intimately vested in the father as head of his autonomous marital family unit, came to be regarded more as a legally transferable parental function. Guardianship - which like wardship had always been concerned with the duties of care, protection and maintenance of children – became the legislative vehicle which first introduced the welfare interests of the child as a criterion for judicial determination of disputed custody arrangements. However, this criterion only came into play after proof of parental death, absence or fault. A judicial finding of fault in matrimonial proceedings, most usually on proof of adultery, would result in a ruling that the spouse was thereby unfit to be a parent.

In public law, fault also came to be the central rationale for disentitling a parent; most usually on proof of child neglect, ill-treatment or abuse. The indices of parental fault established a century ago – such as failure to provide adequate food, shelter, maintenance, being found 'likely to cause' unnecessary suffering or refusal to consent to an operation – still ground judicial decisions to transfer care responsibility. Extending fault liability from parents to third parties was accelerated through an ever broadening swathe of statutes proscribing circumstances and conduct identified as detrimental to the welfare of children. Parental decisions to entrust day care responsibility to third parties were made subject to rules governing the registration and inspection of child-minding arrangements. The legal position of third party carers such as foster parents and voluntary child care organisations was given a degree of statutory protection. Parental relinquishing of children into the long-term care of the state was facilitated and informal adoptions were left unregulated until 1926.

The three legislative strands set the thresholds for intervention in family affairs on matters relating to the welfare interests of children. They and the underpinning indices of welfare, first statutorily identified at least a century ago, are largely still in place today.

Notes

1 (1831) Eng Rep 162; Stone, p 173.
2 (1836) 4 Adolphus & Ellis, p 624.
3 See *Clout v Clout and Hollebone* (1861) 2 Swabey & Tristram 391.
4 (1862) 2 Swabey & Tristram 567.
5 (1865) LR 1 P & D 39 at p 41.
6 See *Bent v Bent and Footman* (1861) 2 Swabey & Tristram 392; *Seddon v Seddon and Doyle* (1862) 2 Swabey & Tristram 640.
7 See *Chetwynd; Milford v Milford* (1869) LR 1 P&D 715.
8 (1878) 4 PD 87 at p 88.
9 *Report of the Royal Commission on Marriage and Divorce*, Cmnd 9678, 1956.
10 *Op cit*, para 366.
11 *Op cit*, para 367.
12 Law Commission, *Arrangements for the Care and Upbringing of Children*, No 15, 1968.
13 [1964] 3 All ER 255.
14 (1876) 4 Ch D 157 p 160.
15 [1897] 1 Ch 786 at p 792.
16 [1970] AC 668 at p 709.
17 See *Re N (Minors)(Parental Rights*, [1974] Fam 40, [1973] 3 WLR 866, [1974] 1 All ER 126, DC.
18 See, for example, Tizzard, B, *Adoption: A Second Chance*, Open Books, 1977.
19 [1900] 2 IR 233 at p 244.
20 *The Report of the Committee on Child Adoption* (Cmnd 1254), 1921.
21 See *Report of the Departmental Committee on the Adoption of Children*, London, HMSO, 1954, Cmnd 9248, p 4.
22 See *Report of the Departmental Committee on the Adoption of Children*, London, HMSO, 1972, Cmnd 5107, para 17.
23 See, for example, *R v Gibbons and Proctor* (1918) 13 Cr App Rep 134 where a woman was found guilty of murder by wilfully neglecting to feed the child of her cohabitee.
24 See, for example, *R v Whibley* [1938] 3 All ER 777 where it was held that a father had not caused his children suffering or injury to health when he abandoned them in a courthouse. Also, see, *Brooks v Blount* [1923] 1 KB 257 it was held that proof of actual suffering was unnecessary; proof of likelihood was sufficient.
25 See *Oakey v Jackson* [1914] 1 KB 216 where 'treatment' was held to be a constituent element of 'care', and blood transfusion was considered a form of treatment. However, account must also be taken of the House of Lords ruling in *R v Sheppard* [1981] AC 394 which held that, when determining recklessness, the standard to be applied is a subjective understanding of the circumstances as perceived by the alleged offender, not the objective assessment of the court. See, also, *Alhaji Mohammed v Knott* [1969] 1 QB 1, which is authority for the view that an objective assessment must also give way to the particular values of the cultural context within which the alleged offender perceives the circumstances.
26 See Bean, P., and Melville, J., *Lost Children of the Empire*, London, Unwin Hyman, 1989 and Platt, A., *The Child Savers*, Chicago, University of Chicago Press, 1969.
27 See *A Treatise on the Law Relating to Infants*, London (1842).

28 See *R v Connor* [1908] 2 KB 26 where Lord Alverstone notes the history of this legislation.

29 [1899] 1 QB 283.

30 [1908] 2 KB 26, per Lord Alverstone CJ at p 30.

31 The preventative duties of a local authority were legislatively introduced by s 1(1) of the Children and Young Persons Act 1963 which required it 'to make available such advice, guidance and assistance as may promote the welfare of children by diminishing the need to receive children into or keep them in care...or to bring children before a juvenile court'.

32 See also the Houghton Report, *op cit*, para 116.

33 See, for example, the Custody of Children Act 1891, ss 1 and 3; Children and Young Persons Act 1933, s 1(1); Children Act 1975, s 12(2)(d); Adoption Act 1976, s 16(2)(d).

34 The Industrial Schools Act 1857 (and associated statutes) and the Prevention of Cruelty to and Protection of Children Act 1889 jointly gave rise to the body of legislation known generally as the Children and Young Persons Act (1933, 1963 and 1969) which in due course was displaced by the Children Act 1989.

35 *Report of the Care of Children Committee*, HMSO, 1946.

36 See *Reformatory Schools for the Perishing and Dangerous Classes and for the Prevention of Juvenile Delinquency*, published in 1851.

37 See Morris, A., and Giller, H., *Understanding Juvenile Justice*, Croom Helm, London, 1987, p 6 where the authors note that on one day in 1814, five children aged between eight and 12 were hanged for petty larceny.

38 In response to the recommendations of the Kilbrandon Committee, HMSO, 1964; see, also, the government White Paper *Children in Trouble*, 1968.

39 The Reformatory Schools Act 1866, s 14.

40 The Industrial Schools Act, s 14.

41 See FM L Thompson, *The Rise of Respectable Society: A Social History of Victorian Britain*, Oxford University Press, 1988, p 23.

42 See *Transactions of the National Association for the Promotion of Social Sciences* (1874), quoted by Pinchbeck, I and Hewitt, M in *Children in English Society* (1973), p 359.

43 See Fox Harding, *Perspectives in Child Care Policy*, Longman, 1997, p 35.

44 See: the Health and Morals of Apprentices Act 1802; the Factories Acts of 1802, 1819, 1833 and 1867; the Workshop Regulation Act 1867 etc.

45 See: the National Insurance Acts 1911 and 1946; the Family Allowances Act 1945; and the National Assistance Act 1948.

Part 2: The Content and Structural Role of the Welfare Principle in the Legal System

Introduction to Part 2

Structure and method condition the functioning of the welfare principle within the legal system. The welfare of the child must, therefore, be examined from the perspective of the actual mechanics for giving effect to it. These range from explicitly prescribed statutory rules binding on all parties, to implicitly acknowledged areas of judicial and professional discretion. They include not only administrative and procedural requirements but extend to the way in which the court system is organised to deal with family matters. Of particular relevance to children are the means whereby their welfare interests are identified and represented before the court, so this Part explores in some depth the processes whereby the legal system facilitates or impedes recognition of those interests.

The content of welfare is often presumed. It is assumed that the nurture needs of children are sufficiently well know to be readily identified and appropriately taken into account when decisions are taken affecting them. It is taken for granted that the courts will be well versed on such matters. This Part examines the judicial indices of welfare interests. It identifies the themes which have emerged with some consistency over several centuries of caselaw.

Evaluating the appropriateness of the existing legal system - as a suitable and efficient means of recognising and responding to the welfare interests of individual children - provides an important theme for this book.

This Part acknowledges a major development in the role played by the welfare principle in the modern law as it relates to children. Part 1 charted the principle's evolution from judicial genesis in the courts of Chancery to eventual incorporation in legislation. The principle then functioned largely as a brake to constrain an irresponsible exercise of rights by parent, guardian or stranger and as a litmus test to identify and legislatively proscribe those circumstances, conduct and materials judged to be harmful to children. Part 2 sees the principle grow from a role as determinant of the subject matter for legal processes to its present position of also governing, to some extent, the means whereby the law relates to children. This Part acknowledges that the principle functions not only as a factor or objective in proceedings, but is now so infused within the legal system that it shapes the appropriate structures, governing principles and particular statutory duties common to both public and private law.

Part 2 consists of four chapters which examine the content and structural role of the welfare principle. It begins with a chapter that takes stock of what is meant by the welfare of the child; it identifies and assesses its primary ingredients as disclosed by caselaw. The next chapter considers the ways in which the principle affects the legal system as it now relates to children under the Children Act 1989; the jurisdiction and operation of the courts, access and the governing rules and principles. The final two chapters focus on the ways in which the legal system gives effect to the principle by providing for the identification and representation, respectively, of matters having a bearing on a child's welfare interests; attention is given to the role of the child, other parties and the range of professionals now engaged in bringing welfare interests before the court.

This Part thereby lays a foundation for Parts 3 and 4 which examine the distinctive operational features of public and private family law in some detail.

4 Welfare Interests and the Child

Introduction

The principle of the welfare of the child is notoriously imprecise. Any elucidation of the principle's content can only be sensibly attempted in relation to the particular needs of the child to whom it is to be applied. Those needs will be defined according to the values of the cultural context to which the child belongs. They will also vary according to the age of the child. It is technically difficult to identify objectively the components of a principle which only acquires a valid meaning when applied subjectively. But the key questions remain - What actually constitutes welfare? Who decides? In what way do welfare considerations affect legal decisions?

This chapter concentrates on examining the substance of welfare, rather than its role or weighting, as interpreted and developed by the judiciary in judgments given on matters concerning a child's upbringing. Its central concern is to identify the main components currently considered by the judiciary to constitute a child's welfare interests. It begins by examining problems of definition and interpretation before considering who has the right to take decisions in respect of a child's welfare interests. It then identifies developments which show how the meaning given to the principle has broadened, noting its susceptibility to judicial rules. This approach reveals that while certain core traditional aspects of welfare continue to be consistently taken into judicial account, some have changed and new dimensions to welfare have been added. It also reveals that perhaps the most significant change in relation to this principle has been in the role played by a child, the subject of proceedings, in assisting the court to define and interpret the meaning of his or her welfare relative to other considerations.

Welfare interests: problems of definition and interpretation

The welfare principle has never been a fixed standard capable of uniform application across diverse circumstances and across the entire age range of childhood. Because it is a value based standard its meaning at any point in time derives from the prevailing cultural context of the society applying it. Parenting and child welfare always reflect cultural values. The welfare of a child is currently construed differently in the barrios of Rio de Janiero and in Surrey and has been construed quite differently over time in the latter.

The fact that it is such an indeterminate concept has allowed it to be used creatively and flexibly by the judiciary of this jurisdiction in many different circumstances for several centuries. Its meaning has had to be derived from its immediate context. This has most usually been a legislative context, where it has been defined by the legislative intent. Where the provisions specified particular aspects of welfare interests, such as health or education, then the courts have been required to interpret a child's welfare in accordance with that specific definition. Other statutes have referred broadly to 'welfare' or 'best interests' etc. This has given the courts great discretion to determine a child's welfare in accordance with the full range of options available. The former objectifies welfare and requires judicial decisions to be tied to the specific legal context. The second employs welfare as a subjective standard and allows judicial decisions to explore the family context and tailor the legal solution to the needs of a particular child. It is this subjective approach which has permitted the judiciary to extend the interpretation of welfare to include not only the traditional elements of physical well-being and maintenance but also religious and moral upbringing and psychological needs such as enduring relationships and notions of risk and security. The judgments contain many illustrations of the judiciary taking into account such subjective aspects of welfare as the stigma attached to illegitimacy, the impact of parental adultery on the child, the desirability of parental access. Increasingly the courts have come to interpret welfare in terms of a child's relationships; establishing those relationships, their viability, quality, the likelihood of their interruption or termination are aspects of welfare of growing importance. While the subjective approach allows judicial discretion to interpret welfare relative to the needs of a particular child the objective approach requires the judiciary to apply the welfare specification to the needs of all children appearing before the court; but the latter rule will often also contain subjective elements[1] and the children involved will each have their own very individual set of needs.

There has never been any uniformity of policy in relation to the role of welfare in legislation.[2] In many instances the legislative intent of a statute is to pursue objectives other than securing or promoting welfare. The policy of an Act affecting children may have nothing to do with the protection or promotion of the welfare of children. Alternatively, the legislative intent may be to safeguard welfare by placing duties on others. Legislation may deal with welfare in the present tense. Reference will then tend to be made to it in relatively objective and precise terms; abandonment, parental unfitness, danger to health and detrimental environment or premises for example. Legislation may also deal with welfare in the future tense. Where it does so the references lack comparable precision. Legislation may or may not require the judiciary to have regard for welfare at the threshold or adjudicative stages of proceedings, but this will always be a factor at the disposal stage.

Welfare interests: the child and the decision-makers

Traditionally, a decision affecting the welfare interests of a child could only be made by the mother of an illegitimate child, by either or both parents of a marital child, by the court or by a guardian or person acting in *loco parentis* with authority from one of the aforementioned. The child and his or her welfare were the subject of decisions taken by others. The consent of the child was not required. The law confined itself to licensing the decision-makers and establishing the terms for the legitimate exercise of their authority. In the space of the past few decades this has changed.

The child

Under the common law a child was defined as such until he or she attained the age of 21. Since the introduction of the Family Law Reform Act 1969, the operative age has been 18. A valid consent for a third party to undertake a course of action affecting the welfare interests of a child could only be obtained from a parent, guardian or court but not from the child. A child was held to be legally incapable of determining his or her own welfare interests and of binding others to respect them. Two cases radically altered the legal standing of a child's welfare interests relative to all other parties: *J v C* [3] and *Gillick v West Norfolk and Wisbech Area Health Authority.* [4]

The first case concerned foster parents in England who had cared for the ten year old son of a Spanish couple for all but eighteen months of his life. In the House of Lords, on appeal from wardship proceedings, their lordships held that even if the parents were 'unimpeachable' the welfare interests of the child were of paramount importance, outweighing all other considerations. In the frequently quoted words of Lord MacDermott in this leading case:[5]

> ...the words 'shall regard the welfare of the infant as the first and paramount consideration' in their ordinary significance...must mean more than that the child's welfare is to be treated as the top item in a list of items relevant to the matter in question, I think they connote a process whereby, when all the

> relevant facts, relationships, claims and wishes of parents, risks, choices and other circumstances are taken into account and weighed, the course to be followed will be that which is most in the interests of the child's welfare as that term has now to be understood. That is the first consideration because it is of first importance and the paramount consideration because it rules on or determines the course to be followed.

Thereafter, this principle was embodied in legislation and has grown to become a benchmark standard for the law relating to the welfare interests of children.

In the second case it was the law relating to the consent of an adolescent that was radically changed; indeed the position of a consenting minor was altered more radically by the decision in *Gillick*[6] than by the provisions of the 1969 Act. In that case, the House of Lords ruled that in some circumstances a doctor could prescribe contraceptives for a child under the age of 16 without consulting the child's parents. Since then the legal standing of a child in any decision-making process affecting his or her interests has depended on their age and their understanding of the issues involved. As Lord Scarman explained:

> ...a minor's capacity to make his or her decision depends upon the minor having sufficient understanding and intelligence to make the decision and is not to be determined by reference to any judicially fixed age limit.

The *prima facie* presumption that a child below the age of 16 is non-competent may be rebutted by evidence based on age and understanding; a child over that age will be presumed to have the necessary competence. But, where a child is aged 16 or is deemed to be '*Gillick* competent', then the law requires that his or her consent is sought in relation to the matter at issue.

In legal terms, the distance between these two cases is enormous. *J v C* marks, perhaps, the apotheosis of a welfare jurisprudence in which the child is objectified to become merely the recipient of a welfare allocation callibrated in accordance with a standardised judicial formula. The *Gillick* ruling may be seen as the first step away from the objectification of the child within a paternalistic welfare philosophy and towards welfare as a matter capable of subjective interpretation, and of justifying action as a right, by the child concerned.

Distinguishing a child's legal interests from those of his or her parents, particularly in private proceedings, has always been a fraught and complicated area of family law. This is less so where the distinction to be made is between a child's interests and those of a third party. In the context of proceedings where an offence involving a child is known or alleged to have been committed, the legal issues at least are usually relatively uncomplicated and will dictate the separation of a child's interests from those of any first or third parties.

Where the child is of an age and understanding to express views[7] on the issues raised these will have a bearing on the judicial task of separating the different sets of legal interests.[8]

The courts most usually have cause to adjudicate on the separateness of the interests of parents and children where the latter are either too young to express any views or are mature enough to have their legal competence recognised when doing so.

In relation to babies, the courts have always held pretty much to the view[9] that the younger the child the greater the weight to be attached to preserving the 'psychological bond' between mother and child, as a factor in determining the welfare interests of that child. The inference being that the welfare of a young child is not readily separable from the legal interests of the mother. In the words of Romilly MR in *Austin v Austin*:[10]

> The welfare of the child is so intimately connected with its being under the care of the mother that no extent of kindness on the part of any other person can supply that place. It is the notorious observation of mankind that the loss of a mother is irreparable to her children and particularly so if young.

This approach has had and continues to have a virtually determining effect on contested private family law proceedings; though it offered little resistance to the 'protectionist' ethos which characterised child care proceedings under the 1968 Act. In relation to a foetus, the courts recognised[11] that a mother owes a duty of care to her unborn child; albeit one that is not actionable until after birth. The significance of this landmark decision, in terms of the light it sheds on judicial rationale for distinguishing between the welfare of the child and the legal interests of the mother, is difficult to judge. It may, perhaps, be seen as a logical extension of the judicial view that the younger the child the more fused are mother/child interests; the greater, therefore, is the maternal obligation to safeguard her own well-being as only by doing so will her child's interests be protected.

The parents

'Parent' has been defined in law as meaning both the mother and father of a legitimate child and the unmarried mother of an illegitimate child.[12] This definition excludes such others as a step-father[13] and an unmarried father. The latter may, however, acquire 'parent' status. Traditionally, in law the welfare interests of a child were to be identified and determined by the parent as so defined and not the child. This most usually occurred when the proposals of a third party, such as those of a medical practitioner to conduct an intimate physical examination or to administer anaesthetic, could lead to a possible charge of trespass to the person of the child unless properly authorised. However, the one hundred years which separate the decisions taken in *Re*

Agar-Ellis[14] and in *Gillick v West Norfolk and Wisbech Area Health Authority and the DHSS*[15] have witnessed a quiet revolution in the relative legal standing of parents and their children in proceedings concerning the latter's welfare. The former case is a reference point for the law's recognition of a father's exclusive rights to determine matters affecting his children, within an autonomous marital family unit (see, further, Chap 2). The latter provides a marker of equal significance for the law's recognition of a 'mature minor's' emerging right to take unilateral decisions on such matters, within or without a marital unit and in relation to matters defined as falling within public or private family law. Now, judicial acknowledgement is readily given to the fact that there will be some circumstances where parental consent will be displaced by a child's wishes and feelings. As was stated in the *Gillick* case:

> An underlying principle of the law....is that parental right yields to the child's right to make his own decisions when he reaches a sufficient understanding and intelligence to be capable of making up his own mind on the matter requiring decision.[16]

The welfare of children may also be protected by conferring rights upon or safeguarding the interests of others, most notably parents. It is axiomatic that to some extent the law relating to children creates a delicate balance between the interests of the child and those of other persons, particularly the child's parents. It is probably a matter of debate whether the conferring of rights upon parents and other persons is intended to benefit the recipient of the right or the child. Most instances probably benefit the parent by complementing parental common law rights, while the others may no doubt be justified as beneficial on the ground that, for example, parental care is *prima facie* preferable to institutional or similar upbringing. Some measures which provide for a child's welfare interests are statutorily made subject to the rights of a parent. So, for example, advance parental consent is required: before an adoption order can be made; before a child can be ordered to attend a special school; or before a child can be operated upon.

Third parties

Prior to the decision in *Gillick* a valid consent for a third party to undertake a course of action affecting the welfare interests of a child could only be obtained from a parent, guardian or court but not from the child. The main statutory exception to this rule was provided by s 8(1) of the Family Law Act 1969:

> The consent of a minor who has attained the age of sixteen years to any surgical, medical or dental treatment which, in the absence of consent, would constitute a trespass to his person, shall be as effective as it would be if he were of full age; and where a minor has by virtue of this section given an

> effective consent to any treatment it shall not be necessary to obtain any consent for it from his parent or guardian.

Since then the courts can be seen looking to this decision as a reference point for determining the consent capacity of an older child in relation to third parties on issues affecting his or her welfare. Distinguishing a child's legal interests from those of a third party has tended to be a fairly straightforward matter.

Welfare: refining the common law legacy

The common law judiciary regarded certain aspects of a child's upbringing as constituting the core elements of welfare. These were: care and maintenance; education; religious upbringing; and, arguably, control. They were of such importance that the safeguarding of each constituted both a right and a duty vested in parent or guardian in respect of a child in their care. In due course they each came to be the subject of a considerable body of legislation and caselaw. As that body developed many other components of welfare were identified, differentiated and regulated by statute. Together they may be grouped under the headings of physical welfare, moral welfare and psychological welfare.

Physical welfare

The composite duty to safeguard a child's welfare by providing appropriate care and maintenance consists of satisfying his or her needs in relation to physical integrity, health, medical and dental care, accommodation, environment, hygiene, food and sanitation. From common law origins, through the period of legislative endorsement in the Poor Laws and the subsequent reforms of the mid-nineteenth century, to the welfare state in the late twentieth century, the law relating to a child's physical and material well-being has remained fundamentally the same. Statute law has steadily raised the required standards for meeting such needs and has increased the range and sophistication of related duties. The law dealing with some of the more traditional aspects of physical well-being, most notably in regard to protection and medical treatment, has burgeoned in volume and complexity. Entirely new branches of law have evolved around such modern determinants of physical well-being as genetics, pre-natal heath care and abortion. But the basic duty owed to children by their parents, or failing them by the state, to provide for their physical needs and safeguard them from any foreseeable harm, has not changed.

The law has always been most clear and objective in its specification of duties in relation to a child's care and maintenance. Most usually this has been achieved by statutorily proscribing the exposure of children to conduct or circumstances held to harm or threaten their physical well-being (see, further, Chap 2). A child has long been held to have an entitlement to an adequate standard of physical care and to protection from an abusive, exploitive or neglectful parent; an entitlement which warrants enforcement, or coercive removal of care responsibility, by the state. Provision of physical care is the primary responsibility of those with parental responsibility; providing a safe home for the child in question, or determining where he or she shall live, is the most basic duty.[17] The ancillary duty, to provide maintenance adequate to meet the care needs of the child, has also long been recognised by the courts and in a body of legislation of increasing complexity.[18]

Moral welfare

For at least the past century the courts have acknowledged that while nurture needs were fundamental to a child's welfare interests, meeting such needs was in itself insufficient to fully discharge the duty in respect of the welfare principle. The quality of welfare implied more than a requirement to fulfill a child's minimal needs for physical and material well-being. Lindly LJ drew attention to this in *Re McGrath (Infants)*:[19]

> The dominant matter for the consideration of the Court is the welfare of the child. But the welfare of a child is not to be measured by money only, nor by physical comfort only. The word welfare must be taken in its widest sense. The moral and religious welfare of the child must be considered as well as its physical well-being. Nor can the ties of affection be disregarded.

The law recognised the moral and religious components of child welfare by enforcing a parental duty to provide education in relation to the former while also acknowledging a parental right to provide religious training. Both came to be addressed, in effect, by the state through mandatory education programmes. Initially an objective within such programmes was to protect or enforce the parent's interest in the child's religion; this has largely given way to provisions which enforce the child's own interest in his religious education. The education of children became an integral aspect of their welfare enforceable in law. Statute law provided for this welfare component by conferring and imposing powers and duties upon parents, education authorities and other educational administrative bodies. A duty was placed upon parents to cause every child of school age to receive efficient and suitable education. A corresponding duty was placed upon an education authority to ensure adequate educational provision. A lack of education became a sufficient ground for care proceedings.

The moral welfare of a child cannot be fully assured solely by statutory provision relating to education and religious upbringing. The common law basis for protecting the moral welfare of children has been extended by a raft of statutes, continuously added to as developments in society's values indicate new areas for protective intervention. Most obviously these have sought to preserve the moral integrity of children in relation to sex and violence by setting threshold criteria of age and consent for access to a range of audio/visual material and involvement in sexual relations particularly homosexual relationships. Many statutes prohibit specific conduct or circumstances considered likely to undermine moral welfare; such as indulgence in or access to alcohol, cigarettes, solvents, betting and gaming. While the legal function of prohibition was directed towards the activities of adults and commercial bodies, the function of enforcement was often also directed towards control of the children concerned. A child subject, of conduct or circumstances statutorily proscribed on moral welfare grounds, could as a result find themselves also becoming the subject of a court order made to control future behaviour.

Psychological welfare

As society has developed a more sophisticated awareness of children's needs and an understanding of the developmental stages of childhood so the law has refined its recognition and protection of welfare interests. Although there have never been any statutory references to emotional or psychological welfare,[20] the judiciary in recent years have demonstrated a willingness to view these as inherent components of welfare. Since the mid-1960s', judicial notice has increasingly been taken of the work of leading child psychiatrists and psychologists and decisions grounded on evidence of the child's emotional and psychological welfare as distinct from material welfare.[21] The case of *In re L (An Infant)*[22] provides a typical example. When the mother was unable to decide whether to give her consent to the adoption of her child, some considerable time after the child had been placed for that purpose, the court took into consideration the psychological and physical harm which could follow if the child were removed from the adoptive home; a *ratio decidendi* to be followed in many cases. Where attachment existed between the adopters and the child, a reasonable parent might be expected to consider whether a refusal to consent would disrupt that attachment with consequent implications for welfare. The concept of a 'psychological parent' emerged from such cases to gain widespread judicial approval. This is defined as follows:[23]

> ...whether any adult becomes the psychological parent of a child is based on day-to-day interaction, companionship, and shared experiences. The role can be filled by a biological parent or by an adoptive parent or by any other caring adult...but never by an absent, inactive adult, whatever his biological or legal relationship to the child may be.

The courts have been reluctant to look at the psychological aspects of welfare in isolation.

Presumptive judicial rules relating to welfare

The role of the welfare principle, ascribed or permitted by the law, has always been conditioned by its context. This is most explicit in a legislative context, particularly in the distinctions between public and private or civil and criminal proceedings (see, Chap 3). It is evident also in a procedural context where it is governed by the relative legal standing of the parties engaged in the proceedings: the role is quite different where the dispute lies between first parties, between third parties or between first and third parties. But, most obviously, because of its intrinsically subjective nature, the principle has leant itself to a range of interpretations in the context of the discretionary use of judicial powers. In this latter context, the formulation of certain judicial rules at first inhibited then positively advanced the role, functions and understanding of the welfare principle. In some instances the rules attained the status of legal presumptions. In other cases they offered little more than optional guidance in certain circumstances. Some were explicitly directed towards the needs of children, others affected their needs implicitly. The judiciary employed such rules and guidelines to remedy actual legislative deficiencies and to counter what they viewed as conservative legislative principles.

Negative judicial rules

The legal standing of the marital family has always had a decisive influence on the potential for the welfare principle to influence judicial determination of issues affecting the upbringing of children. From the era when the law was resolved to uphold the twin principles of patriarchy and matrimony, three areas of parental relationships gave rise to enduring judicial rules which initially inhibited the potential for a more positive application of the welfare principle. These concerned paternal rights, the conduct of the parties and legal status.

The first of these was the rule that a father had a *prima facie* right to the custody of his legitimate child. This common law presumption, that custody vests in the father unless and until a court orders otherwise, found statutory endorsement in s 5 of the Guardianship of Infants Act 1886. It survived the legislative intent that it should provide a counterbalance to paternal rights in judicial considerations of custody issues (see, also, Chap 2). Until the mid-twentieth century, court judgments frequently demonstrated that this presumption had sufficient residual viability to persuade the judiciary to make awards of custody to divorced or separated fathers in the absence of evidence that this would be harmful to the child concerned. Even where a father candidly disclosed an intention to delegate total care responsibility to his mother, the courts would defer to his right to do so rather than give preference to the custody claims of the child's caring mother. Not until Parliament introduced further guardianship legislation nearly a century later was judicial defence of this rule finally quashed and the welfare interests of the child legislatively asserted as the paramount judicial consideration.

The second judicial rule concerned the conduct of the parties. The so-called doctrine of the unimpeachable parent, which required that custody be awarded to a parent only if he or she was without fault in relation to the marital breakdown, once played a determining role in custody disputes[24] (see, Chap 3). So if, for example, a wife had been found to be adulterous[25] or either parent had 'abducted'[26] their child, then that parent would not be awarded custody. The judicial approach to the latter offence may also be seen as an aspect of the more general rule that no guilty party should be permitted to benefit from wrongdoing.[27] The eventual neutralising of the doctrine and with it that whole judicial approach, enabling preference to be given to the parent most effective in safeguarding their child's welfare interests, even if proven to be a culpable spouse, was due in large part to the role played by the judiciary in the wardship jurisdiction. However, where culpability directly affects parental fitness, as when the conduct in question is incest, then the right to custody may still be lost.

The third area, in which judicial rules inhibited the development of the welfare principle, concerned the legal status of the parties. In the case of a non-marital child, or *filius nullius*, the judiciary were free to focus wholly on the child's welfare interests as there were no legal interests to impede judicial discretion:[28] neither child, father or any third party could have an inherent legal right that had to be taken into account; the presumptive rule was that full care responsibility vested in the natural mother. Where a third party, such as a foster-parent or natural father, had acquired sufficient legal interests to challenge a mother's right to possession then nonetheless the court was able to give a determining role to the welfare principle when deciding future custody rights. In the case of a marital child, however, which initially constituted the bulk of custody disputes, the court has always had difficulty in accommodating the welfare principle. When faced with a supervening legal right such as the traditional paternal right to custody, or with the competing legal rights of more contemporary marital parents, the court has had to place welfare considerations in abeyance while it adjudicated the dispute in terms of the rights of the parties; the presumptive rule being that the welfare principle was at best a secondary consideration in first party marital disputes.

Positive judicial rules

An important element in the development of the law relating to the welfare interests of children has been the influence of judicial notice given to certain factors held to be significant and positive determinants of welfare. By reaching behind such statutory synonyms for child welfare as 'best interests', 'well-being', 'for the good of' or 'to the advantage of' etc and using their discretionary powers to inject some specific indicators of what in particular may be held to constitute the substance of 'welfare', the judiciary were able to advance the role of the principle relative to other considerations. This occurred most frequently in wardship and in cases which most often concerned children and/or adults whose *locus standi* was compromised by non-marital status or care orders.

Firstly, the age and gender of children had a consistent bearing on judicial decisions regarding custody arrangements. Until the 1989 Act, there had never been a legislative requirement that a child's age or gender should play any part in the determination of custody proceedings in respect of that child. The judiciary, however, developed certain rules of thumb to guide decision-making on such matters. Although first applied in wardship cases, these rules prevailed to gain a more generalised judicial credence in cases of custody contests. One such rule was that the younger the child the stronger the judicial presumption that maternal rather than paternal care was to be preferred;[29] maternal care for such a child was also preferred to third party care.[30] In due course maternal preference was to mutate to become the 'blood-tie' rule.[31] This was offset by another such rule to the effect that the older the child the stronger the presumption that he or she should be cared for by the parent of corresponding gender.[32] The extent to which these rules of thumb may be compatible with the dictates of the paramountcy principle has become steadily more contentious.

Secondly, the judiciary have consistently emphasised the importance of keeping siblings together.[33] The rationale for this approach has been succinctly expressed as follows:[34]

> ...brothers and sisters should wherever possible, be brought up together, so that they are an emotional support to each other in the stormy waters of the destruction of their family.

Thirdly, the judiciary have stressed the importance of keeping children in a familiar environment. An approach which has been tempered by a view that the younger the child the more this factor diminishes in importance; although a seven year old child would now be considered capable of forming an attachment to his or her surroundings.[35] This approach is sometimes referred to as 'maintaining the *status quo*' and is very evident in a long line of judgments, most often concerning guardianship, going back to at least the late nineteenth century. As Lindley LJ then explained:[36]

> The duty of the court is, in our judgment, to leave the child alone, unless the court is satisfied that it is for the welfare of the child that some other course should be taken (p 148).

Fourthly, judicial weight has long been given to the opinion of the child.[37] Caselaw, particularly from the wardship jurisdiction, reveals a consistent judicial concern to establish a direct relationship with the children who come before the court accompanied by a willingness to solicit, and take into account, their views on matters affecting their welfare.

Fifthly, when making determinations the judiciary will have regard for the children's future welfare. It is a characteristic of the wardship jurisdiction that, unlike statutory law, it has not been tied to past or present circumstances but has had the capacity to consider also the likely bearing of future probabilities. Throughout the judgments, decisions are taken with reference to such projected welfare considerations as the ages, career potential and domestic relationship of the prospective custodians.

Conclusion

From humble beginnings as an inert threshold existing only in statutorily prescribed circumstances, acting no more than as a brake on the enjoyment of the rights of others, to be activated only in retrospect following its breach, the welfare principle evolved to become a powerful weapon for assertively protecting the welfare of a child. This has largely been achieved by the judiciary utilising the inherent flexibility of the principle to extend its interpretation and role in the law relating to children, mainly in a private family law context.

Notes

1 For example, the rule regarding the reasonableness of a parental withholding of consent for adoption carries the caveat that a reasonable parent would take into account the welfare of the child.

2 Until the Children Act 1989 with its checklist of considerations to provide for more judicial consistency in the interpretation and application of welfare indicators. This has diluted the strength of Maidment's observation that:

> The 'welfare of the child' principle is therefore now a deliberately indeterminate standard incorporated into the law in order to allow current social and cultural views about the needs of children, and also, it must be said, of their parents to be embodied in the legal decision-making process…p 3, *Child Custody and Divorce* (1985).

3 [1970] AC 668.

4 [1986] 1 AC 112, [1985] 3 All ER 402 HL.

5 *Op cit* at 710-711.

6 *Op cit*.

7 This has not always been the case: see, *R v Howes*, (1860) CA when Cockburn LCJ, in deciding whether or not a father should recover custody of a teenage daughter, thought the views of the 15 year old to be dangerously precocious and might lead to 'irreparable injury'.

8 See *Hewer v Bryant* [1970] 1 QB 357 at 369 where the court recognised a gradual displacement of parental rights by an adolescent's right of self-determination. Also see: *M v M (Child: Access)* [1973] 2 All ER 81 where the court established that a right of access between parent and child attached more to the latter than the former; *Re H (Minors)(Access)* [1992] 1 FLR 148 where the court held that the test was not - what positive advantages would the child gain by a resumption of contact? but rather - did any cogent reason exist for denying a child the opportunity to have contact with a parent?; and *Re R (A Minor)(Contact)* [1993] 2 FLR 762 where Butler-Sloss LJ emphasised that the companionship of a parent is so important for a child that it gives rise to a basic right in a child to such companionship.

9 See Bowlby et al.

10 (1865) 34 Beavan 257 at p 263. The enduring consistency of the judicial view on this matter can be gauged by the following recent pronouncement by Lord Jauncey for the House of Lords in *Brixey v Lynas* [1996] 2 FLR 499, HL:

> Nature has endowed men and women with very different attributes and it so happens that mothers are generally better fitted than fathers to provide for the needs of very young children (p 504C-5C).

11 See *D (A Minor) v Berkshire County Council* (1987) 1 All ER 33.

12 See *Re M* [1955] 2 QB 479. Note also, that after some uncertainty as to whether the 1886 and 1925 Acts applied to illegitimate children, the position of legitimate and illegitimate children was equated for the purposes of parental custody applications in 1959 (Legitimacy Act, s 14(1); also 1971 Act, s 14(1)).

13 See *Re N* [1974] 1 All ER 126.

14 [1883] 24 CH D 317.

15 [1986] AC 112.

16 *Gillickv West Norfolk and Wisbech Area Health Authority* [1986] 1 AC 112, HL (p 251B).

17 See, for example, *Hitchcock v WB* [1952] 2 QB 561 where the duty was restricted to "the provision of a home".

18 The statutory duty requiring a parent to maintain his or her child is now to be found mainly in the Child Support Act 1991 and also in the provisions of the Social Security Act 1986 and those of the Children Act1989.

19 [1893] 1Ch 143.

20 The first statutory reference to such matters came with the inclusion of 'wishes and feelings' as welfare considerations in the Children Act 1989.

21 See evidence of such a trend beginning with the judgment in *Re C(L) (an infant)* [1965] 2 QB 449 and culminating in the HL judgment in *Re W (an infant)* [1971] AC 682.

22 (1962) 106 Sol Jo 611.

23 See Goldstein, Freud and Solnit in *Beyond the Best Interests of the Child* Free Press, (1980).

24 During the late nineteenth and early twentieth centuries the guilt of a party provided the grounds for both the spouse's divorce action and the rejection of claims for custody. The waning of judicial weight given to this factor began with the judgment in *Stark v Stark and Hitchins* [1910] P 190. The demise of the presumption in favour of an innocent parent in custody disputes was confirmed by Ormrod LJ in *S v S* [1977] Fam 109 at 115, and by Stamp LJ in *Re K* [1977] Fam 179 at 183. In the former case it was noted that although no longer applicable in such issues between parents, this doctrine may still apply where the issue lies between a parent and a third party, per Ormrod LJ at p 116. See, also, MacDermott LJ in *J v C* [1970] AC 668 at 715.

25 See, for example, *Clout v Clout* (1861) 2 Sw and Tr 391.

26 This judicial approach to 'kidnapping parents' was reviewed by Buckley LJ in *Re L (Minors)* [1974] 1 WLR 250 at 265 where he concluded that "the weight to be attributed to it must depend upon the circumstances of the particular case". He formed the view that the court could deduce that notwithstanding the conduct of the 'kidnapper' the child should remain in his or her care. See, also, *McKee v McKee* [1951] AC 352; *In re E (D)(An Infant)* [1967] Ch 287; *In re TA (Infants)* [1972] 116 SJ78; and *R v D* [1984] AC 778, [1984] 2 All ER 449, HL.

27 See, for example, *Re L (Minors)* [1973] 3 All ER 743.

28 Not until the Family Law Reform Acts of 1969 and 1987, together with the Legitimacy Act 1976, did their legal interests acquire statutory recognition.

29 See, for example, *Re K (Minors)(Children: Care and Control)* [1977] Fam 179, [1977] 1 WLR 33, [1977] 1 All ER 647, CA. An approach which owed a good deal to the Bowlby dictum as to the importance of preserving the bonding relationship between mother and baby; see J Bowlby *Attachment*, (1969). Subsequent research has seriously challenged Bowlby's thesis (see, for example, Rutter *Maternal Deprivation Reassessed* (1972)).

30 As Hanna LJ noted in *Re B* (1962) 1 AER 872:

> True it is that the Chancery Judges, and I think those in the Divorce Division also, have in the past years rather taken the view that as long as the child is young enough to need the day to day care of his or her mother, it is better to leave the child with the mother unless the mother is an entirely unsuitable person (p 873).

See also *Re W (A Minor)(Custody)* (1982) 4 FLR 492, CA.

31 An early example of the "blood-tie" presumption can be seen in *Ord v Blackett* (1724) 9 Modern 116 where a putative father succeeded against the executrix and guardian of a child's dead mother "since he owned her to be his child" (p 117). Questioning the validity of this presumption, Dr Kellmer Pringle once said:

> A misplaced faith in blood-tie, and unjustified optimism about the chances of successfully treating the battering parent by casework or psychiatric methods, has placed many a child at risk of repeated injury (The Times, 26th Nov 1973).

32 See, for example, *May v May* [1986] 1 FLR 325, CA.

33 See, for example, *Re Besant* (1879) 11 Ch D 508, 512 CA; more recently, see, *Re C (A Minor)(Custody of Child)* (1980) 2 FLR 163, CA, *B v B (Custody of Children)* [1985]

FLR 166, CA, and also *C v C (Minors: Custody)* [1988] 2 FLR 291, 302 CA.

34 See *C v C (Minors: Custody), op cit*, per Purchas LJ.

35 See *Re Thain* [1926] Ch 676.

36 See *Re McGrath (infants)* [1893] 1 Ch 143. Also, see, *In re X, X v Y* [1899] 1 Ch 526.

37 See *R v Smith* (1734) 2 Strange 982 for an example of a case where the common law considered the child's wishes.

5 The Legal System and Welfare Interests

Introduction

The principle of the welfare of the child is no longer confined to the role and functions assigned to it in substantive law. It now also has a significant part to play in the legal system as it relates to matters affecting the upbringing of a child. However, to identify with any precision the nature and effect of the part it plays is problematic.

This chapter examines the modern structural role of the welfare principle as a determinant of how the legal system relates to children. It begins by reviewing the position in the years between the 1975 and 1989 Children Acts; a period characterised by the ever widening use of discretionary powers by the court and local authorities. It then considers the impact made by the later legislation in terms of organisational change to the legal system. Mostly, however, this chapter concentrates on outlining and examining the changes made to the interpretation and application of the welfare principle. In so doing, this chapter introduces the post-1989 era and the subject matter for the subsequent chapters.

The role of welfare in the legal system

The legal system governs the legitimate use of authority. It does so by setting out the rules for accessing and using the specific grants of power embodied in the court orders statutorily provided by Parliament. The role played by the welfare principle has evolved to the point where it is now beginning to fundamentally change the way in which the legal system accommodates the law relating to children. The principle is being infused throughout the system. Matters of substantive law, procedure and administration have, to a greater or lesser extent, been adjusted to respond to welfare indicators. It is no longer confined simply to a role in the threshold requirements for commencing proceedings and as a discretionary component in judicial disposal of such proceedings. It has also come to acquire a new leverage in the structure as well as in the content of the legal system. From a role previously confined to the fabric of legislation, as a factor in or the objective of a statute, the principle has now grown to assume a role which affects the organisation of courts, puts in place new court processes, new officials and new rules of evidence.

Before the Children Act 1989

The legal system always had difficulty in recognising both the separateness of a child's interests and the need for those interests to be independently represented before the court. Not until certain age specified levels of competence were met could a child then be held to satisfy the legal definition of 'person' as understood by Salmond.[1] Under the common law this had been determined by applying the construct 'age of discretion', as exemplified in the criminal law by rules of *doli incapax* in relation to children under the age of ten, the rebuttable presumption of incapacity for those aged ten to fourteen and the presumption of full adult capacity thereafter (see, further, Chap 9). Under statute law, the stipulated age of majority[2] marked the point at which a 'child' acquired a fully developed legal personality; although the body of statute law relating to children contained an assorted spread of age criteria for participation in different proceedings. Attaining the age of majority brought with it the right to initiate and/or appear as a party in court proceedings. Until then, the law stated that a child:[3]

> ...may not bring, or make a claim, in any proceedings except by his next friend and may not acknowledge service, defend, make a counterclaim or intervene in any proceedings, or appear in any proceedings under a judgment or order notice of which has been served on him, except by his guardian *ad litem*.

He or she had to rely on others to represent their interests within the legal system.

The status of legal 'person' was not so much denied a child as held to be absorbed within the personality of an adult recognised by the legal system as entitled and obliged to speak for the child's interests. Inherently, this responsibility was held to vest in the child's parent, most usually the father,[4] or a guardian appointed to act in their place (see, further, Chaps 1 and 2). Where the parent was unavailable, unable or disqualified from acting on behalf of the child then the court would appoint a 'next friend' to do so.

In the wake of changes wrought within the body of substantive law relating to children (see, further, Chap 3), there eventually followed some related procedural adjustments. The welfare interests of a child began to be brought before the court by persons other than parents, parent substitutes or 'next friends' as recognition was given to the need for independent representation of a child's interests. Mandatory welfare reports were required in an increasing range of public and private family law proceedings for the purpose of providing the court with information relating to the home surroundings, school record, health and character of the child appearing before it. Rules were introduced to disentitle parents from appearing as representatives on behalf of their children in circumstances where there was a clear conflict of interest. The introduction of the juvenile courts was a landmark development in the process of adjusting the legal system to accommodate the welfare interests of children.[5] In civil proceedings, particular arrangements were made to safeguard the welfare interests of children. These included, for example: the separation of children from adults in police stations and courts; hearings could be held in camera; the court could be cleared; in care proceedings whole or part of evidence could be heard in the absence of the child concerned; identity could be hidden by use of serial numbers; and restrictions could be imposed on publishing accounts of proceedings. In criminal proceedings, restrictions were introduced to the fingerprinting of suspected children and young persons, after a finding of guilt the court could take note of any particular welfare circumstances and use its discretion to direct a treatment rather than a punishment disposal option. Duties were placed on the court to explain the nature of care proceedings and the grounds on which they were being brought or to explain the substance of a charge to child or young person in offence proceedings and to allow representation in the case of juvenile offenders. In addition to procedural changes adjustments were also made to the rules of evidence. The rules were made more flexible to assist in promoting the objective of positively advancing the child's welfare by, for example, rendering admissible the depositions of children, the use of video technology and increased reliance on expert witnesses.

Among the ways in which the legal system governs the use of authority is by vesting powers (or giving formal recognition to inherent powers) in decision-makers. This usually means delineating the responsibilities of adults - parents, guardians and others with a *loco parentis* standing - towards children and to some extent identifying the situations and setting out the terms on which the powers may be exercised. But other decision-makers are also important. In the period leading up to the 1989 Act, the legal system conferred considerable discretionary powers on local authorities. Most notably this was the time when very many children, placed in local authority care by their parents on a voluntary basis, found their status changed to compulsory care as resolutions were passed vesting full parental rights in the local authorities. It was also the era when adoption agencies refined their suitability criteria to exclude adoption applicants who did not conform to a preferred model of parenthood. Again, local authorities were escalating their recourse to the wardship jurisdiction, an option not available to parental applicants, in order to supplement their statutory powers in relation to children. New surveillance systems were introduced such as the 'at risk register' and the multi-disciplinary case conference. The period between the introduction of the Children Acts 1975 and 1989 was one in which the coercive intervention powers of local authorities were maximised. Their unilateral use of discretionary powers was greatly eased by the ruling in *A v Liverpool City Council*[6] which thereafter prevented the court from reviewing any local authority exercise of power vested in it.

These are just some illustrations of the type of adjustments that were being made to procedural and administrative law as it relates to children in the decades prior to the 1989 Act. They complemented changes made in the related substantive law but there was no overall strategy to achieve a new coherence of structure, content and process. From time to time the proposal to establish a family court re-surfaced as a means of and bringing such coherence to this part of the legal system and transcending the built-in adversarial nature of proceedings. This movement failed to gain sufficient support and the piece-meal approach of incremental adjustments to procedural and administrative law continued.

After the Children Act 1989

The 1989 Act introduced important changes to the role and functions of the welfare principle within the structure of the legal system; particularly with regard to the organisation, administration, jurisdiction and access to the courts. It had a direct impact upon the way in which courts were organised. It brought new measures to ensure that they became financially accessible, to provide *locus standi* for the children concerned and for the proper recording of decisions reached. It also introduced statutory duties to protect children from the anxiety of enduring avoidable delay or an unnecessary continuance of litigation.

The 1989 Act brought together for civil purposes most provisions of public and private family law affecting the welfare and upbringing of children. This it did through reliance on unifying principles and a common set of court orders and also by introducing certain organisational and administrative changes to the legal system. In particular, the strategic use of the principles of 'parental responsibility' and the 'paramount welfare interests of the child' together with a range of new legal rules and presumptions (see below) are the most obvious of the elements which are now used to bind together certain public and private dimensions of child care law. The fact that s 8 orders are available to the court in both public and private family law proceedings commenced or continued under the 1989 Act is a useful technical device for promoting greater coherence in judicial application of the welfare principle.

In the same way, the involvement of guardians *ad litem* in identifying, safeguarding and representing the welfare interests of children in public proceedings as in adoption, has assisted the legislative intent to introduce greater consistency in court management of welfare related issues.

Ensuring that welfare is always the paramount consideration in family proceedings has also been greatly facilitated by an ideological sea change in legislative intent. Whereas the Children and Young Persons Act 1969 had deliberately provided for the possibility of welfare oriented disposal options being available to the court in respect of child perpetrators as well as child victims of criminal behaviour, where the needs of the former justified such a liberal approach, this overlap ended with the implementation of the 1989 Act. By removing from the definition of family proceedings all residual traces of the criminal jurisdiction, consigning them to be addressed in separate legislation and processed through the youth courts, this legislation permits the welfare principle to more fully govern a restricted range of proceedings. The legislative intent to break the ideological commitment to treating children similarly, whether appearing before the courts on proceedings grounded on their needs or deeds, where justified by their welfare interests, has been achieved.

The 1989 Act provides for the introduction of a concurrent system of jurisdiction covering magistrates courts, county courts and the High Court. This arrangement allows all proceedings relating to a child to be consolidated and heard together and cases to be allocated to courts on the basis of case complexity or gravity. It puts in place the infrastructure necessary to facilitate: ease of access to the appropriate court; greater uniformity in the use of orders; flexibility and consistency in court procedures; and to generally systematise the application of the civil law to the welfare needs of children. Such organisational changes have been accompanied by welfare oriented changes to the administration of court business. Public and private proceedings, for example, commenced in any court under the 1989 Act are now preceded by a direction hearings. In theory, this promotes greater consistency and efficiency in the overall management of the means whereby the courts respond to issues affecting the welfare of children. The decisions of all courts, and the accompanying rationale, must now be recorded; which places a new obligation on all magistrates courts to summarise the grounds for decisions reached. Similarly, the introduction of 'care centres' provide a new mechanism for reviewing efficiency and effectiveness in the conduct of court business and they serve as an appropriate forum for highlighting problems in inter-agency co-ordination. However, the findings from recent socio-legal research projects indicate that the manner and processes, the pace, the multiplicity of officials and the formality of court language and surroundings combine to obstruct the influence of the welfare principle.[7] Although the 1989 Act has given a new priority to the welfare principle, there remains a significant gap between its role in substantive law and in the procedures and administration established to give effect to it.

Access to the courts has been eased by the 1989 Act. Legal aid is now granted in many family proceedings such as applications for injunctions, ancillary relief on divorce and orders relating to the upbringing of children: subject to means and merits tests. The 1989 Act directs that legal aid must be made available to the child concerned in any application for a care or supervision order, a child assessment order, an emergency protection order or for an extension or discharge of an emergency protection order.[8]

Change has also occurred to the *locus standi* of a child in proceedings affecting his or her welfare. The only form of civil proceedings heard in a magistrates court, in which a child may be made a party, are family proceedings commenced under the Children Act 1989. In 'specified' proceedings this is automatic and mandatory but otherwise it is permissible only in circumstances where the child is the applicant with leave of the court. Under the Family Proceedings Rules, in any public law proceedings, the child concerned (in addition to the local authority, parents, any other person with parental responsibility and such other persons as may be granted leave by the court to be joined) will automatically have full party status. Entitlement to full party status brings with it a right to attend court, to be represented in court and to appeal from the decision of the court.[9] It also entitles the court to compel the attendance of a child where necessary. In public proceedings there is a discretion available to the court, under the 1989 Act, to waive the necessity for a child's attendance, even where the child is a party.[10]

The position of a child relative to other parties has been strengthened by a number of other adjustments. The rule against admitting the hearsay of children has been generally disapplied.[11] Removed also, at least in public proceedings, is the rule which permitted a married person to claim a privilege, exempting him or her from the normal obligation to make a full disclosure of information, on the grounds that to do so would be self incriminating or would incriminate the spouse.[12] Further, the welfare interests of a child are now protected by a new rule prohibiting any medical examination or assessment of a child without prior court approval.[13]

The court has a duty under the Children Act 1989 to appoint a guardian *ad litem* to represent a child in specified family proceedings.[14] Where, in such proceedings, a solicitor has not been retained to represent a child and the court considers such an appointment to be necessary then, subject to certain specified conditions, it may make the appointment.[15] The court, it would seem, is precluded from appointing a solicitor where a guardian *ad litem* has already been appointed as it then falls to the latter to make such an appointment (under the Rules).

Arguably, the net effect of the change to the role of the child in family proceedings has been to consolidate the adversarial nature of the framework within which the welfare principle must operate. In particular the measures conferring full party status on a child, giving him or her a right to be heard by the court and providing for more assertive advocacy on their behalf, may have served to re-position the child in the legal system as another combatant. No longer merely the subject and recipient of measures judicially determined to be in keeping with their welfare interests, the child may now have to compete with other parties in defining the nature of such interests and in claiming an entitlement to an appropriate disposal option.

The Children Act 1989 and the welfare principle

The Children Act 1989 laid down a new synthesis of principles, procedures, court orders and court administration in the civil law relating to children. For most purposes, the 1989 Act consolidated the public and private sectors of family law insofar as these affect the care and upbringing of children. The principle of the welfare of the child provided the main tool for shaping this legislation. The concept of parental responsibilities functioned as the natural counterbalance to that principle. Other principles were also at work and important new structures and processes were developed but, primarily, the 1989 Act can be seen as being built on a foundation created by a radical juxtaposition of child welfare and parental responsibilities.

In all family proceedings, whether initiated in a public or private family law context, the same rules now broadly apply to define most aspects of the welfare principle in a judicial determination of issues relating to the upbringing of a child. These are: the concept of parental responsibilities; the new weighting given to the principle of the welfare of the child; other related principles; and the checklist criteria. In marked contrast to previous legislation, the 1989 Act specifies, partialises and differentiates the use of authority in relation to decisions affecting the welfare of children. The legislative intent behind this conspicuous regulatory approach is that by prescribing the indicators for interpreting the welfare principle, and identifying how and when the court and a local authority should apply the principle, some parameters would then be placed on discretionary exercises of authority by both decision-making bodies.

Parental responsibilities and the welfare principle

The 1989 Act replaced the concepts of 'parental rights' and 'parental duties', which for centuries formed the basic constructs of family law in this jurisdiction, with the composite term 'parental responsibilities'. The change signalled a profound difference of approach from a proprietal frame of reference to one which implies that parental use of authority is valid only if employed for the benefit of the child. It also suggests that such responsibilities are exclusively an attribute of parenthood which may be temporarily met by other persons or bodies but can never be wholly shed by a 'parent' to whom, by definition, they must continue to attach. Only those attributes which have a functional bearing upon the nurture needs of the child, rather than those traditionally associated with the status of parent, are now held to comprise such responsibilities. The reframing of this concept allows it to now play a more consistent role in both public and private family law.

The exact nature of parental responsibilities will clearly depend on the age and circumstances of the child concerned. Broadly speaking, however, "the effect of having parental responsibility is to empower a person to take most decisions in the child's life.[16] Bromley, more specifically, suggests that this composite term comprises at least 16 separate areas of responsibility relating to: providing a home; having contact; determining and providing for education; determining religion; discipline; consent to treatment, marriage, adoption, emigration and change of surname; vetoing the issue of a passport; taking the child outside the jurisdiction; administering property; protection and maintenance; representing the child in legal proceedings; burial or cremation and; appointing a guardian for the child.[17]

More than one person may bear such responsibility in respect of the same child at the same time. Having parental responsibility does not entitle the bearer to act in any way which is incompatible with a court order made under the 1989 Act in respect of the child. The mother does not lose parental responsibility merely because the father has it or because he later acquires it. Nor do either or both parents lose it when the court grants a care order to a local authority.

Parental responsibility is juxtaposed in the 1989 Act with the paramountcy principle. The new weight and bearing of the latter is declared in section 1 as follows:

> (1) Where a court determines any question with respect to -
> (a) the upbringing of the child; or
> (b) the administration of the child's property or the
> application of any income arising from it,
> the child's welfare shall be the court's paramount consideration.

This principle, drawn initially from caselaw[18] and first statutorily stated[19] in s 1 of the Guardianship of Minors Act 1971, is now asserted to govern judicial determination of all issues affecting a child's upbringing and administration of his or her property. It ends the uncertainty associated with the fine distinctions previously made between different statutory definitions of the welfare test. From being one among many factors to be judicially considered in family proceedings 'welfare' has now been elevated to become the primary objective of such proceedings. The paramountcy principle, as now statutorily stated, applies to matters of upbringing or administration of property in any proceedings and in any court where related issues arise; the principle is not restricted to proceedings commenced under the 1989 Act. The approach pioneered by the wardship jurisdiction has now been comprehensively endorsed. As Sir Stephen Bown P has said:

> ...the proceedings under the Children Act are not adversarial, although an adversarial approach is frequently adopted by various of the parties. However, as far as the court is concerned, its duty is to investigate and seek to achieve a result which is in the interests of the welfare of the child...Children's cases...fall into a special category where the court is bound to undertake all necessary steps to arrive at an appropriate result in the paramount interests of the welfare of the child.[20]

However, in addition to matters statutorily excluded as not constituting 'upbringing' or administration of property, caselaw has established some further limitations to the principle's applicability. It has been held[21] that the principle does not apply to the issue of whether leave should be granted to allow application to be made for a 'section 8' order under s 10 of the 1989 Act. The principle is expressly excluded from having any bearing on certain statutory procedures where the main issues affect adult interests: on applications for secure accommodation orders, for child maintenance or for ouster orders; on matters falling within the scope of Part III of the 1989 Act, s 6 of the Adoption Act 1976 or s 25(1) of the Matrimonial Causes Act 1973.

The no-delay principle

The 1989 Act introduces other welfare related principles. One of these is the no-delay principle which is given effect by section 1 as follows:

> (2) In any proceedings in which any question with respect to the upbringing of a child arises, the court shall have regard to the general principle that any delay in determining the question is likely to prejudice the welfare of the child.

This is the first legislative statement of a principle which addresses a matter that, for some years now, has been the focus of growing concern to the judiciary and child care practitioners both within and without the United Kingdom.[22] In a number of UK cases in recent years judicial dismay had been expressed at some inordinate, and perhaps deliberately orchestrated delays, which have prejudiced the outcome of proceedings.[23] A child's 'sense of time' is not the same as that of adults and psychological damage may be caused to a child by the anxiety of protracted proceedings. Indeed, it has been claimed[24] that a child's welfare interests are better served by a wrong decision taken swiftly than the right one taken after a lengthy delay. The courts, however, do recognise that there are some circumstances in which a delay is in a child's best interests.[25]

The no-order presumption

Another welfare related principle introduced by the 1989 Act was the no-order presumption and is again given effect by section 1 as follows:

> Where a court is considering whether or not to make one or more orders under this Act with respect to a child, it shall not make the order or any of the orders unless it considers that doing so would be better for the child than making no order at all.

This statement is an important declaration of principle which crystalises the minimal intervention ethic underpinning the 1989 Act. It applies equally to public and to private family law proceedings brought under that statute. The legislative intent is to replace the 'winners and losers' approach with one which instead presumes that the parties should be able to make their own arrangements outside the court. Once the matter comes before the court the presumption will necessitate judicial scrutiny of any proposed arrangements for children to establish whether authority should be exercised by court rather than family. Only if decision-making by others is not possible, and/or if it is necessary to use authority to secure a child's welfare interests, will the court intervene by issuing an order. The onus is then on the judiciary to clearly show why it would not be best for the child if no order was made.

The limiting of litigation principle

This principle, also clearly welfare related, is stated in section 91 of the 1989 Act as follows:

> (14) On disposing of any application for an order under this Act, the court may (whether or not it makes any other order in response to the application) order that no application for an order under this Act of any specified kind may be made with respect to the child concerned by any person named in the order without leave of the court.

This enables the court to prevent further and unnecessary litigation, on a matter upon which it has made a ruling, and so avoid exposing a child to further uncertainty and anxiety.

The welfare checklist

The introduction of the checklist of considerations, all clearly welfare related, was perhaps the most clear and specific demonstration of legislative intent to ensure that the 1989 Act effected change in the judicial approach to child welfare. This checklist must be judicially considered in all public family law cases (though see Chap 8 for application to Part V proceedings) and in private proceedings where the parties are contesting the future arrangements for children. As well as indicating the sort of outcomes the orders should strive to achieve, the legislative intent is that the checklist will promote greater consistency in judicial decisions, practitioner assessments and in the overall coherence of family law.

The first of the checklist considerations is the requirement that judicial account be taken of 'the ascertainable wishes and feelings of the child concerned (considered in the light of his age and understanding)'. The judicial importance attached to this consideration was made clear when it was held that the court should always elicit and respect the views of a child which it may not be able to act on but which may tip the balance in a difficult case.[26] However, following the ruling in *Gillick*, much will depend on the maturity of the child concerned and the possible bearing of decrees of the European Convention must also be borne in mind. This provision gives the child the right to be heard by the court, a right which the latter may direct should be exercised by granting the child full party status with the commensurate freedom to represent his or her own interests.

The second consideration requires the judiciary to take into account a child's 'physical, emotional and educational needs'. The statutory requirement that the court should have regard to the child's physical and educational needs continues the law's concern that these, the basic common law duties of a guardian, must be attended to. The judiciary have consistently singled out these attributes of good guardianship as constituting criteria for granting or removing custody. The similar requirement in respect of emotional needs merely endorses well established judicial practice and lends statutory weight to the approach developed in this jurisdiction in wardship cases which tended to favour maternal care for very young children and paternal for older boys. This approach has received further endorsement in rulings[27] made more recently by Butler-Sloss LJ where she acknowledged the importance of maternal care for very small children, particularly the importance of maintaining the bonding relationship. However, this does not amount to a legal presumption favouring such care arrangements. When considering a child's emotional needs, judicial weight will be given to the significance of sibling as well as parental relationships. Again, judicial practice in wardship cases has traditionally recognised the importance of preserving sibling relationships when determining future care arrangements for a child. Its importance was underlined in a case where Purchas LJ commented "...brothers and sisters should wherever possible be brought up together."[28]

The third consideration affecting the welfare of a child directs that judicial attention be given to 'the likely effect on him of any change in his circumstances'. The strength of a child's attachment to persons, places and things has only in recent years come to be judicially recognised as playing a crucial part in contributing to any child's psychological development. The early acknowledgement of trauma caused by disrupting the ties between a young child and a caring parent has now been extended to include an awareness that a risk of similar trauma exists where the ties are to siblings, grandparents or other relatives and perhaps friends. The dilemma this poses for the court is apparent in the observation made many years ago by Black J who advised that when considering a minor's welfare the court:

> ...must not only address itself to the child's present comfort and happiness but must also look forward and try to consider what is ultimately in the best interests of the child.[29]

In more recent years the courts have tended to favour the parent best positioned to maintain the *status quo*. This key ingredient of judicial thinking was illustrated by Ormrod LJ when he observed:[30]

> ...it is generally accepted by those who are professionally concerned with children that, particularly in the early years, continuity of care is a most important part of a child's sense of security and that disruption of established bonds are to be avoided whenever it is possible to do so.

This principle received further endorsement in a subsequent Court of Appeal decision[31] and now ensures that in by far the majority of contested parenting arrangements the mother retains care responsibility. Again, however, it cannot be regarded as amounting to a legal presumption. The courts have, occasionally, granted an order to a 'snatching' parent despite the entailed trauma to the child resulting from being abruptly uprooted from a familiar environment.

The fourth consideration requires and/or permits judicial attention to be given to the child's 'age, sex, background and any characteristics of his which the court considers relevant'. Age and gender considerations, which have long been evident in caselaw,[32] have now been given explicit statutory approval. Their modern significance has undoubtedly been given considerable weight by the judgment in the *Gillick* case and by the influence of the European Convention. However, it has to be said that this provision is likely to be judicially regarded as representing tacit legislative support for the established practice of awarding primary care responsibility for very young children and older girls to their mothers, where feasible, and older boys to their fathers.

Cumming Bruce LJ, for example, was acknowledging the judicial weight given to these considerations when he commented "...if all...factors are nicely balanced, then probably it is right for a child of tender years to be brought up by his or her natural mother".[33] The reference to 'background' acknowledges the difficulties that have been caused by 'mixed-race' placements made by statutory and voluntary agencies for fostering and adoption purposes.[34] By also including a reference to any other characteristics considered relevant the legislators have again sought to build in some of the discretionary flexibility which has characterised judicial use of wardship and enabled creative decisions to be taken in respect of children's welfare interests.

The fifth consideration imposes a requirement that the judiciary address a child's need for protection by taking into account 'any harm which he has suffered or is at risk of suffering'. Section 31(9) of the 1989 Act defines "harm" as: "ill-treatment or the impairment of health or development". On the question of whether harm is significant ss (10), not very helpfully, suggests that:

> (10) Where the question of whether harm suffered by a child is significant turns on the child's health or development, his health or development shall be compared with that which could reasonably be expected of a similar child.

Section 31(9) offers further definitions: "ill-treatment" is held to include "sexual abuse and forms of ill-treatment which are not physical" while "development" is the "physical, intellectual, emotional, social or behavioural development". In addition to its application in a public family law context (see Chap 8) 'harm' clearly has a bearing on private issues where there is evidence to show that a child has suffered or may be at risk of suffering undue emotional stress or an impairment of their physical, intellectual, social or behavioural development. In the past the courts have had opportunities to consider the significance of 'harm' in relation to children if custody is granted to a parent who, being a Jehovah's Witness, might refuse consent for a blood-transfusion.[35] Such evidence will now play a critical role in determining an application for a residence order.

The court may consider that the harm, or the risk of it, may be alleviated by means of a family assistance order. Alternatively, where that 'harm' appears to be 'significant' then the court may well choose to direct the relevant local authority to undertake an investigation of the child's circumstances which in turn could lead to the issue of a care order or of a supervision order.

Previously wardship was the only satisfactory means of securing the welfare of an unharmed but potentially vulnerable child but now the court may be asked to make a statutory order on the basis of an assessment of predicted risk. This type of situation has in the past often appeared before the courts in cases where immature, inexperienced and perhaps unsupported mothers have been in contest with local authorities in relation to arrangements for the future of their children. Now, this statutory measure rather than wardship is available to a court enabling it to make an early decision before predictable harm to a child demonstrates parental incapacity and rehabilitation is proven to be unrealistic.

The sixth consideration requires the judiciary, when assessing proposed future care arrangements for a child, to pose the question 'how capable of meeting his needs is each of his parents and any other person in relation to whom the court considers the question to be relevant?'. It is probable that in framing this provision the legislators had in mind the contention generated in recent years by the influence of the principle of non-discrimination on judicial and social work practice in relation to arrangements for the custody and placement of children· The extent to which ideology may obscure an objective assessment of the parenting abilities of, for example, a very young mother, a lesbian or homosexual person, an older or disabled person, a couple of mixed race, or perhaps a member of a minority religious group, has caused considerable professional and political debate and resulting media interest.

However, it is in relation to the sexual orientation of the parent that this consideration has most notably exercised the judiciary. Two relatively recent cases, both involving lesbian mothers, have fallen to be determined in the light of the equivalent provision under the 1989 Act. In *C v C (A Minor)(Custody: Appeal)*[36] the Court of Appeal overturned the decision of a county court to grant custody to a lesbian mother because it considered that the judge at first instance had not taken fully into account the significance of the mother's lesbianism; i.e. it was a real factor with a bearing on the welfare of the child concerned, it could not be simply discounted. However, on being remitted for a re-hearing to the High Court the lesbian mother was then granted custody. In *B v B (Minors) (Custody, Care and Control)*[37] the court consulted expert opinion on the issue of whether being reared by a lesbian mother was likely to impair a child's welfare by blurring the latter's sexual identity or by causing the child to be stigmatised. On being advised that neither was necessarily the case and having assessed the mother as loving and mindful of her child's psychological needs the court granted her custody.

This provision also directs the court to assess the parenting abilities of any other person who may have a direct care role in relation to the child. Given the transient relationships which many children are now exposed to, this provision should afford an important protection in situations where the caring and long-standing relationship of a parent or grand parent may be in danger of being legally displaced by a new cohabitee.

The final consideration allows a flexible response to be made to an application for a specific order by inviting the judiciary to utilise, instead or additionally, 'the range of powers available to the court under this Act in the proceedings in question'. This enables the court to look beyond the wishes of the parties, if necessary, to find the court order most compatible with the welfare interests of the child concerned. In doing so, it may also look beyond the above checklist of considerations as this is not intended to be a definitive list. The court may of its own initiative make any of the following orders which are available under the 1989 Act: any s 8 order; a s 16 family assistance order (in exceptional circumstances and with the consent of every person, other than the child, named in the order); a s 5 order, on application, appointing a guardian for the child; or under s 37 it may issue a direction to the local authority requiring it to undertake an investigation of the child's circumstances (where a question arises as to the child's welfare and the court believes that a care or supervision order may be necessary). The court may choose to exercise its authority in a way neither requested nor foreseen by the parties. It is this provision which now provides judicial access to public family law orders in private proceedings; though the responsibility for determining the appropriateness of a care or supervision order is now a matter for local authority assessment not judicial discretion. Again it seems to reflect a legislative intent to provide the judiciary with the range of discretionary authority which would previously only have been available to them in wardship proceedings.

Conclusion

The 1989 Act has changed the role, functions and weighting of the welfare principle in the substantive civil law relating to children, radically as well as specifically and comprehensively. It has firmly confined its application to civil cases; children alleged to be the perpetrators rather than the victims of criminal offences are now diverted away from the welfare oriented family proceedings court. Within the latter court, the welfare interests of a child are assured of being formally awarded priority over other considerations in public and private family law proceedings. The impact of the principle can also be seen in the re-structuring of the courts and in the creation of the many new rules and professional roles which now govern the passage of proceedings.

However, the accompanying procedural and administrative changes have been introduced more to expedite proceedings and co-ordinate professional input rather than to further the welfare interests of the children concerned. The structures and processes of the legal system remain essentially adversarial allowing it to retain its traditional reliance upon precedents, contest and adjudication as the preferred means of conducting business. The continuity of these embedded traditional hallmarks raises the question as to whether the present legal system is appropriately responding to the requirements of the welfare principle.

Notes

1 See Salmond, J., *Jurisprudence*, Sweet and Maxwell, 1947.

2 Altered from 21 years to 18 by the Family Law Reform Act 1969 in response to the recommendations made in the *Report of the Committee on the Age of Majority* (the Latey Report) (Cmnd 3342), 1967.

3 See Rules of the Supreme Court 1965, Ord 80, r 2(1).

4 See *Woolf v Pemberton* (1877) 6 Ch D 19.

5 The Ingleby Committee noted the difficult balancing act to be performed by this court:

> It must try at one and the same time to protect the public, to promote the welfare of the child and to stress the responsibility and respect the legitimate rights of the parents. Finally, it must satisfy public opinion that justice is being done.

Report of the Departmental Committee on Children and Young Persons, London, HMSO, 1960, (Cmnd 1191) p 39.

6 [1982] AC 363, [1981] 2 All ER 3 85, [1981] 2 WLR 948, 79 LGR 621, 2 FLR 222, 145 JP 318, 125 Sol Jo 396, HL.

7 See, for example, Dame Margaret Booth's report *Delay in Children Act Proceedings*. Also, see, Plotnikoff and Woolfson, *The Pace of Child Abuse Prosecutions*, DoH, 1995 and the *Children Act Advisory Committee Final Report* (June 1997), Lord Chancellor's Dept.

8 See the Legal Aid Act 1988, s 15 and the Civil Legal Aid (General) Regs 1989 as amended by the Children Act 1989, s 99.

9 The Children Act 1989, s 94.

10 The Children Act 1989, s 95(1).

11 The Children Act 1989, s 96.

12 The Children Act 1989, s 98(1).

13 See Family Proceedings Rules 1991, r 18(1); Family Proceedings Courts (Children Act 1989) Rules 1991, r 18(10).

14 The Children Act 1989, s 41.

15 The Children Act 1989, s 41(3).

16 See *Introduction to the Children Act 1989*, DoH, (para 2.4).

17 See *Bromley's Family Law* 8th ed, p 301. See Chap 1 for judicial interpretation of the role and responsibility of a parent.

18 See *J v C* [1970] AC 668. Also, see Chap 4.

19 Although it had previously appeared in the UN Declaration of the Rights of the Child 1959, see further Chap 15.

20 See *Oxfordshire County Council v M* [1994] Fam 151, [1994] 2 WLR 393, [1994] 2 All ER 269.

21 See *Re A and W (Minors)(Residence Order: leave to apply)* [1992] 2 FLR 154, [1992] 3 All ER 872. Also, see, *Re SC (A minor)(Leave to Seek Residence Order)* [1995] 1 FLR 96 and *Re C (Residence: Child's Application for Leave)* [1995] 1 FLR 927 which both concerned adolescent girls.

22 See, for example, *H and O v UK* Series A, No 120 where the ECHR ruled that by the undue delay in its litigation process, the UK was in breach of Articles 6 and 8 of the Human Rights Convention.

23 As documented by the Law Commission in Report No 172, para 4.55.

24 See *Re P (A Minor)(Education)* [1992] 1 FLR 316, CA.

25 See, for example, *S v S (Minors)(Custody)* [1992] Fam Law 148 when, despite the equivalent directive under the 1989 Act, it was nonetheless decided to defer making a permanent order until such time as the children concerned had time to adjust and settle down in their 'volatile family situation'.

26 See *Re P (A Minor)(Education)* [1992] 1 FLR 316 CA.

27 See *Re S (A Minor) (Custody)* [1991] 2 FLR 388, 390, CA and *Re A (A Minor) (Custody)* [1991] 2 FLR 394, 400, CA.

28 See *C v C (Minors: Custody)* [1988] 2 FLR 291, 302, CA.

29 See *Re B (An Infant)* [1946] NI 1 at p 4.

30 See *Dicocco v Milne* (1983) 4 FLR 247, 259, CA.

31 See *Re B (Minors)(Residence Order)* [1992] Fam 157 CA.

32 See, for example, *B v B (Custody of Children)* [1985] FLR 166, CA.

33 See *Re W (A Minor)(Custody)* (1982) 4 FLR, 492, 504, CA.

34 See, for example, *Re JK (Adoption: Transracial Placement)* [1991] 2 FLR 340.

35 See *Jane v Jane* (1984) 4 FLR 712.

36 [1991] 1 FLR 223.

37 [1991] 1 FLR 402.

6 Identifying Welfare Interests

Introduction

The Children Act 1989 introduced the requirement to ascertain the wishes and feelings of the child as the first item on a 'welfare checklist'[1] to be judicially applied in all public and some private proceedings instigated under this legislation. It also made some decisions by judiciary and local authority conditional upon their acceptance by the child concerned and required the local authority to involve a child in other areas of decision-making. This chapter considers these and other ways in which the law now identifies the welfare interests of a child. It examines when and to what effect the views of a child may contribute to a decision taken by the judiciary, local authority or others in relation to that child's legal interests. It assesses the inter-relationship between a child's views, welfare and legal interests as provided for within this legislation.

Welfare interests: as identified by the child

The Children Act 1989, in particular s 1(3)(a), is now the primary source of legal authority for the principle that a child's views should be ascertained and taken into account when decisions are to be taken on matters concerning that child's welfare. This important, comprehensive and relatively recent legislative recognition of the changed *locus standi* of a child in family proceedings has been brought about by a gradual convergence of pressures emanating from international sources as well as from local judicial practice.

Indeed, there is considerable evidence to suggest that legislative recognition of the importance of a child's views on matters concerning his or her welfare was a response to pressure from outside the UK.[2] In particular, the United Nations Convention on the Rights of the Child[3] which was adopted by the UN General Assembly in November 1989 and ratified by the UK in

December 1991 probably influenced the contemporaneous shaping of some of the more formative principles governing the 1989 Act.[4] It may be that the assimilation (though not the formulation and development) of the paramountcy principle within the Children Act 1989 owes at least as much to Strasbourg initiative as to indigenous caselaw. The significance of the latter was apparent particularly with the ruling in *Gillick* which was a landmark decision for recognition of the separate legal interests of children.[5] Arguably, however, it may with hindsight be seen as forming a watershed in UK jurisprudence in the area of 'children's rights' as subsequent caselaw reveals, if anything, a steady constriction of the *Gillick* principle. The judicial approach to the views of children, and the weighting accorded to such views, has since remained essentially paternalistic.

The guiding principle, now firmly established by the 1989 Act, is that when in certain circumstances decisions are taken by the state on matters affecting the welfare of a child, those taking such decisions should only do so after having fully assessed the legal interests of the child concerned. The views of the child on the presenting issue should also be sought and taken into account. However, such views are not determinative, and may not even be very relevant, they are merely an ingredient in the totality of factors which constitute an overall assessment of the child's legal interests. As the Court of Appeal pointed out in *Re P (Minors)(Wardship)*[6] although there is a duty to seek out and take into account the views of a child, the court could disregard those views where they were deemed to be in conflict with the child's welfare interests.

The statutory duty placed on the courts is to apply the paramountcy principle in certain proceedings when determining matters affecting the welfare interests of a child. It is stated in section 1 of the 1989 Act as follows:

> (3) In the circumstances mentioned in paragraph (4), a court shall have regard in particular to - (a) the ascertainable wishes and feelings of the child concerned (considered in the light of his age and understanding).

There are many issues on which the court will seek the views of a child of sufficient age and understanding. There are also some few issues where consent rather than views will be sought. This is an important statement of principle but as a legal duty it has its limitations. Although binding on the courts it has no application to others, in particular this provision does not apply to decisions taken by local authorities. The duty does not come into play until after problems have arisen and decisions then need to be taken in the particular circumstances allowed for under the 1989 Act. There is no general principle in UK law that a child has a right to participate in decisions affecting his or her welfare.

The limits to the application of this provision can be appreciated from a brief examination of its key clauses. Firstly, 'the circumstances' are those where contested proceedings are commenced to make, vary or discharge a s 8 order and proceedings to make, vary or discharge an order under Part IV. The mandatory application of this duty in all public but only in contested private family law proceedings reflects the legislation's underpinning philosophy of minimal judicial intervention in consensual family law matters, but comprehensive and consistent judicial scrutiny of public law matters, where the welfare interests of children are involved. Secondly, 'shall have regard' gives statutory effect to the trenchant observation made by Butler-Sloss LJ:

> The child is a person and not an object of concern...Children are entitled to a proper explanation appropriate to their age...The views and wishes of the child, particularly as to what is to happen to him/her, should be taken into consideration by the professionals involved....and should be placed before whichever court deals with the case.[7]

However, this requirement stops well short of importing any suggestion that a child's consent should be sought. Indeed, the court may over-rule a *Gillick* competent minor[8] and the parents or any professional. Finally, 'ascertainable wishes and feelings' clearly implies that while the judiciary are to be guided by this provision when applying the paramountcy principle, their discretion is not to be fettered in the interpretation and relative weighting they give to the different factors which will constitute the welfare of the child in each case. The wishes and feelings of the child are not synonymous with his or her legal interests. The first may inform judicial appreciation of the latter but they may also be biased, wrong and obscure the legal issues.

This composite duty heads the checklist of factors to be considered by the court when giving effect to the paramountcy principle. But it remains only one of seven such factors all of which require judicial consideration and none of which will necessarily weigh more than any other in the circumstances of a particular case. The judicial checklist is clearly not a definitive slide rule to be uniformly applied in all cases.

Parties: the child

In the Children Act 1989 the law now explicitly and systematically addresses the circumstances in which the child's views should be sought and taken into account on matters affecting his or her welfare interests. But the effect of the ruling in *Gillick* has also become very apparent in recent caselaw. For example, the court has indicated that it would respect the wishes of a 14 year old regarding his education but also commented that had he been 11, it would not have hesitated to 'pack him off to boarding school'.[9] The critical factor in this and many similar cases is the age and understanding of the child concerned. As Sir Thomas Bingham MR has observed:

> Children have different levels of understanding at the same age. And understanding is not absolute. It has to be assessed relative to the issues in the case.[10]

The child's 'wishes' and 'feelings' are not seen as the sole indicators of his or her appreciation of the matters at issue, nor are these necessarily accorded the same weighting in each case. The subjects on which a child refuses to communicate, or refers to obliquely, may be of greater importance. An assessment of a child's wishes and feelings is acknowledged to be a difficult task. It can only be sensibly achieved by taking into account factors such as: particular attributes and/or needs; personality and character development; attachments; and each child's understanding of where he or she fits into the family dynamics. In court proceedings intermediaries such as the guardian *ad litem*, the social worker, the Official Solicitor and/or expert witnesses such as psychologists and child psychiatrists may be available to assist the court to ascertain a child's wishes and feelings. It should be noted, however, that the court has held[11] that evidence, in the form of such views and wishes, could only be withheld from a party to proceedings (the mother) in the most exceptional circumstances: disclosure to all parties is the normal rule.

The importance now attached to hearing the views of a child was the subject of judicial comment in *Re W (A Minor) (Contact)*[12] where the children, aged 10 and 12, expressed a wish to see the judge to explain why they wanted to live with their father. Butler-Sloss in the course of her judgment stated that:

> If children of 10 and 12 express the view that they wish to see the judge, that is in line with Section 1(3)(a) of the 1989 Act... If children have views which they wish the court to hear that is entirely in accordance with Parliament's requirement for the first time that courts should ascertain the wishes and understanding of children who are of an age and maturity to give them.

Where the child is aged at least 16, or though if younger is deemed to be of an age and understanding to give an informed consent, then parents, the court and other third parties will be legally obliged to do more than ascertain and have regard to his or her views. If the child satisfies the 'competence test' then he or she may assert their views by instigating proceedings (though sometimes leave of the court is required), instructing a solicitor and/or by participating as a full party in proceedings (see, also, Chap 7). Such a child may also give or withhold consent in relation to the proposals of such others as parents and local authority. There are circumstances in which others may have to defer to the views of a child: some of these circumstances are stated in or arise from the Children Act 1989.

Parties: the parents

The position of parents or those with parental responsibility, in relation to the authority necessary for a valid consent to be given on matters affecting their child's welfare, is not as clear and simple as formerly. It can at least be stated with some certainty that where a child is aged 16 or satisfies the competence test then the courts will be extremely reluctant to impose a parental decision against the wishes of that child. Further, where parental consent is unavailable, for whatever reason, then a third party would be entitled to rely on the authorisation of such a child. However, it is when a third party is faced with a clear contradiction between the wishes of parent and such a child that legal certainties become hardest to find. The decision in *Re W (A Minor)(Medical Treatment: Court's Jurisdiction)*[13] provides authority for the limited proposition that where a child, aged 16 or *Gillick* competent, has given a valid consent then this cannot be subsequently overridden by the parent. Indeed, s 8 of the Family Law Reform Act 1969 has long provided children aged at least 16 with the right to give an independent consent to surgical, medical or dental treatment.

The judiciary also acknowledge that in some circumstances parental consent will be congruent with a child's wishes and feelings. In keeping with the spirit of the Children Act 1989, particularly the approach which has substituted for the previous exclusivity of parental rights a new concept of shared parental responsibility, the courts have since been interpreting consent in relation to welfare related decisions as a power which may be vested jointly in a number of office-holders. The significance of this being that either parent or a competent child could unilaterally exercise their joint authority to give a valid consent. It would thus be open to a third party to choose the office-holder from whom they would seek authorisation; a refusal by one would not debar the other from granting authorisation.[14]

Parties: other third parties

Consent, for a course of action relating to the welfare interests of a child, can only be given by a parent, the court, someone or body with parental responsibility or by the child concerned if he or she is of an age and understanding to do so. Among the third parties who would be recognised as having capacity to give consent are: any local authority vested with a care order; a putative father, if he has legally acquired parental responsibility; a guardian, or; any person in whose favour the court has made a residence order.

Public family law: the duty to identify welfare wishes

The Children Act 1989 gives more prominence to the views of the child in public family law proceedings than in private. Whereas the application of s 1(1) is selective in relation to the latter it is universal to all public proceedings.

This provision places a double duty on the court when hearing public law proceedings commenced under the 1989 Act. Firstly, the court has a duty to ascertain a child's wishes and feelings. How these are to be ascertained will to some extent vary in accordance with the age and assertiveness of the child concerned. Where a guardian *ad litem* (GAL) is appointed, which will be in virtually all public law cases, that person will ascertain and present such wishes and feelings to the court. In a minority of cases the child will be the applicant and proceedings will in effect be driven by their views. In many their views will represented by a solicitor engaged by the GAL and/or be the subject of assessment by expert witnesses. Whether elicited by intermediaries, sought by judicial interview or directly expressed at the insistence of the child, the 1989 Act now requires the latter's wishes and feelings to be ascertained by the court. Secondly the court has a duty to have regard for wishes and feelings. This requirement clearly leaves to judicial discretion the crucial issue of how much weight is to be attached, in any particular instance, to the views of a child when determining a matter affecting his or her welfare. The fact that such a consideration will seldom be the deciding factor was apparent in a ruling of the Court of Appeal.[15] In considering the equivalent provision of the 1989 Act, it was held that the court should always elicit and respect the views of a child which it may not be able to act upon but which may tip the balance in a difficult case.

Local authorities also incur duties in relation to the identification of welfare wishes. Once a local authority incurs responsibilities in respect of a child it will now, thereby, incur an obligation to ascertain the wishes and feelings of that child. This may arise by implication in the context of service provision for children with special needs. It may arise by explicit statutory directive in relation to children being either accommodated or being 'looked after' by a local authority. It may also arise from the considerable body of regulations which detail a local authority's implementation of its various statutory duties towards children, including those being adopted. There are several different and specific sets of circumstances in which such duties may arise.

Firstly, the duty to identify a child's welfare wishes will arise in relation to children being accommodated by a local authority. As is stated in s 20 of the 1989 Act:

> (6) Before providing accommodation under this section, a local authority shall, so far as is reasonably practicable and consistent with the child's welfare -
>
> (a) ascertain the child's wishes regarding the provision of accommodation; and
>
> (b) give due consideration (having regard to his age and understanding) to such wishes of the child as they have been able to ascertain.

The form of words relied upon in this and the following provisions to delineate the duty of a local authority differs slightly from that used above in respect of the equivalent judicial duty. It may be that the change from "have regard" to "give due consideration", and the occasional absence of a local authority's duty to do so in relation to "feelings", is intended to imply a subtle distinction in the extent and weighting to be attached to the views of a child by local authority and judiciary.

The regulations governing the agreements made between a local authority and parents, in respect of arrangements for a child being accommodated, provide for the views of the child concerned to be ascertained. The requirement is that every local authority shall record the arrangements it makes for ascertaining the views of the child in relation to the matters dealt with in the accommodation agreement.

Secondly, the duty will arise in relation to children being 'looked after' by a local authority. Under s 22 of the 1989 Act:

> (4) Before making any decision with respect to a child whom they are looking after, or proposing to look after, a local authority shall, so far as is reasonably practicable, ascertain the wishes and feelings of -
>
> (a) the child
>
> and
>
> (5) In making any such decision a local authority shall give due consideration -
>
> (a) having regard to his age and understanding, to such wishes and feelings of the child as they have been able to ascertain.

When so considering a child's views, in the context of such decision-making, a local authority is further directed to consider also the child's religious persuasion, racial origin and cultural and linguistic background. This requirement, that a local authority consult, where practicable, with a child before making decisions affecting that child and before making arrangements regarding his or her future home, ensures that the child is at least briefed and at best given a chance to participate in the choices to be made as to the manner in which he or she is looked after by the local authority.

Thirdly, the duty will also arise in relation to the reviews of children being 'looked after' by a local authority. Under s 26 of the 1989 Act:

> (1) The Secretary of State may make regulations requiring the case of each child who is being looked after by a local authority to be reviewed in accordance with the provisions of the regulations.
> (2) The regulations may, in particular, make provision -
> (d) requiring the authority, before conducting any review, to seek the views of -
> (i) the child.

The regulations emanating from this provision provide comprehensively for the responsibility of local authorities to ascertain and take into account the wishes and feelings of children across the full range of settings in which they may be accommodated; including those of children in secure accommodation. How this is achieved, so as to ensure that the child is therapeutically engaged, his or her legal interests are effectively and assertively represented while welfare interests are not uncompromised, remains a principal challenge for the practice of a local authority as much as for the court.

Finally, the duty will also arise when a local authority receives representations, including complaints, from children. The duty of a local authority to establish a complaints procedure in relation to children whom it is 'looking after' is addressed in regulations which derive from the authority of s 36: -

> (3) Every local authority shall establish a procedure for considering any representations (including any complaint) made to them by -
> (a) any child who is being looked after by them or who is not being looked after by them but is in need.

In addition to the above duties of court and local authority, the duty to identify the welfare wishes of a child may also fall on other bodies and persons. For example, s 61 of the 1989 Act places such a duty on voluntary organisations:

> (1) Where a child is accommodated by or on behalf of a voluntary organisation, it shall be the duty of the organisation -
> (c) to advise, assist and befriend him with a view to promoting his welfare when he ceases to be so accommodated.
> (2) Before making any decision with respect to any such child the organisation shall, so far as is reasonably practicable, ascertain the wishes and feelings of -
> (a) the child
> regarding the matter to be decided.
> (3) In making any such decision the organisation shall give due consideration
> (a) having regard to the child's age and understanding, to such wishes and feelings of his as they have been able to ascertain.

This provision extends to voluntary organisations the duty to identify and take into account a child's views regarding his or her welfare. Under s 64(1)(c), (2)(a) and (3)(a) of the 1989 Act, the stated duties of any person carrying on a private children's home replicate those outlined in the corresponding provisions of s 61 above. The inclusion of private children's homes within the scope of this mandatory duty thereby ensures its uniform legal application across both the statutory and voluntary sectors of child care. Under s 46 a constable has the power to remove, and provide accommodation for, a child in an emergency. The exercise of this power is subject to a requirement in (3) of the same section that, as soon as is reasonably practicable after the child has been taken into police protection, the designated officer shall -

> (d) take such steps as are reasonably practicable to discover the wishes and feelings of the child.

However, under s 46(10), the issue of whether the child is then to have contact with parents or any other stated persons is a matter to be determined by the designated officer in the light of his assessment of the child's best interests; there is no requirement that he seek the views of the child on this matter. Again, under Part III, Schedule 3, of the 1989 Act, the duties of a supervisor in respect of a child the subject of an education supervision order include the power to give such directions to the child as may be necessary to ensure that he or she is properly educated. This power is subject to the instruction that the supervisor:

> ...so far as is reasonably practicable, ascertain the wishes and feelings of -
>
> (a) the child.

Sub-para (3) adds the further instruction that:

> ...when settling the terms of any such directions, the supervisor shall give due consideration -
>
> having regard to the child's age and understanding, to such wishes and feelings of his as the supervisor has been able to ascertain.

These instructions do not lie solely in relation to the child; they are exactly replicated in respect of the child's parents. Not only are the views of the child thus accorded no greater weight than those of the parents but there is no suggestion in this provision that the supervisor should comply with the views of either party.

Public family law: the duty to defer to the views of a child

There is no such thing as a sweeping statutory duty directing that a child's views, as opposed to his or her legal interests, must prevail over all other considerations in the determining of issues affecting the welfare of that child. The essential point of the paramountcy principle, after all, is a recognition that the responsibility for decision-making is to be placed not in the hands of a child but in the hands of certain authorised others. Additionally, the party primarily bound by the outcome of any decision to which the principle applies, is the child concerned.

However, there are now some areas of decision-making governed by the 1989 Act where such authority has been extended to enforce the views of a child that in effect responsibility for a decision rests with that child. There are also other areas which, because decisions turn on the consent rather than the views of a *Gillick* competent child, the outcome will be the same.

The court, for example, has certain duties in regard to the non-consensual medical treatment of a child in care. The circumstances in which the wishes and feelings of a child may, in public family proceedings, be permitted to override a refusal of parental consent is an area of law which seems set to experience an exponential increase in litigation. The issues arise most commonly, and most urgently, in relation to medical treatment where consent of parent or child is an essential pre-condition for doctors to commence treatment: except in an emergency. Such cases most usually appear before the courts in private family proceedings where the criteria to be applied and the appropriate forum for hearing them have greatly exercised the judiciary in recent years. In public family proceedings, where the child is in care, then it is evident[16] that the appropriate forum is the inherent jurisdiction of the High Court. Occasionally, circumstances arise in which the person whose consent is required to authorise treatment lacks the capacity to do so; usually due to mental illness. This was the situation in a case[17] where a local authority sought permission to disconnect a life support system which was sustaining the life of a severely brain damaged child. The High Court, exercising its inherent jurisdiction, provided the necessary authority (see, also, Chap 7). Where the child is a mature minor and parental consent is, for whatever reason unavailable, then there is authority under the ruling in *Gillick* for the courts to endorse the consent of the child.

Local authorities are frequently faced with problems in relation to older adolescents in care who make reasoned decisions which are not in keeping with their welfare interests. An adolescent will often hold strong views as to what he or she believes constitutes their welfare interests and what should be done to further those interests. The question then arises as to what power a local authority might have to override the decision of a *Gillick* competent minor.

In *Re W (A Minor)(Medical Treatment: Court's Jurisdiction)*[18] the court considered an application made in respect of a 16 year old anorexic girl in care, for permission to arrange medical treatment, and for this to be provided without her consent if necessary. The Court of Appeal unanimously gave its consent. It held that: it had authority to do so under the court's unlimited inherent *parens patriae* jurisdiction; the authority of those holding 'parental responsibility' for a child would be insufficient to override the decision of a '*Gillick* competent' child; its authority when exercising this jurisdiction exceeded that which came within the definition of 'parental responsibility' and; that the High Court's inherent jurisdiction may apply regardless of whether or not the child in question was a ward.

Where the views of a mature minor in care are being unreasonably opposed by a parent the court will not hesitate to give precedence to the views of the child if the evidence shows that to do so would be compatible with welfare interests. This approach is very much in keeping with the decision in *Re O (A Minor)(Medical Treatment)*[19] which provides authority for the view that the inherent jurisdiction is the most appropriate forum to authorise a blood-transfusion for a child against the wishes of the child's parents who, in the latter case, were Jehovah Witnesses.

The fact that a court is bound by the paramountcy principle in its determination of most proceedings arising under the 1989 Act, does not of itself give rise to any presumption that other factors must give way to the views of a child. Indeed, quite the opposite is the case. However, in certain circumstances the courts have little or no option when faced with a resolute child.

Firstly, this can occur in relation to child assessment orders. Under s 43 of the 1989 Act, the court is empowered, on the application of a local authority or authorised person, to make a child assessment order if satisfied that the requirements stated in that provision have been met. However, under para (8) "if the child is of sufficient understanding to make an informed decision he may refuse to submit to a medical or psychiatric examination or other assessment". This effectively gives the child a power to determine his or her welfare interests and to veto an entire court order.

Secondly, it may occur in relation to assessment conditions attached to other court orders. Under s 44(1) of the 1989 Act the court may make an emergency protection order which can be subject to a direction made under ss (6)(b) requiring a medical, psychiatric or other form of assessment for the child. However, ss (7) adds that the child concerned may "if he is of sufficient understanding to make an informed decision, refuse to submit to the examination or other assessment". The child is thus given a power of veto, restricted to an ancillary aspect of the order and to that extent may determine his or her welfare interests. Also, under Sched 3 para 4, the power of a court to attach a direction to a supervision order made under s 31(1), requiring the child to attend for psychiatric or medical examination, is subject to: -

> (4) No court shall include a requirement under this paragraph in a supervision order unless it is satisfied -
>
> (a) where the child has sufficient understanding to make an informed decision, that he consents to its inclusion.

The case of *Leeds City Council v C*[20] demonstrates the difficulties presented by this provision.

Finally, it can occur in relation to applications for the discharge and variation etc of certain orders. Under s 39(1) and (2) the court may discharge a care order or a supervision order, respectively, on the application of the child concerned. Under s 45(8)(a) the court may do the same where the child's application is in respect of an emergency protection order. Similarly, under Sched 3, the court may do so where the child's application is in relation to an education supervision order. These provisions require the court to treat an application from a child in the same way it would if the application had been made by a local authority, parent or a person with parental responsibility: if the applicant satisfies the conditions then the court must defer and discharge the order.

In certain circumstances the duties of a local authority leave it with little or no option other than to defer to the wishes of a child. Under the 1989 Act and other legislation, a local authority may find that its obligation to defer to the views of a child are such that in effect it is recognising and conceding a right held by that child. This may occur, for example, in relation to the provision of accommodation. Section 20(11) of the 1989 Act removes both a local authority's right not to provide accommodation and the right of any person with parental responsibility to remove a child from local authority accommodation 'where a child who has reached the age of sixteen agrees to being provided with accommodation under this section'. Effectively, this provision would seem to place a duty on the local authority to provide accommodation to such a child or allow him or her to remain in local authority accommodation if that child has determined that this is in accordance with his or her welfare interests. The independent legal status of such a child is further recognised by s 29(4)(b) under which a local authority is authorised to recover from that child contributions towards the maintenance costs incurred in looking after him or her.

Private family law: the duty to identify welfare interests

The requirement to ascertain the wishes and feelings of a child has a restricted application to private family proceedings. It falls as a statutory duty on the judiciary only in respect of contested proceedings and its bearing on local authority procedures is virtually limited to forming an item in the court reports of social workers and GALs in adoption and some wardship and matrimonial proceedings.

The judiciary have virtually no obligation to identify welfare interests in the context of uncontested private family law proceedings. The welfare 'checklist' has no application and therefore there is no statutory requirement that the wishes and feelings of the child concerned be ascertained. This non-interventionist stance is well illustrated by the two provisions in the 1989 Act relating to the intention to change a child's surname. Section 13 states that:

> (1) Where a residence order is in force with respect to a child, no person may -
>
> (a) cause the child to be known by a new surname; without either the written consent of every person with parental responsibility or the leave of the court.

Under s 33(7)(a) 'no person shall cause the child to be known by a new surname' - except in the same circumstances. In neither instance is there a requirement to seek the child's views. Indeed, where the child's views are brought before the court[21] they may be discounted. This was precisely what occurred in *Re B (Change of Surname)*.[22] The unequivocal wishes of three children (aged 12, 14 and 16), supported by mother and social worker, then proved insufficient to convince the court that a change of surname to that of their step-father would be justified. An approach which contrasts with that advocated in Articles 2 and 9 of the Convention.

In adoption, wardship and matrimonial proceedings where an application is being contested the judiciary have a well established practice of seeking the views of the children concerned. Information on their views will also be made available to the court in the form of reports from local authority social workers in respect of all such proceedings, augmented by reports from GALs in adoption applications and in all cases by occasional evidence from expert witnesses.

In adoption proceedings, the statutory requirement in s 6 of the Adoption Act 1976 to "...ascertain the wishes and feelings of the child...and give due consideration to them, having regard to his age and understanding", is binding on both court and local authority in relation to any decision. The significance attached to this requirement was apparent in *In Re B*

(Minor)(Adoption: Parental Agreement)[23] where the court's decision to dispense with the need for parental agreement was significantly influenced by the wishes of the 11 year old subject.

In matrimonial proceedings, the checklist considerations as stated in s 1(3) of the 1989 Act now apply to any disputes concerning the parties proposed care arrangements for their children. Such is the significance attached to the requirement to seek the views of the children concerned that it has been held[24] that a failure to do so ought to be a ground of appeal. It is, however, a matter of some concern that this requirement only applies when such proceedings are contested. By far the majority of judicial determinations affecting the future upbringing of children occur in the context of matrimonial proceedings. Most of these are undisputed. In the majority of cases affecting child welfare, therefore, the law does not require the views of the children involved to be heard in settling the arrangements for their future upbringing. This is a significant constraint on the application of the welfare principle (see, further, Chap 12).

The Family Law Act 1996 requires the welfare interests of the child concerned to be identified in divorce proceedings: s 8(9)(b) states that information must be given to parents about 'the importance to be attached to the welfare, wishes and feelings of the child'; s 11(4)(a) obliges the court to have particular regard to the wishes and feelings of the child. However, there is no reason to believe that these provisions will alter the established practice of leaving the ascertainment of a child's wishes and feelings to the routine enquiries of solicitors and/or court welfare officers (and, in the future, 'mediators'), usually directed towards parents rather than the child concerned, and discouraging the participation of children in court proceedings.

In the wardship jurisdiction, the caselaw reveals a consistent judicial concern to establish a direct relationship with the children who come before the court. In recent years this has been accompanied by a judicial willingness to solicit, and give more weight to, their opinions.

Private family law: the duty to defer to the views of a child

In private family proceedings the duty upon others in relation to the views of a child is at its weakest. This is balanced by the powerful right of a child in such proceedings to assert his or her views at the expense of others. After all, the decision in *Gillick* resulted from private family proceedings and remains the leading case and reference point for a developing body of jurisprudence on the autonomous legal interests of children and the weighting of such interests relative to those of parents and others. It is private family proceedings which have since witnessed the emergence of such child 'rights' as: to sue for damage caused while a foetus; to 'divorce' parents; to have access to parents;

and to have access to information on pre-adoption family background. This is in keeping with the general philosophy underpinning the 1989 Act that state intrusion in family matters should be minimised while the capacity of family members to assert their autonomous legal interests should be facilitated. However, it is possible that the decision in *Re B* (see, above) indicates a firming-up of the judicial approach towards children's 'rights': where a child's wishes are in conflict with rights traditionally regarded as hallmarks of parental status (the right to determine religious upbringing, surname etc) they may not prevail.

The duties of the court in relation to leave to apply for section 8 orders are outlined in s 10:

> (8) Where the person applying for leave to make an application for a section 8 order is the child concerned, the court may only grant leave if it is satisfied that he has sufficient understanding to make the proposed application for the section 8 order.

This would seem to imply that where the condition is satisfied the court is then virtually required to grant the leave sought.

Their duties in relation to contact arrangements have been established since the decision in *M v M (Child: Access)*.[25] The courts will defer to the views of a child, where these are judged to be compatible with his or her welfare interests, when faced with a conflict between such views and those of a parent in respect of contact arrangements.

In relation to applications for the termination of guardianship appointments the court may, under s 6(7) of the 1989 Act, at any time order the termination of an appointment of a guardian made under s 5-

> (b) on the application of the child concerned, with leave of the court.

Again, the court is required to treat the application on its merits and will be obliged to accede to the child's wishes if satisfied that to do so would be in keeping with his or her welfare interests.

Finally, in private law cases the assessment of a *Gillick* competent child is dependent upon the prior consent of that child. However, his or her right to refuse might depend upon mental competence.[26] This may also be overriden by the court if the latter should be of the opinion that an examination is in his or her best interests.[27]

Conclusion

It is paradoxical that as the law specifies an increased range of welfare indicators to be taken into account when determining matters affecting a child's upbringing it also drastically reduces the opportunities for applying them. The removal of the mandatory welfare test as a condition for a judicial order terminating a marriage, has removed professional scrutiny from the largest category of proceedings in which the future welfare of children needs to be safeguarded. The retreat of state intervention across the range of private family law has been a new development in family law and one which in effect abandons decision making on welfare issues to the families concerned.

Notes

1 See Article 3 -
(3) In the circumstances referred to in paragraph (4), a court shall have regard in particular to - (a) the ascertainable wishes and feelings of the child concerned (considered in the light of his age and understanding).

2 For example, in 1984 the Parliamentary Assembly made a recommendation to the Ministers of the Council of Europe on the subject of 'parental responsibilities' and incorporated advice in relation to the views of children. It then argued that when decisions are to be taken affecting the legal interests of children, the latter 'should be consulted if their degree of maturity with regard to the decision so permits'.

3 See in particular, Article 12(1).

4 Article 5 of the Convention, for example, recognises the inherent mutuality between the rights of parents and the welfare of their children in its declaration:

> States Parties shall respect the responsibilities, rights and duties of parents....to provide, in a manner consistent with the evolving capacities of the child, appropriate direction and guidance in the exercise by the child of the rights recognised in the present Convention.

See also Article 12 which deals with the right of a child to freely express his or her opinion, and have that opinion taken into account, in any matter or procedure affecting him or her.

5 *Gillick v West Norfolk and Wisbech Area Health Authority* [1986] 1 AC 112, HL.

6 [1992] FCR 261.

7 See *Report of the Inquiry into Child Abuse in Cleveland* 1987, at p 245.

8 See *Re R* [1991] 4 All ER 177.

9 See *Re P (A Minor)(Education)* [1992] 1 FLR 316 CA.

10 See *Re S (A Minor)(Independent Representation)* [1993] 2 FLR at p 444H.

11 See *Re M (Minors)(Disclosure of Evidence)* [1994] 1 FLR No 6.

12 [1994] 2 FLR 441.

13 [1992] 3 WLR 785, [1992] 4 All ER 627.

14 This approach can be seen in *Re R (A Minor)(Wardship: Medical Treatment)* [1992] 1 FLR 190 where Donaldson LJ held that a parent retained the right to consent to treatment on behalf of a child, even though the child was of age and understanding and had refused her consent.

15 See *Re P (A Minor)(Education)* [1992] 1 FLR 316 CA.

16 See *Re R (A Minor)(Blood Transfusion)* [1993] 2 FLR 757.

17 See *Re TC (A Minor)*, [1994] 4 BNIL.

18 [1992] 3 WLR 785, [1992] 4 All ER 627.

19 [1993] 2 FLR 149.
20 [1993] 1 FLR 269.
21 See *W v A (Child: Surname)* [1981] 1 All ER 100.
22 [1996] 1 FLR 791.
23 [1990] 2 FLR 383.
24 See *M v M (Minor: Custody Appeal)* [1987] 1 WLR 404.
25 [1973] 2 All ER 81.
26 See *R v Waltham Forest London Borough ex parte G* [1989] 2 FLR 138.
27 See *Re W (A Minor) (Consent to Medical Treatment)* [1993] 1 FLR 1.

7 Representing Welfare Interests

Introduction

Audi alteram partem – the right of a person directly affected by the outcome to put their case to the court – is a right of natural justice which, traditionally, has been denied to children. Instead, a person below the age of eighteen has been construed as *sui juris*,[1] their legal interests subsumed within those of a parent or guardian. The latter would therefore be the party named in proceedings to represent the welfare interests of a child. In more recent years, where it was considered appropriate by the court, (most usually in wardship proceedings) the Official Solicitor might be invited to 'speak for the child'. Occasionally, such a duty might have been assigned to a guardian *ad litem* (in adoption proceedings) or to a local authority social worker (in matrimonial or child care proceedings). Neither court nor legislation required a child's wishes or their perception of their welfare interests to be brought before a judge. The duty of official intermediaries was to provide factual information and advice as to what, in the presenting circumstances, they considered to be a child's best interests. Their views were often at variance with the wishes of the child concerned, did not necessarily take full account of his or her particular welfare interests and had no regard for what are now recognised as the legal rights of children.

The Children Act 1989, together with other legislation within and without the jurisdiction, has significantly altered the law relating to the representation of children's interests. There is now a considerable range of statutorily designated circumstances in which a child's welfare interests are recognised as warranting protection. A number of specific officials and bodies are statutorily charged with representing a child's welfare interests. Certain statutorily specified forums, including the family proceedings court, are identified to hear and determine such representations. But, perhaps most importantly, legislation now requires that the voice of the child concerned be heard by those with a responsibility for determining issues relating to the welfare interests of that child.

This chapter identifies and examines the means whereby the modern interpretation of a child's welfare interests are represented and given effect.

The child

The United Nations Convention on the Rights of the Child has, in recent years, provided an inescapable reference point for Westminster legislators drafting provisions relating to the treatment of a child in court.[2] This is particularly true in relation to Article 5 which gives recognition to the evolving capacities of the child,[3] Article 8 which acknowledges a child's right to an identity and Article 12 which declares the right of a child to representation.

Representing the welfare interests of a child is dependant upon those interests being accurately identified. The law has always had difficulty in leaving that responsibility to the child concerned. The younger the child the stronger the legal presumption that he or she lacks the competence to understand fully and objectively the nature of their particular welfare interests. This problem is acknowledged by the inclusion of the caveats 'capable of forming his or her own views' in Article 12 and 'of sufficient understanding' in the 1989 Act which condition the exercise of a child's right to be an advocate on behalf of their own welfare interests. The leave of the court for a child to apply for a s 8 order,[4] the retaining of a solicitor by a child and the right of a child to participate in proceedings without a next friend or GAL are each dependent upon the statutory requirement (s 10(8), s 41(4)(b) and Rule 9.2A(6)[5] respectively) that the child concerned first satisfies the 'sufficient understanding' test.

In recent years there have been a number of important judicial decisions which offer some measures for determining when a child's understanding may be construed as 'sufficient'. Firstly, in considering whether a child is competent to instruct a solicitor the courts have ruled that much will depend on the age and maturity of the child concerned.[6] Secondly, the court will be concerned to establish a child's understanding relative to the issues. A crucial point was made by Sir Thomas Bingham in *Re S and B (Minors)(Child Abuse: Evidence)*[7] when he observed that understanding "has to be assessed relative to the issues in the case". An approach he later returned to in a case[8] where the Court of Appeal considered whether an 11 year old boy should be granted leave to apply for the removal of the Official Solicitor. The latter had been appointed to represent the boy's interests in a bitter dispute between parents who each sought a residence order in respect of him. In ruling that leave should not be granted, Bingham MR reasoned that the child did not have the maturity to sufficiently understand the complex emotional context of the dispute and thus would be unable to undertake the role of a party in the proceedings. Two years later Johnson J took the view that S had attained sufficient maturity to instruct his own legal representative and, dismissing the Official Solicitor, gave S permission to leave the jurisdiction and live with his father. Again, in *Re K,W, and H (Minors)(Medical Treatment)*[9] the Court of Appeal was unconvinced that children had the capacity to give independent instructions. Finally, the court will take into account any possible emotional disturbance which might effect a child's understanding of the issues. The fact that a child is emotionally disturbed will necessarily affect that child's capacity to instruct a solicitor.[10] The judgment as to whether the emotional disturbance is affecting rationality to the extent that a capacity to issue valid instructions is impaired, is one for a doctor to make.

The proceedings

Article 12 of the United Nations Convention on the Rights of the Child declares that:

> 1. States parties shall assure to the child who is capable of forming his or her own views the right to express those views freely in all matters affec ting the child, the views of the child being given due weight in accordance with the age and maturity of the child.
>
> 2. For this purpose the child shall in particular be provided with the opportunity to be heard in any judicial and administrative proceedings affecting the child, either directly or through a representative or an appropriate body, in a manner consistent with the procedural rules of national law.

Contrary to the direction in Article 12(2) that representation be provided in 'any judicial and administrative proceedings' this is currently only obligatory in judicial proceedings of a public nature. There is no legal entitlement, under the 1989 Act, to representation in such administrative proceedings as case conferences or reviews of children in care.[11] Nor is there any such entitlement in uncontested private proceedings. In the latter case this omission is significant as they constitute the majority of proceedings in which children's welfare interests are a factor (see, further, Chap 12). Only in adoption and contested private family proceedings is there an obligatory requirement that the welfare interests of children be represented before the court. In the future, s 64 of the Family Law Act 1996 provides the means for regulations to be introduced which could allow separate representation for the interests of children in matrimonial proceedings.

Recognition of the right of a child to representation in public proceedings, commenced under the Children Act 1989 and affecting his or her welfare interests, is a natural corollary of the recognition given to their right to appear as a party in such proceedings. Under the Family Proceedings Rules, in any public law proceedings, the child concerned (in addition to the local authority, parents, any other person with parental responsibility and such other persons as may be granted leave by the court to be joined) will automatically have full party status. In private law proceedings the child concerned may, with leave of the court, acquire full party status; this is a comparatively rare occurrence. Entitlement to full party status brings with it a right to attend court, to be represented in court and to appeal from a decision of the court (s 94 of the 1989 Act). It also entitles the court to compel the attendance of a child where necessary. However, the warning sounded by Thorpe J has received widespread judicial support:

> The balance to be maintained between recognising and upholding the rights of children who are parties to Children Act 1989 litigation to participate and be heard and the need to protect children from exposure to material that might be damaging is a delicate one, and one essentially to be performed by the trial judge with a full perspective of the issues and the statements and reports, at a relatively early stage in the proceedings.[12]

Representation

Representation, properly understood, can only be provided by a solicitor acting on and abiding by instructions from the client. Whether or not the solicitor is in agreement with the instructions is beside the point.

The child with 'sufficient understanding' is entitled to retain and instruct a solicitor to act as their representative in any family proceedings; with leave of the court in some circumstances. Where entitlement is established but the child is not of 'sufficient understanding' or chooses not to instruct a solicitor then the court will require that a guardian *ad litem* or local authority social worker be appointed as a 'court officer' to advise it on matters relating to the child's best interests. Where representation is provided, it will rarely be controlled by the child; though in private proceedings is more likely to be so. Allowing or expecting a child to exercise such control, or even to attend the proceedings, may in some circumstances amount to 'secondary abuse' of that child. In public proceedings there is a discretion available to the court, under s 95(1) of the 1989 Act, to waive the necessity for a child's attendance, even where the child is a party.

There is an important distinction to be made between representation in public and in private proceedings. The difference in the roles of solicitor and guardian *ad litem* and the rules governing when which role has priority are crucial to the way in which a child's interests are brought before the court.

The right of a child to directly assert his or her legal interests, as opposed to having a guardian *ad litem* present an assessment of their welfare interests, is dependent upon representation by a solicitor. The rules governing when a child may elect to instruct a solicitor and prevent the involvement of a guardian *ad litem* are not the same in public and private proceedings. In 'specified' proceedings in public law the role of the guardian, whether or not accompanied by a solicitor, is virtually mandatory. In contrast a child with sufficient understanding to instruct a solicitor may more readily do so in private proceedings.[13]

In public law proceedings there are now opportunities for a child to directly assert his or her own welfare interests before the court: by challenging the making of an emergency protection order; by applying for contact when in care; and, under s 39(1)(b) of the 1989 Act, by applying for the discharge of a care or supervision order. The latter provision has given rise to controversy in relation to the right of the child to make application without first obtaining leave of the court. In *Re A (Care: Discharge Application by Child)*[14] the High Court considered the question, which had arisen in the county court, as to whether a 14 year old boy could apply as of right for the discharge of the care order relating to him. It also considered the further question as to the extent to which he should be allowed to participate in the discharge hearing. The court held that the provision did not suggest a requirement that the applicant first obtain leave to apply. It would fall to the county court judge, when the applicant appeared before the court, to then determine whether or not the child was of sufficient understanding to make representations under the Rules. In making this decision the judge would take into account the fact that the child had already been accepted by a solicitor as a client with sufficient understanding to give direct instructions. This was an important ruling marking a significant point of difference between the *locus standi* of a child applicant in public and private family proceedings commenced under this legislation. Unlike the situation in respect of applications for s 8 orders, a child of 'sufficient understanding' to instruct a solicitor will not require prior leave of the court to commence proceedings to discharge a care order. Given that the distinction between private and public family law in this legislation seems to rest, to a considerable extent, on a pervasive legislative intent to facilitate autonomous decision-making by family members in the former while requiring this to be subjected to prior authorisation from court or local authority in the latter, there is now arguably a logical inconsistency in the legal standing accorded to child applicant in each area.

The court also held that the right of a child, who is a party to public proceedings instigated under this legislation, to participate must be balanced against the risk that in doing so he or she may be exposed to harm. The decision as to whether the child should participate was one for the court to make as soon as practicable after the commencement of an action. This was in keeping with the view expressed by Waite J in *Re C*[15] that "the presence of children should not be encouraged to develop into settled practice". However, this is at variance with the approach followed by the judiciary in private proceedings (see above) but readily facilitated by the discretionary judicial power, available under s 95(1) of the 1989 Act, to waive the necessity for a child's attendance. In practice children will rarely be in a position to either control the representation of their interests or to even be present in the courtroom when decisions affecting them are taken.

The evidence of children[16]

The principle of the welfare of the child has increasingly, in recent years, been brought to bear on the manner in which the legal system accommodates the evidence of children and the evidence of others in relation to children. The relevant law is to be found mainly in the Children (Admissibility of Hearsay Evidence) Order 1993, the Civil Evidence Act 1995, sections 96-98 and 41(1) of the Children Act 1989, the Magistrates' Courts Act 1980 and the Rules. The law relating to the evidence given by children revolves around three central issues: should a child be compelled to attend court; what weight should be attached to hearsay evidence; and how competent is the testimony of a child? Other ancillary issues concern the use of modern technology in the presentation of evidence and the rules regarding disclosure.

The legal system has only recently acknowledged a difficulty with the preliminary question of whether a child should appear in proceedings where their welfare interests are at issue. The traditional rule was always that plaintiff and respondent should be physically present before the court. Children were therefore compellable witnesses and, in keeping with this rule, s 2 of the Children and Young Persons Act 1969 required the attendance of a child subject of care proceedings. Since the introduction of the 1989 Act,[17] however, the attendance of a child witness has become a matter to be determined at the discretion of the court and the assumption is that although this will seldom be necessary in care proceedings or in private law proceedings it will be required in criminal prosecutions. The difficulties in reconciling welfare interests and legal rights arise most starkly and frequently in child abuse cases where the sole or main evidence rests on the testimony of the child concerned. When in such circumstances the child victim is very young, the court (or other involved professionals at an earlier stage) will often elect not to proceed with the prosecution of an alleged abuser. The younger the child the more probable the prevailing view that requiring him or her to give evidence, and face possible cross-examination, would be to unjustifiably jeopardise their welfare interests.[18] This general assumption has been coming under sustained attack in recent judgments. In *Re P (Witness Summons)*[19] it was held that the paramountcy principle had no part to play in the exercise of judicial discretion; as the issue of a summons was not a matter affecting a child's upbringing, welfare was no more than one of the factors to be taken into account when deciding whether attendance is necessary. In the type of proceedings most likely to be damaging to welfare interests, attendance of the child concerned will usually be required.

The law governing hearsay in the context of children's evidence has long been problematic. The common law required the judge to warn a jury about the dangers of finding a defendant guilty on the basis of the uncorroborated evidence of a child. This rule has been removed except where the offence alleged is one of sexual abuse. Under sections 96(3)-(7) of the Children Act 1989 the Lord Chancellor was given authority to make orders to provide for 'the admissibility of evidence which would otherwise be inadmissible under any rule relating to hearsay' and under s 41(1) the court was given a broad discretion to take into account evidence which would similarly be in breach of that rule. Judicial notice was taken of this authority in *R(J) v Oxfordshire County Council*[20] where the court held that hearsay evidence could be admitted in all proceedings instituted under the Children Act 1989 including proceedings for secure accommodation and child assessment orders. The Children (Admissibility of Hearsay Evidence) Order 1993 then gave effect to the Lord Chancellor's authority by abolishing the hearsay rule in all civil proceedings affecting children. Any remaining doubt was laid to rest by the Civil Evidence Act 1995 which now permits the general admission of hearsay evidence in all civil proceedings. The weight given to such evidence remains a matter for judicial discretion.

The courts have also been greatly exercised by the issue of 'competence' when faced with the evidence of children. Judicial reluctance to require the court attendance of a child arises not only because of welfare considerations but also because he or she may be judged too young for their evidence to be reliable; in terms of providing the corroboration necessary to satisfy the burden of proof and likely to secure a conviction. The child's competence to identify their welfare interests will often in effect be neutralised by an adult judgment of the child's non-competence to represent those interests in court (see, further, above).

The law relating to the use of video technology in the context of children's evidence has attracted controversy in recent years. The Pigot Committee,[21] in addition to recommending the abolition of the exception to the corroboration rule relating to sexual abuse cases, also advocated the use of closed-circuit television technology as a means of reducing stress for children giving evidence in abuse cases. This recommendation found endorsement in the Memorandum of Good Practice on Video Recorded Interviews with Child

Witnesses for Criminal Proceedings 1992. More recently, the decision of the Court of Appeal in *Re N (Child Abuse: Evidence)*[22] serves as a reminder that evidence from a videotaped interview will have to comply with certain quality standards if the court is to accept that it meets the standard of proof required in sexual abuse cases. The Court of Appeal ruled that the judge at first instance should have: reminded himself that the video recording was a form of hearsay evidence; treated the videotape as unreliable evidence because the child was in the presence of a parent and exposed to leading questions; and the GAL had strayed beyond his area of expertise when giving evidence.

The law relating to the evidence of others in relation to children and to the influence of the self-incrimination rule has been clarified by s 98 of the 1989 Act:

> (1) In any proceedings in which a court is hearing an application for an order under Part IV or V, no person shall be excused from -
> (a) giving evidence on any matter; or
> (b) answering any question put to him in the course of his giving evidence, on the ground that doing so might incriminate him or his spouse of an offence.

This provision disapplies the privilege against self-incrimination from emergency proceedings and also from proceedings concerning care and supervision orders. In return for giving evidence which would otherwise have been incriminating, the person concerned shall be excused by the court from the consequences of any admission or incriminating statement made, except where the offence disclosed is one of perjury. This exemption may be of considerable significance in care proceedings grounded on allegations of child abuse.[23]

Again, as regards the onus to make a full disclosure of evidence, the court has the power to direct that evidence be withheld from a party to proceedings brought under the Children Act 1989.[24] This power should only be exercised in exceptional circumstances.[25] As Butler-Sloss stated in *Re M (Minors)(Disclosure of Evidene)*[26] when considering whether to order non-disclosure:

> The test was not one of significant harm, but of whether disclosure would be so detrimental to the welfare of the children as to outweigh the normal requirement of a fair trial that all evidence must be disclosed.[27]

In *Oxfordshire County Council v M*[28] the Court of Appeal ruled that the court has the power to override legal professional privilege and order disclosure of an otherwise privileged expert's report. This continues the approach Wall J outlined earlier[29] when he endorsed the view of Thorpe J in *Essex County*

Council v R[30] that there is a positive duty of disclosure. It is clear that the judiciary are no longer to be neutral umpires as counsel field their expert witnesses but are resolved to play a positive part in the business of protecting children in the course of court proceedings. More recently, the House of Lords in *Re L (Police Investigation: Privilege)* [31] has taken this approach a step further by ruling that the right of a party to proceedings not to produce documents is an incident of adversarial proceedings which can have no place in the inquisitorial proceedings of the Children's Act 1989. The report of an expert witness, adverse to the interests of the party who held it, was ordered to be disclosed to the police.

The representatives

The *audi alteram partem* principle, which found authoritative recognition in Article 12 of the UN Convention,[32] has to some extent been incorporated into the civil law of this jurisdiction. The statutory authority for the appointment of professional representation on behalf of a child in family proceedings is now governed by the Children Act 1989. Section 41 provides for the representation of a child by the appointment of a guardian *ad litem* and a solicitor in public law proceedings. This 'tandem' model of representation in such proceedings, allowing welfare interests to be represented by a guardian *ad litem* and legal rights by a solicitor, has been extolled as ideal and unique within Europe.[33]

The Official Solicitor

The role of this person may be of crucial importance. The circumstances in which the Official Solicitor may act are governed by a direction issued by the Lord Chancellor under s 90(3) of the Supreme Court Act 1981. Traditionally, his appointment has been associated with wardship, adoption and occasional child care proceedings where he would undertake the role of guardian *ad litem* or, subsequently, be assigned responsibility to act as guardian of the child's estate. More recently his involvement has been usual in cases involving a clear conflict of interests between the child and another party, an international dimension or some complex legal issue such as may arise from time to time in the legal/medical field. Since the introduction of the 1989 Act, his role has been considerably restricted in public proceedings (but, see further below) both because of the virtual disappearance of wardship in that context and because of displacement by the GAL of responsibilities which previously fell to the Official Solicitor. However, as the GAL panel is not available to the court in private proceedings, the Official Solicitor is on occasion invited to fill the gap. He also has a role in wardship which continues to be a growth area in private family law. When, in exceptional circumstances, the Official Solicitor is appointed to act in proceedings instigated under the 1989 Act or in wardship then he acts as both solicitor and as GAL.

The duties of the Official Solicitor can be of crucial significance for a child's future welfare. This official has been described as:

> ...much more than a mere guardian *ad litem*. He is at once *amicus curiae*, independent solicitor acting for the children, investigator, advisor and sometimes supervisor.[34]

He has a duty to communicate a child's wishes to the court but he is not obliged to follow 'instructions' if these do not coincide with what he believes to be in the child's best interests. His role is, therefore, a hybrid one.[35] On the one hand he is obliged to 'give the child a voice in proceedings' by representing the child's views, defending his or her legal interests, instructing specialist consultants, or negotiating with overseas officials and generally acting as a solicitor to his client the child. On the other hand, as an officer of the court his primary duty is directed towards discovering and then representing to the court that which he conceives to be the child's best interests, which may conflict with the child's wishes.[36] He may, with his consent, be appointed as GAL to defend the interests of a minor with a disability. A solicitor may ask the court to invite the Official Solicitor to act or, in adoption proceedings involving an alleged illegal placement, he may be appointed by the High Court.[37] He may also be appointed by the county court.[38] His appointment must be on terms which do not attempt to fetter his traditional discretion to determine how he may best give effect to his functions. He may be dismissed by the appointment of a solicitor.[39] Despite the importance of his role, the ultimate decision remains for the court; the latter may override the wishes of the child concerned.[40]

The guardian *ad litem*

The duties of a guardian *ad litem* may also have a vital bearing on a child's future welfare. This court official is appointed in specified proceedings, usually child care cases but also, most notably, in adoption proceedings. The primary responsibilities of this official include a duty to communicate a child's wishes to the court, to advise the court as to what he considers are in the child's best interests and to appoint a solicitor to represent the child as a client. The guardian *ad litem* conducts extensive investigatory enquiries, independently of all other parties, into any matter considered to have a bearing on the child's welfare interests. This person acts as a court official rather than as a representative of the child and their primary duty is to advise the court on what, in their professional opinion, is in the child's best interests. Older children may often chose to have their own interpretation of their best interests forcefully advocated before the court, rather than rely on a guardian. Where there is conflict between the views of the child and those of the GAL, the latter may present his separate views personally or through a solicitor, and thereby continue to assist the court. The child may, however, choose to dismiss the GAL and prosecute or defend the remainder of the proceedings by directly instructing the solicitor[41] (see, also, Chap 8).

Section 41(9) of the Children Act 1989 provided the authority for the setting up of GAL panels. The constitution, administration and procedures of these panels and appointment of panel managers are among the matters which are addressed by the Regulations.[42] Although there is provision to appoint a GAL in private family law proceedings such an appointment cannot be made from the GAL panel and hence there is no public provision for payment.

The issue of the independence of GAL panels has been the focus of some debate. The courts have on occasion demonstrated the importance they attach to the principle that the independence of this court officer should not be compromised by the terms of his employment.[43]

The duties of a solicitor are most often of immediate importance in ensuring that a child's welfare interests are represented before the court. Under the 1989 Act, the court of its own motion may appoint a solicitor to represent a child in any private proceedings or in any public proceedings where a GAL has not been appointed, the child is of sufficient understanding and if such an appointment is in the child's best interests. A solicitor may be retained by and take instructions from a child whenever, in 'specified proceedings', the child has 'sufficient understanding' or in private proceedings has such understanding and chooses to make that appointment.[44] A solicitor will take instructions from the GAL only when the child is not sufficiently mature to directly instruct or the mature child's views do not conflict with the views of the GAL. A preliminary interview will be necessary to establish 'sufficient understanding' on the basis of whether the child fully comprehends the nature of the proceedings and appreciates the likely long and short term consequences of the proceedings. Where a child instructs a solicitor (which may occur either in specified proceedings when the wishes of a mature child conflict with those of the GAL or in private proceedings, where no GAL involvement is necessary), then such instructions must be followed even if they conflict with the solicitor's views. Though, as in any other case, the solicitor must remember his duty to the Legal Aid Board in respect of unreasonable instructions.

As the true representative of the child and advocate of the latter's wishes, the solicitor must ensure that proceedings are at the child's pace and must give the child space and permission to express their views. The solicitor must at all times act on behalf of the child and defend the latter's interests in all dealings with other parties. The responsibility to provide the child with independent and impartial advice, and to equip him or her with sufficient information to make an informed decision, falls on the solicitor. As with any other client, the solicitor is under a general duty of disclosure to a child in respect of documentary evidence held by the solicitor in preparation for the case; but discretion is called for in the manner in which this is done[45] (see, also, Chap 8).

The court welfare officer

The interests of a child may also be brought before the court by a court welfare officer. This person is most usually a probation officer attached to the court with responsibility for furnishing the court with family background information when so requested in the context of family proceedings. Alternatively, where the family concerned is already known to a local authority, then the relevant social worker will provide the required report; this will occur as a consequence of an investigation directed by the court under s 37(1) of the 1989 Act or initiated by a local authority under s 47. When reporting to the court, whether as court welfare officer or local authority social worker, this role is not as a representative of the child. The duties require that he or she gather and place before the court a body of factual information which comprehensively addresses all circumstances of child and family which are relevant to the proceedings. This 'welfare report' is of particular significance in private family law proceedings where it most often provides the only means by which the interests of the child concerned can be brought before the court. Any responsibility to provide representation for the child's welfare interests, as disclosed by the reported facts, will fall to a solicitor though the report may conclude with a substantiated opinion or recommendation. There is a view that the court welfare officer, or occasionally the local authority social worker, should have a greatly enlarged role which would provide an intake screening service in respect of all private law cases to establish the wishes and feelings of the children concerned and to advise the court as to whether or not legal representation would be appropriate.[46]

The expert witness

The contribution of expert witnesses to elucidating the welfare interests of a particular child has often been controversial. The role of such a witness is to provide the court with specialist information and, where appropriate, with a considered opinion on matters which lie within the witness's area of specialist expertise. Their evidence to the court results from an examination of a child which has been conducted with prior court approval. As stated in the Rules:

> (1) No person may, without leave of the court, cause the child to be medically or psychiatrically examined, or otherwise assessed, for the purpose of the preparation of expert evidence for use in the proceedings.[47]

It has been said that expert witnesses should only express opinions genuinely held and which are not biased towards one party or the other.[48] The contribution of an expert witness is confined to illuminating the court's understanding of complex factors and cannot be permitted to usurp the court's responsibility to determine the weighting to be given to such factors when deciding the matters at issue. Significant problems, arising in relation to the evidence of children resulting from disclosures made to professionals, have been apparent in a number of cases in recent years.

Representation in relation to service provision by a local authority

A right and a procedure has been provided, under the 1989 Act, for those affected by the provision or lack of provision of services governed by child care legislation, to make representations (including complaints) about such services. These afford important new avenues for representing a child's interests where his or her welfare has been adversely affected by the decisions of local authority officials.

A complaints procedure has been introduced by s 24 of the 1989 Act:

> (14) Every local authority shall establish a procedure for considering any representations (including any complaint) made to them by a person qualifying for advice and assistance about the discharge of their functions under this Part in relation to him.

This provision requires that complaints procedures be set up, publicised and operationalised by all local authorities in respect of the services they provide. This duty is extended to all voluntary organisations and children's homes. A person is deemed to be 'qualifying for advice and assistance' under the terms of this provision if he or she is under 21 and if at any time after reaching the age of 16 had been looked after by a local authority or accommodated in any of the settings specified under s 24(2). Those entitled, under s 26, to make a complaint or representations to a local authority include: children, parents and any person with parental responsibility; any local authority foster parent and; any other person whom the local authority considers has good reason to be interested in a child's welfare. The services in respect of which representations may be made include accommodation and those provided, or needed but not provided, by any local authority, voluntary organisation or registered children's home. Under s 26(2)(g) a local authority is required to inform any child, so far as is reasonably practicable, of the steps he or she may take under the 1989 Act to seek redress for any perceived grievance and in particular:

> (3) Every local authority shall establish a procedure for considering any representations (including any complaints) made to them by -
>
> (a) any child who is being looked after by them or who is not being looked after by them but is in need - about the discharge by the authority of any of their functions under this Part in relation to the child.

Such representations may, for example, be in relation to a local authority's failure to meet its obligation under s 26(2)(d)(i) to seek the views of a child being looked after by a local authority before conducting any review in respect of him or her. The representations are made in the first instance in writing or in person to the appropriate local authority where they are considered by local authority officials and an independent person.

A response must be made within 28 days and must be accompanied by guidance as to the procedure to be followed in the event of continued dissatisfaction. The complainant then has the right to request that the matter at issue be referred to a Representations Panel for further consideration. This panel is constituted to provide a formal hearing for any person who has registered their dissatisfaction with the local authority response to initial enquiries. The panel must include an independent person and must meet to consider the matter at issue within 28 days of notification. It must receive any written or oral submission made by the complainant, the local authority or by the independent person involved in the initial enquiry (if different from the panel representative). The Legal Aid Board may provide financial assistance to enable a child to be legally represented at such a panel. When the panel has reached a conclusion this must be recorded, together with the reasons for it, within 24 hours of the meeting. All parties, and any other person judged to have a *bona fide* interest, must then be notified by the panel of the conclusion reached. The local authority, assisted by the independent appointee, must then consider what action if any it should take in relation to the child or children, the subject of the enquiries, in the light of the conclusions reached by the representation panel. Finally, a complainant seeking further redress may consider an application to the court for a judicial review.

Conclusion

The occasions and means whereby a child's welfare interests can be brought before a determining body have been greatly increased by recent legislation, most notably the Children Act 1989. But there continues to be profound uncertainty as to the function of representation in relation to such interests. The distinction between legal rights and welfare interests lies at the heart of this uncertainty. The law has yet to clarify the rationale for determining the relative priorities of welfare interests and rights in particular circumstances. It has yet to satisfactorily bridge the gap between recognising the legal capacity of children as bearers of rights and acknowledging their competence to assert those rights. The discretionary right of the judiciary to decide whether or not to hear directly from a child is illustrative of this problem. The assertion by a child of his or her rights may well impair their welfare interests. Should the child concerned bear the responsibility for choice of representation?

Children are now more fully a part of the adversarial court system than previously. They can, and frequently are, compelled to appear as witnesses in criminal proceedings brought because they have been the victims of cruel abuse. They will then be required to recount painful experiences and may well be cross-examined on the veracity of their evidence, their honesty, their past and present relationships etc. Where the court's central concern is proof of the guilt or innocence of an adult, then the child's welfare interests afford little or no right to avoid full participation in proceedings. Where that concern is about future parenting arrangements for a child, the latter's welfare interests seem to confer little or no right to be heard by the court in person.

Notes

1 Beneath the law.

2 The issue of the Draft Convention on Children's Rights by the Council of Europe in November 1994 serves to emphasise the importance of the influence from outside the jurisdiction (see, further, Chaps 15 and 16).

3 Article 5:

> States Parties shall respect the responsibilities, rights and duties of parents or, where applicable, the members of the extended family or community as provided for by local custom, legal guardians or other persons legally responsible for the child, to provide, in a manner consistent with the evolving capacities of the child, appropriate direction and guidance in the exercise by the child of the rights recognised in the present Convention.

4 Applications for leave are not governed by the paramountcy principle, see: *Re C (Residence: Child's Application for Leave)* [1995] 1 FLR 927.

5 The Family Proceedings Rules 1991. Rule 9.2A details circumstances exempting a child from the general prohibition, stated in RSC Ord 80, r 2(1), against commencing or acquiring party status in proceedings (see, also Chap 5, fn 4A).

6 In *Re T (A Minor)(Wardship: Representation)* [1994] Fam 49, [1993] 3 WLR 602; *sub nom T (A Minor)(Child: Representation), Re* [1993] 4 All ER 518 the court upheld the right of a 13 year old girl to instruct a solicitor. In *Re S (A Minor)(Independent Representation)*, [1993] 2 FLR 437 the court denied the same right to an 11 year old boy (see, also, Chap 15).

7 [1990] 2 FLR 489 at p 444H.

8 See *Re S (A Minor)*, supra.

9 [1993] 1 FLR 854.

10 This was the view of the court in *Re H (A Minor)(Care Proceedings: Child's Wishes)* [1993] 1 FLR 440 where Thorpe J ruled that a child must be rational as well as having 'sufficient understanding'.

11 This deficiency is a matter of concern to such voluntary organisations as the Voice of Children in Care (VOYPIC), the National Youth Advocacy Service (NYAS) and the Children's Law Centre.

12 See *Re A (Care: Discharge Application by Child)* [1995] 1 FLR 599, at p 601B.

13 See, for example, *Re T (A Minor)(Child:Representation)* [1993] 4 All ER 518 FLR 440, *Re S (A Minor)(Independent Representation)* [1993] 2 FLR 437, CA) and *L v L (Minors)(Separate Representation)* [1994] 1 FLR 156. But note that s 64 of the Family Law Act 1996 makes provision for regulations to be introduced to permit the separate representation of children in proceedings under Parts II and IV of the 1996 Act and under the Domestic Proceedings and Magistrates Courts Act 1978.

14 [1995] 1 FLR 599.

15 [1993] 1 FLR 832 where the attendance of a 13 year old girl was viewed with judicial disapproval. See, also, *Re W (Secure Accommodation Order: Attendance at Court)* [1994] 2 FLR 1092 where attendance of a 10 year old boy was not permitted to attend.

16 See JR Spencer and R Flin, *The Evidence of Children*, Blackstone Press, 1993, for a fuller account of the law and issues.

17 s 95(1).

18 See, for example, *R v B County Council, ex parte P* [1991] 1 WLR 221.

19 [1997] 1 WLR 221; see, also, *R v Highbury Corner Magistrates Court ex parte D* [1997] 1 FLR 683 where a witness summons, requiring the attendance of a nine year old at the trial of his parent for assault on the latter's cohabitee, was held to be justified notwithstanding the possible negative effect on the child's welfare.

20 [1992] 3 All ER 660.

21 See *Report of the Advisory Group on Video Evidence* (Home Office), 1989.

22 [1996] 2 FLR No 2. See, also, *G v DPP* [1997] 3 All ER 909 and *Re D (Child Abuse: Interviews)* [1998] 2 FLR10; in the latter case it was ruled that standards laid down in the *Memorandum of Good Practice on Video Recorded Interviews with Child Witnesses for Criminal Proceedings* (HMSO, 1992) applied equally to criminal and civil proceedings.

23 See *Rochdale Borough Council v A and Others* [1991] 2 FLR 192, *Re A and Others (Minors)(Child Abuse: Guidelines)* [1992] 1 FLR 439 and *Cleveland CC v F* [1995] 2 All ER 236. Also, see Spencer and Flin *The Evidence of Children* (Blackstone, 2nd ed, 1993).

24 See *Re B (A Minor)(Disclosure of Evidence)* [1993] 1 FLR 191.

25 See *Re G (Minors)(Welfare Report: Disclosure)* [1993] 2 FLR 293, also see *Re C (A Minor: Irregularity of Practice)* [1991] 2 FLR 438.

26 [1994] 1 FLR No 6.

27 See also *Official Solicitor v K* [1965] AC 201.

28 [1994] 1 FLR 175.

29 See in *Re DH (A Minor)(Child Abuse)* [1994] 1 FLR 679.

30 [1993] 2 FLR 826.

31 [1996] 1 FLR 731.

32 Article 12:

1. States Parties shall assure to the child who is capable of forming his or her own views the right to express those views freely in all matters affecting the child, the

views of the child being given due weight in accordance with the age and maturity of the child.
2. For this purpose, the child shall in particular be provided the opportunity to be heard in any judicial and administrative proceedings affecting the child, either directly, or through a representative or an appropriate body, in a manner consistent with the procedural rules of national law.

> In their recent audit of the implementation of the Convention in the UK, the UN Committee on the Rights of Children recommended that "greater priority be given to incorporating the general principles of the Convention especially the provisions of....Article 12 concerning the child's right to make their views known and have those views given due weight, in legislative and administrative measures and in policies undertaken to implement the rights of the Child" (CRC/C/15Add.34 Feb 1995).

33 See report by Professor Ludwig Salgo, commissioned by the German Federal Government to make a comparative assessment of representation provided in child protection cases in several different European jurisdictions.

34 See *Re G* [1982] 1 WLR 438.

35 See *Re T (Child: Representation)* [1993] 3 WLR 602 where Waite LJ said of the Official Solicitor -

> He owes a loyalty which has by its very nature to be divided: to the child whose views he must fully and fairly represent; and to the court, which it is his duty to assist in achieving the overriding or paramount objective of promoting the child's best interests.

36 See *L v L (Children: Separate Representation)* [1994] 1 FLR 890 at p 893.

37 See *Practice Direction* [1986] 2 All ER 832 and *Practice Note: The Official Solicitor: Appointment in Family Proceedings* [1995] 2 FLR 479.

38 See *Re M (Official Solicitor's Role)* [1998] 2 FLR 815.

39 See *Re H (A Minor)(Role of Official Solicitor)* [1993] 2 FLR 552.

40 See *Re CT (A Minor)(Wardship: Representation)* [1993] 2 FLR 278.

41 As in *Re H* [1993], supra.

42 See The Guardians *ad litem* and Reporting Officers (Panels) Regulations 1991.

43 For example, in *Oxfordshire County Council v P* [1995] 1 FLR 552 the court held that the GAL had been wrong to divulge to his employers information concerning child protection matters received while acting in his capacity as GAL. Again, in *R v Cornwall County Council* [1992] 1 WLR 427, the court quashed a decision made by the Boards counterpart in England which purported to limit the number of hours which a social worker could spend on his GAL duties.

44 See *Re H (A Minor)(Care Proceedings: Child's Views)* [1993] 1 FLR 749, where Thorpe J emphasised the 'sufficient understanding' requirement and ruled that a child suffering from emotional disturbance would not satisfy this test.

45 See M I'Anson, *Guide to Good Practice*, SFLA, PO Box 302, Orpington BR6 8QX, DX 86853 Locksbottom.

46 See Association of Lawyers for Children, *The Future of Representation for Children*, Family Law, Vol 28, p 403-411, where it is suggested that a new unified welfare service should be established which would incorporate and more effectively co-ordinate the roles of solicitor, guardian ad litem, court reporter with the enlarged brief of the court welfare officer.

47 Rule 18 of the Family Proceedings Courts (Children Act 1989) Rules 1991; Rule 4.18 of the Family Proceedings Rules 1991.

48 See *Re R (A Minor)(Expert's Evidence)(Note)* [1991] 1 FLR 291 per Cazalet J.

Part 3: Public Family Law

Introduction to Part 3

Where a child was brought before the court, for reasons of a public rather than a private interest in matters affecting his or her welfare, then traditionally the exercise of judicial authority has been closely circumscribed by statute. Any question of altering the legal status of a child, by vesting future care responsibility outsidc the family of origin, required judicial attention to focus firstly on a technical legal dissection of the rights and duties of the respective parties. The whole approach to the welfare of a child, in this context, has traditionally been treated as subsidiary to the primary issues concerning the legal standing of the adults involved.

From the outset the core statutory proceedings constituting this strand have been those concerning the care, protection and control of children. These blanket proceedings included issues which grew to become separate proceedings in their own right: training; supervision; access; non-consensual adoption placement; secure accommodation and others. In this public family law context, the use of authority as provided for by statute and judicially applied, has changed since the proceedings were first introduced. The 'discovery' of child sexual abuse and the increase in child protection measures have brought ever widening permutations of care and protection issues before the courts. But, as with private family law, the fundamental distinguishing characteristics of the use of authority have also remained relatively intact.

The distinguishing legal hallmarks of public family proceedings, in relation to the welfare principle, may again be generally and crudely summarised as: coercive; resting on threshold criteria of prescriptive grounds; determined by adjudication; and disposed of by relatively fixed disposal options in relation to which judicial discretion is restricted.

Firstly, coercive intervention is the means by which welfare related issues are brought before the court in a public family law context. Criminal proceedings for injuries caused to a child and civil proceedings in respect of care, protection or control issues are a consequence of state initiated intervention in the family. The instigation of such proceedings is mandatory by police or local authority respectively on receipt of relevant information. Consent of the family is immaterial, the alleged offender or person suspected of being in breach of a duty of care has the *locus standi* of defendant in proceedings which are conducted in prosecutory manner.

Secondly, the intervention threshold is set by prescriptive grounds which identify, directly and objectively, the circumstances and conduct held to damage or endanger a child's welfare interests. The grounds for both criminal and care and protection proceedings share the common feature that they are largely retrospective in effect; they provide mainly for circumstances in which a child's welfare has already been breached. The criminal law is used to proscribe certain types of behaviour construed to be so detrimental to a child's welfare as to justify criminal sanctions. The civil law of care and protection is used to proscribe situations of risk to children (e.g. parental inadequacy or incapacity) from which they need protection. The grounds in both sets of laws create the threshold for access to measures which may safeguard a child's welfare interests; but in civil law these are identified in broad terms which are capable of some degree of subjective interpretation in relation to an individual child's particular needs. The law has slowly changed from resting on grounds proscribing specific indicators of welfare needs to employing less precise more generalised terms such as 'unreasonable', 'unfit' or 'moral danger'. More recently, this has trend has been further refined with the substitution of 'avoidable prevention of proper development and need of care and control' in the 1969 Act with 'significant harm' in the 1989 Act. Also, a prospective dimension is now more often present in the grounds; intervention to prevent a likelihood of welfare being damaged is often authorised.

Thirdly, public family law proceedings have a definite adversarial nature. Under the 1989 Act, such proceedings are required to be conducted as enquiries rather than prosecutions but in fact they more often closely resemble the latter. Extending full party status to children has also brought in train the use of representatives and expert witnesses, the practice of cross-examination and many other features typical of adversarial prosecutions. In this context, the first stage of judicial decision-making is an adjudication of the issues. This concludes with a determination that the welfare interests of the child before the court have or have not been damaged, or placed at risk, in relation to the statutorily specified grounds.

Fourthly and finally, the second stage of judicial decision-making deals with disposal options. Once the threshold criteria have been met, the adjudicative role exercised and all legal issues fully addressed in the course of proceedings conducted in an adversarial manner then the function of the court changes to focus on welfare interests. The judicial role at the disposal stage of public family law proceedings has changed significantly during the latter half of the twentieth century. Initially legislation had directed the court to address two matters when determining disposal: the welfare of the child and the statutorily fixed disposal options. Welfare was to be taken into account, without any indication of the priority to be accorded it nor what weighting it should receive relative to other considerations. Disposal was to be made from a short list of specific options, largely involving a choice between training, supervision or local authority care. Judicial discretion was minimal. The 1989 Act has greatly changed the judicial role. The fact that welfare has been accorded paramountcy status throughout the proceedings, and is reinforced by the checklist at the point of case disposal, would itself have transformed the judicial role by placing a responsibility and power on the court to subordinate all other factors to welfare considerations when determining disposal. But the ambit of judicial discretion at point of disposal in public family law proceedings has also been significantly broadened under the 1989 Act to permit use of private law orders. At the final stage it may now creatively employ discretionary powers to address the subjective position of a particular child's welfare interests rather than the objective specifications of the public law proceedings.

The authority of the court ends with the conclusion of proceedings. Any uncertainty regarding the availability of a residual power of judicial review in relation to local authority decisions in respect of children subject to public law orders, existing prior to the ruling in *Liverpool*, and to some extent subsequently in the wardship jurisdiction, has been removed. The 1989 Act specifically confines judicial use of authority to the duration of proceedings.

8 Care and Supervision

Introduction

This chapter examines the current role of the welfare principle in proceedings for care and supervision as governed by Part 1V of the Children Act 1989. It does not consider child protection (see, Chap 10) as this is now legislatively and professionally treated as a separate and distinct process. Nor does it deal with matters of 'control' (see, Chap 9) as they raise welfare issues which are sufficiently different to warrant separate consideration. In the present context, the welfare principle is represented by the concept 'significant harm'. This, the new coercive welfare threshold, in fact continues to rest on the traditional legal functions of 'care' and 'protection' (and indeed 'control'). The new threshold, like the old, is operationalised by measures of coercive intervention leading to the familiar court orders which in effect transfer differing levels of parental responsibility from family to state.

This chapter takes as its primary themes the prescriptive but negative duties owed by first and third parties to a child in relation to objectively stated circumstances. These circumstances are defined by the fault or default of a person owing a duty of care to a child. State intervention most often occurs after the duty has been breached. The determination of that which is held to constitute a child's welfare is in accordance with statutorily prescribed indicators together with certain judicial and agency criteria as interpreted and applied by those professionals with a duty to advise the court. A statutory weighting is given to the wishes of child in determining his or her welfare. The selection of the most appropriate disposal option is accompanied by a degree of discretion.

The welfare principle and the roles of court and local authority

The Children Act 1989 has radically adjusted the role and weighting given to the principle of the welfare of the child in public family law. This has affected the responsibilities of both court and local authority.

The relationship between local authority and parent, in a public family law context, is now governed by the principle stated in the 1989 Act that the interests of children will be best served if the former make every effort to achieve a partnership with the parents. When this is considered in conjunction with the directive in s 17(1)(b) of the 1989 Act to 'promote the upbringing of such children by their families', the 'no-order' presumption of s 1(5) and the absence of any requirement to give priority to the separate interests of a child, the cumulative effect is to place an onus on a local authority to safeguard the welfare interests of a child by maintaining that child in parental care wherever possible. Moreover, even where the 'significant harm' threshold has been breached a local authority now has a discretion (s 47(8)), not previously available, to waive its power to instigate care proceedings if they should view such proceedings as not 'reasonably practicable'.[1] As was stated by Sir Stephen Brown P in *Nottinghamshire*:

> if a local authority doggedly resists taking the steps which are appropriate to the case of children at risk of significant harm it appears the court is powerless.

The fact that initiating action to secure the safety of a child known to be at risk is now a local authority discretion rather than a duty leaves a child's welfare interests at this stage more vulnerable under the 1989 Act than under the 1969 Act; welfare is now seen first and foremost as a matter for the family not the state.

A local authority has no statutory obligation to apply the paramountcy principle. The principle, as stated in s 1(1) of the 1989 Act, is binding on the judiciary, not on a local authority. There is no statutory requirement on a local authority under this legislation that it should give any priority to the welfare interests of a child.[2] Indeed, if a local authority were required in the course of its family support duties to give automatic precedence to the interests of children, this would be in conflict with the whole partnership ethos. The legislative intent is to leave a local authority free to negotiate the best compromise possible between the conflicting interests of family members which still enable it to safeguard and promote the welfare of any children involved. Only when conciliation has failed, the issues are transferred to the court and the latter is required to consider changes in the legal status of a child, does the paramountcy principle come into play. Paradoxically, a local authority may now find the court employing this principle to restrain rather than facilitate its intervention. In circumstances where, according to the statutory grounds, a local authority could intervene and is entitled to be granted a care order the court may rule that it should not do so and decline to grant the order sought. This may occur, for example, where the court determines that it is of paramount importance, not to cause further damage to the psychological bond between child and parent.

The legislative synchronisation of the roles of court and local authority in relation to the welfare interests of a child is far from seamless (see, also, 'care plan' below). Judicial determination of issues concerning parental responsibilities in most court proceedings has been significantly altered by the 1989 Act. This has upgraded the principle of the welfare of the child to paramountcy status and has comprehensively applied it to guide judicial decision-making on matters affecting a child's upbringing. It reinforced this new normative approach with a battery of ancillary welfare related directives including the 'welfare checklist' (s 1(3)). While in private family law the checklist has a mandatory application only to contested cases it must be applied to all public proceedings. Coercive intervention by a local authority under Part 1V proceedings, will not be authorised until the court has applied the checklist criteria to the particular circumstances giving rise to the local authority application and is then satisfied that an order is necessary.[3] Three other statutory directives, ancillary to the welfare principle, and having a direct bearing on both court and local authority are the 'no-order presumption', the 'no-delay' requirement and the 'limited litigation' principle. As regards the first, s 1(5) of the 1989 Act requires that a court when considering an application for an order that it 'shall not make the order or any of the orders unless it considers that doing so would be better for the child than making no order at all'. This places a firm onus on a local authority applicant, not only to satisfy the court that the specified statutory grounds can be met, but to also convince it that in the particular circumstances not to grant an order would result in greater harm to the child than to do so. Definite evidence has to be produced to rebut the presumption that no order is best. This approach has been neatly summarised in the observation made by Templeman LJ:[4]

> The best person to bring up a child is the natural parent. It matters not whether the parent is wise or foolish, rich or poor, educated or illiterate, provided that the child's moral and physical health is not in danger. Public authorities cannot improve on nature.

As regards the second directive, the no-delay principle is declared in s 1 of the 1989 Act in the following terms:

> (2) In any proceedings in which any question with respect to the upbringing of a child arises, the court shall have regard to the general principle that any delay in determining the question is likely to prejudice the welfare of the child.

This in itself places no onerous burden on the courts: while they are required to have regard to it and presumably to act in accordance with it wherever possible, they are also free to act otherwise whenever circumstances dictate. It is, however, given teeth by s 32. This imposes a mandatory duty on a court hearing an application for an order under Part 4 to draw up a timetable 'with a view to disposing of the application without delay'. The importance of this directive was emphasised by the Court of Appeal when it overturned the decision of the court at first instance to adjourn care proceedings pending the outcome of a criminal trial.[5] One reason for this statutory requirement was to address the problem of orchestrated delay which by favouring a continuation of the settled care arrangements provided by an applicant, effectively pre-empted judicial discretion and did not necessarily permit a decision which would best promote the long-term interests of the child concerned. Now, once an application is lodged in court, it will in theory be for the court and not a local authority to determine the pace at which proceedings progress. However, adhering to the time constraints continues to prove problematic for local authorities.

The third directive, the limited litigation principle is declared in s 91of the 1989 Act in the following terms:

> (14) On disposing of any application for an order under this Act, the court may (whether or not it makes any other order in response to the application) order that no application for an Order under this Act of any specified kind may be made with respect to the child concerned by any person named in the order without leave of the court.

Although more directly relevant to private family law proceedings, this provision also serves to remind local authority applicants that the court will not permit repeated litigation on the same issues as this is not conducive to the stabilisation necessary for promoting a child's welfare interests.

The parties

Any person with parental responsibilities and the child concerned are automatically the parties in care proceedings instigated under the 1989 Act. Other persons may apply, or the court may direct that they be joined, to become parties to such proceedings.

The applicants are restricted, under s 31 of the 1989 Act, to a local authority or an 'authorised person'. No others may apply for a care order or for a supervision order. For the purposes of this Act, an 'authorised person' is restricted to mean an officer of the NSPCC. The respondents to a care order application are each parent, with parental responsibility, of the child concerned. Any other parent and certain other persons must be notified and may then elect to become respondents: an unmarried father or person currently caring for the child, for example, must be notified and may then decide to apply to be joined to the proceedings.

The subject of such proceedings can be any child below the age of 17 (or 16 if married). Any such person may be the subject of proceedings instigated to obtain a care, supervision or interim order. Under s 41(6) any such proceedings are designated 'specified proceedings' and the child concerned is, therefore, automatically made a party. This will be the case regardless of whether the child does or does not wish to make application for any of these orders.

Representation

In Part 1V proceedings the welfare interests, the legal interests and the factual circumstances of a child are respectively represented by a guardian *ad litem*, a solicitor and a social worker.

The appointment of a guardian *ad litem* is governed by s 41 of the 1989 Act:

> (1) For the purposes of any specified proceedings, the court shall appoint a guardian *ad litem* for the child concerned unless satisfied that it is not necessary to do so in order to safeguard his interests.

This provision for the appointment of a guardian *ad litem* in all specified (public family law) proceedings, unless the court deems it unnecessary, has proven to be one of the most significant developments for identifying and asserting the welfare interests of children in family law. Under s 41(6) of the 1989 Act, a guardian *ad litem* must be appointed, regardless of the level of court (unless the court is satisfied that it is unnecessary), in all applications to make, vary, extend and discharge a care or supervision order. The appointment must be made in all private family proceedings where the court is considering making a care order and all proceedings relating to emergency protection orders, child assessment orders and secure accommodation. Similarly, such an appointment is obligatory in all cases concerning a possible change of name, contact, emigration or removal from the jurisdiction. All appeal proceedings regarding these matters also require a guardian.

A guardian *ad litem* has an important but time-limited role in proceedings. He or she should be appointed at the commencement of proceedings but should cease involvement with the child at the close of proceedings[6] or at the close of that part which are designated 'specified proceedings'.[7] There can be no on-going monitoring role for a guardian *ad litem*. The court will not routinely make such an appointment in all cases.[8]

As stated in s 41(2)(b) the guardian *ad litem* is primarily under 'a duty to safeguard the interests of the child'. This is achieved by conducting an investigation on such interests and compiling a report to the court which the latter, under s 41(11), "may take account of". The guardian *ad litem* is obliged to represent the best interests of the child even if the latter holds contrary views as to what constitutes those best interests. The child concerned may not wish to have such interests represented by a guardian *ad litem*. This has been a source of contention.[9] The powers and duties of a guardian *ad litem* are further specified in the Rules. These require that official to appoint a solicitor, if one has not already been appointed, give such advice to the child as is appropriate having regard to his age and understanding and instruct the solicitor as appropriate. The guardian must attend all directions appointments and hearings in relation to the proceedings, advise the court on certain matters, notify certain parties, serve and accept service of documents on behalf of the child and carry out such investigations as may be necessary.

The guardian *ad litem* is entitled to require disclosure of documents. A guardian is empowered by s 42 to have access to records and may seek expert advice. He or she may examine and take copies of any records held by a local authority which are relevant to the welfare of the child concerned; including adoption records.[10] A guardian *ad litem* may seek out expert advice, co-ordinate the pooling of information from experts and analyse the issues for the court.[11] Though able to require others to disclose information, this official is protected from any reciprocal obligation. This was stressed in *Oxfordshire County Council v P*[12] when the court held that the guardian *ad litem* had been wrong to disclose information obtained from a parent concerning child protection matters to the police. The guardian *ad litem* was accountable to the court, which should have been appraised and whose permission should have been sought, prior to the divulging of *sub judice* matters to a third party. Once proceedings are over any further disclosure of information in a guardian *ad litem's* report, for example to the staff of a family centre,[13] is a matter for the court.

The appointment of a solicitor is governed by s 41 of the 1989 Act:

> (3) Where -
>
> (a) the child concerned is not represented by a solicitor; and
>
> (b) any of the conditions mentioned in subsection (4) is satisfied, the court may appoint a solicitor to represent him.
>
> (4) The conditions are that -
>
> (a) no guardian *ad litem* has been appointed for the child;
>
> (b) the child has sufficient understanding to instruct a solicitor and wishes to do so;
>
> (c) it appears to the court that it would be in the child's best interests for him to be represented by a solicitor.

The appointment is mandatory in proceedings for a secure accommodation order. Most usually, a solicitor will be appointed by and take instructions from the guardian *ad litem*. However, there will be cases where a child of sufficient understanding will wish to exercise his or her right to appoint and directly instruct a solicitor. There will also be those cases envisaged by the above provisions where the initiative will come from the court. The solicitor is required to represent the child, in furtherance of the latter's best interests, or in accordance with instructions received from either child or guardian *ad litem* (see, also, Chap 7).

The appointment of a social worker may be directed by the court under s 37 of the 1989 Act:

> Where, in any family proceedings in which a question arises with respect to the welfare of any child, it appears to the court that it may be appropriate for a care or supervision order to be made with respect to him, the court may direct the appropriate authority to undertake an investigation of the child's circumstances

Alternatively, a local authority may itself initiate an investigation where, under s 47, it has 'reasonable cause to suspect that a child who lives or is found in their area is suffering or is likely to suffer significant harm' (see, also, Chap 7).

The welfare threshold

Significant harm is declared a threshold condition for Part IV proceedings by s 31 of the 1989 Act:

> (2) A court may only make a care or supervision order if it is satisfied -
>
> (a) that the child concerned is suffering, or is likely to suffer, significant harm

Section 31(9) defines 'harm' as 'ill-treatment or the impairment of health or development' and states that 'ill-treatment' 'includes sexual abuse and forms of abuse which are not physical'. The latter term clearly allows for the inclusion of emotional abuse within the definition of 'harm'.[14]

The first requirement of this provision is that 'harm' or the 'likelihood of harm' exists. It is evident that 'ill-treatment', the 'impairment of health' and the impairment of 'development' are each independent and alternative conditions all or any one of which would be sufficient to establish 'harm' or the 'likelihood of harm' and thus satisfy the terms of this requirement. The court considered the meaning of harm in a case[15] where a 15 year old girl had obdurately refused to attend school for three years. The court made a care order holding that harm included social, educational and intellectual development.

The degree to which such conditions must exist in order to constitute 'significant' harm and thereby satisfy the 'significance' test is problematic (i.e.

just how bad does the harm have to be for it to be judged 'significant'?). Clearly, at one extreme, if the harm can be considered very grave as in a case[16] where the 'harm' involved the death of an abused child (see, further below) then there is little difficulty. The uncertainty increases in proportion to the decrease in gravity of harm.

The 1989 Act does not provide any definition for the term 'significant'. The only statutory guidance available is that this be determined by making a comparison with a 'similar' child. Again, the exact meaning of 'likelihood' has given rise to considerable contention. It has been held[17] that the 'likelihood' test would be satisfied by evidence that there was a real risk of future harm. The House of Lords have consolidated this view in a judgment which, by rejecting the argument that 'likelihood' should be equated with 'probability', has significantly eased the threshold test. The fact that the mere 'likelihood' of a future occurrence of harm could be sufficient to justify coercive intervention provides an important extension to the protective reach of a local authority's statutory powers.

Under s 31(2)(b) of the 1989 Act, the 'harm' or 'likelihood of harm' must be attributable to:

> (i) the care given to the child, or likely to be given to him if the order were not made, not being what it would be reasonable to expect a parent to give to him; or

as this section goes on to state:

> (10) Where the question of whether harm suffered by a child is significant turns on the child's health or development, his health or development shall be compared with that which could reasonably be expected of a similar child.

The requirement, therefore, is that the 'harm' or 'likelihood of harm' is attributable to, rather than caused by, either an unreasonable standard of parenting or the child being beyond parental control. In the former instance, the standard of parental care will be judged by an objective application of the 'reasonableness' test i.e. not what that parent in those circumstances could be expected to provide but what a reasonable parent would provide. However, it has been held[18] that the statutory reference to 'care' (as in s 31(2)(b)(i) above) referred to the actual parent or carer whose lack of care caused the harm not to that of the hypothetical reasonable parent in that situation.

Parental fault or default is not the issue, it is the bare fact that there has been a breach of the significant harm threshold, whether by child or parent, which is of concern to the court (see, Chap 9 for 'beyond parental control').

The tenses used in this provision have been a source of considerable uncertainty as they refer only to present and prospective harm. However, the decision of the House of Lords in *Re M (A Minor)(Care Order: Threshold Conditions)*[19] would seem to have brought certainty. The operative time for adducing evidence of significant harm is not the date of hearing. In the words of Lord Mackay:

> ...the relevant date with respect to which the court must be satisfied (that the child is suffering significant harm) is the date at which the local authority initiated the procedure of protection under the Act.

The spirit behind this ruling, and the authority now attached to it, became evident in *M v Birmingham City Council*[20] where the Court of Appeal held that the court was not tied to the facts existing at the time of the hearing but should consider the state of affairs - in the past, in the future or in the present - according to the context in which it fell to be applied.

The orders

Responsibilities in relation to the welfare interests of a child are transferred, in varying degrees, from a parent to an authorised body by the issue of one of the court orders available under the Children Act 1989. The order made by the court will be the one affording the minimum degree of coercive intervention in the affairs of a family necessary to safeguard the welfare interests of the child concerned.[21]

Care and supervision orders

Both care and supervision orders are available under the 1989 Act if the two stages of the application process are completed. Firstly, the threshold criteria of s 31 must be met. Secondly, the court must also be satisfied that the order if made would be compatible with the child's welfare interests; this is ascertained by the court applying s 1(2), (3) and (5).

The 1989 Act upholds the spirit of the *Liverpool*[22] ruling by preventing the court from exercising any discretionary power to supervise, review or in any way intervene in a local authority's exercise of the powers granted to the latter by a care order or supervision order.[23] The legislative intent is that it should be for a local authority and not the court to implement the authority conferred by a care order or supervision order; subject only to the power reserved to the court by s 34(1). In the words of Butler – Sloss LJ:

> After a care order is made, the court has no continuing role in the future welfare of the child.[24]

A statement which, as she goes on to acknowledge, is subject to some specific exceptions (e.g. applications for contact or for leave to refuse contact, for the discharge of care order or application for a residence order).

Before the court passes responsibility to a local authority by way of a care order, however, it has been held[25] that the court should satisfy itself that all the facts are known as fully as possible. Such facts should be presented to the court by way of a care plan which deals with contact arrangements and addresses the headings outlined in the regulations.[26] If the court is not satisfied that the care plan is in the child's best interests then, the advice of Wall J[27] is that the court may refuse to make a care order or supervision order. The court may conclude that a local authority has provided sufficient evidence to establish that the significant harm threshold of s 31 has been breached but, because its care plan is insufficient to meet the requirements of the welfare test in s 1, the order sought cannot be granted. The fact that a local authority has applied for a supervision order will not prevent the court from instead issuing a care order[28] or from making an interim care order when the application is for a care order.[29] The determining factor will be a combination of the gravity of the prospective harm and the likelihood of it occurring. So, to a considerable extent, the court also has a discretion in the exercise of its statutory powers even where satisfied that the threshold conditions of s 31(2)(a) and (b) have been met. This discretion is provided by the welfare principle.

The making of an order ends court involvement in responsibility for decisions affecting the welfare of the child. The local authority is thereafter free to change or abandon its care plan without leave of the court. The principle judicially expressed in the *Liverpool* decision has now been given full legislative endorsement.

A care order, like a supervision order, is only available on evidence of a breach of the significant harm threshold. Their functions in relation to the welfare interests of a child are therefore essentially negative. The supervision order imposes reciprocal legal obligations on three parties: the supervisor (most often a local authority social worker); the child or young person and; the 'responsible person' who, most usually, is the person with parental responsibility for the child. This order provides the means whereby an offer of broad professional support to parents and to a child, supplemented by certain specific powers, may be sufficient to maintain the latter in the community. Because it leaves all parental responsibilities with thc parent, its capacity to further a child's welfare interests remains dependent upon parental co-operation.

In care

Under s 33(1), a care order places a duty on the named local authority to take the child concerned into its care. The order vests parental responsibilities for the child concerned in the local authority: not to the exclusion of those responsibilities that remain with the parents but to the exclusion of any further court responsibility. This is in keeping with the principle under the 1989 Act, unlike the position previously, that a clear line be drawn between the authority of the court and that of the local authority.

Under s 22 of the 1989 Act, the making of a care order gives the named local authority the duty to safeguard and promote the welfare of the child concerned. It is significant that decisions taken by a local authority, unlike those of the court, are not statutorily governed by the paramountcy principle. The clear legislative intent is not to impose as onerous a burden on a local authority as is placed on the court but the former is now required to meet specified welfare standards. Whereas previously it was statutorily required to apply the primacy of the welfare principle in relation to children in care[30] the current reference to the basic threshold of 'safeguard' implies that if a local authority strives to ensure the health and safety of a child in its care then it is fulfilling an important statutory duty; one which was not always attended to within the previous broad discretionary duty. Should it fail in that duty, however, it is clear from the ruling of the House of Lords in *X v Bedfordshire CC*[31] that a local authority will escape liability; it cannot be liable for a breach of statutory duty, for negligence nor even for a breach of the common law duty of care. This and subsequent rulings[32] constitute a significant setback for welfare interests. If a breach of the most basic threshold, by the public authority specifically and statutorily entrusted with safeguarding it, cannot ground an action by or on behalf of the child concerned then the latter's welfare interests have been seriously devalued. The litany of public enquiries into the gross and long-term abuse of children in local authority care by local authority staff, throughout the UK, strongly suggests that the welfare interests of children in care need to be amenable to external monitoring.

The concept of partnership in the context of care arrangements has been operationalised through the following approach: all children in respect of whom a local authority provides away from home care, whether or not under the terms of a court order, are now regarded as being 'looked after' by that local authority; and a parent whose child is being 'looked after' retains parental responsibility for that child. The effect of the first is, essentially, that a local authority must be guided by the same principles when making arrangements for a child who is the subject of a care order as for one for whom it is merely providing accommodation. This, for example, requires a local authority, before taking any decisions in respect of that child to give due consideration to the wishes and feelings of the child, depending on his or her age and understanding, and of certain others. It must also respect the child's religious persuasion, racial origin and cultural and linguistic background (s 22(5)).

The 1989 Act, more so than previous legislation, places an obligation on a local authority to maintain and facilitate the relationship between a child in care and his or her family of origin because of the presumed importance of that relationship to the continued welfare of the child. Therefore, insofar as it is practicable and consistent with the child's welfare, a local authority must ensure that the accommodation it provides is near to the child's home and caters also for any other sibling that the local authority might be looking after (s 23(7)). Also, a duty is placed on a local authority to return any child which it may be looking after to family care unless this would not be reasonably practicable or consistent with his welfare (s 23(6)). The effect of the second is to impose upon both parent and local authority a sense of shared responsibility for important decision-making in respect of any child subject to a care order. Parents do not wholly shed responsibility for their children on the making of an order and a local authority does not thereby attain exclusive rights to determine matters affecting the welfare of the children concerned. It is highly probable that these new statutory presumptions together with the partnership ethos are having a combined an unforeseen effect which is working to the detriment of the welfare interests of many children; they reduce the likelihood of children in care being placed for adoption. Despite evidence that local authority care at best places children at a disadvantage relative to their peers[33] (even according to such basic indices as health and education) and at worst exposes them to serious risk of abuse and that the number of prospective adopters is far greater than that of children waiting to be adopted, only a very small minority of children in public care become available for private adoption (see, also, Chap 14).

The power of the court to make a contact order in respect of such a child also illustrates the legislative intent to safeguard relationships judged to be of importance to the welfare of the child concerned. Indeed, by exercising its powers under s 34(5) and (7), the court may of its own motion require a local authority to permit contact between a child and parent and by attaching specific conditions can, if necessary, significantly alter a care plan to ensure that this aspect of the child's welfare is appropriately provided for. Finally, the absence of any statutory duty requiring local authorities to provide specific after care services for children remains an area where the latter's welfare interests are particularly vulnerable. The eligibility under s 24(2) of the 1989 Act, of a person under the age of 21 who was in care after he or she became 16, to claim advice and assistance from the relevant local authority places a weak and inappropriate onus on the wrong party; the local authority should be charged with a specific duty to provide a service programme tailored to facilitate the particular rehabilitation of each child being discharged from care.

Interim order

Under s 38(1) of the 1989 Act the court is empowered to grant either an interim care order or an interim supervision order when:

> (a) in any proceedings on an application for a care or a supervision order, the proceedings are adjourned; or
> (b) the court gives a direction under section 37(1).

The principal effect of this order is to provide a holding operation, permitting a local authority to carry out its enquiries, gather evidence and prepare reports so as to bring a case before the court in as short a time as possible. The court must restrict itself to maintaining the *status quo* between the parties by authorising and controlling the minimum level of intervention required in the circumstances for a local authority to prepare its case.[34] A local authority will be entitled to an interim care order in circumstances where its need to carry out the initial investigations necessary to establish whether or not a child is at risk of significant harm is being obstructed by a lack of parental co-operation.[35]

An interim care order can allow the court, for a limited period, to impose its own care plan on a local authority instead of granting a care order application by that authority This is achieved by the court making an interim care order subject to directions designed to provide the information necessary for a valid care plan to be compiled. The court is thereby placed in a position to decide, when the interim care order has run its course, whether the making of a full care order would be in the child's best interests.[36] This discretionary judicial power, to make the order considered by the court rather than the applicant to be most appropriate to the welfare of a child, has also been used to give preference to interim care orders instead of child assessment orders at the early stages of coercive intervention. It offers the court a last opportunity to require a professional evaluation of the welfare interests of a child, and submission of evidence that such interests are being or are in danger of being so impaired as to justify a care order, before full responsibility for decisions relating to those interests passes to a local authority with the issue of a care order.

The court may make an interim supervision order linked to a residence order, instead of making an interim care order. It must do so when making a residence order in care proceedings, unless satisfied that this is unnecessary. However, it cannot use an interim supervision order to achieve objectives statutorily reserved to an interim care order.[37]

In keeping with the full care and supervision orders, an interim order has a negative functional relationship with welfare. The 'reasonable grounds for believing' test may not require evidence of an actual breach of the welfare threshold but grounds must still exist before the order can be made. However, in practice the functions of the interim care order are quite complex. It has a proven capacity to act as a judicial bridgehead into local authority decision-making affecting the welfare interests of the child concerned. This, together with the judicial power to add to the order such discretionary conditions as it sees fit, makes an interim order a potentially very powerful exercise of authority in respect of a child's welfare interests. However, as Professor Hayes has succinctly stated:

> ...a care order is still a care order, whether it is an interim or a final order. By drawing a distinction between the two orders the courts are in grave danger of blurring the law and departing from the clear principles relating to the proper exercise of judicial power which were established in *A v Liverpool City Council*.[38]

Although, if such a departure allowed the court to exercise a degree of on-going monitoring of arrangements agreed with a local authority then, arguably, the welfare interests of the children concerned could only benefit.

Education supervision order

This is the only interventionist order that is not grounded on 'significant harm' as a basic pre-requisite. A fact which reflects the distinctive nature of the legal relationship between parental responsibilities and welfare interests in the context of compulsory education. Arguably, it is in this context of undoubted importance to the welfare of children that the law remains most ambivalent about whether it is primarily pursuing public or private functions. All statutory duties to comply with compulsory education requirements rest on parents rather than children. All formal opportunities for choices to be made and consents given are for parents not children. The formal requirement that local authority social workers at least seek and take into account the views of children where decisions are to be taken affecting them, would seem to have no counterpart where such decisions are taken by teachers. The law has not moved far from its traditional respect for the core parental right to decide matters relating to the education of children.

Under s 36 of the 1989 Act the court may, on the application of a local education authority, make an education supervision order in respect of a child where that child 'is of compulsory school age and is not being educated'. Proceedings for an education supervision order are defined as 'family proceedings' under s 8(3) and (4) of the 1989 Act. The court must, therefore, apply the paramountcy principle, the welfare checklist, the no-delay principle and the no-order presumption. The fact that they are designated 'family proceedings' also means that the court is free to exercise its discretion and make any s 8 order instead of an education supervision order. It may call for welfare reports and for a hearing to be adjourned for preparation of such reports.

The order does not carry any attached directions from the court but instead it delegates the power to make such directions to the supervisor; these may be made at any time while the order is in force.

In *Re O (A Minor)(Care Order: Education Procedure)*[39] the court considered the possible bearing of the significant harm threshold on a situation of chronic non-attendance. The court found that where a child is not attending school without good reason he or she is either suffering harm due to a lack of adequate parental care or is beyond parental control. In that case it was held that the court at first instance had been right to impose a care order rather than an education supervision order where the 15 year old child had been truanting for three years and had only attended school for 28 days in the previous year. This is an important ruling which endorses the pre-1989 Act view of Denning MR in *Re S (A Minor)* that '...if a child was not being sent to school or receiving a proper education then he was in need of care'.[40]

The fact that there should now be an order which solely addresses school non-attendance marks a significant change in the legislative approach to non-attending children. Previously, the child with a record of poor school attendance was statutorily defined as vulnerable, the behaviour indicative of welfare needs and the court required to consider a care disposal option. Under the 1989 Act, such a child is viewed as ill-disciplined, the behaviour indicative more of deviancy than of care needs and as such warranting a regulatory form of supervision.

Private orders

Of considerable importance is the fact that the court may respond to an application for a care or supervision order by instead making a s 8 order. This discretionary power to re-interpret public law proceedings as providing grounds for exercising private law remedies is a power which the court did not possess under previous legislation and which it cannot exercise in reverse. For example, in *Re B (Care: Expert Witness)*[41] the Court of Appeal held that the rejection of a care order application by a local authority and the substitution of a residence order with attached conditions in favour of the child's parents was an appropriate response to the particular welfare interests of a child.

Conclusion

The 1989 Act has imposed some firm and clear lines of demarcation in the law relating to children: between the remit of court and local authority; between care and offence proceedings; and between the jurisdiction of the family proceedings court and all other courts. It has narrowed the scope for judicial discretion while increasing that of local authorities. It has introduced definite thresholds for coercive and consensual intervention and proscribed conduct and circumstances construed as likely to cause a breach. It has underpinned judicial interpretation of welfare issues with a checklist of indicators and reinforced the court's welfare focus by requiring compliance with a number of governing rules and presumptions. In such ways this legislation has substantively altered the law relating to child care.

From the perspective of the child concerned, however, some of the technical changes introduced by the 1989 Act have had a more direct impact upon their welfare interests. Of these the most notable has been the change to the *locus standi* of the child in public proceedings. Granting a child party status together with rights of representation by a solicitor, working in tandem with a guardian *ad litem*, has transformed the capacity of the court to be informed on matters relating to the welfare interests of a child. Also, the ability of the court to grant an order or orders other than that applied for, in particular to grant private law orders, broadens the scope to tailor disposal to suit the needs of the child concerned.

However, the inability of the court to affect planning for a child's future welfare after the issue of a care order, except in the context of proceedings for a contact order, remains a serious gap. This is compounded by the lack of any formal mandatory procedure for ensuring that a child's rights and welfare interests are represented in any decision-making processes affecting him or her while the subject of a care order. The record of local authority care for children in the UK is sufficiently well documented to warrant legislative provision of independent safeguards to protect, monitor and review the welfare interests of children while they are in care.

Notes

1 Such was the conclusion of the court in *Nottinghamshire County Council v P (No 2)* [1993] 2 FLR 134, p 148.

2 In fact, the 1989 Act explicitly reduced the onus on a local authority when it removed the obligation placed on it by s 18(1) of the Child Care Act 1980 to give 'first consideration' to welfare interests.

3 See *Humberside County Council v B* [1993] 1 FLR 257.

4 See *Re KD (A Minor)(Ward: Termination of Access)* [1988] 1 AC 806 at 812.

5 See *Re TB (Care Proceedings: Criminal Trial)* [1995] 2 FLR 80.

6 As was demonstrated in *Kent County Council v C and Another* [1993] Fam 57.

7 See *Re S (Contact: Grandparents)* [1996] 1 FLR 158.

8 As is illustrated by the decision not to do so in *Re J (A Minor)(Change of Name)* [1993] 1 FLR 699 where it was held that a GAL could do no more than others had already done.

9 See, for example, *Re S (A Minor)(Independent Representation)* [1993] 2 FLR 437 where the Court of Appeal upheld the earlier judicial decision to over-rule the wishes of an 11 year old boy who sought to dismiss his GAL in what was a complex case.

10 See *Re T (A Minor)(Guardian ad Litem)* [1994] 1 FLR 632, CA.
11 See *Re C (Expert Evidence: Disclosure: Practice)* [1995] 1 FLR 204.
12 [1995] 1 FLR 552.
13 See *Re C (Guardian ad Litem: Disclosure of Report)* [1996] 1 FLR 61.
14 See *Report of the Inquiry into Child Abuse in Cleveland* (1987) Cmnd 412 p 4.
15 See *Re O (A Minor)(Care Order: Education: Procedure)* [1992] 2 FLR 7.
16 See *Re D (A Minor)(Care or Supervision Order)* [1993] 2 FLR 43.
17 See *Newham London Borough Council v AG* [1993] 1 FLR 281.
18 See *Re S and R (Minors)(Care Order)* [1993] Fam Law 43.
19 [1994] 2 FLR 577.
20 [1994] 2 FLR 141.
21 See dicta to that effect in *Re O (Care or Supervision Order)* [1996] 2 FLR 755 and in *Re B (Care or Supervision Order)* [1996] 2 FLR 693.
22 See *A v Liverpool City Council* (1982) FLR 222. Also, see, Chap 15 and the implications arising from the judgment of the European Court of Human Rights in *Osman v UK* [1999] 1FLR 193.
23 See, for example: *Re W (A Minor)(Care Proceedings: Wardship)* [1985] FLR 879; *Re B (Minors)(Care: Contact: Local Authority's Plans)* [1993] 1 FLR 543; *Kent County Court v C* [1993] 1 FLR 308; *Re T (A Minor)(Care Order: Conditions)* [1994] 2 FLR 423); and *Re S (Contact: Prohibition of Applications)* [1994] 2 FLR 1057.
24 See *Re B (Minors)(Contact: Local Authority's Plans)* [1994] 1 FLR 543 at pp 550 and 551.
25 See *C v Solihull Metropolitan Borough Council* [1993] 1 FLR 290 and *Hounslow London Borough Council v A* [1993] 1 FLR 702.
26 See *Manchester City Council v F* [1993] 1 FLR 419.
27 See *Re J (Minors)(Care: Care Plan)* [1994] 1 FLR 253 at p 258F-G.
28 See *Re D (A Minor)(Care or Supervision Order)* [1993] 2 FLR 423 where the court made such a substitution because it considered that the risk to the children of a current relationship, posed by a father who had previously abused his own children (causing the death of one), was too great to warrant a SO.
29 See *Re M and R (Child Abuse: Evidence)* [1996] 2 FLR 195 where the court substituted interim orders for the sought care orders even though satisfied that the s 31 requirements had been met.
30 See s 12(1) of the 1948 Act and s 20(1) of the 1969 Act.
31 [1995] 2 FLR 276. Also, see, *Nottinghamshire County Council v P (No 2)* [1993] 2 FLR 134, CA and *Re S and D (Children: Powers of Court)* [1995] 2 FLR 456, CA.
32 See *H v Norfolk County Council* [1997] 1 FLR 384 where the plaintiff had been sexually abused by his foster father while in care, and *Barrett v Enfield London Borough Council* [1997] 2 FLR 167 where a young man who had spent 17 years in care alleged that as a result of the local authority's 'catalogue of errors' he had been left with psychological and psychiatric problems. However, in the more recent decision of the Court of Appeal in *W v Essex County Council* [1998] 2 FLR 278 there is evidence of a retreat from the virtual blanket immunity for any local authority liability implied in the *Bedfordshire* ruling. In the *Essex* case the court was prepared to hold that a local authority could be liable for the abuse of children in foster care caused by the wrongful placing of a known abuser in the foster home without informing the foster parents of his abusive record.

33 See Sir W Utting, *Putting Children First*, (The NFM Lucy Faithfull Memorial Lecture), 13th November 1997, where he quotes the following statistics from the Social Services Inspectorate report for that year:
More than 75% of care leavers have no academic qualifications of any kind.
More than 50% of young people leaving care after the age of 16 are unemployed.
17% of young women leaving care are pregnant or already mothers.
10% of 16-17 year old claimants of DSS severe hardship payments have been in care.
23% of adult prisoners and 38% of young prisoners have been in care.
30% of young single homeless people have been in care.

34 See *Re G (Minors)(Interim Care Order)* [1993] 2 FLR 839 where Waite J states that:

> Parliament intended the regime of an interim care order to operate as a tightly run procedure closely monitored by the court and affording to all parties an opportunity of frequent review closely monitored by the court and affording to all parties an opportunity of frequent review as events unfold during the currency of the order (p 846).

Also, see, G Brasse *A Tightly Run Procedure? Interim Care Orders Under Strain*, May [1994] Fam Law.

35 See *Re B (A Minor)(Interim Care Order: Criteria)* [1993] 1 FLR 815.

36 This was the course of action approved by the Court of Appeal in *Buckingham County Council v M* [1994] 2 FLR 506 when the court rejected a care plan which had as its objective the placing of a child for adoption and instead substituted a phased rehabilitation programme underpinned by an interim care order.

37 See *Re R and G* [1994] 1 FLR 793.

38 *The Proper Role of Courts in Child Care Cases*, Child and Family Law Quarterly, Vol 8 No 3, 1986.

39 [1992] 2 FLR 7.

40 [1978] QB 120.

41 [1996] 1 FLR 667.

9 Control

Introduction

'Control', as a legal function in the context of child welfare, is essentially negative, is rooted in private family law and owes its origins to the doctrine of parental rights. As such it acknowledges that the recipient of parental care has a corresponding duty to the provider not to obstruct or make impossible the provision of such care by their own wilful behaviour. This continues to be a matter for the civil jurisdiction of the courts. But 'control' also represents a public law interest in the protection of third parties from the unreasonable behaviour of children and young persons inadequately supervised by their parents. This public law dimension, a natural corollary to the parental duties of care and protection, has grown to become a significant and contentious area for modern social policy. Depending on the nature of the uncontrolled behaviour and its consequences, this may be a matter for either the civil or the criminal jurisdiction of the courts.

The responsibility to exercise control, so as to ensure that the behaviour of a child or young person does not breach socially acceptable norms, is in law distributed with some uncertainty between child, parent and state. Once such a breach has occurred then the role to be played by the welfare principle will depend very much on whether the issues of liability for the consequences and imposition of measures to provide for future control arise for judicial determination in civil or in criminal proceedings. A particularly revealing dimension to the evolving legal role of the welfare principle is provided by the history of its application to the criminal behaviour of children and young persons. An examination of the law relating to juvenile justice is, however, outside the scope of the present study.

This chapter examines the current role of the welfare principle in the civil law governing provision for the control of those children and young persons brought before the family proceedings court; or, more specifically, with 'control' in a 'care' context as defined by the Children and Young Persons Act 1989. It confines its consideration of juvenile justice to areas of overlap between the civil and criminal jurisdictions, to identifying the role of the welfare principle in relation to 'control' in an 'offence' context and to comparing the defining characteristics of the welfare principle in both. It includes an assessment of provision for secure accommodation where control facilities are applicable to children and young persons from both 'care' and 'offence' contexts.

The background: children, the law and the principles

Responsibility for controlling the behaviour of children and young persons, and liability for any harm or loss incurred as a consequence of a failure to exercise such control, has long been governed by both civil and criminal law. The welfare principle has played a critical role within each and in managing the interface between both. Other principles have also played a part. Ultimately, however, differentiating between behaviour in terms of its relative appropriateness to civil or criminal proceedings varies according to prevailing social values and falls to be determined by the social policy of the government of the day.

Civil law

In civil law, responsibility for the consequences of a child's behaviour was traditionally held to rest solely with the parent but is now best viewed as shared between child and parent; the proportional distribution varying in accordance with the age and understanding of the child. Uncertainty regarding the grounds for apportioning responsibility between them is particularly apparent in the caselaw relating to the legal capacity of minors in matters of contract, torts and property. Family law reflects the same uncertainty as that prevalent in the broader civil jurisdiction of which it forms a part.

The body of legislation comprising successive Children and Young Persons Acts has provided, and continues to provide, the statutory framework for resolving control issues arising in a public family law context. In this context the role of the principle in relation to the control function broadly follows the typical pattern of such other functions as 'care' and 'protection' (see, Chaps 8 and 10 respectively). The threshold of coercive and mandatory intervention by a local authority is legislatively set in prescriptive terms. The grounds underpinning the threshold are objectified; what matters is that the behaviour is uncontrolled, the fact that either parent or child is too ill or otherwise too disabled to exercise adequate control is beside the point. Judicial determination provides adjudication on the issues but is discretionary in relation to disposal. The disposal options are essentially of a treatment and rehabilitative nature the choice of which is governed by considerations for the welfare interests of the child concerned.

Criminal law

In criminal law, responsibility for the consequences of a child's behaviour was traditionally held to rest solely with the child; unless parental involvement, as accomplice or through the usual rules governing the acts of principal and agent, could be proven. Children found guilty of criminal activity were treated by the legal system as adults and flogged, imprisoned, transported overseas or hanged in accordance with the prevailing statutory tariff for criminal offences. More recent legislation has broadened liability to also hold parents accountable for the criminal activity of their children.[1]

The age of the child concerned plays a crucial part in determining criminal liability. In England and Wales, in keeping with traditional common law rules, the commission of a crime requires that the *actus reus* (or physical act), be accompanied by the appropriate *mens rea* (or malicious intent). The *doli incapax* presumption sets the age of criminal responsibility at 10 years;[2] below which a child cannot be held to have the requisite *mens rea* to commit a crime and proceedings, if appropriate, must be of a civil nature. A child between the ages of 10 and 14 was presumed to be incapable of committing a crime but this presumption could be rebutted by evidence[3] demonstrating that he or she knew the activity was wrong. The younger the child the stronger the presumption.[4] In respect of a young person aged between 14 and 16 a reverse presumption applied i.e. from the age of 14 a person was presumed to have intended the consequences of his or her actions. Thereafter, young persons were held to have full capacity and to be as criminally liable for their actions as any adult. The Criminal Justice Act 1991 reasserted the *doli incapax* presumption; children below the age of 10, not possessing the *mens rea* necessary for criminal intent, are deemed incapable of committing criminal offences. The 1991 Act altered the law to the extent that the presumption of wrongful intent has now been extended to the age of 17; all children and young persons, aged 10 but less than 18, possess the necessary *mens rea*, are liable for criminal conduct and fall within the jurisdiction of the youth court but, on conviction, may be treated differently than fully mature adults. The Crime and Disorder Act 1998 abolished the rebuttable presumption favouring those aged 10 to 14; effectively making all offenders, aged between 10 and 17 inclusive, amenable to the youth court.

The law relating to juvenile offenders, is to be found mainly in that body of legislation comprised of successive Criminal Justice Acts. While an assessment of the role and functions of the principles governing the criminal justice system is outside the scope of this study, some of its more prominent distinguishing characteristics and their effect on the welfare principle can be noted. The threshold for coercive and mandatory intervention is legislatively explicit. The grounds underpinning the threshold are objective; once the uncontrolled behaviour results in a crime then prosecution must follow. The judicial role is firmly adjudicatory, there is little if any scope for discretion. Disposal options are governed by considerations of justice and public protection, they are pre-set in accordance with a 'tariff' which matches orders available with crimes on a proportionality basis, and they have a definite punishment and deterrent orientation.

Welfare needs and criminal behaviour

Justice and welfare are the two competing frames of reference governing the legislative response to the problem of a child whose behaviour is both out of parental control and criminal. The extent to which the welfare needs of such a child should be taken into account by the criminal justice system, if at all, is determined by a social policy which periodically oscillates between placing an emphasis on welfare or justice. As has been observed, "our juvenile justice system tends to swing uneasily between the 'justice' and 'welfare' models".[5] The present firm endorsement of the justice model is the result of just such a swing.

The Children and Young Persons Act 1969 made a significant shift from the traditional approach of treating juvenile offenders as simply young adults, deserving of little more than a diluted interpretation of the same criminal justice system. Instead it established the principle that it was appropriate to differentiate between them on the basis of their needs and deeds and ascribe welfare and justice oriented disposals respectively. This legislation was considerably influenced by the principles expressed in the White Paper *Children in Trouble* which stated, for example:

> It has become increasingly clear that social control of harmful behaviour by the young, and social measures to help and protect the young, are not distinct and separate processes. The aims of protecting society from juvenile delinquency, and of helping children in trouble to grow up into mature and law-abiding persons, are complementary and not contradictory.[6]

In particular, 'discretion' as a *modus operandi*, justified by the concept of individualised justice and the principle of the welfare of the child, was developed by many professionals as an appropriate and sufficient rationale for judicial disposal in proceedings for compulsory care and juvenile justice. The welfare principle was employed, at judicial discretion, to permit a treatment order to be made under the Children and Young Persons Acts rather than a punishment order under the Criminal Justice Acts. This occurred where, in relation to a particular instance of criminal behavior, the welfare of the child was of more pressing concern to the court than satisfying the requirements of justice by rigorously applying the tariff of punitive sanctions. Ironically, however, the indeterminate duration and intrusiveness of the welfare option was often less welcome to child and family than the fixed penalty approach of juvenile justice.[7] The 1969 Act also generated controversy among the professionals involved because of its perceived failure to deal adequately with 'criminal' juveniles. Squaring the circle between an approach emphasising the needs of the individual child (favoured by the social work profession) and one affording greater weight to the interests of the general public (as favoured by magistrates) proved difficult.

The current legislative framework

Proceedings relating to the control of the behaviour of children and young persons are available in two distinct sets of statutes. The Children and Young Persons Act 1989 governs the civil family proceedings jurisdiction. The Criminal Justice Act 1991, together with such ancillary legislation as the Criminal Justice and Public Order Act 1994 and the Crime and Disorder Act 1998, structures the equivalent criminal jurisdiction. These provide the largely separate and alternative 'care' and 'offence' contexts in which the legal system defines and responds to the uncontrolled behaviour of children and young persons.

The 'care' context

By abolishing care orders in criminal proceedings, s 90 of the Children Act 1989 made a clear and firm legal distinction between care and criminal behaviour. Those whose uncontrolled behaviour is such that state intervention is indicated on care grounds are now the subject of proceedings governed by the 1989 Act. All other children and young persons, aged 10 or older, the perpetrators rather than the victims of criminal offences, will be the subject of proceedings governed almost exclusively by other legislation.

The 'offence' context

The clear legislative intent to define the uncontrolled and criminal behaviour of children and young persons as a matter to be governed more by justice than welfare considerations found expression in the Criminal Justice Act 1991. The perpetrators of such behaviour are presumed to have intended the consequences of their actions. The responsibility for exercising control and liability for failure to do so are seen as rooted in the family of origin rather than attributable to a more general social malaise. Both child and parent are to be held accountable before the court. The prevailing ethos of the 1989 Act – returning responsibilities to the family – is also evident in the 1991 Act. The latter requires a parent to accompany their child,[8] aged between 10 and 16 and accused of a criminal offence, to the court hearing and to pay any fines and/or costs.[9] The parent may be bound over by the court,[10] with or without recognisances,[11] to exercise control over such a child. This approach, designed to hold parents responsible for exercising proper control over juveniles and make them financially accountable for the consequences of failing to do so, has since been further reinforced.[12]

The Crime and Disorder Act 1998 builds upon the established principle of parental responsibility by introducing the 'parenting order' enabling the court to require the parent of every convicted juvenile to attend counselling programmes and if necessary to control the future behaviour of the juvenile in a specified manner. Where the juvenile is aged between 16 and 18 the court will hold him or her, rather than the parent, directly responsible and accountable for criminal offences.

Overlap of care and criminal jurisdictions

The behaviour requiring control may bridge both care and offence contexts. The standard of significant harm is the determinant of whether behaviour otherwise criminal will be treated by the legal system as more appropriately dealt with by care proceedings. Usually this arises in individual cases where a child's uncontrolled behaviour - resulting in criminal harm, damage or loss – becomes the subject of proceedings under the 1989 Act instead of the 1991 Act because clear evidence exists that the behaviour also harmed or threatens to harm the welfare interests of that child to a significant degree. This will also be the outcome where the harm, damage or loss results from the uncontrolled behaviour of a child below the age of 10 and therefore falls outside the legal definition of 'criminal'. The child is then treated as in need of care not as an offender. The same logic applies to categories of behaviour *per se*, rather than just to their individual manifestations. While the process of criminalising and de-criminalising categories of behaviour is a general process legislatively calibrated in accordance with the changing priorities of unfolding social policy, it has recently been particularly evident in the context of the law governing adolescents and sexual activity. Child prostitution, for example, is currently being removed from the statute books as a criminal activity and in future children engaged in prostitution will be amenable only to care proceedings. Homosexual relations may well also be de-criminalised for those aged 16-18. On the other hand rape, offences involving sexual intercourse and buggery have now become criminal activities for boys aged 14 or less.[13]

Prevention

The consequences of the uncontrolled behaviour of a child or young person may give rise to either civil or criminal proceedings. Accordingly, the statutory duty to put in place measures designed to reduce the likelihood of children and young persons becoming the subjects of proceedings, due to their behaviour being out of control, is one which falls on both local authorities and on the police. However, this duty is only to assist those with primary responsibility – parents and the children at risk of offending – to cope more effectively with problematic behaviour.

Local authorities

The local authorities have a duty under the Children Act 1989 to assist parents in exercising control over children and young persons by making such provision as is likely to prevent the latter from entering the youth justice system. Under Sched 2, para 7, of the 1989 Act:

> Every local authority shall take reasonable steps designed -
> (a) to reduce the need to bring -
> (ii) criminal proceedings against such children
> (b) to encourage children within their area not to commit criminal offences; and
> (c) to avoid the need for children within their area to be placed in secure accommodation.

This specific statement requires local authorities to be proactive in their prevention duties. As such it complements and gives focus to their general duty under s 17(1)(b) to provide 'a range and level of services appropriate to those children's needs'. However, there is no indication of any overall strategy nor of precisely what services they might deploy in giving effect to these duties. But s 20 does link a preventative duty to specific objectives and services:

> (3) Every local authority shall provide accommodation for any child in need within their area who has reached the age of 16 and whose welfare the authority considers is likely to be seriously prejudiced if the authority does not provide him with accommodation.

By requiring local authorities to provide accommodation for such young persons 'in need', this provision offers the possibility of assistance being made available to those at risk of being drawn into the youth justice system.

The Crime and Disorder Act 1998 placed further preventative duties and conferred certain powers on local authorities. Section 39 requires every local authority to set up at least one 'youth offending team' in its area while under s 38-41 youth justice services must be made available. The legislative intent is that such teams and services will be deployed so as to maximise the opportunities for preventing youths from committing offences and being drawn into the criminal justice system. In addition, local authorities have been given the power under s 14 to create local child curfew schemes which can be used to designate specified public places 'out of bounds' to children below the age of 10 unless accompanied by a responsible adult; this curfew will be enforced by the police. It is of considerable significance that the lead role for this preventative strategy has been given to local authority social workers rather than to the probation or police services. The governing principle for crime prevention in relation to children and young persons is to be welfare rather than justice and is to be supported by an infrastructure of professionals and services.

Police

The strategy to prevent children and young persons entering the criminal justice system has for some time rested on a diversionary policy. The centrepiece of this policy has been the scheme for the administration of a formal police caution to any child or young persons guilty of a minor offence as an alternative to criminal proceedings. Because it rested on the consent of all parties, particularly that of the parents, it may be seen as a discrete means of reinforcing the latter's responsibility and powers in relation to the control of minor offenders. It was ended by the Crime and Disorder Act 1998 which substituted a scheme for administering a formal police reprimand and final warning together, where appropriate, with an offer of a place in a programme designed to dissuade offenders from re-offending. This scheme differs from its predecessor in that it is enforced by stiff sanctions for any failure to comply.

Intervention in a care context

The governing authority is provided by the Children and Young Persons Act 1989. Under s 31(2)(b), the threshold of significant harm may be breached where the 'harm' or 'likelihood of harm' is attributable to:

> (ii) the child's being beyond parental control.

The requirement, therefore, is that the 'harm' or 'likelihood of harm' is attributable to, rather than caused by, the child being beyond parental control. A child may be in need of control because the significant harm threshold has been or is being breached either by the child's own conduct or by the fault or default of a parent. It is the bare fact that the child is found to be beyond parental control which is all important.[14] This may arise, for example, from drug or alcohol abuse, sexual promiscuity or *anorexia nervosa*.

The grounds for intervention and the role of welfare

The welfare principle may well come into play at an early stage by identifying a child as being 'in need' within the definition of the 1989 Act. This will trigger local authority service provision duties. The principle is also given effect by s 11 of the Crime and Disorder Act 1998 which enables the court to make a 'child safety order' in respect of a child below the age of 10 whose behaviour is giving rise to a concern that he or she is in danger of becoming engaged in activities which would be criminal for an older child.

Once the threshold of 'significant harm' is breached, however, then the relevant local authority has a corresponding duty to consider bringing care proceedings. The courts have held that this threshold may be breached by a child's persistent refusal to attend school. A distinctive characteristic of local authority powers at this point is that it has a discretion not to commence proceedings (see, further, Chap 8).

The court, judicial options and the role of welfare

The family proceedings court is the appropriate forum for hearing issues relating to the behaviour of a child out of control in a care context. Where the behaviour is such that the significant harm threshold has been breached then normally proceedings will be commenced under s 31(2)(b) of the 1989 Act. In making this determination the court will have regard to a further provision in this section which states that:

> (10) Where the question of whether harm suffered by a child is significant turns on the child's health or development, his health or development shall be compared with that which could reasonably be expected of a similar child.

In so doing the Court of Appeal has held that that the court is not tied to the facts existing at the time of the hearing but rather the term 'being beyond parental control' should be viewed as describing a state of affairs - in the past, in the future or in the present - according to the context in which it fell to be applied.[15] The conduct of proceedings, role of the parties, provision of reports and the representation and weighting of the child's welfare interests will be as for other care proceedings (see, Chap 8).

The appropriate judicial disposal option will be a public or private family law order, or combination of orders, available under that Act; except in those exceptional circumstances where urgent recourse to wardship is indicated. A care order is not available in respect of children who have committed offences or are only in breach of statutory education requirements.[16] It is available in respect of a child beyond parental control, but 'significant harm' must first be established. The full authority of a care order is often necessary where the behaviour constitutes a possible threat to the general public. The narrowly defined and explicitly control oriented disposal options may be sufficient; these include the child assessment order and supervision order in public law proceedings, and the prohibited steps order or specific purposes order in private proceedings. The more generic scope of the residence order with attached directions, perhaps accompanied by other orders, may also offer the basis for an overall package of statutory authority tailored to control the behaviour of a particular child in particular circumstances (see, further, Chap 8).

Local authority options and the child in care

The issue of a care order vests parental responsibility in a local authority which thereby also acquires responsibility for controlling the behaviour of the child concerned. Many adolescents, having become the subject of care orders because of their uncontrolled behaviour, pose serious management problems for the staff of children's homes. How to impose reasonable restraints on the activities of a *Gillick*[17] competent minor, who has chosen to behave in a way which threatens their welfare interests or those of others, is a recurring and well-documented dilemma for local authorities.[18] Since the introduction of the 1989 Act, the secure accommodation provisions have provided judicial protection for all parties when formal recourse must be had to constraint measures (see, further, below).

Intervention in an offence context

A child may be in need of control because his or her criminal behaviour is endangering others. The governing legislation is provided by an array of statutes including not only the Criminal Justice Act 1991, the Criminal Justice and Public Order Act 1994 and the Crime and Disorder Act 1998 but also the residual provisions of statutes such as the Children and Young Persons Acts of 1933 and 1969.

The grounds for intervention and the role of welfare

Police intervention may initially have been made in pursuance of their preventative duties and have concluded in a formal reprimand (see, above). A decision to arrest for criminal activity will be taken purely on the basis of whether evidence exists to satisfy the prescriptive grounds for the alleged crime and the resulting procedure will be governed by the provisions of the Police and Criminal Evidence Act 1984. Any decision not to bring an offending child before the court, unlike the equivalent decision in respect of a child with welfare needs, is amenable to judicial review. A local authority is free to choose not to initiate care proceedings where the significant harm threshold has been breached and will be shielded by the ruling in *Liverpool*[19] from having to account to the court for that decision. The Court Prosecution Service, however, may find itself judicially challenged should it choose not to initiate criminal proceedings where a juvenile has committed, or is suspected of committing, a criminal offence.[20] In both instances the public interest in ensuring that the welfare of a child is fully taken into account, by those charged with responsibility for deciding on the appropriateness of court proceedings, may be avoided.

From the time of arrest, the welfare principle has a role to play in moderating the approach of the criminal justice system towards juveniles. The special requirements, differentiating the treatment of juveniles and adults, include measures for: notifying parents and the relevant local authority; an 'appropriate' adult to be present during police questioning; keeping juveniles apart from adult offenders; being held on remand in local authority accommodation; and a presumption of entitlement to bail.

The court, judicial options and the role of welfare

The youth court[21] is the appropriate forum for hearing issues relating to the behaviour of a child out of control in an offence context. Unlike the pre-1989 era, the court will now not hesitate to prosecute child offenders, is permitted to do so in relation to those aged 10-14 and is also now unable to order a care disposal on the grounds of a child's particular welfare interests. These justice oriented changes are offset slightly by the new rule that those aged 17 are to be made amenable to the youth court instead of, as formerly, being prosecuted as adults. The procedures of this specialised magistrates court, established to deal with charges of criminal activity brought against juveniles ages in the 14 to 17 age group, are governed by special rules differentiating the treatment of juveniles from adults in the criminal justice system. Protection is given to juveniles by measures which: confer anonymity; limit those who may be present; impose reporting restrictions; and makes adjustments to the use of language. It has jurisdiction to hear and determine summary offences and also has authority to deal summarily with indictable offences (except murder) if it is considered expedient to do so by the court and with the agreement of parents and subject. However, where a child is charged with a very serious offence then he or she will be tried by judge and jury in the Crown court in accordance with the same procedures as apply to adults. Any child aged 10 or older, charged with murder or manslaughter, will be exposed to the full rigour, formality and ritual of the legal system in a manner which makes little allowance for his or her welfare interests.

The way in which the welfare interests of a juvenile are brought before the youth court are important. The court will always have the benefit of a 'welfare report' which will provide it with factual information on the child, his or her family and home surroundings and some general guidance as to which disposal options might be most appropriate. This is usually filed by the relevant local authority, following the mandatory service of notice of prosecution, though in particular circumstances this may be compiled by a probation officer or court welfare officer. The juvenile's interests will not be represented by a guardian *ad litem* nor necessarily by a solicitor; he or she has no entitlement to legal aid nor to legal representation.[22] The child must, however, be given copies of all reports and/or the court must explain the issues to the child. The court may then make such order as would have available to it if the case had been tried on indictment. In reaching its decision the court is obliged 'to have regard to the welfare of the child or young person...'.[23] By not requiring it to give either first consideration nor a paramount weighting to the latter's welfare interests leaves, the legislative intent is to leave the court free to give overriding priority instead to the interests of justice.

A critical test for the way in which the legal system relates to children is the role permitted the welfare principle in determining the appropriate sentence for young children convicted of serious criminal behaviour.[24] Given its pivotal role across the centuries - identifying, articulating and giving weight to the developmental needs of children in the context of legal issues affecting their upbringing – what part does it now play in enducing the judiciary to take into account the welfare needs of very young criminals? The House of Lords recently had cause to consider the role played by the welfare principle in the sentencing policy governing convicted juveniles.[25] It concluded that a clear historical strand of legislative intent could be detected, differentiating between the rationale for sentencing juveniles and adults, which required the principle to be taken into account in relation to the former.[26] Their lordships held that the Secretary of State had been wrong when he had advised that an inflexible application of the tariff system would be sufficient in computing the sentence for two ten year old offenders; their needs as children required a different approach. Unlike adults, the sentencing of juveniles necessitated making provision for a regular review of their needs and allowing for the possibility of welfare considerations contributing towards their early release.

The disposal options available in respect of offending juveniles are, in the main, set out in the Criminal Justice Act 1991.[27] The majority of offenders are the subject of 'diversion policy' options. They are formally reprimanded and diverted away from the juvenile justice system in circumstances where the offence is a first and/or a minor transgression and either guilt has been admitted or may be readily proven. Many others found guilty of minor offences will be absolutely or conditionally discharged or they and/or their parents will be the subject of directions requiring the payment of fines, compensation or depriving them of all rights to offence related property. The 1998 Act has introduced a new focus on reparation whereby an offender may be required to make amends directly to the victim whose views will be taken into account by the court prior to sentencing. It also provides that an 'action plan' will be required from the offender explaining how he or she intends to 'mend their ways'. Only those found guilty of serious or repeated offences will, following determination, be retained within the system by an order requiring that they undertake treatment in either a community or custodial setting. The court will then draw from the tariff of disposal options, ranging from supervision in the community to long term custodial confinement, available under the criminal justice legislation.

Community treatment options

The wider range of community disposal options introduced by the 1991 Act now allows the rehabilitation of juvenile offenders to be individually tailored to a greater extent than ever before. These include community service orders, attendance centre orders, curfew orders, supervision orders, combination orders and probation orders. In practice, the majority of juvenile offenders are made the subject of supervision orders with attached judicial directions suited to individual circumstances. As providing supervision is a duty which falls to local authority social workers, professionally more concerned with the needs than the deeds of juveniles, it may be construed that most offenders continue to benefit more from welfare oriented than punishment oriented disposals.

Custodial treatment options

Custodial treatment options are reserved for those young offenders who persistently re-offend or whose offences are so grave that no other option is justified.[28] The courts are increasingly relying on custodial sentences[29] which, since the introduction of the Criminal Justice and Public Order Act 1994, has reduced the age of the children amenable from 14 to 10. Of these options the courts resort most frequently to detention in a young offender institution, where the offender is over the age of 15. Another alternative, introduced by the 1994 Act, is the secure training order which provides for the detention of persistent offenders aged 12-14 in a secure training centre followed by supervision in the community. The latter option has been broadened by the Crime and Disorder Act 1998 to become a detention and training order which is to replace other custodial orders and become the basic disposal option for all young offenders. The most extreme custodial option, available under s 53(1) of the Children and Young Persons Act 1933 and reserved for convictions of murder, is to be sentenced to be detained 'at Her Majesty's pleasure'. Other custodial options include detention for treatment under the Mental Health Act 1983 and detention in secure accommodation.

Secure accommodation

There are two different forms of secure accommodation: for children and young persons being 'looked after' by a local authority; and for those convicted of, or on remand in relation to, a criminal offence. Both can be accessed only by order of the court and result in serious constraints being imposed upon the children concerned.

Secure accommodation in a care context

Any child already being accommodated by a local authority is eligible for a judicially sanctioned removal to, or retention in, secure accommodation. This is so whether the accommodation is provided on a voluntary basis or as the consequence of a care order and regardless of the type of accommodation being provided (foster home, psychiatric hospital, hostel, children's home etc). In *A Metropolitan Borough v DB*[30] Cazalet J held that a hospital maternity ward, which was kept locked and to which the only inmate, a 17 year old pregnant crack-cocaine addict, had no key, met the definition of secure accommodation.

Authority to provide secure accommodation is to be found in the Children Act 1989 and supporting regulations.[31] Under s 25(1) of the 1989 Act 'secure accommodation' means 'accommodation provided for the purpose of restricting liberty'. Whether or not a particular place or practice meets the terms of this definition is ultimately a matter for the court to determine. Any practice which prevents a child from leaving a room of his or her own volition, however, could amount to a restriction of liberty. It has been held[32] that a behaviour modification unit in a hospital, where the programme entailed a restriction on person liberty, was a form of secure accommodation.

Under s 25(1), a child who is being looked after by a local authority may not be placed, and, if placed, may not be kept, in secure accommodation unless it appears:

> (a) that-
>
> (i) he has a history of absconding and is likely to abscond from any other description of accommodation; and
>
> (ii) if he absconds, he is likely to suffer significant harm; or
>
> (b) that if he is kept in any other description of accommodation he is likely to injure himself or other persons.

Intended as a 'last resort',[33] there are thus only two types of situation in a care context which justify secure accommodation.

The role of the welfare principle can be seen in the restrictions placed on the use of secure accommodation. It is never justified as a punishment[34] nor by the lack of an alternative. Under regulations provided for in s 25(7), the Department of Health has excluded certain categories of children and young persons from eligibility for placement in secure accommodation: no child being accommodated for 24 hours or less; any child already detained under the Mental Health Act 1983;[35] no child under the age of 13 years without the prior approval of the Secretary of State; no child convicted of a grave offence whose detention is subject to the discretion of the Home Office; and no young person aged between 16 and 21 years who is being provided with accommodation by a local authority in order to safeguard or promote that person's welfare, or who is the subject of a child assessment order and is being kept away from home pursuant to that order. Under s 25(2) provision is made for regulations to specify a maximum period during which a child may be retained in secure accommodation without recourse to the court.[36] It should be noted that the previous prohibition on the use of secure accommodation in a voluntary or registered children's home has been abolished.[37]

The court has an important role in safeguarding the welfare interests of children. Where a child is to be detained in secure accommodation for a period exceeding 72 hours then authority to do so must be sought from a family proceedings court (or county or High Court where a secure order is made in the course of civil proceedings being heard in either court). As stated in the Guidance:

> It is the role of the court to safeguard the child's welfare from inappropriate or unnecessary use of secure accommodation...[38]

However, as Butler-Sloss LJ observed in *Re M (Secure Accommodation Order)*,[39] the action of the court in making such an order "may be inconsistent with the concept of the child's welfare being paramount". She then ruled that welfare is a relevant but not a paramount consideration in determining whether or not a secure accommodation order should be made and the welfare checklist had no application. The court also held that the no-order presumption had no role to play in such proceedings. This finding has the effect of reversing the presumption: once it is satisfied that all formal requirements have been met, the court is required to then make the order sought. This is an interesting deviation from the usual rule that once threshold requirements are met, the making of an order (whether or not the one sought) is a matter of judicial discretion to be determined on the basis of the particular welfare needs of the child concerned. Instead, this provision deals with the control function of welfare in a prescriptive manner.

The role of the welfare principle may be constrained in the context of secure accommodation proceedings but the normal rules for acknowledging and representing a child's welfare interests in family proceedings must be respected. The court has ruled that the child concerned must be given the opportunity to properly present his case. In *Re AS (Secure Accommodation Order)*[40] an appeal was allowed because the 12 year old boy had not been notified of the proceedings and a guardian *ad litem* had not been appointed. In *Oxfordshire County Council v R*[41] the court advised that as secure accommodation proceedings were family proceedings for some purposes of the 1989 Act, hearsay evidence was therefore admissible. Under s 41, they are also 'specified proceedings' and therefore the court must appoint a guardian *ad litem* unless satisfied that it is not necessary to do so in the interests of the child. Having determined that the criteria for detention are met, then it is for the court, under s 25(4), to 'make an order authorising the child to be kept in secure accommodation and specifying the maximum period for which he may be so kept'.[42] Before so doing, however, the court must, under s 25(6) ensure that legal representation is provided for the child 'unless, having been informed of his right to apply for legal aid and having had the opportunity to do so, he refused or failed to apply'.[43] Once the criteria cease to be met the child should be removed. After placement in secure accommodation, the welfare interests of the child fall to be protected by the local authority not the court. Thereafter, it is most unlikely that those interests will be represented by a guardian *ad litem* or solicitor and they will not arise for review before the court.

In addition to the responsibilities it has in respect of all children whom it is looking after, a local authority also has other duties which are specific to children in secure accommodation. In particular it must establish a review panel of at least three members, one of whom at least must not be employed by the local authority, which shall conduct a review of every child in secure accommodation within one month of a child's admission and at not less than three month intervals thereafter. The panel should address not only the matters relating to the child's welfare as detailed in s 26, but must also satisfy itself that the criteria for retention in secure accommodation is still being met. When making its deliberations the panel is required to ascertain and take into account the wishes and feelings of the child and those of any person bearing parental responsibility or having had care responsibility in respect of him or her. All involved must be advised of the outcome of the review and proper records must be maintained.

Secure accommodation in an offence context

Section 23(5) of the Children and Young Persons Act 1969,[44] provides authority for children and young persons held on remand, or following committal, in respect of a criminal offences, to be placed in secure accommodation. It states that before making such an order the court must first satisfy itself that it is necessary for the protection of the general public from serious harm. More specifically, to be eligible a juvenile should have been either:

1. detained by the police under section 38(6) of the Police and Criminal Evidence Act 1984; or
2. remanded to local authority accommodation under section 23 of the Children and Young Persons Act 1969;
    (a) having been charged or convicted of an offence of violence (or having been previously convicted of such an offence), or
    (b) having been charged with or convicted of an offence which would be imprisonable for fourteen years or more if they were aged twenty-one or over.

The eligibility criteria were broadened further by interim arrangements put in place by s 60 of the Criminal Justice Act 1991. This enabled a court, after it had consulted with the local authority or probation service, to remand a fifteen or sixteen year old, with a 'security requirement', to local authority secure accommodation where the juvenile:

1. is charged with, or convicted of, a violent or sexual offence or an offence punishable, in the case of an adult, with imprisonment for fourteen years or more; or
2. has a history of absconding while remanded to local authority accommodation and is charged with, or has been convicted of, an imprisonable offence alleged or found to have been committed while he was so remanded.

The welfare principle comes into play in a negative sense by restricting access to secure accommodation. In either of the above cases the court must be convinced that protecting the public from serious harm is only possible by so remanding the juvenile. As s 60 became fully implemented it replaced s 23 of the 1969 Act and the above judicial power became available together with conditions which can be attached when remanding juveniles. The maximum period a young offender can be retained in secure accommodation is for the duration of the remand, or for 28 days, whichever is the longer. Thereafter, court authorisation must be sought.

Secure accommodation and welfare interests

The welfare principle has a very restricted role in judicial determination of an application for a secure accommodation order: no paramount weighting; no checklist; and no no-order presumption. It is also compromised by the fact that the order can be made in respect of children whose behaviour requires control for very different reasons. Local authority use of secure accommodation is, in theory, for the welfare of the child concerned: to protect him or her from the possibility of self-inflicted harm. In practice it is most often utilised to protect others from the possibility of harm being inflicted upon them by the child. These are very different sets of needs: the introverted anorexic and the belligerent vandal have little in common with each other and require very different regimes from that which is appropriate for the criminal youths referred by the youth justice system. Secure accommodation facilities can only meet the welfare test if they appropriately differentiate between these different sets of needs; in particular by providing a safe, therapeutic environment suited to the health care needs of children at risk of self harm.

Conclusion

There has clearly been a quite dramatic and comprehensive change in the law relating to the control of the behaviour of children and young persons in recent years. New legislation has carefully teased apart the legal response to such behaviour occurring in 'care' and 'offence' contexts. The result, when fully fleshed out, will be two distinct and largely separate systems – one for child care and another for youth justice. Although there are some provisions which will, to some degree, have the effect of bridging the two systems; most notably those relating to remand and secure accommodation.

At first sight the role of the welfare principle in this change would seem to have been wholly eclipsed by that of justice supplemented by considerations of punishment, proportionality and deterrence. The creation of a specific youth court, the extension of its remit at either end of the age range, together with the removal of the care disposal option and the increase in the number of powers available to it, all certainly serve to consolidate a much more coherent and independent justice model than existed previously. There is also the inescapable fact that once proceedings are underway there is far less scope for the principle in the youth court than in the family proceedings court to influence the course of events, the decision made and the disposal option chosen. The difference in the representation available to the child is particularly apparent.

However, it is also evident that there is to be a new focus on preventative intervention spearheaded by a new and comprehensive youth justice service. This will be welfare led, well resourced and, by operating on a nation wide, inter-disciplinary and inter-agency basis, should have the desired effect of ultimately reducing the numbers of children and young persons charged with criminal offences.

A real change has been the shift from the focus on the offender in isolation to a broader approach by holding parents accountable for their failure to exercise adequate control, by making room in proceedings for the views of victims and by requiring offenders to make direct reparation.

Perhaps the change of most concern is the removal of welfare oriented protections for those in the 10-14 age range who are charged and later convicted of serious offences.

Notes

1 Signalled by the White Paper *Crime, Justice and Protecting the Public* (Cmnd 965) 1990, in which the government indicated its resolve to firmly place on parents the responsibility for control of wayward children by making it a criminal offence if they should 'fail to prevent their children from committing offences'.

2 At common law this was initially fixed at aged 7, was raised to 8 in 1933 and to 10 in 1963.

3 As in *JM (A Minor) v Runeckles* (1984) 79 Cr App Rep 255.

4 See *X v X* [1958] Crim LR 805. The law on this matter was well scrutinised more recently by the courts in *C v DPP*[1994] QBD 3 All ER 191 which concerned a 12 year old boy charged with the offence of tampering with a motor vehicle. In the magistrate's court he was convicted, it being held that on the evidence the presumption of *doli incapax* was rebutted. He appealed to the Divisional court by way of case stated on the issue of whether there was any or sufficient evidence that at the time he knew his act to be seriously wrong. The appeal was denied it being held that the *doli incapax* presumption was out-dated and could no longer be regarded as a part of the law of England. But, see, *C v Director of Public Prosecutions* [1995] 1 FLR 933 HL where on appeal to the House of Lords, the *doli incapax* presumption was re-affirmed: it may only be rebutted by showing showing clear positive evidence - not consisting merely in the evidence of the acts amounting to the offence itself - that the child knew the act was seriously wrong.

5 See Brenda Hoggett, *Parents And Children* (4th ed), London, Sweet and Maxwell, 1993, p 215 where she references 'Parsloe, 1978; cf. Priestly, Fears and Fuller, 1977; Taylor, Lacey and Bracken, 1979; Morris, Giller, Szwed and Geach, 1980'.

6 See *Children in Trouble*, Home Office, Cmnd 3601, HMSO, 1968; also, see *The Child, the Family and the Young Offender*, Home Office, Cmnd 2742, HMSO, 1965.

7 See Parker, H., *Receiving Juvenile Justice*, Blackwell, 1981.

8 s 58 of the Criminal Justice Act 1991.

9 s 57 of the Criminal Justice Act 1991.

10 s 58(1)(a) of the Criminal Justice Act 1991.

11 s 58(2) and (3) of the Criminal Justice Act 1991.

12 See the White Paper *No More Excuses – A New Approach to Tackling Youth Crime in England and Wales* (Cmnd 3809) 1997. Note, also, the Criminal Justice and Public Order Act 1994 which extended the judicial power to bind over parents.

13 Sexual Offences Act 1993.

14 See, for example, *Re O (A Minor)(Care Order: Education: Procedure)* [1992] 2 FLR 7 where it was considered to be irrelevant to determine whether this established fact was attributable to the fault of child or parent.

15 See *M v Birmingham City Council* [1994] 2 FLR 141.

16 But see *Re O (A Minor)(Care Order: Education: Procedure), op cit*, where the court ruled that obdurate and persistent school refusal, maintained over a period of years, constituted a breach of the significant harm threshold.

17 *Op cit.*

18 See, for example, A Levy and B Kahn *The Pindown Experience and the Protection of Children*, Stafford, Staffordshire CC (1991).

19 *Op cit.*

20 See, for example, *R v Chief Constable of Kent and Another ex parte L* [1991] Crim LR 841 where the decision of the police to institute criminal prosecution, rather than comply with the recommendation that a caution was sufficient, in respect of a juvenile who had allegedly inflicted serious injuries on his victim, was judicially reviewed and upheld.

21 Under s 70 of the Criminal Justice Act 1991, the juvenile court was renamed the 'youth court'.

22 The court has a discretion to direct that legal aid be made available; and under r 5 of the 1992 Rules it has a discretion to permit a parent or other person to represent the child.

23 S 44(1) of the Children and Young Persons Act 1933.

24 See, for example: *R v Fuat and Others* (1973) 57 Cr App R 840; *R v Fairhurst* [1986] 1 WLR 1374; and *R v Wainfur* [1997] 1 Cr App R (S) 43.

25 See *R v Secretary of State for the Home Department ex parte Thompson and Venables* [1997] 2 FLR 471.

26 Evident in the Children Act 1908 and in s 44 of the Children and Young Persons Act 1933.

27 But also see the Children and Young Persons Act 1933, the Powers of Criminal Courts Act 1973, the Magistrates' Courts Act 1980, the Criminal Justice Act 1982 and the Crime and Disorder Act 1998.

28 The Criminal Justice Act 1991, s 1(2).

29 The Home Secretary in the 'Green Paper' *Strengthening Punishment in the Community* has indicated that while the range of community disposal options in England and Wales will remain as they are, the custodial options may well be strengthened

30 [1997] 1 FLR 767.

31 See the Children Act 1989, s 25, the Children (Secure Accommodation) Regulations 1991, the Children (Secure Accommodation)(No 2) Regulations 1991 and the Children (Secure Accommodation) Amendment Regulations 1995.

32 See *R v Northampton Juvenile Court, ex parte London Borough of Hammersmith and Fulham* [1985] FLR 193.

33 See *Guidance,* Vol 4, Residential Care, para 8.5.

34 See Regs, Vol 4, para 8.5.

35 In this context, the decision of Wall J in *Re C (Detention: Medical Treatment)* [1997] 2 FLR 180, concerning a suicidal 16 year old girl suffering from anorexia nervosa, should be noted. Faced with resistance from the hospital for a detention order under the 1983 Act and from the local authority for a care order under the 1989 Act, Wall J used the court's inherent *parens patriae* jurisdiction to authorise detention in the hospital.

36 Under Reg 10(1) a child in care may only be so retained for a maximum period of 72 hours in any period of 28 days, unless a further period has been sanctioned by the court. Also, see, the Children (Secure Accommodation) Regulations 1991; and Reg 11(3) for exceptional arrangements at weekends and public holidays.

37 See Reg 6 of the Children (Secure Accommodation)(Amendment) Regulations 1995.

38 Children Act 1989, Guidance, vol 1, para 5(7).

39 [1995] FLR 418, at pp 423-442.

40 [1999] 1 FLR 103.

41 [1992] 1 FLR 648.

42 Under Reg 13(2), the order may authorise the retention of a child for a period not exceeding 3 months. Under Reg 13, on subsequent applications, a local authority may seek six month extensions.

43 Legal aid for secure accommodation proceedings is provided for under Part 1V of the Legal Aid (General) Regulations 1989.

44 As amended by the Criminal Justice Act 1991 and supplemented by the Children (Secure Accommodation) Regulations 1991.

10 Protection

Introduction

Protection has long been the first threshold of state intervention. The principle of the welfare of the child has always required, as a basic minimum, that protection be given to the bodily integrity of a child. The role played by the principle in public family law proceedings commenced to secure protection for a child is now governed almost exclusively by the provisions in Part V of the 1989 Act. These authorise coercive state intervention in the affairs of a family by a local authority and/or certain others.

This legislative concern, to provide for the protection of children in circumstances of abuse or neglect at the hands of their parents or third parties, represents the earliest expression of the welfare principle and continues the most basic function of the law relating to children. This function is essentially reactive and negative in nature. It is usually activated after the welfare threshold has been breached and a child harmed. It is most often given effect through the removal of the child concerned from a familiar environment (containing supportive as well as harmful relationships). Being designed and utilised to deal with the effects of a welfare breach, in itself it does nothing to address the causes.

This chapter examines the child protection process and considers the different stages at which professional or judicial intervention endeavours to secure a child's welfare interests.

Child abuse

The phenomenon of child abuse is represented most often by domestic maltreatment, in the form of a physical or sexual assault, on a child by either a member of that child's family, a close relative or by a family friend. The legal response in civil law is provided by s 43(1)(a) of the 1989 Act which defines a child as an abused child when he or she 'is suffering or is likely to suffer, significant harm'. 'Harm' under s 31(9) is defined as including both ill-treatment (which 'includes sexual abuse and forms of ill-treatment which are not physical') and the impairment of health ('health' meaning physical or mental health) or development ('development' means physical, intellectual, emotional, social or behavioural development).

In this context a child is defined as someone who has been born but has not yet reached the age of 18; a definition which caselaw has consistently held to exclude a foetus.[1] In recent years this exclusion has been examined and significantly re-interpreted by the House of Lords in judgments which seemed to indicate a trend with profound implications for extending the application of the welfare principle.[2] An emerging thread of logic suggested that harm inflicted upon a pregnant mother, and the subsequent birth of a child suffering on-going impairment directly resulting from that harm, would be sufficient to ground proceedings against the perpetrator of the harm alleging liability for impairing the welfare interests of the child. Much media speculation ensued as to the prospect of maternal accountability for child born with a health impairment caused by the mother's excessive smoking, drinking etc while pregnant. The viability of this new approach has received a setback with the decision of the Scottish courts in *Kelly v Kelly*[3] that an estranged husband had no right to intervene, as 'next friend' of his unborn child, to prevent his wife from having an abortion. However, the trend towards viewing the welfare interests of a mother and her very young child as being inextricably fused is hardening. This decision may prove insufficient to prevent an eventual recognition of a presumptive duty of care owed to a foetus as an extension of that trend.

While a breach of the welfare threshold will activate child protection proceedings it also continues to attract criminal law sanctions. The 1989 Act, understandably, has done nothing to lessen the fundamental conflict between the legal system's obligation to protect the welfare interests of a child and to ensure that the requirements of criminal justice are satisfied. The latter has always remained grounded on general considerations of public interest, has assiduously guarded against any obscuring or diminution of a defendant's rights and has insisted on a high standard of proof to secure a conviction. This continues to sit uncomfortably alongside the individualised welfare interests of a child. Where, as is most often the case, a child is involved as a witness in criminal proceedings instigated against his or her alleged abuser, this conflict is glaringly evident with welfare interests routinely subordinated to justice considerations and often seriously impaired as a consequence. More often than not the interests of justice can only be satisfied by an examination of the evidence of the child concerned – including probing his or her character, motives and previous experience – as that child is the only witness to the alleged abuse. An inevitably distressing experience will be made harrowing where the child is required to give evidence against an abusing family member.

Affording some immediate safeguards for the welfare interests of a child witness, while also allowing for measures which will in the long-term minimise the destruction of relationships upon which the child is psychologically dependant and permit rehabilitation within his or her family, are among the most serious challenges now facing all professionals working in the field of child protection.

The professional response recognises and differentiates between four different types of abuse: neglect, physical abuse; sexual abuse; and emotional abuse.[4]

Neglect

The liability of a parent, a person with parental responsibility or someone with *loco parentis* standing, for any harm which befalls a child as a consequence of their failure to afford him or her an adequate standard of care or protection is well established. Traditionally, this liability arose in circumstances where the failure in parenting was associated with low standards of care, maintenance or safety due perhaps to poverty, immaturity or parental incapacity resulting from illness, injury or learning disability. The introduction of the 1989 Act has seen this liability assimilated within the definition of "harm" in s 31(9) and allows it to be grounded equally on the fault or default of a culpable person.

It has always been the actual consequences for the child not the intentions of the carer which are of primary concern to both local authority and court. The standard of child care required is judged objectively in the sense that the measure applied is that of a hypothetical caring parent i.e. no allowance can be made for the fact that the actual parent is too young, inexperienced or distressed to cope any better. The standard applied is also subjective in the sense that the level of care expected from such a parent is that actually required to meet the particular needs of the child in question i.e. the fact that the level of care provided would be adequate for an average child is irrelevant if the child in question requires care of a higher standard due perhaps to a disability.

Evidence of parental failure to provide, or permit others to provide, essential medical treatment for a seriously ill child has repeatedly been found sufficient to ground court intervention.

Physical abuse

Child abuse clearly falls within the definition of 'ill-treatment' given in s 31(9). As has been said:

> Physical abuse implies physically harmful action directed against a child; it is usually defined by any inflicted injury such as bruises, burns, head injuries, fractures, abdominal injuries or poisoning.[5]

This is the most frequently recorded form of abuse. The legal issues are most often relatively straightforward as evidence in the form of injuries and testimonies from victim and perpetrator are readily available. However, it is the deliberate harm inflicted by a well-intentioned parent, or someone acting on his behalf, for the purposes of disciplining a child, that gives rise to most contention. The common law right[6] of a parent to administer 'moderate and reasonable chastisement' continues to govern the law in this difficult area and to generate debate as to what constitutes 'moderate' or 'reasonable'. It has long been held to be justifiable for a parent to demonstrate disapproval of a child's unacceptable behaviour and to discourage its repetition by physically chastising such a child. But parental discretion in this area is subject to a legal test of reasonableness. Paradoxically, it was acceptance of its status as a legal incidence of parenthood that enabled the European Court of Human Rights to rule in favour of parent petitioners who objected to the use of corporal punishment in state schools.[7]

The issue as to if and when third parties have a right to administer such chastisement has concerned the courts. This arose for consideration in the ECHR[8] in a case where a seven year old boy had been punished by the headmaster. The chastisement took the form of three strikes on his bottom, through his shorts, with a rubber soled gym shoe. He alleged breach of Article 3 of the European Convention of Human Rights 1950. The ECHR held that the following factors to be considered in determining whether or not a breach had occurred: the nature and context of the punishment; the manner and method of its execution; its duration; its physical and mental effects; and, in some cases, the sex, age and state of health of the victim. It was decided, by a majority verdict of 5:4, that the punishment had not been so severe as to constitute a breach of Article 3. The court also decided, unanimously, that the punishment had not adversely affected the child's physical or moral integrity to a degree that would have constituted a breach of Article 8 (respect for private and family life) and held that the applicant had an adequate route to a remedy under domestic law. The headmaster was found to have been acting within the scope of his *loco parentis* responsibilities as, subsequently, was a childminder[9] who admitted smacking a child in her care but with parental permission. However, a stepfather[10] who had beaten a nine year old boy on more than one occasion, causing bruising on his legs and bottom, was found to have inflicted excessive punishment which breached Article 3. It is clear from these cases that chastisement will only be regarded as coming within the legally permitted parameters of Article 3 if it is administered with moderation, this being determined with regard to factors such as the type and severity of the punishment relative to the age and gender of the child.

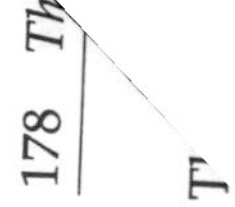

Sexual abuse

This is recognised in s 31(9) of the 1989 Act as constituting
ill-treatment and has been defined as follows:[11]

> Sexual abuse is defined as the involvement of dependen
> immature children and adolescents in sexual activities they do not fully comprehend and to which they are unable to give informed consent or that violate the social taboos of family roles

The media attention given to serious abuse by predatory paedophiles has now resulted in the introduction of the Sex Offenders Act 1997 with its mandatory requirement for the registration of all future convicted offenders. In fact, however, the perpetrators are more likely to be parents or other family members than third parties. The main legal problems in securing future protection for the welfare interests of a child victim of alleged sexual abuse have been to do with satisfying the standard of proof and providing sufficient corroborative evidence.

The normal standard of proof, resting on the balance of probabilities, applicable in all civil proceedings, applies also to cases of child sexual abuse. However, the courts have tended to place a heavy burden on the party alleging such abuse to produce a convincing weight and range of evidential material in support of the allegations. The House of Lords examined this approach in what has now become the leading case[12] on the standard of evidence applicable in cases of alleged sexual abuse. This was a case which rested on the single issue of whether the elder of four sisters had been sexually abused by her step-father who had been acquitted of rape on that issue. The court, subsequently, had to consider an application for care orders in respect of the other three sisters on the grounds that they were 'likely to suffer significant harm' (as per s 31(2)) if the orders were not made. Having considered possible different interpretations of the requisite standard and reviewed related caselaw, the House concluded that the correct rule was to apply the simple balance of probabilities test. The ruling in *Re H and others* also serves to underline the basic obligation of applicants in such cases to discharge the burden of proof lying on them to show that the child concerned is likely to suffer significant harm; this requires actual evidence.

In the absence of an admission of guilt, allegations of child sexual abuse present the court with greater difficulties than other forms of abuse. In the words of Browne -Wilkinson LJ:

> Child abuse, particularly sex abuse, is notoriously difficult to prove in a court of law. The relevant facts are extremely sensitive and emotive. They are often known only to the child and to the alleged abuser.[13]

…here is a school of thought[14] which holds that this ruling has raised the threshold of proof by requiring a somewhat higher standard of evidence in sexual abuse cases and that this therefore works to the disadvantage of children's welfare interests. But, in fact, the courts have for some years been more assiduous in their demands for proof in this category of case than in relation to other abuse cases and this ruling is more likely to stem than increase any tendency toward incrementally raising the standard of proof. The grievousness of the consequences for the child, as much as for the perpetrator, of a finding of guilt in such cases cautions against any relaxation in the existing standard. Reliance solely on the testimony of a victim is particularly fraught with legal difficulties. Corroboration must sought in the form not only of medical evidence but also in verifiable psycho-social disturbance.

A central issue in *Re H and others* was whether, even if the abuse had occurred in respect of one child, that it would provide sufficient evidence to ground a finding of risk of future abuse to that child's siblings. As Browne - Wilkinson LJ stated:

> If legal proof of actual abuse is a prerequisite to a finding that a child is at risk of abuse, the courts will be powerless to intervene to protect children in relation to whom there are the gravest suspicions of actual abuse but the necessary evidence legally to prove such abuse is lacking.[15]

The House of Lords held that the issue of whether the girl's siblings were exposed to - 'harm, or the likelihood of harm...attributable to ..the care given to the child, or likely to be given to him if the order were not made, not being what it would be reasonable to expect a parent to give to him' (as per s 31(2)(b) of the 1989 Act) - was not dependent upon the initial finding. The two parts of this provision may stand separately: 'the likelihood of future harm does not depend on proof that disputed allegations are true' (per Lord Lloyd of Berwick). In principle, it was possible for the court to find that a risk of future abuse existed to a child's siblings despite there being insufficient evidence to confirm past abuse in respect of the child concerned.

Emotional abuse

This type of abuse is clearly intended for inclusion within the 'forms of ill-treatment which are not physical' for the purposes of s 31(9) of the 1989 Act. Like neglect, emotional abuse is more frequently a sin of omission than commission. Unlike neglect it has only gained legal recognition as a form of abuse, requiring coercive state intervention to protect a child's welfare interests, comparatively recently. Whether resulting from deprivation or deliberation, emotional abuse like all other forms of child abuse is a consequence of the misuse by adults of the authority they bear as such in their relationships with children. Once the level of abuse breaches the threshold of significant ha satisfies the grounds for coercive intervention by a local authority or 'author person'. The consequent problems in providing sufficient evidence to convi the court of a cause and effect linkage between a child's emotional disturbance and the particular conduct of a specific adult are well established. This form of abuse, which may take the form of an absence of normal behaviour rather than an infliction of the abnormal (e.g. parental refusal to talk to a child), can often present the most difficult challenge for the professionals and judiciary seeking to protect a child's welfare interests.[16]

Investigation

The intervention threshold is set by the legal benchmark 'significant harm' as defined in s 31(9) of the 1989 Act. Only a breach or suspected breach in this threshold will authorise representatives of the public interest in the welfare interests of children to investigate private standards of care.

Both the court and a local authority may initiate an investigation. Under s 37 of the 1989 Act, the court in the course of any family proceedings may require a local authority to conduct an investigation of a child's circumstances with a view to determining whether grounds exist to make application for a care or supervision order. This is an important discretionary power which provides the judiciary with a capacity to direct intervention for child protection purposes. It is supplemented with a power to make an interim care or supervision order pending the results of the investigation. Under s 47 of the 1989 Act, a local authority has a duty to investigate when it has reason to believe that a child in its area is suffering, or is likely to suffer, significant harm.

Mandatory reporting of actual or suspected incidents of child abuse, an uncontroversial public law requirement for the protection of children's welfare interests in other modern western societies, is not part of the law in this jurisdiction. However, failure to disclose to the proper authorities knowledge of criminal conduct, is itself an offence. An informant is entitled to have his or her anonymity protected by the investigating local authority.[17] Once a referral has been received then, under s 47(9), certain specified agencies have a duty to assist a local authority in its inquiries 'by providing relevant information and advice'.

The child must be seen by the investigating officer from the local authority and, if the child is of sufficient age and understanding, should be interviewed in relation to the presenting issues. The stress of interview may further compromise a child's welfare. Butler-Sloss LJ offered guidance in the Cleveland Report on interviewing children[18] and has more recently observed:[19]

> Generally, it is desirable that interviews with young children be conducted as soon as possible after the allegations are first raised, should be few in number and should have investigation as their primary purpose.

The decision whether or not to place the name of a child on the child protection register is taken at a multi-disciplinary case conference after evidence has been heard from all professionals who have been involved with the child. Factors determining registration are: certainty that abuse or neglect had occurred; its seriousness; the characteristics of the parents indicating a future risk to the child; and 'chronic concern on the part of community agencies'. The main function of the register is to provide a central record of those children defined by a panel of inter-agency professionals as currently in need of an inter-agency protection plan.

As a means of facilitating the protection of a child's welfare interests, it is doubtful whether the placing his or her name on such a register achieves very much. Research findings indicate that this practice provides little assurance that thereafter effective professional intervention will ensure either adequate protection for the child concerned or appropriate support services for the family.[20] The link between a local authority's investigative/coercive intervention duties and its powers under Part III (specifically, the link between sections 47 and 17 in which the circumstances described and the services are the same) may not be readily made.[21] Alternatively, s 17 enquiries are seen by some professionals as a 'passport to services'.[22]

Assessment

Under the 1989 Act, the legislative intent is to provide a local authority with a broad range of options at the conclusion of its protective procedures.

An investigating local authority may determine that a child is vulnerable but the significant harm threshold has not been breached. The local authority will then consider whether the circumstances are such as to require it to treat the child as coming within the definition of 'in need'. If so then this will give rise to a duty under s 17 to provide a 'range and level of services appropriate to those children's needs.' This, in effect, is a decision that the impairment of welfare interests does give rise to a public interest in the quality of care arrangements but is such as to require consensual rather than coercive intervention (see, further, Chap 11). Again, a local authority investigation may conclude that a child is vulnerable, the significant harm threshold has not been breached but that no one person has parental responsibility for the child. Then, in keeping with the 'family care is best' principle, that authority could support a private proceedings application from a suitable member of the family for a s 8 order (e.g. a residence order). The local authority itself has no right to apply for a s 8 order.

A local authority may decide that there is cause for concern and more time is needed for a thorough investigation. Under the 1989 Act it will then consider whether an application for an interim care order or for a child assessment order will best enable it to complete its inquiries. Although both orders are public family law measures they each allow a local authority to hold a fairly neutral position in relation to the child and family and permit the *status quo* care arrangements to continue while inquiries are being pursued.

Alternatively, it may decide that although there is sufficient cause for concern to warrant commencing proceedings under Part IV of the 1989 Act it will not do so. A local authority has a discretion to decide whether or not a child which it has found to be in need of protection should be brought before the court. While s 47(8) places an onus on an investigating local authority 'to take action to safeguard or promote the child's welfare' this duty is conditional upon it being 'within their power' and 'reasonably practicable' for the local authority to do so. A local authority will, therefore, be justified in concluding that although the significant harm test is satisfied it will not commence proceedings as it would not, for example, be in a position to allocate the staff or resources necessary to implement any order granted. It is clear that such an exercise of local authority discretion will not be open to judicial challenge.[23] Where it decides not to initiate any court proceedings, a local authority must nevertheless consider whether it should review the case at a later date. In the event of it determining that such a review would be appropriate then, under s 47(7), it must fix a date for that review.

This discretionary capacity of a local authority, enabling it to choose not to respond to a breach of the welfare threshold, is new. The discretion would appear to give a local authority the ability to circumvent the public interest by not using coercive intervention powers in circumstances for which they were legislatively provided. The protection of children's welfare interests, in circumstances where they may have suffered or be at risk of suffering significant harm, by the public agency specifically vested with child protection duties, now rests on the discretionary decision of the latter to bring the matter to court. The law can offer no protection to a child unless the relevant local authority elects to initiate proceedings and it can impose no sanctions on the local authority which chooses not to do so.

Where there is clear evidence of significant harm and it is 'within their power' and is 'reasonably practicable' for it to do so, then the local authority is required to initiate the appropriate proceedings. This it may do by ensuring that appropriate care arrangements are made for the children concerned away from the family home. The local authority may achieve the latter either on a consensual basis by 'looking after' such children within the meaning of s 27, on a coercive basis by applying directly for a care order or supervision order or it may need to intervene coercively and immediately using the powers of Part V.

:ection: the principles and consequences

As the Court of Appeal has firmly emphasised[24] intervention is not permissible unless and until the threshold criteria of 'significant harm' have been met. In many if not in most cases it will be found that this threshold has not been breached, or if it has that the breach is repairable and on-going local authority intervention is unnecessary. A feature of the 1989 Act is the moral authority vested in the presumption favouring family care. Welfare under the 1989 Act, unlike under the 1969 Act, is seen first and foremost as a matter for the family not the state.

Proceedings commenced under the Children Act 1989, Part V, are excluded from the s 8(4) definition of 'family proceedings'. When hearing Part V proceedings the court is unable to make any s 8 order: not on its own motion nor in response to an application. It can only make or refuse to make the order applied for with the exception that it may make an emergency protection order instead of a child assessment order. When considering an application for an order under Part V, the court must have regard to the paramountcy principle but is not required to apply the 'welfare checklist'. Child protection is statutorily set aside to facilitate urgent professional intervention and prompt judicial determination as to whether or not emergency powers should be used to secure a child's immediate protection. However, the actions of the court are governed by the 'no delay' principle, by the 'no order' presumption and the requirement to draw up a timetable to expedite the proceedings.

The sense of urgency which characterises these proceedings prompted the Court of Appeal[25] to rule that such applications should not be delayed by an unduly legalistic analysis of whether or not the presenting evidence fully satisfied the significant harm test. However, the House of Lords in a judgment[26] which overturns the approach in *Newham* has now fully restored significant harm as a condition precedent in applications for an emergency protection order or a child assessment order or an order for the police to exercise their powers of protection.

Removal from home

Traditional child protection practice, entailing the removal of the child concerned, ensured that it had at least one serious consequence for the subject's welfare interests. This 'child rescue' approach wrenched the child from home and from his or her network of positive relationships as well as from the source of abuse. The following precipitate immersion in a strange new foster care or residential care setting added trauma to the loss of relationships upon which the child, for better or worse, had been emotionally dependant. The 1989 Act sought to change this practice by clearly stating that local authorities should give preference to facilitating the removal of the abuser or suspected abuser rather than the child.[27] The subsequent introduction of non-molestation orders and occupation orders under the Family Law Act 1996[28] serves to emphasise the desirability of effecting such a change in practice by providing the means whereby family members can initiate the action necessary to remove offender rather than child from their home. Again, this could be viewed as another instance of a public law issue being re-defined as private; which, when resulting in responsibility being borne by those victimised by criminal behaviour, may be neither just nor feasible.

Proceedings: the orders

The proceedings available under Part V of the 1989 Act are applications for a child assessment order, an emergency protection order, a recovery order and a police protection order. Part V also makes provision for the setting up and running of children's refuges.

Child assessment order

This order, like an emergency protection order, is a tightly defined grant of authority to an applicant, intended to license coercive intervention in family affairs for a specific purpose and for a restricted time period. It provides a less interventionist option than the emergency protection order, interim care order and interim supervision order. The legislative intent is to provide positive welfare intervention, to which all parties could give their agreement, and thereby forestall a judicial necessity to impose a more draconian protection order. Of all the orders designed to directly affect the welfare interests of a child, this one has the singular characteristic of being vulnerable to the veto of the child concerned. By refusing to co-operate, the child is able to quite legitimately assert his or her view of how their welfare interests should be advanced.

A child assessment order is available under s 43 of the 1989 Act on the grounds specified in s 43(1). Only a local authority or an "authorised person" (as defined by s 31(9)) are permitted to apply. It may be utilised in conjunction with private but not public law orders (though it may co-exist with an education supervision order). Its function is to authorise the means whereby a local authority can establish whether or not the subject is suffering or is likely to suffer significant harm. By issuing a child assessment order the court can permit an applicant to bring a child to a named assessor and ensure that such assessment as the court specifies is conducted by that assessor. A child assessment order does not give the applicant any degree of parental responsibility. Section 43 stresses the limitations of the authority conferred by this order: the court is prohibited from granting a child assessment order in situations where an emergency protection order would be more appropriate (para (4)); the child, if of sufficient understanding to make an informed decision, may refuse to submit to the assessment (para 7 and 8)) and; the child may only be kept away from home for the period or periods specified in the order (para 9).[29] The necessity for the child to be away from home will only arise if the court is convinced that this is necessary for the purposes of the assessment (and not, for example, to ensure the child's protection), can be limited to a period or periods less than the statutory maximum and can otherwise be accomplished within such directions as the court may decide to attach to the order, including directions regarding contact arrangements with family and others.

Emergency protection order

The tightly defined powers of an emergency protection order reflect the professional and public disquiet aroused by the Cleveland affair and the guidance offered in the subsequent *Cleveland Report*.[30] Unlike its predecessor, the place of safety order, an emergency protection order is of much shorter duration and focusses attention on the child rather than the place. If, having located the child, the bearer of an emergency protection order should discover that he or she is no longer at risk then the child should not be removed. An emergency protection order allows for continued contact between child and family and is not to be used as an expedient means of commencing care proceedings. Available under s 44 of the 1989 Act, this order is intended to provide court authorisation for urgent protection to be given to a child by ensuring his or her immediate removal to, or retention in, a secure place. There are two sets of grounds. The first, specified in s 44(1)(a), rest solely on the test of prospective harm: evidence of past or present harm is insufficient but may be relevant to indicate the likelihood of a future occurrence; there is no requirement relating to fault for, or causation of, such harm. The second, under s 44(1)(b) and (c), is relevant only to applications from either a local authority or from an authorised person where inquiries are being urgently pursued in relation to actual or suspected significant harm and those enquiries are being frustrated by access to the child being unreasonably refused. The court may, under s 44(9), issue a warrant permitting a constable to accompany the applicant and to use such reasonable force as may be necessary to ensure entry to premises or access to the child. The second set of grounds are restricted to applications from a local authority or from an 'authorised person' and represent a legislative response to the case of Kimberley Carlile and others.[31] In such circumstances, s 47(6) places a strict duty on a local authority or other 'authorised person' to apply for an emergency protection order, or other public law order, unless satisfied that the child's welfare may be otherwise safeguarded.[32]

The court is also required to make an emergency protection order, in the context of proceedings for a child assessment order, where it considers that the grounds for the former exist. It is significant that the court has been given the power to question a local authority's grounds for optimism, which may lie behind the latter's application for a child assessment order, and is empowered of its own motion make instead an order giving absolute priority to the protection of the child concerned. On the other hand, even if the grounds are satisfied the court need not make an emergency protection order. The court may conclude, after applying the paramountcy principle and the no-order presumption, that the child's interests would be best served by not granting the order sought. This is an important judicial discretion enabling the court to avoid licensing coercive intervention even though the welfare threshold has clearly been breached.

The power vested in the holder of an emergency protection order to exercise parental responsibility is hedged around with restrictions. There is a requirement to establish and take into account the views of the subject of an emergency protection order. The s 44(13) provision requiring contact arrangements to be facilitated, is framed more as a right of the child rather than of the parent or other persons. The total possible period of retention is 15 days (as opposed to 15 weeks under a place of safety order). Indeed, an important principle behind this order, as is clear from s 44(5)(b), is that discretionary action is limited to the minimum necessary to "safeguard the welfare of the child". It would, therefore, be inappropriate to seek to make any decisions which would have a long-term effect on the child's life. Similarly ss (10) and (11) place an onus on the bearer of an order to arrange for the child to return home to the care of the person from whom he or she was removed, or returned to a parent, a person with parental responsibility or someone judged (by the bearer of the order and the court) to be appropriate, just as soon as this is reasonably practicable.

Recovery order

There is no legislative precedent for this order which was introduced with the 1989 Act. It represents another tightening up of the public law regime to permit direct and immediate coercive intervention to retrieve a child whose status as being in need of protection is not in doubt. Where the court has confirmed a breach of the welfare threshold it can now prescribe the manner of his or her recovery. The order is available under s 50 of the 1989 Act and applies to a child, defined in s 49, as being either in care, the subject of an emergency protection order or in police protection, who needs to be physically retrieved. It authorises a constable to enter and search specified premises for the child, using reasonable force if necessary.

Police protection

Again, this power is new to statute law and illustrates the legislative intent to ensure that welfare in the context of protection is afforded prompt recognition followed by direct coercive intervention. Under s 46 of the 1989 Act this power may be used in circumstances where either the police are the first to discover that a child is suffering or is likely to suffer significant harm or the urgency is such that immediate intervention is required. As there are no powers to search it may only be used where the police have already located the child. Having taken the child into police protection, a constable may (under s 46(3)(f)) remove him or her to accommodation provided for such children under s 21.[33] Although the police do not thereby acquire parental responsibility they must nonetheless do all that is reasonable to safeguard and promote the child's welfare while he or she remains in their care. Such steps as are reasonably practicable must be taken to ascertain the wishes and feelings of the child (under s 46(3)(d).

Refuges

By enabling a local authority to ensure the provision of a safe haven for children whose welfare is threatened, this provision seeks to further broaden local authority's protective capacity. Once a child's safety is secured by means of an emergency protection order, for example, the local authority may then give effect to its duty to provide reception and accommodation facilities by means of provision within a designated refuge for children at risk.

Conclusion

The law and practice relating to child protection has traditionally served to fence off our society's more fundamental need to preserve the life and safety of children from a more general concern for their growth, development and well-being. In this context, children are more obviously the objects of intervention rather than legal subjects. Child protection constitutes a focus for specialist professional, judicial and agency expertise which is now quite separate from all other rationale for involvement in the lives of children.

The Children Act 1989 challenges the specialists to adjust that focus to accommodate both the principle of partnership with parents and the presumption that care in the family of origin is in every child's best interests. Child protection and family care are not legislatively addressed as separate entities and positioned as alternatives. Professional concern and agency resources are to be channeled by the concept of 'children in need' to pre-empt or bridge any such gap. Indeed, there are no statutory directives which require social workers (as opposed to the judiciary) to give a priority weighting to the welfare interests of a child.

This challenge to the professions is unlikely to succeed. The machinery of inter-agency collaboration, intra-agency structures, management priorities, staff training and hard won expertise continues to resist any inducement to fudge the boundaries between child protection and other forms of intervention in the lives of children. The child protection system and ethos remain intact.

Notes

1 See, for example, the judgment of Sir George Baker in *Patton v Trustees of British Pregnancy Advisory Service* [1979] QB 276.

2 See *D (A Minor) v Berkshire County Council* [1987] 1 All ER 33 where the House ruled that for the purposes of care proceedings it may be appropriate to take into account a mother's treatment of her child while it was still a foetus in the womb. Also, see, *Attorney-General's Reference (No 3 of 1994)* [1997] 3 WLR 421 where it ruled that a cohabitee was guilty of manslaughter when the child, which he had wounded while it was still a foetus in the womb, died of its injuries some three months after its premature birth.

3 [1997] 2 FLR 828.

4 See *Working Together*, HMSO, 1991.

5 See Kempe C, Silverman F, Steele B, Droegmueller W and Silver H 'The battered child syndrome', *Journal of the American Medical Association*, 181, 4-11 (1962).

6 See *R v Hopley* (1860) 2 F&F 202.

7 See *Cambell and Cossans v UK* (1982) 4 EHRR 293.

8 See *Costello - Roberts v United Kingdom* [1994] ELR 1, ECHR. Note, also, Article 37 of the UN Convention on the Rights of the Child, ratified by the UK in 1991.

9 See *London Borough of Sutton v Davies* (No 2)[1995] 1 All ER 65; also see Chap 5.

10 [1999] 2 FLR 959.

11 See Schechter M and Roberge L. 'Sexual Exploitation' in Helfer R and Kempe C (eds) *Child Abuse and Neglect,* Balinger, pp 127-142, (1976).

12 See *Re H and R* supra.

13 Supra, [1996] 1 All ER p 4.

14 See Fortin J, *Children's Rights and the Developing Law*, Butterworths, 1998, pp 383-387.

15 Supra, [1996] 1 All ER p 4.

16 See, for example, *Re M and R (Child Abuse: Evidence)* [1996] 2 FLR 195, CA where the court of Appeal upheld the finding of emotional abuse by the court at first instance and the making of interim care orders.

17 See the House of Lords ruling in *D v NSPCC* [1977] 1 All ER 589.

18 See *Report of the Inquiry into Child Abuse in Cleveland*, 1987, HMSO (1988) (Cmnd 412).

19 See, *Re M (Minors)(Sexual Abuse: Evidence)* [1993] 1 FLR 822. See, also, Chap 15.

20 See Bell etc (p116). See, also, Gough et al, (1987); Corby, (1987).

21 See Gibbons et al *Operating the Child Protection System: A Study of Child Protection Practices in English Local Authorities*, HMSO, (1995, where a study of CPRs revealed that in more than 50% of the cases though a finding had been made of grave concern, no services were provided.

22 See Dingwall and "diagnostic inflation".

23 See, for example, *Nottinghamshire County Council v P (No 2)* [1993] 2 FLR 134, CA and *Re S and D (Children: Powers of Court)* [1995] 2 FLR 456, CA. But see, also, Chap 15 and the implications arising from the judgment of the European Court of Human Rights in *Osman v UK* [1999] 1 FLR 193.

24 See *Nottinghamshire County Council v P (No 2)* [1993] 2 FLR 134.

25 See Sir Stephen Brown P in *Newham London Borough v AG* [1992] 2 FCR 119 at 120.

26 See *Re H and R (Child Sexual Abuse: Standard of Proof)* [1995] 1 FLR 643.

27 See Sched 2, para 5(1).

28 See ss 42(2)(a), 62(3) and 63; and s 33(3)(f) respectively.

29 It may be queried whether both the CAO and the EPO are in accord with Article 51(d) of the European Convention on Human Rights; detention is not for the purposes of educational supervision nor is it for the purposes of bringing the child before the competent legal authority.

30 *Report of the Inquiry into Child Abuse in Cleveland 1987* (1988) (Cmnd 412).

31 *A Child in Mind: Protection of Children in a Responsible Society*, Report of the Commission of Inquiry into the Circumstances surrounding the death of Kimberley Carlile (1987).

32 Ensuring prompt access to a child suspected of being abused was a primary legislative objective following the report in respect of Kimberley Carlile and such others as: *A Child in Trust: Report on the Death of Jasmine Beckford*, London Borough of Brent (1988).*Whose Child: Report on the Death of Tyra Henry*, London Borough of Greenwich (1987).

33 s 21: (2) Every local authority shall receive, and provide accommodation for children - (a) in police protection whom they are requested to receive under section 46(3)(f).

11 Prevention and Promotion

Introduction

'Prevention' and 'promotion' are legal functions which give effect to a very modern interpretation of the welfare principle. Traditionally, when the law had to authorise intervention to safeguard the welfare of a child from circumstances, activities or relationships identified as being prejudicial to his or her interests, it did so by removing or insulating the child from that harmful context. A neglectful parent or an exploitive form of employment, relationships of a contractual or sexual nature, the availability of alcohol, drugs, cars, cigarettes and fireworks and many other such sources of harm were (and often still are) legally addressed by removal of the child, either literally or by the use of legal prohibitions. The significance of 'prevention' and 'promotion' is that they now ground the legislative intent to require local authorities to provide the support and safeguards necessary to retain and protect the child within a context which carries some risk of harm but is otherwise beneficial to their welfare interests.

This chapter deals with the modern positive functions of the welfare principle, in a public family law context, as embodied largely in Part III of the Children Act 1989. In that statute the principle is now represented by the consensual intervention threshold 'children in need' which rests on the functions of 'prevention' and 'promotion' and is operationalised through the general and specific responsibilities placed on local authorities to provide services for children and their families. These are now examined.

Duty of the state to assist children and their families

The broad socio-legal context of contemporary paternalistic state assistance for children and their families evolved from the ancient *parens patriae* responsibilities of the king for the welfare of his more vulnerable subjects (see,

Chap 1). It now provides an important backdrop to any view of the particular functions of prevention and promotion. There are several significant features to this backdrop. Firstly, there is the framework of services that constitute the present 'welfare state'. Secondly, the influence of the United Nations Convention on the Rights of the Child and the ensuing caselaw precedents established by the European Court of Human Rights. Thirdly, the special protection afforded a child in relation to particular circumstances, activities and products. Finally, there is the legal standing of children in certain areas of civil law.

The framework of national services, developed after the second world war under the guidance of Sir William Beveridge,[1] continues to make a vital contribution to the preventative and promotional functions of the welfare principle. Without the basic underpinning provided by such services as health, housing, education and child support the level of poverty and ill-health would be such as to make any discussion regarding the legal role of the welfare principle totally beside the point. The effectiveness of this contribution has been made much more focussed and potent by the present requirement under the Children Act 1989 that where possible the services be co-ordinated to address the circumstances of a child in need when so requested by a local authority.

The United Nations Convention on the Rights of the Child, 1989, which received UK ratification in 1991, is exercising an increasingly important influence on our legal system. Primary responsibility for the upbringing and the development of children is ascribed to parents. It requires that 'State Parties shall render appropriate assistance to parents and legal guardians in the performance of their child-rearing responsibilities' and 'ensure that children of working parents have the right to benefit from child care services and facilities for which they are eligible'.[2] It further requires State Parties to 'recognise the right of every child to a standard of living adequate for the child's physical, mental, spiritual, moral and social development'.[3] This is now becoming a benchmark document against which present and potential UK family law legislation must be tested.

The law providing protection for children in relation to specific circumstances, activities and products is evident across a vast range of disparate statutes each dealing with a specific product or circumstance known to pose particular dangers. The range of statutes includes: the Protection of Children (Tobacco) Act 1991 and the Licensing Act 1964 which, respectively, prohibit the sale of tobacco and alcohol to children; the Horses (Protective Headgear for Young Riders) Act 1990 which makes it an offence for a child to go horseriding without wearing headprotection; the Tattooing of Minors Act 1969 makes it an offence to tattoo a person under the age of 18 and the Explosives (Age of Purchase etc) Act 1976 which seeks to prevent the sale of fireworks to children. These statutes have in common a prescriptive approach to welfare, in which a breach of a particular aspect of the welfare threshold constitutes an offence. The provisions are directed towards the actions of an offender, the related proceedings are concerned with prosecution and the child is very much the object rather than the subject of legislative intent.

The law imposing a duty on others to respect the welfare interests of children because of their relative lack of competence is to be found in three key areas of civil law: tort, contract and employment.

In tort, the law gives recognition to the vulnerability of children through such means as imposing on others a particular duty of care when dealing with them, by requiring others to be aware of the dangers that an 'allurement' might present to a child and by restricting their use of corporal punishment. The corollary to this legal recognition of third party duties is that the law also requires parents to protect a child from entering situations where he or she could incur harm and a third party incur a related liability.

In contract, the law is relatively clear. Generally speaking, minors are held not to have contractual capacity. Again, this rests on a child's presumed lack of competence and reflects a concern to protect children from financial harm and third parties from incurring liability.

In employment, the general and universalist protective measures designed to regulate the circumstances in which young persons, as opposed to children, could be employed, remain as articulated in sections 18-21 of the Children and Young Persons Act 1933.[4] These provide that: no child shall be employed: (a) so long as he is under the age of 13 years; or (b) before the close of school hours on any day on which he is required to attend school; or (c) before seven o'clock in the morning or after seven o'clock in the evening on any day; or (d) for more than two hours on any day on which he is required to attend school; (e) for more than two hours on a Sunday; or (f) to lift, carry or move anything so heavy as to be likely to cause injury to the child. Other legislation prohibits the employment of children in a range of specific settings such as shops, mines, factories, ships and quarries. Where children can be employed, their employment is subject to certain conditions. The first of these rests on the definition of 'child' as 'a person who is not over school-leaving age' which in turn means 'the upper limit of school-leaving age'. This implies that it is the actual age at which a particular child is entitled to leave school, rather than a standard application of the 16 year rule, which is all important. In effect this will vary from 15 years and eight months to 16 years and seven months. The restrictions on the employment of children in the performing arts are the subject of considerably detailed provisions in the 1933 Act and under the Children and Young Persons Act 1969. Basically, before children can be so employed a licence will have to be obtained from the relevant local authority.

Prevention and promotion: concept and function

Prevention and promotion may be viewed as conceptual opposites, both equally removed from the welfare principle's cutting edge of coercive intervention. They are additions, representing legal refinements to the traditional welfare threshold, governed equally by the Children Act 1989.

'Prevention' requires action to avoid any further deterioration in the circumstances of a particular child or children such as might otherwise result in a breach of the welfare threshold. It identifies a form of state intervention that rests in the main on a negative monitoring of child care standards and on a defensive resource input. As a public law function, it neither authorises nor seeks to achieve anything further than the maintenance of the basic welfare threshold and is predicated on a principle that welfare is best assured by parental care. Although a relatively new addition to public law, it has been given a broad and consolidated application under the 1989 Act.

'Promotion' is a function with little application in a public law context. It requires action to create opportunities for further enhancing the welfare of a particular child or children whose circumstances are already well above the coercive intervention threshold. As such it requires the degree of authority, freedom of choice and command of resources appropriate to a person or body vested with parental responsibility. Precisely because it is a function which only comes into play when the choice to be made is intended to achieve more than the mere maintenance of the welfare threshold, it belongs to private rather than pubic law (see, Chaps 12 and 13 for the function of 'promotion' in a private law context). While local authorities do have responsibilities to promote the welfare of children in accommodation under a care order (see, further, Chap 8) the scattered statutory references in the 1989 Act to promote welfare are otherwise without any specific functional content.

The Children Act 1989: consensual statutory intervention

The 1989 Act places a clear but minimalist responsibility on local authorities in respect of the welfare threshold. Central to the Act is the requirement that support be given to vulnerable parenting arrangements and that a child's relationships with the members of his or her family of origin should be safeguarded. This finds expression in three different approaches. Firstly, the legislative intent is now to preserve the legal integrity and privacy of the family unit wherever possible. This is to be achieved by restricting coercive intervention to circumstances where a local authority can convince the court that evidence exists to overcome the 'no-order' presumption and to satisfy the 'significant harm' test. Secondly, the legislative thrust is for parents and local authority to work in partnership to secure the welfare interests of children.

In furtherance of this aim the local authority is to make certain support services available to parents. Finally, specific importance is attached to maintaining a child's links with the members of his or her family of origin. To this end a duty is placed on a local authority to promote the upbringing of children by their families and to promote contact between a child and his or her parents in circumstances where a child is being accommodated by that authority.

Legislative intent is given effect through two different sets of provisions. There are those which are 'universalist' in nature in that they have a broad application to all children and essentially continue the established responsibility of local authorities to maintain an overview of service spread and related standards and to ensure the protection of children in certain circumstances. Then there are those provisions which, by placing new specific duties on a local authority in relation to the support requirements of vulnerable family units, positively discriminate in favour of 'children in need'[5] (see, further, below).

Prevention: the broad support responsibilities of a local authority

The Children Act 1989 outlines a local authority's preventative responsibilities in respect of children who, without support, might become 'children in need'. This may be seen as establishing a minimum baseline from which a local authority may ratchet up the deployment of its consensual and coercive intervention resources. They consist of certain powers which are employed at local authority discretion to alleviate the difficulties of those whose circumstances are not so extreme as to satisfy the 'children in need' test (see, further, below). They consist, also, of certain duties which a local authority owes in general to the children resident in its area. These support responsibilities are an important means of giving effect to the preventative function of the welfare principle. However, the requirement imposed on a local authority is not to put in place support services but merely to regulate such provision as may be made by others. The families and children using such services are assured that quality standards will be set, inspected and reviewed but, necessarily, the availability and financial accessibility of such services are also determinants of this function's effectiveness. The fact that regulatory requirements only apply in respect of children aged 8 years or less (instead of 12 years as in Northern Ireland) is also a limiting factor. In effect the powers and duties of local authority under the 1989 Act in relation to support services largely take the form of registration and monitoring responsibilities in respect of privately run day care, child-minding or private fostering facilities for children.

Child minding and day care

The protection afforded a parent who privately places a child with persons providing child minding or day care services is governed by sections 17, 18 and 19 of the 1989 Act and is provided by the system of registration, certification, notification and inspection. These are implemented through duties placed on the local authorities under Part X (sections 71-79) of the 1989 Act and under the *Children Act 1989 Guidance and Regulations*.[6] They provide for a duty to register and thereafter inspect any domestic premises used for child minding purposes within a local authority's area. It is the place as much as the person which must be registered and, therefore, where a person provides day care in more than one place separate registration is required for each place. There are certain requirements to be met by child minders if they are to be registered by their local authority. These include provisions relating to the total number of children, the number within each age group, the safety of the premises, the keeping of records and the equipment to be provided. The powers and responsibilities of the local authorities in relation to the inspection of registered premises and the working arrangements within are outlined.

It is the service per se, rather than the service as it affects an individual child, which is the subject of these provisions. So, the person providing care for more than two hours in a day, even if no individual child is being looked after for more than one hour and no charge is made, will come within these statutory controls.

In determining whether the service meets the criteria for registration a local authority will assess separately the fitness of the care provider and the fitness of the premises.

Whether a person is fit to provide a child minding or day care service will be determined according to the advice of the DoH in the Guidance and Regulations. In making an assessment a local authority will have regard to such matters as: previous experience; qualifications and training; ability to provide warm and consistent care; multi-cultural awareness; capacity to treat each child as an individual; physical health; attitudes and; the existence of any criminal record involving the abuse of children. These criteria must be applied not only to every applicant seeking registration but also to all persons living or working on the premises to be registered.

Whether premises are fit for the purpose of child minding or day care will also be determined in accordance with the advice provided by the DoH under the above mentioned Guidance and Regulations. In making its assessment a local authority will have regard to such matters as the suitability of the premises in the light of its situation, construction and size.

Under s 71 of the 1989 Act certain persons may not be registered as either a child minder or day care provider. The reasons relate to prescribed offences, orders and requirements made under this or other prescribed provisions. An application for registration will be refused if the applicant, or any person living in or employed on the premises to be registered and who may be involved in caring for children, is 'not fit to look after children under the age of eight' or, in certain circumstances, is 'not fit to be in the proximity of children under the age of eight'. Breach of this requirement may ground an action for negligence.[7] Registration, for example, was refused to a Mrs Davis,[8] a graduate with primary school teaching experience and child-minding experience, because she refused to comply with the 'no-smacking' requirement in the Guidance on the Children Act 1989. But the parent had given permission and smacking was viewed as not constituting a breach of Article 3 of the Convention ('inhuman and degrading punishment').[9] Anyway, as Wilson J observed, in relation to the status of the Guidance, it:

> ...is not intended to be applied so strictly that, if an application for registration is in conflict with part of it, there should automatically be a finding of unfitness.

Under ss (11) a local authority may also refuse registration if the premises to be used for child minding or for day care 'are not fit to be used for looking after children under the age of eight, whether because of their condition, or the condition of any equipment used on the premises or for any reason connected with their situation, construction or size'.

Private foster care

Part 1X, sections 66-70, of the 1989 Act deal with the responsibilities of a local authority in relation to private arrangements for fostering children.[10] Under s 66(1) of the 1989 Act a 'privately fostered child' means a child who is cared for, and provided with accommodation by, someone other than:

> (i) a parent of his;
> (ii) a person who is not a parent of his but who has parental responsibility for him; or
> (iii) a relative of his.

Section 66(1)(b) defines the term 'foster a child privately' somewhat unhelpfully as meaning to 'look after the child in circumstances in which he is a privately fostered child'.

For the purposes of this provision 'a child' means a person under the age of 16 or, if he is disabled, under the age of 18. To meet the definition the child must be cared for and accommodated for a period of at least 28 days. These and the other provisions of Part 1X of the 1989 Act dealing with private arrangements for fostering children are subject to further re-definition under Sched 8 the effect of which is to harden the distinction between domestic and fostering arrangements.

The responsibility for ensuring that the arrangements made do in fact safeguard and promote the welfare of the child concerned rests with the parent.

Under s 67 a local authority is responsible for ensuring that the welfare of any child privately fostered in its area is being 'satisfactorily safeguarded and promoted' and that those providing care are appropriately advised.

In respect of any proposed private fostering arrangement, the persons making the arrangement, making the placement and receiving the child must all serve advance notice of their intentions on the local authority. It must then investigate the suitability of any arrangement prior to placement and is required to carry out inspection visits thereafter. A local authority may stipulate requirements in respect of the number, age and sex of the children who may be privately fostered and it may require special equipment and medication to be available. Further, Sched 7 of the 1989 Act includes private foster parents within its strictures relating to limits on the number of foster children and related complaints procedures.

Children in need: the consensual intervention threshold

The concept of 'children in need' sets the threshold for consensual intervention by a local authority in family affairs on child welfare grounds just as 'significant harm' does in respect of coercive intervention. Eligibility for preventative support services has been tied to the former threshold. Once the threshold criteria are met the welfare principle comes into play. The statutory requirement that local authorities be proactive in seeking out and offering assistance to those in need, without any inference that the latter are at fault for their circumstances, provides a positive legal reference point for the welfare principle's preventative function. The singular legal characteristic of this threshold is that it mandates state intervention before the welfare principle is compromised rather than retrospectively after a child has suffered significant harm.

It is a concept intended to place both an onus on a local authority to be proactive in seeking out such children and a duty to target sufficient resources to maintain them, where practicable, in their families. The legislative intent is that the role of a local authority, in relation to its preventative responsibilities, should be to develop a needs led rather than a demand led approach to service provision. This approach is very much in keeping with that advocated in Article 18 of the UN Convention which emphasises the desirability of state intervention being in the form of partnership with parents so as to enable them to give effect to their parental responsibilities.

'Children in need' are defined under s 17 of the 1989 Act as follows:

> For the purposes of this Part a child shall be taken to be in need if -
> (a) he is unlikely to achieve or maintain, or to have the opportunity of achieving or maintaining, a reasonable standard of health or development without the provision for him of services by a local authority under this Part'
> (b) his health or development is likely to be significantly impaired, or further impaired, without the provision for him of such services; or
> (c) he is disabled,
> and 'family' in relation to such a child, includes any person who has parental responsibility for the child and any other person with whom he has been living.

This provision reflects a legislative intent to incorporate a number of not wholly compatible objectives. For example, a primary objective would seem to be to place inclusive service responsibilities on a local authority; so certain categories of need are 'defined in'. At the same time it is apparent that there is a wish to avoid granting reciprocal service entitlement rights to those who may meet this definition; so there is a lack of specificity in defining eligibility criteria. The provision specifies three different categories of 'children in need'.

Firstly, there are those children who are 'unlikely to achieve or maintain ....a reasonable standard of health or development' etc. Under s 31(9) of the 1989 Act 'health' is to be interpreted as meaning 'physical or mental health' and 'development' as 'physical, intellectual, emotional, social or behavioural development'. The significance of the word 'unlikely' is that it clearly imports a requirement that a local authority acts in a preventative fashion to forestall the prospect of a child becoming a 'child in need'. The legislative intent is to prompt local authorities to correct the approach they had previously adopted towards their preventative and protective duties. In order to redress the balance struck in favour of resource investment for the latter at the expense of the former (on the grounds that in the long-run this may prove to be a more cost effective form of intervention) a firm duty is now placed on local authorities to ensure the early identification of children in need, including the disabled and, by providing services appropriate to their health and development, promote the upbringing of such children by their families. Experience indicates that this provision is being interpreted as a licence to lower the 'significant harm' threshold, thus allowing agency resources to be targeted at those already within the ambit of coercive intervention, rather than as an obligation to prevent private vulnerable parenting arrangements from becoming matters of public concern.[11] As Dingwall has observed, there is a tendency towards 'diagnostic inflation' in child protection cases in order to access resources.[12]

Secondly, the provision identifies those children whose 'health or development is likely to be significantly impaired' etc. Again the 'likelihood' factor implies that a duty rests on local authorities to invest resources in a preventative strategy. However, the degree of risk necessary to constitute a likelihood and the extent to which an 'impairment' may need to deteriorate before this becomes 'significant' are both open to question. It may be that a local authority could offer a good defence for not investing preventative resources by claiming that its interpretation of a situation did not lead it to believe that, relative to other situations already within its child protection remit, the level of risk or the significance of probable impairment warranted a diverting of funds.

The third category of children identified by the provision as being in need are the 'disabled'. Under s 17(11) of the 1989 Act 'disabled' means 'blind, deaf or dumb or suffering from mental disorder of any kind or is substantially or permanently handicapped by illness, injury or congenital deformity or such other disability as may be prescribed'. The inclusion of children who are disabled within the general definition of children in need is an important landmark in the development of the law relating to children. It reflects an acceptance of the principle that for children a recognition of what they share in common by virtue of their childhood is of greater importance than that which may, for whatever reason, separate them.[13] Legislating specifically for the difference between 'normal' and disabled children, and then between disabled children on the basis of disability type, is now seen as an inappropriate form of discrimination which can be associated with a degree of stigma and is unacceptable in a modern pluralist culture. However, differentiating between children on the basis of the gravity of their needs within the same legislation is seen as acceptable. To that extent this provision does positively discriminate in favour of children in need.

Identification of children in need

Sched 2 of the 1989 Act requires that every authority shall take reasonable steps to identify the extent to which there are children in need within the authority's area. A local authority is empowered to assess the needs of any child appearing to be a 'child in need' at the same as any assessment is being made under any other statutory provision. The requirement 'shall take reasonable steps' emphasises the obligation on the local authorities to be proactive rather than reactive in the delivery of its preventative services.

Children in need: the duties of a local authority

The service provision duties of a local authority in respect of vulnerable children are restricted to those whose circumstances bring them within the definition of 'children in need'. Intervention, whether consensual or coercive, is now statutorily authorised only in respect of prescribed welfare thresholds.

Once authorised, intervention places both general and particular duties on local authorities.

General duties

These are stated in s 17 of the 1989 Act as follows:

> (1) It shall be the general duty of every local authority (in addition to the other duties placed on them by this Part) -
>
> (a) to safeguard and promote the welfare of children within their area who are in need; and
>
> (b) so far as is consistent with that duty, to promote the upbringing of such children by their families,
>
> by providing a range and level of services appropriate to those children's needs.

The use of the word 'general' is intended to indicate that the duty on a local authority is to plan and deliver services broadly appropriate to the needs which vulnerable children as a group would have in common. Its effect is to statutorily over-rule the decision in *AG (ex rel Tiley) v London Borough of Wandsworth*[14] which determined that a local authority would be expected to anticipate the consequences of its actions for the welfare of a particular child. In that case the agency was held to be liable to a claimant who, having met the agency specified eligibility criteria, had nonetheless been denied the corresponding service.

The first such duty is towards children in need but a 'child in need' may also be a 'child at risk of significant harm'. Such an overlap of thresholds may occur in situations where it comes to the attention of a local authority that a child particularly susceptible to harm (perhaps due to 'special needs') is exposed to a level of stress which, though insufficient to require protection for an 'average' child, carries a significant level of risk for that child. An assessment by a local authority social worker, of a breakdown in parenting arrangements occurring in a public or private context, may reveal no statutory duty of coercive intervention but may alert the local authority to the presence of a particularly vulnerable child for whom the 'family' require support services.

The second general duty is to promote upbringing within families. 'Family', as defined in s 17, includes any person with whom the child has been living, whether or not a relative. It will not extend to include a person - relative or friend - no matter how close the relationship, unless the child has in fact also been living with them. This very wide definition will apply to situations where direct care responsibility for a child has been borne for some time by a carer such as a neighbour, foster parent or by a relative such as a grandparent. Any service which serves to safeguard and promote the welfare of a child may be provided to the 'family' as a whole or to any member of it.

The third of the general duties is to provide a range and level of appropriate services. It is a duty to which it is the collective responsibility of the constituent parts of a local authority to respond; because any or all of its services may be required, a multi-disciplinary team approach is required. This is also likely to have important consequences for entitlement in other areas i.e. success or failure in meeting the terms of the definition will trigger an entitlement to all or none of the spectrum of such related public services as housing, phones and benefits. Under s 27 of the 1989 Act a number of agencies are directed to co-operate with a local authority requesting assistance for any child in need:

> (2) An authority whose help is so requested shall comply with the request if it is compatible with their own statutory or other duties and obligations and does not unduly prejudice the discharge of any of any of their functions.
>
> (3) The authorities are -
>
> (a) any local authority;
>
> (b) any local education;
>
> (c) any local housing authority;
>
> (d) any health authority or National Health Service trust; and
>
> (e) any person authorised by the Secretary of State for the purposes of this section.

For these reasons full implementation of the 1989 Act will only be successful if it is accompanied by a local authority child care policy and strategy which sets a priority on the management of integrated teams of health and social service professionals accompanied by systems for co-ordinating its service provision with that of such other public service agencies as those listed above.

Particular duties

The 1989 Act imposes nine separate and particular specific preventative duties upon a local authority. But these are mostly permissive, only a few are mandatory. The prescriptive directives are those with a more marginal bearing on welfare such as the strict duty to publish information. Of considerable significance to the modern role of the welfare principle is the legislative definition of 'family' and therefore the range of persons whom a local authority should consider when assessing possible service provision to children in need. This public law recognition of persons bearing direct care responsibilities for a child, regardless of whether or not that person is related in any way to the child, as being thereby entitled to local authority assistance, greatly widens the potential of the welfare principle to consolidate the *status quo* care arrangements of children in circumstances which may be far removed from the marital nuclear family which traditionally qualified for state protection.

The first preventative duty is to provide assistance. This may be provided as a cash grant, a loan or as a grant of 'necessities' and may be subject to such conditions as a local authority shall see fit to make. Further, as outlined in Sched 2 of the 1989 Act, more specific assistance may be offered.

Secondly, under Sched 2(9) a local authority has a duty to provide such family centres as it considers appropriate within its area for a child, parents of that child, person with parental responsibilities or who may be caring for that child. The facilities offered by such a family centre should include: occupational, social, cultural or recreational activities; advice, guidance or counselling or; accommodation while receiving advice, guidance or counselling. In relation to disabled children, Sched 2 requires a local authority to provide services to minimise the effects of their disabilities and opportunities to lead as normal lives as possible.

Thirdly, a local authority is now statutorily obliged to take steps to avert the necessity for coercive intervention in family care arrangements. The directive in s 17(1)(b) that a local authority should seek to 'promote the upbringing of such children by their families' is an important statement of principle which serves to reinforce the 'no-order' presumption embodied in s 1(5). It is further addressed by a directive in Sched 2(6) requiring every local authority to 'take reasonable steps' to reduce the need to bring proceedings in respect of children, encourage them not to commit criminal offences and avoid the need to place them in secure accommodation.[15]

Fourthly, the preventative duties of a local authority are specifically addressed by Sched 2 which requires that:

> (1) Every local authority shall take reasonable steps, through the provision of services under Part 111, to prevent children within their area suffering ill-treatment or neglect.

A duty is also placed, under Sched 2(4), on any local authority, which believes that a child within its area but living or proposing to live elsewhere, is likely to suffer harm, to notify the relevant local authority accordingly.

Fifthly, a local authority must certain provision to enable children to remain at home. Sched 2(9) places a duty on a local authority to provide the following services, as appropriate, in respect of children in need who are living with their families:

> (a) advice, guidance and counselling;
> (b) occupational, social, cultural or recreational activities;
> (c) home help (which may include laundry facilities);
> (d) facilities for, or assistance with, travelling to and from home for the purpose of taking advantage of any other service provided under this Order or of any similar service;
> (e) assistance to enable the child concerned and his family to have a holiday.

This is the first explicit legislative statement of the services considered appropriate to the role of a local authority in the context of consensual intervention. It indicates the extent of public investment which is now considered reasonable in order to reinforce the coping capacity of vulnerable families.

Sixthly, where a child in need is not living with his or her family and is being accommodated but not being looked after by a local authority, then the latter is required under Sched 2(11) to take such steps as are reasonably practicable to enable the child to live with that family or promote contact between them if, in the opinion of the local authority, this is necessary to safeguard or promote the child's welfare.

Seventhly, alternative accommodation may be provided for any member of a household posing a risk to a child in that household. Sched 2(5) of the 1989 Act gives a local authority a discretionary power to provide financial assistance to enable a person who may be causing a child to suffer, or who may do so in the future, to find alternative accommodation away from that child. This provision acknowledges the long-standing sense of grievance attached to the practice whereby, in order to afford future protection to a child at risk of abuse from a member of the household, the child was removed from the home. The fact that this is a discretionary responsibility and is not linked to a local authority power to apply for an exclusion order in respect of such a suspected abuser has attracted criticism.

Eighthly, under Sched 2(6) of the 1989 Act, every local authority is required to publish information about the support services it has a duty to provide for children in need and their families. It is also permitted to do so in respect of such services provided by other agencies, particularly by voluntary organisations, which it has a power to provide. Every local authority is specifically directed to 'take such steps as are reasonably practicable to ensure that those who might benefit from the services receive the information relevant to them'.

Finally, under Sched 2(11) every local authority in making arrangements for day care or for the recruitment of foster parents shall: 'have regard to the different racial groups to which children within the local authority's area who are in need belong'.

Liability for non-provision of services

The local authority's plea of insufficient finance in *AG (ex rel Tiley) v London Borough of Wandsworth* was found to be an inadequate defence to the charge that it had failed to meet the claimant's statutory entitlement to support services. In the intervening years caselaw demonstrates a steady judicial retreat from this position.[16] In *R v Cambridge District Health Authority ex parte B (No 2)*,[17] the Court of Appeal acknowledged that the court was not empowered to review the basis upon which a local authority elected to use its resources; the latter was entitled to prioritise the services it was prepared to fund as it saw fit. Nor does the court have any power to direct a local authority to recognise a child as being in need within the definition of s 17 for the purposes of ensuring a service entitlement.[18]

Children in need: specific support services

The linking of welfare to a range of specified family support services is another indicator of the positive legislative influence on the modern role of the welfare principle. This objectification of incidences of welfare, allowing them to become a listing of duties owed to children, also has a negative history dating back at least to the mid-nineteenth century criminal law of child cruelty and neglect. In respect of most services listed in the body or schedules of the 1989 Act, a claimant may clear the first hurdle by satisfying the threshold criteria only to fall at the second when their claims are nullified by a local authority's considered decision not to exercise a discretionary duty in favour of that claimant. The two main sets of specific support services relate to day care and accommodation.

Day care

This type of support service is defined by s 18(4) of the 1989 Act as:

> ...any form of care or supervised activity provided for children during the day (whether or not it is provided on a regular basis).

In this context 'supervised activity' 'means an activity supervised by a responsible person'. A local authority's basic preventative strategy will rest on the range of services it has available to help and support those children in need resident in its area and their families. Most usually this involves providing direct financial assistance, or it may involve a local authority paying for places with childminders, playgroups or family centres.

In relation to pre-school children, s 18 places on a local authority: a strict duty to provide appropriate day care for children in need within their area who are under the age of five and not at school; but only a power to provide day care for other children of that age who are not in need. In relation to school aged children the duty similarly placed is to provide day care outside school hours and during school holidays for those in need and attending school while it may also do so for those who are attending school but are not in need. A local authority is required to have regard to any local day care services provided by the appropriate local education authority or other body or person when exercising its functions under this provision. A local authority is empowered to provide such facilities as training, advice, guidance and counselling for persons caring or accompanying children in day care settings.

Section 19 makes elaborate provision for reviews and review procedures in relation to day care services. These must include registered child-minding services and other day care services provided by registered persons. Every local authority must conduct a comprehensive review of day care services provided in its area in respect of children under the age of eight. The review should take account of services provided in schools, hospitals and in other such establishments which are exempt from the registration requirements; the local authorities are themselves exempted from registration requirements. It should be conducted in conjunction with the appropriate local education authority or other body at three year intervals. The results of each review, including information about any proposals affecting the day care services, must then be published as soon as is reasonably practicable.

Accommodation

The new provisions relating to accommodation restore the initial basis of the voluntary admission to care service. These remove the long-standing iniquity whereby a parent having voluntarily placed their child in local authority care, on what they believed would be a short-term basis, found their efforts to retrieve the child blocked by a local authority resolution which had divested the parent of all relevant rights and vested these instead in the local authority (subject to routine court endorsement). Very many children, placed voluntarily in care by their parents, were subsequently placed for adoption by local authorities. This change is one of the most tangible expressions of the new partnership between parents and a local authority and one with considerable potential for the welfare principle.

The duty now placed on a local authority, as stated in s 20 of the 1989 Act, is that:

> (1) Every local authority shall provide accommodation for any child in need within their area who appears to them to require accommodation as a result of -
>
> (a) there being no person who has parental responsibility for him;
> (b) his being lost or having been abandoned; or
> (c) the person who has been caring for him being prevented (whether or not permanently, and for whatever reason) from providing him with suitable accommodation or care.

Further:

> (3) Every local authority shall provide accommodation for any child in need within their area who has reached the age of sixteen and whose welfare the

authority consider is likely to be seriously prejudiced if they do not provide him with accommodation.

Because this duty rests so unequivocally on the voluntary consent of all parties an objection from a parent or from someone with parental responsibility will relieve a local authority of its obligation to provide accommodation. A discretionary power exists under s 20(5) enabling a local authority to provide accommodation for a person between the ages of 16 and 21 where it considers that to do so would safeguard or promote his or her welfare. The general duty of a local authority to co-ordinate its activities in respect of children in need with those of other statutory and voluntary agencies finds specific expression in s 27. Among the agencies required to lend their co-operation to a local authority is any local housing authority.

The legislative intent in s 21(1)(c) and (3) is clearly to grant a right to homeless young persons (at least to those aged 16-18) to claim accommodation from their local authority. A corresponding duty is placed jointly on that local authority and the local housing authority to make such provision. The indications (from Char, the national charity for the homeless and from New Horizon, the oldest such charity in the UK) are that this provision, designed to assist such children in need, is not being fully implemented. This age group is debarred from claiming Income Support. The availability of accommodation to destitute homeless young adolescents unable to claim welfare benefits could be of crucial importance. In theory, such persons now have the right to make their claims against the appropriate local authority which in turn (if convinced that the young persons welfare is likely to be 'seriously prejudiced') will be obliged to act jointly with the local housing authority to meet those claims.[19]

Caselaw[20] has established that a housing authority has no duty to provide accommodation for a homeless family under housing legislation. However, it is clear that such a duty does arise under child care legislation if the application comes not from a family but from a local authority on behalf of that family. In a case where a local authority was faced with a refusal from the local housing authority to its request that accommodation be provided for a family of five children, whose parents had rendered them intermittently homeless, the court held that the refusal to consider the request was wrong. The housing authority must consider the request and must comply with it unless compliance would be incompatible with its own obligations and/or it would unduly prejudice the discharge of any of its functions. It was not enough that the housing body had decided that the request did not meet its own criteria.

Section 21 requires a local authority to receive, and provide accommodation for, children who have been removed or kept away from home under a child assessment order or who have been taken into police protection.

Parents, if they satisfy the above eligibility criteria, are to be provided with relief as of right without any implication that they have been in any way deficient or at fault (evidenced also by the phrase 'for whatever reason') in the execution of their parental duties. The accommodation must now be the subject of a written and signed agreement between the parties. At no time do the parents lose, nor the local authority acquire, any parental responsibilities. The child is not 'in care' and may be removed by the parent/s, or by someone with parental responsibility (under s 20(8)), from local authority accommodation at any time. If the child has reached the age of 16 then, under s 20(11), he or she may not be removed from such accommodation without his or her consent.

The 1989 Act has transformed the role of a local authority in relation to a claimant and the provision of accommodation services. There can now be no question of a local authority assuming parental responsibilities, and possibly initiating freeing proceedings for adoption, in respect of a child voluntarily admitted to its care. Indeed, a local authority no longer has the right to delay yet alone deny a parental request for the immediate return of a child for which it is providing accommodation. However, the requirement in s 22(3)(a) that any authority (e.g. a local authority) when looking after any child (e.g. by the provision of accommodation) should 'safeguard and promote his welfare' may permit a local authority to resist such a parental request until satisfied that compliance would not be in breach of that duty. Alternatively under s 3(5)(b) the local authority, having care but not parental responsibility for the child, would be entitled to 'do what is reasonable in all the circumstances of the case for the purpose of safeguarding or promoting the child's welfare'. If all else fails a local authority could always call upon the police to exercise their powers under s 46(1)(b) to prevent the removal of an accommodated child in circumstances where there is reasonable cause for a constable to believe that such a removal would be likely to expose the child to significant harm.

Section 20 also makes some stipulations regarding the position of the child to be accommodated. In particular:

> (4) A local authority may provide accommodation for any child within their area (even though a person who has parental responsibility for him is able to provide him with accommodation) if the authority considers that to do so would safeguard or promote the child's welfare.

A local authority is thereby granted maximum discretion to interpret whether, in relation to any particular child, the proposed accommodation would meet the welfare interests of that child. It may have a particular application to private family law circumstances where, for example, either or both parents are so absorbed in mutual acrimony while pursuing divorce proceedings that neither objects to the child's wish to be accommodated elsewhere. Under s 20(6) a duty is placed on a local authority, insofar as is reasonably practicable and consistent with the child's welfare, to ascertain and give due (having regard to his age and understanding) to the latter's providing accommodation. If that child is aged 16 or more ar being accommodated (and this is judged to be necessary on welfare grou or to being discharged from accommodation, then a local authority is obliged to give effect to that consent regardless of any opposition from a parent or from elsewhere. The legal situation now has, if anything, firmed since the decision in *Krishnan v Sutton London Borough Council*[21] when the court refused to discharge a child against her wishes to the care of her father. The position regarding the ascertained wishes of a child aged under 16 is less certain. Much would depend on the extent to which such a child could be judged to be '*Gillick* competent'. However, given the fact that this provision rests on the consent of all parties, it is unlikely that the wishes of a child under the age of 16 would be allowed to prevail in the face of parental opposition.

Conclusion

Welfare is a relative term. The functions of prevention and promotion in relation to welfare compound the uncertainty. But the fact that they have been given statutory recognition, underpinned by the concept of 'children in need' as a consensual threshold for intervention, is a very significant step forward for the welfare interests of children. Both functions have a definite positive bearing on welfare which is a new departure in child care law. The 1989 Act goes further by linking these functions to specific family support services; as with the 'significant harm' threshold, legislation has narrowed the ground for discretionary interpretation by providing lists of welfare indices.

There are many aspects of the inclusive approach to the threshold of 'children in need' which are to be welcomed as broadening the definition of those whose welfare interests require consensual intervention. Perhaps the most important is the explicit reference to children with a disability as being *per se* in need. But, although couched in terms of duties, a local authority will escape liability for non-provision of the services required to be made available. This is a serious weakness in the statutory approach to the functions of prevention and promotion. The pressures on local authorities to give urgent attention to children whose welfare interests may be critically impaired following a breach of the 'significant harm' threshold will always work to the disadvantage of those who should receive the support necessary to forestall a breach of the 'children in need' threshold. This will only be overcome when local authorities receive considerable additional funds and formalise the inter-disciplinary, multi-agency structures necessary to dedicate resources to prevention and promotion.

Notes

1 See further, Fraser, D., *The Evolution of the British Welfare State*, London, Macmillan, 1973.

2 Article 18

3 Article 27.

4 See also, the Employment Act 1989. Also note Article 7(3) of the European Social Charter which states that "persons who are still subject to compulsory education shall not be employed in such work as would deprive them of the full benefit of their education".

5 See David Utting, *Family and Parenthood: Supporting Families, Preventing Breakdown*, Rowntree Foundation, (1995). This reveals that preventative services continue to be concentrated on parents whose children are on the child protection registers rather than those identified as vulnerable due, for example, to family pressures or material deprivation. There was little evidence that the anticipated partnership between statutory and voluntary agencies had generated any effective strategies for targeting localised preventative services towards vulnerable families.

6 See Vol 2, Family Support, Day Care and Educational Provision for Young Children, DoH, 1991.

7 See *T v Surrey County Council* {1994] 4 All ER 577.

8 See *London Borough of Sutton v Davies* [1994] 1 FLR 737.

9 See also *Costello-Roberts v UK* [1994] ECR1 and *R v Hopley* (1860) 2 F and F 202.

10 Further detail is given in the Children (Private Arrangements for Fostering) Regulations 1991.

11 This is apparent, for example, in Table 3.1 of the annual Children Act Report (1992) which shows that, in the first year of the Children Act, local authorities were directing resources towards families for whom they already had some level of responsibility rather than towards those whose vulnerability was indicated only by difficulties such as rent arrears, disconnected services or school attendance problems.

12 Eekelaar, J., and Dingwall, R., *The Reform of Child Care Law – A Practical Guide to the Children Act 1989*, London, Routledge, 1990.

13 It also reflects the principles embodied in Article 23 of the *United Nations Convention on the Rights of the Child*, (1989).

14 [1981] 1 All ER 1162.

15 See also the local authority preventative duties introduced by the Crime and Disorder Act 1998; discussed in Chap 9.

16 See, for example, *Re C (Family Assistance Order)* [1996] 1 FLR 424 where the court was forced to discharge the order on being informed that the local authority lacked the resources to comply with it.

17 [1995] 1 FLR 1055.

18 See *Re J (Specific Issue Order: Leave to Apply)* [1995] 1 FLR 699.

19 See *R v Northavon DC ex parte Smith* [1993] 2 FLR 897, which seems to continue the rationale of *AG (ex rel Tilley) v Wandsworth London Borough Council* supra, where it was held that it was not possible to set aside a duty to provide for a child and family purely on the basis that they had been found to be intermittently homeless.

20 See the House of Lords decision in *R v Oldham Metropolitan Borough Council ex parte Garlick and Related Appeals* [1993] 2 FLR 194 where the court held that a local

housing authority had no duty to a homeless dependant child under Part 111 of the Housing Act 1985.

21 [1969] 3 All ER 1367.

Part 4: Private Family Law

Introduction to Part 4

The role of welfare differs according to whether the matter at issue is being contested by first parties, between first and third parties or between third parties. Where parents are not involved there is greater scope for welfare to play a prominent role in determining the outcome of private proceedings. However, parents have always been the litigants most frequently bringing such issues before the courts. The core statutory proceedings, constituting this strand from the outset, have been those concerning parental responsibility for, or access to, children following marital breakdown; and actions relating to custody, education, religious upbringing and maintenance following separation. In addition, proceedings for guardianship, wardship and adoption have also formed part of private family law. The use of authority in this context, as provided for by statute and judicially applied, has clearly changed since the proceedings were first introduced; the huge increase in volume of litigants, matched by the ever broadening definition of 'family' and the resulting multiple permutations of private law issues has forced the pace of change. But the fundamental distinguishing characteristics of the use of authority in private family law proceedings have remained relatively intact.

The authority governing the role played by the welfare principle in these proceedings has traditionally been distinguishable from its use in other contexts by a set of typifying characteristics. These have had in common a capacity to offer a flexible and more balanced approach to welfare relative to other considerations. The distinguishing legal hallmarks of private family proceedings, in relation to the welfare principle, may be generally and crudely summarised as: consensual; resting on threshold criteria of permissive grounds; determined by a mixture of mediation, adjudication and adjustment; and disposed of by an exercise of judicial discretion.

Firstly, the proceedings may be characterised as consensual because they commence with the private initiative of one of the parties rather than by the state. At times of marriage breakdown, death of a parent or voluntary relinquishment of a child for adoption, proceedings begin when a parent or guardian invites a court ruling on future care responsibility for a child. The court then exercises its powers within a parental rights framework, in the context of proceedings which involve the welfare interests of a child for whom responsibility will remain vested in a family and most usually with members of the family of origin. This consensual frame of reference for the exercise of judicial powers, where parental parties have the *locus standi* of petitioner and/or respondent rather than as defendants, allows the proceedings to be conducted in an enquiring rather than adversarial manner.

Secondly, the threshold for a judicial hearing in relation to welfare matters in a private family law context rests essentially on permissive grounds. Under each set of proceedings, an applicant is legislatively permitted to invite the court to formally validate an exercise of their rights as spouse, parent or guardian etc. Increasingly, it has become a feature of the grounds in private family law proceedings that they are broadly framed, entitling an applicant to be heard by the court on a matter which may change the status of family member/s without having to first satisfy rigorous criteria of eligibility. Objectively stated grounds such as those requiring proof of fault, have been displaced by grounds such as 'reasonableness' which permit a subjective interpretation. The significance of a public interest in defending the legal integrity of the marital family unit (evident in the long-standing influence of the fault based grounds in matrimonial proceedings) or the permanency of adoption (evident in the non-use of conditions and the secrecy requirements) has greatly diminished. The initial importance attached to formal status in private family law has faded and been replaced by a policy of facilitating autonomous action by family members whose decisions to enter and exit marital and other family relationships should encounter the minimum of legal hindrance.

Thirdly, within the constraints of what traditionally has been an adversarial process, the judicial role in private family law proceedings has gradually developed an approach which now rests more on mediation and adjustment of the parties legal interests than an adjudication on the respective rights of the parties in relation to the presenting issues. The 'win-or-lose' approach to determining issues, particularly evident in matrimonial proceedings, has given way to compromise. In this context, several developments have occurred in relation to the resolution of issues affecting the welfare interests of a child. Identifying such interests, in relation to the particular circumstances of each individual child, has now acquired a higher priority and the court may be advised by a number of professionals making representations about or on behalf of a child. The court is more likely than formerly to hear directly from a child their views on matters believed to constitute their welfare interests. When such interests arise for judicial consideration, or where they are in conflict with the legal interests of other parties, the judiciary are now required to accord them a paramount weighting.

Fourthly and finally, judicial determination in private family law proceedings will now be primarily characterised by exercises of discretion rather than the simple fixed choice between order, no order, or set package of orders that typified earlier determinations. In keeping with the trend towards compromise, the preferred judicial disposal option will be one which achieves a balance between the legal interests of the adult parties while affording optimal recognition and protection for the welfare interests of a child. Judicial discretion and flexibility, rather than adjudication, will be employed to adjust the respective legal interests of the parties and provide the most suitable and secure care arrangements for the child or children concerned.

12 Parenting Arrangements: Uncontested Proceedings

Introduction

Uncontested proceedings, initiated by a parent/parents or a substitute, involving decisions which determine the future care arrangements for a child or children, have been largely re-absorbed into private family law. Recent years have witnessed state withdrawal across a broad front of such proceedings. Where previously child welfare would have been submitted to judicial scrutiny, usually supplemented by that of other professionals, this is now a rare occurrence. The legal presumption is that the responsibility for ensuring future care arrangements for children satisfy their welfare interests is a private matter for parents. A presumption rebutted by notice that proceedings will be contested.

This chapter examines those proceedings which involve parental decisions to make, break, suspend or significantly alter the legal ties of family membership. The focus is on the law relating to the decisions taken when the proceedings are uncontested and where the future care arrangements for a child are determined. It considers the legal rules which then come into play in respect of the welfare interests of such a child.

The child

The definition of 'child' in the 1989 Act is restricted to mean a person below the age of 16 years for the purposes of making a s 8 order,[1] below 17 when making a care or supervision order[2] and is otherwise to mean a person below the age of 18 years. A child will be a 'child of the family' when in the care of a person who has parental responsibility for him or in the care of any other person with whom he has been living[3] and, for the purposes of any proceedings, is the child who is the subject of those proceedings.[4]

A child may, in private law proceedings and with leave of the court, acquire full party status. The Family Proceedings Rules make provision for a solicitor to provide representation in private proceedings. The child concerned may independently initiate some proceedings (e.g. for a residence order) and his or her wishes may in others (e.g. where an adoption order is made subject to a contact condition) have a determining effect on any decision regarding their welfare. The role a child plays in proceedings is dependent upon a 'competence test' (see, Chap 6).

In recent years the courts have had to adjudicate on the separateness of the interests of parents and children where the latter have been either too young to express any views or are insufficiently mature to have their legal competence recognised when doing so.

The significance of the landmark decision by the House of Lords in *Re D (A Minor)*, in terms of the light it sheds on judicial rationale for distinguishing between the welfare of the child and the legal interests of the mother, is difficult to judge. It may, perhaps, be seen as a logical extension of the judicial view that the younger the child the more fused are mother/child interests; the greater, therefore, is the maternal obligation to safeguard her own well-being as only by doing so will her child's interests be protected. This interpretation would seem to have been reinforced by the more recent decision of the House in *Attorney-General's Reference (No 3 of 1994)*[5] where a cohabitee was found guilty of manslaughter when the child, which he had wounded while it was a foetus in the womb, died some months after its birth. In its judgment the House referred to mother and foetus as 'two distinct organisms living symbiotically' which expresses the high degree of interdependence that the courts have customarily held to be characteristic of the maternal bond.

In relation to adolescents, the two landmark decisions which have done most to shape the modern role of the child in proceedings affecting his or her welfare are *J v C*[6] and *Gillick v West Norfolk and Wisbech Area Health Authority*[7] The first firmly established that a child's welfare must be judicially treated as the factor of paramount importance in any case affecting the care, custody or upbringing of that child. The second held that the decision of a 'mature minor' could prevail over the contrary views of a parent and be binding on a third party (see, also, Chap 4). It is significant, however, that English statute law continues not to give a child of any age the right to be consulted by his or her parents in relation to decisions taken by the latter which may affect his or her welfare interests. In the context of uncontested proceedings, the absence of such a right may place a child who is unhappy about the agreed arrangements in the position of having to contest them in order to have their welfare interests taken into account. This contrasts with legislation in Scotland which imposes a duty on any person exercising parental responsibilities to have regard to the views of the child concerned when making any major decision.[8]

The parent/s

Perhaps the most significant development of the welfare principle in recent years has been its withdrawal from areas of law where it previously played an important role. In a sense the welfare threshold in private family law has been raised to leave a greater range of parenting decisions to parents, or at least to raise the presumption that they will not require judicial scrutiny.

One example of this trend can be seen in the way the Child Support legislation has absorbed the duty of a divorced or separated parent on low income to provide maintenance for his or her child. This circumstance is now catered for by state machinery which calibrates maintenance in accordance with standardised rules and provides uniform methods for its collection and payment rather than it being left to the discretion of parent or court where the role of welfare could, and often did, lead to wide variations in levels of payment. In effect this system has provided statutorily benchmarked standards for the payment of maintenance which are recognised as welfare-proofed levels for the guidance of all parents.

Another example is the resurgence of judicial interest in the 'blood tie' as the rationale for preferring first party to third party care arrangements for a child. The presumption in the 1989 Act, that the welfare of a child is best furthered by care within his or her family of origin, is deeply rooted in family law and has now come to acquire broad acceptance as a benchmark for giving effect to the welfare principle. As Waite J stated in *Re W (A Minor)(Residence Order)*:[9]

> ...the welfare of the child is indeed the test, but there is a strong supposition, other things being equal, that it is in the interests of the child to be brought up by his natural parents (p 639).

This reliance on the blood-tie as the welfare rationale for removing a child from third party carers and returning him or her to their natural parents is also very evident in cases such as in *Re B (Adoption: Child's Welfare)*[10] and *Re M (Child's Upbringing)*.[11]

Again, an example of the state leaving welfare matters to parents can be seen in its avoidance of a legislative initiative to eliminate the common law right of a parent to chastise their child by administering reasonable corporal punishment. This was left untouched by the 1989 Act and continues to be as stated in earlier legislation:[12]

> Nothing in this section shall be construed as affecting the right of any parent, teacher, or other person having the lawful control or charge of a child or young person to administer punishment to him.

The continuance of this right was demonstrated in a case[13] where a registered child-minder, authorised by the mother, smacked a child and the resulting case caused the DoH to revise its guidelines to advise staff that such authorised chastisement was permissible. Subsequently, the case of *Costello-Roberts v United Kingdom*,[14] where a seven year old was chastised by the headmaster of a private school, using a gym shoe, confirmed that parentally authorised corporal punishment in non-state schools was not prohibited.

It may also be argued that the state has in effect withdrawn from the more fundamental issues affecting welfare interests. Whether children are conceived by artificial means and whether they are born rather than aborted are now essentially matters of private choice. A comprehensive genetic counselling service is available to inform such choices. Accessing treatment in circumstances where without it a grievously ill child may die, is also a matter which, as recent cases demonstrate, is a responsibility resting on a parent rather than the court.[15] If a parent fails to give effect to this responsibility by seeking medical advice then he or she may be guilty of criminal neglect, but having received that advice it will remain a private matter between parent and professional as to whether the treatment is provided; unless either party chooses to involve the court. Needless to say, the court can only take decisions where proceedings have been instigated. These will be lodged by parent, child, person or body with parental responsibility or a professional and be grounded on evidence that the decision of one of them, on a matter affecting the upbringing of the child, is invalid because it is not in the child's best interests. Most usually the parties are parents and medical practitioners, the issue is whether or not vital treatment is to be available to a child and the decision is one which the medical practitioners want the court to make. It would seem that such cases, invariably involving very difficult and painful choices, are being brought before the court with increasing frequency. This should not, however, obscure the fact that the vast majority of decision-making in this area does not reach the court. Only where the child involved suffers from a severe learning disability, and invasive treatment is being proposed, is there a requirement that court authorisation be sought. Otherwise, life and death treatment decisions affecting foetuses, neonates, newly borns with complex health problems and seriously ill children are constantly being taken, jointly and privately by parents and medical staff. Decisions to prescribe palliative care only seldom come before the courts. Where there is no disagreement about treatment and welfare interests the decisions remain private and confidential. The question has to be raised as to whether this should be so. Should a decision, manifestly crucial to a child's welfare interests, only warrant court attention when decision-makers disagree? Given the accompanying context of shock, trauma, distress and exhaustion within which parents have to take such decisions are they always the best decisions that can be taken – just because they accord with medical opinion? If professional independent representation is seen as necessary for children in 'care' cases and possible in 'custody' cases should it not also be available in 'life or death' treatment cases? The possibility of guardians *ad litem* in paediatric units is perhaps far fetched, but there is a case to be made for 'the child's voice to be heard' through the provision of independent representation in all life or death treatment decisions affecting children, whether or not parents and medical staff are in agreement (see, further, Chap 13).

The general health, treatment and religious upbringing of children, at least until adolesence, are entrusted to parental care. The compulsory requirement to ensure the education of children, to a standard and an age set by statute, falls on parent rather than child; considerable discretion being left to parents to chose how best to give effect to this duty.

Welfare still functions as a discretionary power but it is now to be exercised more by parent than court. The law would seem to be set on confining the function of welfare and making it more a matter for administration than adjudication. Rights, on the other hand, are matters for the court and proceedings are perhaps being gradually re-drawn around a welfare/rights fault-line. Rights, however, are actionable at the initiative of the individual affected, which may leave children who do not have the information, maturity or resources necessary to assert them, more vulnerable than under the paternalistic but protectionist ethos of welfare.

Blood-tests

Traditionally the importance of conducting blood tests to determine a child's paternity was two-fold. Firstly, it provided the means whereby the status of the child as legitimate or illegitimate could be ascertained. Secondly, it provided the evidence for holding a putative father liable for the maintenance of his child. Neither are now important. An application for court leave for blood tests to be undertaken is currently most likely to arise in the context of contact proceedings initiated by a man claiming paternity; a claim denied by the child's mother. In responding to the application, or in deciding to act of its own motion, the court will apply the welfare test only insofar as it is presumed to be in the best interests of the child concerned that the truth regarding paternity is clearly established; welfare is not the paramount consideration. Where it appears that this information would be unlikely to affect existing care arrangements, or may adversely affect them, then the court will be more inclined to take the view that the test is not justified.[16] Where it decides that the test is in the child's best interests but parental co-operation is not forthcoming, the court may then order the child to be delivered to the Official Solicitor to ensure that the test is conducted.[17]

Proceedings

In uncontested proceedings for guardianship or divorce or nullity or judicial separation, and in a number of circumstances in which adults may carry immediate care responsibility, decisions will be taken regarding the welfare interests of any child involved. The principles, decision-makers and bearers of parental responsibility will then determine the welfare of the child. The discretionary judicial power to re-define a private law issue regarding future care arrangements for a child, whether arising in a consensual or contested application, as a matter for coercive public law intervention has been removed. The 1989 Act replaced the judicial power to make an order, in the course of matrimonial and other private law proceedings, committing a child into the care or supervision of a local authority with a power under s 37 to request a local authority to carry out an investigation of such a child's home circumstances. It also introduced a new judicial option by providing a power under s 16 to make a family assistance order, requiring a local authority to provide short-term support to a family.

The most important principle introduced by the 1989 Act is that when determining any issue affecting the upbringing of a child the court must, as stated in s 1(1), regard the welfare of that child as the paramount consideration. There is no requirement that the welfare checklist, as stated in s 1(3), be considered in any uncontested private family law proceedings. So, for example, in an uncontested adoption application the court is not obliged to refer to the checklist and therefore is not under a duty to consider alternative orders.

Parental responsibility

The 1989 Act has replaced the concepts of 'parental rights' and 'parental duties', which for centuries have formed the basic constructs of family law in the UK, with the composite term 'parental responsibilities'. This is defined in the Act as follows:

> (1) In this Act 'parental responsibility' means all the rights, duties, powers, responsibilities and authority which by law a parent of a child has in relation to the child and his property.

The change signalled a profound difference of approach from a proprietal frame of reference to one implying that parental use of authority is valid only if employed for the benefit of the child. It also suggests that such responsibilities are exclusively an attribute of parenthood which may be temporarily met by other persons or bodies but can never be wholly shed by a 'parent' to whom, by definition, they must continue to attach. An unmarried father, however, is not *per se* a 'parent' for the purposes of the above provision. Arguably, this withholding of parental status unfairly differentiates between marital and non-marital children; the latter's welfare interests being compromised by the non-entitlement to automatic inclusion in a fully legally constituted two-parent family.

Broadly speaking, "the effect of having parental responsibility is to empower a person to take most decisions in the child's life.[18] The responsibilities of a parent may be held by someone other than the parent of the child concerned and more than one person may hold such responsibility in respect of the same child at the same time. The role of this legal construct 'parental responsibilities' has the effect of clarifying who is entitled to take what decisions in respect of a child's welfare interests at any point in time. One clearly discernible legislative intent underpinning the 1989 Act is to leave such decisions with the bearers of parental responsibility and to minimise intervention, whether by local authority or court, in private family law matters.

Another clear legislative intent was to introduce discretionary judicial options enabling the most appropriate order or combination of orders to be made as indicated by the particular needs of a child rather than as determined by the nature of the proceedings instigated by a parental applicant. The availability of s 8 orders under the 1989 Act, together with the supplementary powers to attach conditions, directions, time frames etc, have introduced a capacity for considerable judicial discretion to be exercised in private family law proceedings. Because the need to use such flexibility generally arises in contested proceedings, they are considered more fully in the following chapter (see, Chap 13).

The parental responsibility order

This provides the means whereby an unmarried father, who is unable or unwilling to acquire parental responsibility for his child by making a voluntary agreement with the mother, may be vested with such responsibility by the court. As is explained by s 4 of the 1989 Act:

> (1) Where a child's father and mother were not married to each other at the time of his birth -
>
> (a) the court may, on the application of the father, order that he shall have parental responsibility for the child.

The making of an order is clearly a matter of judicial discretion to be exercised according to the welfare interests of the child concerned. The order vests parental responsibility in the bearer; though not necessarily to the exclusion of others. It lasts until terminated by the court on the application of any person with parental responsibility for the child or, with the leave of the court, the application of the child concerned (see, also, Chap 4). The court has decided[19] that where the following tests are satisfied then it would *prima facie* be in the child's best interests for a parental responsibility order to be made: (a) the degree of commitment which the father had shown to the child; (b) the degree of attachment which existed between them; and (c) the reasons of the father for applying for the order.[20] Where a father has been previously convicted of violence against the mother and of cruel behaviour towards the child[21] or where he is in prison and there is little evidence of attachment[22] then the court will refuse his application for this order.

Guardianship

Guardianship has its origins at the heart of private family law. A guardianship appointment is most likely to be uncontested and, whether made by parent or court, confers a *de jure* duty of care on a named adult in respect of a specific child. This distinguishes it from a number of other *de facto* care relationships (see, 'carers' below). Such *de facto* arrangements can leave the responsibility for safeguarding the welfare interests of a child in some uncertainty. A problem addressed first by the Law Commission[23] and then by the Children Act 1989.

The law of guardianship is now wholly governed by sections 5 and 6 of the 1989 Act. A guardian may be appointed by the court or by a parent. A court appointment may be made under s 5(10) where:

> (a) the child has no parent with parental responsibility for him; or
> (b) a residence order has been made with respect to the child in favour of a parent or guardian of his who has died while the order was in force.

The court may make such an appointment either on application or of its own motion in any family proceedings.
A parent appointment may be made under under s 5(3):

> A parent who has parental responsibility for his child may appoint another individual to be the child's guardian in the event of his death.

The provision requires the appointment to be made by will or deed or by means of some other such properly attested legal document i.e. no special document is needed.

Guardianship has now been statutorily assimilated, along with wardship, into that category formally defined in the Children Act 1989 as 'family proceedings' (for all practical purposes). It now shares with other such proceedings some specific characteristics in relation to welfare. For example, the criteria governing appointment are statutorily prescribed, the common welfare threshold of the paramountcy principle determines any change in the child's status in relation to the applicant and if granted the order vests parental responsibility in the applicant.

To be appointed guardian, whether by parent or court, is to be vested with full parental responsibility for the child. Just like a parent, the guardian must ensure that the child's welfare interests are catered for by providing adequate food, clothing, medical aid and lodging and by making appropriate arrangements for the child's education and religious upbringing. The role of the guardian is to 'stand in the shoes of the parent' and undertake responsibilities for the child to the extent and in the manner that the parent would have done. Therefore, under s 3(1) of the 1989 Act, the guardian assumes the role of the parent in relation to "all the rights, duties, powers, responsibilities and authority which by law a parent of a child has in relation to the child and his property". Like a parent, a guardian will be liable to criminal charges for any neglect, ill-treatment or failure to educate the child. Again, like a parent, if parental responsibility is shared between a number of guardians, or between a parent and a guardian, then each has an equal and independent right of action and right of access to the court to resolve disputes. In a sense, guardianship is unique in that it does not divest a parent of authority but rather it is a trust relationship which empowers an appointed person to act for the parent.

However, there are limits on the extent to which a guardian 'stands in the shoes of the parent'. A guardian is not expected to shoulder the full private family law responsibilities of a parent. The public sector provides a 'guardianship allowance' to defray maintenance expenses and special provision is also made in the Child Support Act 1991 for guardians. Nor is he permitted to benefit from his appointment by, for example, inheriting the property of the child in the event of the latter pre-deceasing him. A guardian has no rights of succession. Nor will the appointment have the effect of conferring on the child the citizenship of the guardian. Among the attributes of parental authority which vest in a guardian, but not in the holder of a residence order, are the right to consent or withhold consent to adoption and the right to appoint a testamentary guardian.

Where the parents are divorced and the one with care and possession of the children wishes to ensure that in the event of his or her death the other does not remove them, then a guardianship appointment could be made in favour of a third party (perhaps the grandparents on that side of the family). This will have the effect of placing the guardians on the same legal footing as the surviving parent who, of course, retains parental responsibility. They will then be able to resist any threatened premptory removal by that parent; at least until the matter is brought before the court. This, in fact, was more or less what occurred in a case[24] where the Court of Appeal, overturning a decision favouring a surviving divorcee, ordered that the children remain with the appointed guardians pending an assessment by a social worker.

Divorce, nullity and judicial separation

Prior to the introduction of the 1989 Act, parties to a marriage breakdown had a general expectation that legal proceedings would conclude with a judicially brokered package including orders in respect of their children (for custody or access). This expectation owed a lot to s 41 of the Matrimonial Causes Act 1973. The court then had a strict duty, before making absolute any decree of nullity or divorce, to be satisfied that the parties proposed arrangements in respect of the future welfare interests of their children were 'satisfactory' or 'the best that could be devised in the circumstances' or that 'it is impractical for the party or parties appearing before the court to make any such arrangements'. Effectively, this gave the judiciary the power and duty to play a very positive role in respect of a child's welfare; the private interests of the parties could only be realised if they first undertook to satisfy a public interest in ensuring the future welfare interests of that child.

However, s 41 was amended by the 1989 Act to remove the mandatory welfare test. With the test has gone the assumption that proceedings need necessarily conclude with judicial orders in respect of any children of the marriage. Its removal has combined with the additional influence of the 'no-order presumption' contained in s 1(5) of the 1989 Act to produce the result that in consensual proceedings, for divorce or nullity or for judicial separation, the court no longer has a strong positive function in relation to welfare. A previous strict duty, central to the 'welfare proofing' of future care arrangements, has been significantly watered down. The link is broken between the private right of parents to obtain an order dissolving the legal basis of their spousal relationship (or settling the terms of their separation) and the duty of the court to ensure that the exercise of that right is compatible with the public interest in adequate care arrangements being made for the future welfare of any children concerned. Instead, two discretionary powers have been introduced, each with a marginal capacity to affect a child's welfare interests: a power under s 37 to request a local authority investigation into a child's circumstances; and a power under s 16 to make a family assistance order.

Where the parents were never married, or if married they choose to separate *de facto* but not *de jure*, then the court will have no opportunity to consider the future welfare of any children involved.

S 8 orders: judicial initiative

The court has a power under s 10(1)(b) of the 1989 Act to intervene and on its own initiative make a s 8 order in 'any family proceedings in which a question arises with respect to the welfare of a child'. In theory this provides a powerful safety net to ensure that private law proceedings are concluded in a manner compatible with the welfare interests of the children involved. However, the opportunity for such intervention is dependant upon information being placed before the court alerting it to the existence of grounds for concern regarding welfare matters. This may not happen.

Even the full formal divorce process offers no guarantee that the court will scrutinise care arrangements for children. Under s 41 of the Matrimonial Causes Act 1973 (as substituted by the Children Act 1989, Sch 12, para 31) the court is still prevented from making absolute a decree of divorce, nullity or separation unless, by order, it declares itself satisfied that: there are no children of the family, or; the arrangements for the welfare of the children that have been made, are satisfactory or are the best that can be made in the circumstances, or; it is impracticable for the party or parties appearing before the court to make any such arrangements for the children. The court will initiate enquiries only where a disclosure of information obviously calls into question the adequacy of proposed arrangements. If the court is able to make a finding of satisfaction it may then issue an order to that effect and need not be concerned about the possible bearing of the provisions available under the 1989 Act. This will follow almost automatically where the proceedings are uncontested.

Because most divorces are uncontested, and proceedings are conducted entirely on the basis of affidavits, the judge will usually only see the plaintiff's 'statement of arrangements for children'. This statement is frequently perfunctory with few details and there is no means whereby the court can check the accuracy of the facts presented therein. Even where the facts give rise to some judicial disquiet in relation to proposed care arrangements, the no-order presumption of s 1(5) will militate against any initiative by the court to exercise its discretionary power under s 10(1)(b) to issue a s 8 order. There will very seldom be any opportunity for the court to hear the views of the children concerned.

The Family Law Act 1996

This situation has been reinforced by the Family Law Act 1996, which by removing the fault grounds for divorce, leaving only the ground of irretrievable breakdown and emphasising the importance of mediation, has ensured that fewer divorce proceedings will be contested.

The 1996 Act introduces very little in the way of change to the role played by the welfare principle in divorce proceedings. Allowance has been made for the welfare interests of any children involved to affect the length of the waiting period. The nine month period which must elapse between the filing of the statement of marital breakdown and the hearing, is compulsorily extended by a further year where divorcing parents have a child below the age of sixteen. This extended period can be waived in circumstances where the court is satisfied that such a delay would be significantly detrimental to the welfare of a child. Where the offer of mediation is accepted or directed by the court, and is being provided under the legal aid scheme, the mediators are required under s 13B(8) of that scheme:

> to have arrangements designed to ensure that the parties are encouraged to consider –
>
> (a) the welfare, wishes and feelings of each child; and
>
> (b) whether and to what extent each child should be given the opportunity to express his or her wishes and feelings in the mediation.[25]

This provision does no more than meet the basic requirements of Article 3 of the European Convention on the Exercise of Children's Rights. When the matter comes before the court and consideration is given to whether the provisions of the 1989 Act need to be utilised, the court is then required, under s 11(4), to have regard to a checklist of factors which includes the child's wishes and feelings, the parties conduct in relation to the upbringing of the child and the general principle that the child's welfare is best served by promoting a good continuing relationship with both parents. These new welfare provisions neither add significantly to the existing law nor are they readily operationalised.

S 8 orders: parental initiative

Before the introduction of the 1989 Act, the parties to marriage breakdown when seeking an order governing the future status of their marital relationship would also petition the court for orders in relation to the future care arrangements for their children. Often the latter were simply requests for a judicial endorsement to confirm care arrangements already privately agreed and these would be routinely granted. Since the 1989 Act, orders relating to children are only granted where there is an actual dispute regarding care arrangements. There is no scope for a parental initiative to obtain a s 8 order in uncontested proceedings; most divorce proceedings are uncontested (see, further, Chap 13).

Carers

In public law, there are now a proliferation of care relationships (baby sitters, child-minders, foster-parents, playgroup organisers, teachers, supervisors in creche and nursery school facilities etc) which are not individually endorsed by a specific grant of authority. In private law, the more complex relationships associated with the modern role of the family in society, particularly those resulting from second and third marriages, have also generated many care relationships (most obviously, step-parents and cohabitees) similarly ill-defined in law.

The introduction of custodianship orders under the Children Act 1975 gave the judiciary access to a statutory means of protecting and providing on-going security for established care relationships. The legal construct 'parental responsibilities', introduced by the 1989 Act, is now central to identifying the rights and duties of carers. As stated in s 2 of the 1989 Act:

> (9) A person who has parental responsibility for a child may not surrender or transfer any part of that responsibility to another but may arrange for some or all of it to be met by one or more persons acting on his behalf.

This provision allows informal arrangements to be made whereby parental responsibility may be shared with another person. The person with care of the child but without full parental responsibility is required, under s 3(5)(b), to do "what is reasonable in all the circumstances of the case for the purpose of safeguarding or promoting the child's welfare". This will include taking decisions such as to remove a child in need of protection to a safe place and to authorise treatment in the event of an accident. The act of delegation will not affect the continuing liability of the delegator for ensuring the safety and well being of the child concerned.

Care by a relative is defined by s 105(1) of the 1989 Act which states that:

> ..."relative" in relation to a child, means a grandparent, brother, sister, uncle or aunt (whether of the full blood or half blood or by affinity), or step-parent.

Arguably, one reason for this definition is to mark a legislative distinction between the *locus standi* of those entitled to be heard by the court on a matter affecting the welfare of a child and those not so entitled; though there are no provisions explicitly to this effect. Unarguably, it serves to place the respective rights of all those mentioned on an equal footing.

In general the courts look more favourably on arrangements which keep responsibility for the care of a child within the family, albeit the extended family, rather than arrangements which require local authority involvement. The 1989 Act, with its statements of principle requiring the courts and local authorities to give preference to family based care and through the s 8 range of orders, enables the judiciary to give new security to carers and child.

Grandparents, in common with all others defined as 'relatives', are entitled to apply for residence and contact orders under the 1989 Act. Where the child has lived with them for a minimum of three years, and they have the consent of anyone with parental responsibility, then the application may be made without leave of the court; leave must, otherwise, be obtained. In private family law proceedings, an application by a grandparent for a residence order will stand a greater chance of success if supported by a natural parent and conversely will be more likely to fail if contested by such a parent. Where the evidence demonstrates that contact would be to the child's best interests, even where the child is in care, then the court will need to be dissuaded from making an order.[26]

A step-parent has long been denied recognition as coming within the legal definition of parent.[27] The fact that such a person lacked legal rights in respect of their spouse's children, despite voluntarily undertaking maintenance and other responsibilities, has often been the subject of judicial concern. However, legislative unease about the use of adoption by a step-parent to acquire with a spouse joint exclusive custodial rights to the latter's children of a previous marriage, has also been apparent. The s 8 orders were created with the circumstances of step-parents very much in mind.

Residence orders are seen as offering an enduring degree of status, protection and security commensurate to the care responsibilities of a step-parent and not necessarily foreclosing a child's relationships with the 'other side of the family'. Where a child is 'a child of the family', as defined by s 105(1) of the 1989 Act, then a step-parent is entitled under s 10(5) without leave to apply for a residence or contact order and with leave to apply for a specific issue or prohibited steps order. The effects of such orders are the same as for any carer.

The position of a child, who is unrelated in any way to a third party into whose care or under whose supervision that child has been placed, has been considerably improved by the 1989 Act. Providers of child minding and day care services, private foster parents and school teachers are now all under a firmer duty than formerly to safeguard the welfare interests of any child in their care.

Conclusion

Family law has always had difficulty in disentangling public and private interests. In recent years the principle of the welfare interests of a child had itself become accepted as a sufficient threshold to warrant public intervention into private family affairs across the broad front of family proceedings. Where parent initiated consensual proceedings alerted the court to the fact that decisions were to be taken, likely to significantly impact upon a child's best interests, then the intervention threshold was crossed by a judicial, if not also a social work, scrutiny of the welfare implications arising from those decisions. The court would require the outcome of a parent's proceedings to be at least compatible with the welfare interests of any child involved. It might even become the decision-maker in respect of any welfare related issues. Ultimately, it could become the arbiter of a child's welfare by directing that he or she be committed into the care of a local authority.

However, the approach to children and their families introduced by the 1989 Act has ended the legislative paradigm that construed welfare and the intervention threshold as synonymous in matrimonial proceedings. Welfare no longer necessarily requires public intervention. Parent initiated, consensual proceedings are now essentially re-privatised and the welfare interests of the children concerned left to be assured by private rather than public scrutiny. The state has not only retreated from this field, it has also reinvested authority in parents to answer for the welfare interests of children whether or not such proceedings are commenced. There is an absence of any legal requirement for a parent to consult with a child before taking a major decision affecting the latter's welfare interests.[28] There is judicial authority for the view that, despite *Gillick*, a parent as well as or instead of their adolescent child may give a valid consent to a course of action by a third party on a matter affecting the child's welfare interests[29] (see, further, Chap 13). The welfare interests of a child are becoming more firmly wrapped up by the legal concept of parental responsibility.

Marriage breakdown is the single most significant factor to affect the welfare interests of children in England and Wales. For most children this occurs without any judicial scrutiny of proposals for their future care. Family law has conceded that the right of a parent to change his or her legal status is not conditional upon first satisfying prescribed welfare criteria. Parental discretion rather than judicial adjudication will determine the consequences of the proceedings for the children concerned. The minimalist residual judicial role is confined to a negative vetting of welfare interests and is in practice now detached from the primary function of the proceedings.

This rolling back of formal public intervention on welfare grounds has been accompanied by a considerable growth in informal types of intervention for the same purpose but now exercised at parental discretion. One manifestation of this is the raft of different types of carer who may be invited by a parent to undertake differing degrees of responsibility in respect of a child. Another is the rapidly growing platform of professionals now in place and offering mediation and conciliation services.

Notes

1 See s 9(6).

2 See s 31(3).

3 See s 17(10). See, *Re A (Child of the Family)* [1998] 1 FLR where a grandchild was held to be a 'child of the family' for the purposes of s 41 of the Matrimonial Causes

Act 1973 in the context of divorce proceedings commenced by grandparents who had cared for the 18 month old child since birth.

4 See *Birmingham City Council v H (No 2)* [1993] 1 FLR 883.

5 [1997] 3 WLR 421.

6 [1970] AC 668, HL.

7 [1986] 1 AC 112, HL.

8 See s 6(1) of the Children (Scotland) Act 1995.

9 [1993] 2 FLR 625.

10 [1995] 1 FLR 895.

11 [1996] 2 FLR 441.

12 See s 1(7) of the Children and Young Persons Act 1933. But note that s 293 of the Education Act 1993 removes the right to administer corporal punishment in state schools.

13 See *Sutton London Borough Council v Davis* [1994] 1 FLR 737.

14 [1994] ELR 1. But see, *A v United Kingdom (Human Rights: Punishment of Child)* [1998] 2 FLR 959 where the European Court of Human Rights held that English law did not provide sufficient protection for the human rights of a nine year old boy who had been beaten with a stick by his stepfather (see, further, Chap 15).

15 See, for example: *Re R v Cambridge District Health Authority, ex parte B* [1995] 1 FLR 1055 and *Re T (Liver Transplant: Consent)* [1997] 1 FLR 502.

16 See, for example: *S v S, W v Official Solicitor* [1970] 3 All ER 107; *Re F (A Minor: Paternity Test)* [1993] 1 FLR 598; *Re G (A Minor)(Blood Test)* [1994] 1 FLR 495; *Re CB (A Minor)(Blood Tests)* [1994] 2 FLR 762; and *Re H (Paternity: Blood Test)* [1996] 2 FLR 65.

17 See *Re R (Blood Test: Constraint)* [1998] 1 FLR 745.

18 See *Introduction to the Children Act 1989*, DoH, (para 2.4).

19 See *Re H (Illegitimate Children: Father: Parental Rights)(No 2)* [1991] 1 FLR 214.

20 This approach was later endorsed by the court in *Re G (A Minor)(Parental Responsibility Order)* [1994] 1 FLR 504.

21 As in *Re T (A Minor)(Parental Responsibility: Contact)* [1993] 2 FLR 450.

22 See *Re P (Parental Responsibility Order)* [1997] 2 FLR No 5.

23 See Law Commission, *Family Law, Review of Child Law: Guardianship*, Working Paper 91, (1985).

24 See *Re H (A Minor)(Custody: Interim Care and Control)* [1991] 2 FLR 109.

25 As inserted by s 27 of the Family Law Act 1996.

26 See *Re F and R (A Minor)(Section 8 Order: Grandparent's Application)* [1995] 1 FLR 524 and *Re M (Care: Contact: Grandmother's Application for Leave)* [1995] 2 FLR 86.

27 See *Re N* [1974] 12 All ER 126.

28 Unlike the situation in Scotland; see, s 6(1) of the Children (Scotland) Act 1995.

29 See, for example: *Re R (A Minor)(Wardship: Medical Treatment)* [1991] 4 All ER 177; *Re W (A Minor)(Medical Treatment)* [1992] 4 All ER 627; *Re K, W and H (Minors)(Medical Treatment)* [1993] 1 FLR 854; *A Metropolitan Borough Council v DB* [1997] 1 FLR 767; *Re C (Detention: Medical Treatment)* [1997] 2 FLR 180.

13 Parenting Arrangements: Contested Proceedings

Introduction

The modern role of the welfare principle is most evident in contested private law proceedings. These are usually brought for judicial determination of an aspect of a child's upbringing, the contesting parties are parents or a parent and a carer of the child concerned and the outcome is the issue of a s 8 order or orders. But private family law in the UK is now a good deal more complex than for previous generations. This is evident in the range of litigation and litigants appearing before the courts. For example, the child may be both applicant and subject in a dispute concerning his or her welfare interests and need not have any blood relationship with the contesting parties. Proceedings regarding where a child is to live may be disputed not by a first party but by a grandparent, step-parent, foster parent or any person with parental responsibility or with an established direct care relationship with the child concerned. The type of issues which attract litigation in a modern and more fluid world (in terms of relationships, careers, homes etc) are no longer concerned almost exclusively with where and with whom a child is to live but extend to include issues regarding names, health care, travel arrangements, variety of relationship contacts etc.

This chapter examines the nature, role and weighting of the welfare principle in contested private family proceedings occurring largely but not exclusively under the aegis of the Children Act 1989.

Principles, parties and proceedings

The role played by the welfare interests of the child is explicitly articulated in certain principles, is apparent in the rules governing the *locus standi* of the parties and has been largely consolidated in contested private proceedings by the 1989 Act.

Principles

The most important principle introduced by the 1989 Act is that when determining any issue affecting the upbringing of a child the court must, as stated in s 1(1), regard the welfare of that child as the paramount consideration. There are other significant duties arising in the context of contested proceedings. The welfare interests of a child are to be ascertained by reference to a stated checklist of considerations. The concept of parental responsibilities rather than parental rights will guide judicial determination of any such contest. No parent is to lose or be wholly absolved of future responsibility for a child, other than by way of a third party adoption. At any time, more than one person may hold parental responsibility in respect of a child. An order shall not be made in respect of a child unless it would be better for the child to make the order than to make no order at all. Any order must be made with the minimum of delay and litigation should be the least required in the circumstances.

Parties

Private family law orders in relation to contested arrangements for children are available under the 1989 Act and may be sought with or without leave of the court or following intercession by the court.

Without leave of the court the following are entitled to apply for any s 8 order under s 10(4) of the 1989 Act:

> (a) any parent or guardian of the child;
> (b) any person in whose favour a residence order is in force with respect to the child.

Then, under s 10(5), there are those who may apply only for a residence or contact order. Such persons are any party to a marriage (whether or not subsisting) in relation to whom the child is a child of the family and any person with whom the child has lived for a period of at least three years. This category also includes those who make application with the consent of a person in whose favour a residence order has been made in respect of the child concerned or the local authority in whose favour a care order has been made in respect of the child concerned. Any and every person who has parental responsibility for such a child will always be so entitled.

Also, an application for a s 8 order with respect to a child may be made by any person, under s 10(2) who:

> (b) has obtained the leave of the court to make the application.

Where the child is the applicant then, under s 10(8), in determining whether or not to grant leave, the court may only do so when satisfied that he or she 'has sufficient understanding to make the application'. This provision has proven to be a powerful legal tool for positively advancing the welfare interests of children.

Where the applicant is a person other than the child concerned then, under s 10(9), the court is required to have particular regard to:

> (a) the nature of the proposed application for the section 8 order;
> (b) the applicant's connection with the child;
> (c) any risk there might be of that proposed application disrupting the child's life to such an extent that he would be harmed by it; and
> (d) where the child is being looked after by a local authority -
> (i) the authority's plans for the child's future; and
> (ii) the wishes and feelings of the child's parents.

That s 10(9) does not present a finite checklist of factors was emphasised in *Re A (A Minor)(Contact: Leave to Apply)*.[1] The court may not, however, apply the paramountcy principle. A s 10(9) applicant must demonstrate a sufficiently strong case to give a reasonable chance of success, if leave is granted.[2]

Section 9(3) prohibits any person who is, or has been within the previous 6 months, a local authority foster parent from applying for any s 8 order unless that person has the consent of the local authority, is a relative of the child in question or the child has lived with him for the immediately preceding three years.

Parties: natural parents

The law clearly differentiates between the *locus standi* of unmarried parents in respect of their child. A natural mother is held to be inherently vested with full parental responsibilities for the child. A natural father will have no parental responsibilities unless he acquires same or they are vested by court order in him. As an ever increasing proportion of annual births occur in a non-marital family context, this disparity between the legal positions of a child's parents is an important factor in any resulting private law dispute between them, or between either of them and a third party, on a matter concerning the upbringing of that child.

The increased importance of the welfare principle in such disputes is particularly evident where the contest lies between first and third parties. It would seem, for example, to be displacing the legal weighting traditionally attached to 'the blood-link'. This is no longer as determinative a factor as formerly in judicial determination of disputes between first and third parties.[3] Indeed, in such disputes, there is some evidence to show that the judiciary will also discount the bearing of legal status; parental responsibilities, whether vested inherently or by court order, will not outweigh the judicial importance attached to the child's welfare interests.[4]

Where the contest lies between first parties then, unless an unmarried father can demonstrate the existence of a relationship bond with his child, the presumption that a mother with care should continue in that role will be very difficult to refute. As the House of Lords have advised, there is a particular onus on an unmarried father to show that an order made in his favour would bring benefits to the child concerned.[5]

Child of the family

The proceedings, whether uncontested or otherwise, may apply in respect of any child either of the parties or treated as one of the family who is aged less than 16 (though the court may direct that an older child be included).

Most obviously, a child of the parties is one born to both spouses during the course of their marriage. The natural child of either spouse, or one adopted by either or both, who has lived with them in the family home, also meets this definition. Conversely, a child of either spouse who has been adopted into another family, as opposed to being placed by them in a private foster care arrangement, can no longer be regarded as a child of the parties. The anomalous common law rule that the father is the natural guardian of his legitimate child[6] was removed by s 2(4) of the 1989 Act.

The term 'child of the family' remains largely unchanged by the 1989 Act except that, in relation to children in the care of a local authority and fostered with a family, it is now interpreted as applying to children who are 'placed' rather than 'boarded-out'. The relevance of related caselaw, which previously defined the boundaries of this term, remains applicable. So, for example, an unborn child would not be included within this definition. This was the effect of the ruling in a case[7] where a pregnant wife left her husband within a week of their marriage and it was proven that he was not the father of the resultant child. Bagnall J held that there was no sense in which the deserted spouse could be regarded as having treated the then unborn child as a child of the family. The duration of the marriage may be very short, as in a case[8] where it lasted a fortnight, yet still allow children to fall within the definition. However, there must be proof that the family unit actually existed before a child can be regarded as having been treated as a member of it.

Proceedings

The 1989 Act brought a new coherence to private family law proceedings. By far the majority of all private family law disputes concerning a child's welfare interests are now brought before the court in the form of applications for s 8 orders. Most usually these occur in the course of proceedings for divorce, separation or nullity though they may also occur as free standing applications, for example by grandparents, step-parents or foster-parents under the 1989

Act. Sometimes disputes may instead be the subject of wardship proceedings. At other times welfare interests will be addressed by applications for certain 'hybrid' orders.

The law governing contested arrangements for children arising in the context of proceedings for divorce, nullity and separation is now as stated in the Family Law Act 1996 together with s 44 of the Matrimonial Causes Act 1973, as amended by Sched 12, para 31 of the 1989 Act. Under the latter provision, and in keeping with the new minimalist approach to judicial intervention, the judiciary are now bound to do no more than consider:

> (a) whether there are any children of the family to whom this section applies; and
> (b) where there are any such children, whether (in the light of the arrangements which have been made, or are proposed to be, made for their upbringing and welfare) it should exercise any of its powers under the Children Act 1989 with respect to any of them.

Only in 'exceptional circumstances' will the court delay the granting of a decree absolute. In most instances the court will determine a divorce application without examining the parties on the detail of their proposed care arrangements. Later, in fresh proceedings, most typically for residence orders perhaps combined with other s 8 orders, one of the parties may bring this matter before the court. In that small minority of cases, where there is clear conflict regarding proposed care arrangements, the court will issue a s 7 direction to the local authority or a probation officer requesting a report on the welfare of the child or children concerned.

Where an application for an order is contested the court will normally wish to hear from any child involved, if he or she is sufficiently mature to have formed a considered view regarding future care arrangements. These views will not be regarded as determinative.

Under s 10(1) in any family proceedings in which a question arises with respect to the welfare of any child, the court may make a s 8 order with respect to the child if -

> (b) the court considers that the order should be made even though no such application has been made.

Under s 11(3) it may make such an order at any stage during the course of family proceedings even though not in a position to finalise the proceedings. It may even do so in respect of a child in care, though this is restricted to the making of a residence order.

The court will resort to using the powers of wardship, only where statutory powers are unavailable or inappropriate, to assist mainly parental applicants negotiate equitable arrangements for the upbringing of their children or determine a particular issue affecting the welfare interests of a child. Before the introduction of the 1989 Act, and despite the greater reporting of public law wardship cases, the majority of wardship applications were private. It then also provided a forum where the legal interests of persons (such as an unmarried father, grandparent, step-parent etc) who would have had difficulty in finding representation in statutory proceedings could be taken into account when determining matters of custody or access. It also offered any applicant with an interest a 'court of last resort' when a particularly urgent, unusual or complex issue arose in relation to the welfare of a child. Since the 1989 Act, which imposed no constraints on private applicants, wardship continues to offer a limited role for determining contested issues affecting a child's welfare interests.

Finally, some private law disputes concerning a particular aspect of a child's welfare can be addressed through narrowly defined proceedings for orders which are neither wholly public or private in nature. These include parental responsibility orders, orders for financial relief and orders relevant in contexts such as domestic violence and child abduction and directions for local authority investigations.

The s 8 orders

In private family law disputes the main orders now available to deal with arrangements for the future upbringing of children are those listed in s 8 of the 1989 Act. Each s 8 order may be made for a specific or for an unlimited period of time and otherwise end on the child's 16th birthday unless exceptional circumstances require an extension. Unlike their predecessors these orders are intended to be flexible and a number of s 8 orders may be made to provide a comprehensive package tailored to fit the particular circumstances of an individual child. Under s 11(7) conditions may be attached, additional judicial directions given and their duration specified. Instead of a s 8 order the court may make a parental responsibility order, a family assessment order, or an order appointing a guardian.

The residence order

The first and most significant of the s 8 orders available to the court is a residence order. This is defined by s 8(1) of the 1989 Act as follows:

> "residence order" means an order settling the arrangements to be made as to the person with whom a child is to live.

The order gives parental responsibility for a child, most often accompanied by actual physical possession, to a named person or persons. It replaces the previous custody order.

A residence order is most usually made in favour of one person, a parent. Under s 10(4) and (5) a parent or guardian may be applicants as of right. Under s 9(3) and (4), all others require leave of the court. A local authority foster parent may also apply but, depending on duration of care, will require the authority's permission before seeking leave of the court. An order can be made out to two or perhaps more persons, none of whom may be a parent.[9] Thus grandparents, foster-parents, uncles and aunts or any combination of same, whether living together or not, may be eligible for such an order. Section 9(1) of the 1989 Act enables the court to make a residence order in respect of a child in the care of a local authority which will have the effect of discharging the latter. In contrast a local authority is prohibited by s 9(2) from being either an applicant or recipient in respect of such an order. This lack of reciprocity across the private/public divide demonstrates the different weighting statutorily allocated to the welfare principle in the two sectors.

Significantly, a residence order may also be made in favour of a child applicant.[10] This possibility at first attracted considerable media speculation that it would provide the means whereby children in this jurisdiction would be able to emulate the example set by their counterparts in the USA and 'divorce their parents'. However, in cases such as *Re C (A Minor)(Leave to Seek Section 8 Orders)*,[11] where a 14 year old girl sought a residence order to allow her to live with her friend's family, the court has indicated that it will not licence unilateral use of this order by children when to do so would threaten the interests of the family as a whole. Despite the ruling in *Gillick* and the growing international thrust towards recognising children's rights, the courts still hold to the view that the welfare interests of a child are best assured by protecting the legal integrity of the family unit, in the absence of grounds which prove otherwise. Significantly, the local authority saw no sufficient reason to treat the matter as one giving rise to issues of public law and indicated that it would not be applying for a care or supervision order.

Under s 12(2), the making of a residence order automatically vests parental responsibility in the person named in the order. Its primary effect is to decide where a child is to live and it is most usually made in favour of one person, a parent. However, a residence order does not vest parental responsibility exclusively in the bearer. As between first parties: where one parent is granted an residence order, both will nonetheless retain full parental responsibility, and with it the capacity to take most decisions independently of each other in regard to the child concerned. As between first and third parties: s 12(2) provides that a parent or guardian with parental responsibility will not lose it on the making of a residence order in favour of a non-parent. Finally, s

2(6) provides that in any circumstance a person with parental responsibility will not lose it merely because a residence order has been granted to another.

The hallmark of a residence order is that it authorises more than one person to hold parental responsibility for a named child at the same time.

The scope of authority vested by a residence order is not coterminous with its predecessor the custody order. In particular s 13(1) prevents the child's removal from the jurisdiction; though the courts may be prepared to recognise exceptional circumstances when this is permissible.[12] The Court of Appeal has held[13] that the law governing this matter remains the same as before the introduction of the 1989 Act. The court confirmed the views earlier expressed by Bracewell J[14] that while the welfare test must now be satisfied by reference to the checklist it is not necessary to methodically apply and satisfy each item on that list.

Section 13 also prevents any change being made to the child's surname without the consent of all those with parental responsibility. This particular prohibition has recently been judicially endorsed.[15] The singular importance now attached to this matter is apparent from the comment jointly made by Thorpe and Hurst LJJ in *Dawson v Wearmouth*:

> ...the registration or change of a child's surname is a profound and not a merely formal issue, whatever the age of the child.[16]

The court will apply the paramountcy principle to determine whether or not a child's surname should be changed. Caselaw reveals that little judicial weight may then be given to the views of the children concerned.[17]

In keeping with the principle of parental responsibility, a residence order does not vest authority exclusively in the named party. The other parent continues to hold and share with the named party all responsibilities in respect of the child except for those which are covered by the order. Section 12 directs that where any court is making a residence order in favour of a father who does not yet have parental responsibility the court shall then also make an order under s 4 of the 1989 Act giving him that responsibility; where the person vested with a residence order is not a parent or guardian then, under s 12(4), that person shall have parental responsibility for the duration of the order and thereafter until revoked. Each parent retains the right to act independently of the other and the right to delegate their responsibility to another e.g. a child minder.

Under s 11(7), the court may attach conditions to a residence order. These may be in relation to matters such as blood transfusions, medical treatment or as regards specific living arrangements. In respect of the latter, if the court issues a joint residence order it may specify the periods the child is to spend in each household. It may also specify the duration of the order. The use of shared residence orders has proved contentious.[18] Section 11(5) provides that a residence order shall cease to have effect if the parent in whose favour it was made lives together with the other parent for a continuous period of six months or more. Under s 91(10), it will cease when the child concerned attains the age of 16 (18 in exceptional circumstances).

The residence order has become a vitally important mechanism for giving effect to the principle of the welfare of the child in contested private family law proceedings. It offers the primary means for determining the major issue for child welfare, identifying the place the child will call 'home', following family breakdown. It is accessed by meeting threshold criteria which permit a wide range of applicants. It allows the court to exercise a broad ambit of discretion in determining the party or parties in whose favour the order should be made, the variety of directions and conditions to be attached and their duration. Most applications, however, are uncontested. Only in that small minority of divorce, nullity or separation cases where the parties disclose a disagreement in relation to future care arrangements for a child will the welfare test be judicially applied to determine in whose favour the order should be made. This seldom occurs because such a disclosure could delay the legal dissolution of the marriage.

The contact order

The second most significant s 8 order, in terms of degree of authority, is the contact order; in numerical terms, however, it is the one most frequently made. This order gives recognition to the authority of Article 8(1) of the European Convention on Human Rights and Fundamental Freedoms which states that 'Everyone has the right to respect for his private and family life, his home and his correspondence'. It is defined by s 8(1) of the 1989 Act as follows:

> ...a 'contact order' means an order requiring the person with whom a child lives, or is to live, to allow the child to visit or stay with the person named in the order, or for that person and the child otherwise to have contact with each other.

It has a more comprehensive and flexible application than its predecessor the access order. It is also enforced, most usually in favour of a non-resident parent, more assiduously by the courts than was its predecessor.

Under s 10(4) and (5), any parent or guardian or any other person who has a residential order in respect of the child concerned, may apply as of right for a contact order. Under s 9(3), others must first seek leave of the court. A local authority cannot apply. In the case of grandparent applicants, there is a requirement under s 10(1)(a) that leave of the court be obtained before application is made. Having been granted leave, however, the courts will not recognise any presumption entitling a grandparent to contact: the applicant must demonstrate good reason.[19]

Like its predecessor the access order, a contact order vests rights in a named adult. It allows defined contact or communication between the child and a named person or persons; that person need not be a parent or relative; and more than one contact order may be in effect at the same time in respect of the same child. Contact may be direct; providing for person-to-person meetings, at such times and perhaps places as specified by the court. Contact may also be defined as indirect; this could take the form of communication by letter or phone instead of or as well as a person-to-person meeting.[20] It may allow for overnight stays, specify visiting arrangements and provide for 'reasonable contact' or contact at such intervals as determined by the court. A contact order made under s 8 differs from a contact order made under s 34. The former is a positive order which enables contact between a child and a named person and cannot be made in respect of a child who is the subject of a care order; the latter limits, removes or re-defines such contact. Under s 11(7) of the 1989 Act, the court may attach conditions or make such directions as it thinks fit which allows this order to be a particularly flexible and directive mechanism for the court to address the welfare interests of a child. Section 11(6) provides that the order will cease to have effect if the parent in whose favour it was made returns to live with the other parent for a continuous period of at least 6 months. Under s 91(10), it will cease when the child concerned attains the age of 16 (18 in exceptional circumstances). A care order discharges a contact order.

Continuing contact with both parents is presumed to be essential for a child's emotional stability. The contact order is a strategically important means of giving effect to the welfare principle in contested private family law proceedings. Its modern welfare significanc has its roots in the decision in *M v M (Child: Access)*[21] where the court held that access is essentially a right of the child rather than of the parent. Caselaw has since continued the presumption that in fact the inherent right is that of the child to maintain relationships.[22] In maintaining a child's presumed right to parental contact, the courts have been very alert to any initiative by one parent intended to deprive the other of contact. The Court of Appeal has ruled that even 'eccentric, bizarre behaviour' should not deprive a father of contact with his children unless this behaviour presented a risk of harm.[23] The fact that a father is in prison, is not recognised as such by his son and that the mother and her family refuse to co-operate will not deter the court from making an order for indirect contact on the grounds that this in the child's long-term welfare interests.[24] However, as Balcombe LJ has observed[25] the essential point is not whether contact is beneficial for the child but whether there exists any good reason why the child should not have access. Where the application for contact occurs against a background of violent behaviour from the applicant towards a child's mother, with a real prospect of this recurring in the future, then the court will be justified in denying a father's request for contact with that child.[26] As before the introduction of the 1989 Act, disputes relating to contact continue to present the courts with the most litigated and hotly contested problems in the law as it relates to children. These problems are exacerbated when one of the parties refuses to comply with the order.

The parent with a residential order, or with possession, who flatly refuses to comply with contact arrangements agreed by the court, fundamentally challenges the capacity of the latter to safeguard the welfare interests of the child concerned. In the pre-1989 Act era the judicial response was expressed with typical good sense by Ormrod LJ who observed[27] when ruling out enforcement by imprisonment:

> These cases are exceedingly intractable. They can only be dealt with by tact not force. Force is bound to fail.

Since the introduction of the 1989 Act such cases are governed more firmly by the rule that access between child and parent is presumed to be in the welfare interests of the child concerned and the court will not flinch from using imprisonment where it believes that an obdurate parent is obstructing contact. As Balcombe LJ has stated[28] the test now applied is "are there any cogent reasons why a child should be denied the opportunity of access to his natural father?" Where the conditions are satisfied, the welfare checklist has been applied and contact is found to be in the child's interests then it would seem the court must make the order;[29] conversely, where the benefit of contact to the child it is not clear then the order should not be made.[30] The principle being that though a parent may ultimately frustrate the court's intentions he or she cannot be permitted to foreclose the court's duty to make an order giving effect to the child's best interests. However, there is a very fine line to be drawn between the parent who is plainly and simply obstructing the court and the parent who by doing so is also prejudicing the welfare of the child to the point where an order would be counter productive. For example, a mother's implacable hostility, fuelled by the attitudes of her mother and her second husband, was such that the court considered it to be futile to make an order which would only place the child concerned under considerable pressure.[31] A view which was questioned by the Court of Appeal but ultimately allowed to prevail. Where the parent flagrantly and persistently refuses to comply with court orders allowing contact then the court will treat this as contempt.[32]

Among the measures which the court may take to buttress a contact order in the face of parental hostility are: the use of specific issue orders and prohibited steps orders; the attachment of conditions to a residence order;

and a direction that a court officer, constable or local authority social worker undertake and supervise contact arrangements.

The child who refuses to comply with the court's contact arrangements presents a double problem - firstly, is the refusal a genuine reasoned or felt response emanating solely from the child or has it been produced as a result of pressure or prejudice from the child's carer? Secondly, in either case will the child's welfare be best furthered in the long-term by continuing, re-adjusting or severing the contact? The Court of Appeal has ruled[33] that the following test should be applied - is the fundamental emotional need of every child to have an enduring relationship with both parents outweighed in this case by the depth of harm which the child will be at risk of suffering as a consequence of the court making the contact order? In this way the court has raised a presumption of contact, underpinned by the welfare principle, evidenced by a basic tenet of developmental psychology[34] which can only be displaced by evidence that such contact will breach the significant harm threshold.

The specific issue order

This order enables the parties, usually parents, to appear before the court to seek direction in relation to a specific aspect of parental responsibility. It is defined by s 8(1) of the 1989 Act as follows:

> ...a 'specific issue order' means an order giving directions for the purpose of determining a specific question which has arisen, or which may arise, in connection with any aspect of parental responsibility for a child.

The aim, however, is not to give one parent or the other a general 'right' to make decisions about a particular aspect of the child's upbringing. Instead it is to enable a particular dispute over such a matter to be resolved by the court, including the giving of detailed directions where necessary. Under s 10(4), a parent or guardian may apply as of right as may any person who has a residential order in respect of the child concerned. All others may only do so with leave of the court.

The order directs that the named party or parties then behave in a specified manner in regard to the issue raised. It replaces the flexible powers previously available to the judiciary in wardship proceedings with a narrower discretionary power which may be applied to any specific difficulty between the parties. It may be made in conjunction with contact or residence orders and may be made instead of the latter where its comprehensive authority is unnecessary to resolve a limited area of contention. The court may attach conditions.

The specific issue order has a limited application to a child's welfare interests but, because of its directive nature, is often of vital importance in circumstances where such interests are in need of urgent protection. Like a prohibited steps order, it is confined to dealing with narrow issues which relate to specific aspects of parental responsibility. Most commonly, such issues have concerned a child's education[35] or their return to the jurisdiction.[36] An extreme example of an aspect of parental responsibility, which has in the past from time to time required judicial action in wardship proceedings, occurs when a child needs urgent medical treatment against parental wishes. That it is appropriate for the court to use this order in such a context is evident from the ruling in *Re R (A Minor): Blood Transfusion)*[37] (see, further below and also, Chap 12).

The prohibited steps order

This replaces the prerogative power previously available to the judiciary in wardship proceedings. It is defined by s 8(1) of the 1989 Act as follows:

> 'a prohibited steps order' means an order that no step which could be taken by a parent in meeting his parental responsibility for a child, and which is of a kind specified in the order, shall be taken by any person without the consent of the court.

Under s 10(4), a parent or guardian may apply as of right as may any person who has a residence order in respect of the child concerned. All others may only do so with leave of the court. It may be made *ex parte*.

A prohibited steps order enables the court to place a veto against the exercise of specific aspects of parental responsibility, such as a threatened removal of the child in question from the jurisdiction,[38] from a particular school or prohibiting a specific medical operation. It replaces the traditional use of wardship to restrain contact between children and undesirable third parties. While the issue in question must relate to an aspect of parental responsibility the order can be made against any person whether or not they are vested with such responsibility. It may, therefore, be made against an unmarried father or a former cohabitee to restrain that person from contacting the applicant. Under s 11(7), the court may attach conditions to a prohibited steps order.

There are limitations to the use of a prohibited steps order. It cannot, for example, be made in respect of a child in care. Unlike the range of powers available in wardship, a prohibited steps order in common with all s 8 orders, may have to be buttressed by a separate application for an injunction where the offending matter or behaviour cannot be construed as strictly parental. Where the authority required is to prevent parents from contacting each other,[39] then an injunction rather than a prohibited steps order is appropriate. When one parent wishes to bar the other from their home then, as was pointed out by Sir Stephen Brown P,[40] "it is very doubtful whether a prohibited steps order could in any circumstances be used to 'oust' a father from the matrimonial home". Under s 9(5)(a), neither a prohibited steps order nor a specific issue order may be made where the objective is one which may be achieved by making a residence order or a contact order. The Court of Appeal[41] had cause to examine the relative merits of a contact order and a prohibited steps order as the means for providing a mother with the authority necessary to prevent a former cohabitee from contacting children in respect of whom he was judged to considered to pose a risk. Butler-Sloss LJ, giving judgment for the court, held that a prohibited steps order would be more appropriate as liability for a breach would then lie against the cohabitee whereas under a contact order it would lie against the mother.

Like the specific issue order, a prohibited steps order is a strictly limited legal means for giving effect to the welfare principle. It makes available a particular power, drawn from the wardship jurisdiction, to provide a narrowly defined authority for the protection of a child's welfare interests.

The wardship order

As is clear from its history (see Chaps 1 and 4) the jurisdiction of wardship is based on safeguarding the welfare interests of a child and for many years has done so through application of the paramountcy principle. The authority of the court when exercising the wardship jurisdiction is not quite the same as that vested in a parent. In some respects its scope is not so extensive. Authority for the adoption of a ward, for example, will not necessarily rest on judicial consent. However, when exercising its inherent and unlimited *parens patriae* jurisdiction (which encompasses wardship) its authority is more extensive than that of a parent. It may, for example, prohibit the publishing of information[42] concerning a ward, override the refusal of a parent or mature minor to consent to medical treatment,[43] override legal or professional privilege to obtain evidence[44] or attach a direction to an adoption order[45] requiring the Registrar General not to divulge certain information.

Wardship is rooted in private family law and is not governed by the restrictions on its use as listed in s 100 of the 1989 Act. However, the range and flexibility of orders, introduced under s 8 of the 1989 Act, have had their intended effect of countering the attractions of wardship in private family law as an alternative to statutory proceedings.[46] As Waite LJ has stated:

> ...the courts' undoubted discretion to allow wardship proceedings to go forward in a suitable case is subject to their clear duty, in loyalty to the scheme and purpose of the Children Act legislation, to permit recourse to wardship only when it becomes apparent to the judge in any particular case that the question which the court is determining in regard to the minor's upbringing or property cannot be resolved under the statutory procedures...[47]

He went on to express the view that there has to be a special justification for giving a child 'the status - an exceptional status under the modern law as it must now be applied - of a ward of court'.

Although the annual number of private wardship applications has fallen since the 1989 Act came into effect, there have nonetheless been a significant number and range of cases where the jurisdiction has been exercised. Foremost in terms of growth have been that category of cases where medical practitioners seek the consent of the court in relation to the treatment needs of a child where their proposed action is being contested by a parent. The cases divide into two categories: those where a hospital wishes to deny treatment and those where it wishes to provide it.

In the first group, the cases of *R v Cambridge District Health Authority ex parte B*[48] and, more recently, *Re C (Medical Treatment)*[49] provide not untypical examples. The first concerned the well publicised case of the 10 year old child Jamee Bowen who had leukaemia. Her wishes and those of her parents that certain expensive, painful and experimental treatment be provided was resisted by the medical authorities on the ground that it could not be justified as it was unlikely to lead to a successful outcome. The Court of Appeal approved the medical approach. The second case concerned a child aged 16 months, in intensive care, diagnosed as having a fatal spinal disease and dependant upon a ventilator. The medical practitioners sought the consent of the court to permanently withdraw the life support system against the wishes of loving parents who, as orthodox Jews, firmly believed that palliative care was sinful; every effort should always be made to sustain life. Again, the court overruled parental objections and endorsed the medical approach. In the course of his judgment, Sir Stephen Brown P quoted with approval from caselaw in which the judicial view was expressed that the court would not force medical practitioners to adopt a treatment approach which was contrary to their clinical judgment.

In the second group, the religious beliefs of parents have often been a factor. For example, Johnson J in *Re O (A Minor)(Medical Treatment)*[50] ruled that the inherent jurisdiction was the most appropriate forum to authorise a blood-transfusion for a child against the wishes of the child's parents who were Jehovah Witnesses and caring, committed and capable people.[51] In *Re T (Liver Transplant: Consent)*[52] the court considered the case of a baby suffering from a life threatening liver defect whose parents were opposed to treatment. Evidence was admitted which indicated that with a transplant the prognosis for recovery was good, without it the child would die within eighteen months. The parents, unmarried but in a stable relationship, who were both health care professionals with experience in the care of sick children, maintained that it was not in their child's best interests to suffer the pain and distress of a major operation. The Court of Appeal agreed. The court held that it could not be in the child's best interests to order caring, well-informed parents to facilitate an operation with which they so profoundly disagreed. The significance of this decision lies in the judicial readiness to assimilate the welfare interests of a very dependent baby and those of a devoted caring mother. This fusion of the legal interests of parent and child carries resonances of a judicial logic not dissimilar to that which last prevailed at *Agar-Ellis*[53] (see, also, Chap 10 and the law relating to a foetus).

As Fortin has pointed out[54] it is troubling that the court finds itself bound to take decisions which do not place medical practitioners in a position of carrying out invasive treatment programmes which conflict with their clinical judgment. *Re T* may be an exception to this policy but perhaps it only indicates that a decision which does so conflict, but results in non-treatment, is not imposing any positive duties on medical practitioners and is therefore not a true exception. It is odd that the court would adopt such a policy in respect of the decisions of one specific professional group; it certainly would not regard itself as being so bound in relation to social workers and care orders, for example. Also troubling is the indication of a willingness to assimilate the interests of parent and child. If there has been one dominant trend in family law in recent decades it has been the painstaking untangling of their separate sets of interests. It would seem important, particularly in issues where there could be a conflict, that the judiciary resist any return to an approach which aggregates the interests of parent and child.

Another area in which the judiciary have developed a use for the inherent *parens patriae* powers of wardship is where a child suffers from a condition which does not meet the definition of a recognised mental disorder under the Mental Health Act 1983, is judged not to have the competence to make a reasoned decision and whose veto of treatment is endangering his or her welfare interests. There have recently been a small number of cases where wardship has been used to override the veto of an adolescent and authorise compulsory detention and treatment.[55] Arguably, for example, in *Re W (A Minor)(Medical Treatment)*[56] such behaviour could have been appropriately addressed by coercive proceedings under the 1989 Act, but instead the court chose to construe the circumstances as raising issues of private rather than public law. This use of wardship to substitute the court's views for the child's, on the issue of what is in the latter's best interests, has been questioned.[57] Of perhaps more fundamental significance is the question – Who has authority to take decisions regarding the welfare interests of an adolescent?

From the judgments delivered, particularly in *Re W*, the answer would appear to be the child, the parent and any person or body (e.g. a local authority or court) vested with parental responsibility. Where parental responsibility rests with the court, as when the child has been warded, then its decision will override that of the child, and indeed that of the parent. Where the child is non-competent then a parent or other person or body with parental responsibility may decide. Where the child is *Gillick* competent then he or she may decide but so may a parent and, presumably, any other person or body with parental responsibility. It is not clear to whom a third party must look for a final decision on a matter affecting a child's welfare interests where the child, parent and/or other with parental responsibility disagree on the best course of action.

There are also certain powers such as protection from publicity[58] which may on occasion require recourse to wardship. Although this is most usually initiated by parents or guardians seeking injunctions to prevent unwelcome media attention being focussed on their children, it may also be imposed by the court against the wishes of a parent.[59]

As has been noted (see, Chap 4) no order has been of greater value to the judiciary, in giving effect to the welfare principle, than wardship. The use of the paramountcy principle in the wardship jurisdiction has had the most far reaching effects on the legal development of the meaning, role and weighting given to the welfare interests of children which in turn have had profound consequences for all of family law. The unique feature of wardship has lain in its capacity to transcend thresholds of intervention and prescriptive rules regarding applicants eligibility, grounds for orders, disposal options available etc. The effect of a wardship order is to establish the welfare of the child as the over-riding objective, to permit a broad exercise of judicial discretion in pursuance of it and to ensure that welfare is determined not by a brief adjudicative process but by on-going and permissive judicial management.

Other orders and powers

In addition to the s 8 orders, the court has other powers and orders available to it under the Children Act 1989. Some may be used at judicial initiative to supplement, or substitute for, the issue of s 8 orders; see Chap 12 for parental responsibility orders. Others may be used in response to an application by a parent or other person with parental responsibility.

In short, the court now has available to it a flexible array of orders and powers which it can employ on a 'pick and mix' basis to address the particular welfare interests of a child in contested private family law proceedings.

The family assistance order

The court has the power to direct a local authority to carry out an investigation of the child's circumstances and may make orders for the financial relief of children. Under s 16 of the 1989 Act, in exceptional circumstances and with the consent of the relevant adult, the court may make an order directing a probation officer or directing the relevant local authority 'to make an officer of the authority available' to 'advise, assist and (where appropriate) befriend any person named in the order'. This may be coupled with a residence order and be made for a period not exceeding 6 months.

The court may also make orders for the financial relief of children who are the subject of residential orders; though not in favour of a parent or step-parent. Authority to do so is available under s 15 and Sched 1 of the 1989 Act.

Welfare reports

The discretionary judicial power to require a local authority to carry out an investigation of a child's circumstances has proved to be of great value as a means of identifying welfare needs of children undisclosed by the parties to private family law proceedings. Under s 7 of the 1989 Act:

> (1) A court considering any question with respect to a child under this Act may
>
> (a) ask a probation officer; or
>
> (b) ask a local authority to arrange for -
>
> (i) an officer of the authority; or
>
> (ii) such other person (other than a probation officer) as the authority considers appropriate,
>
> to report to the court on such matters relating to the welfare of that child as are required to be dealt with in the report.

In any family proceedings, though most probably for contested s 8 orders, where the court considers the arrangements to be questionable it may issue such a s 7 direction.

Domestic violence and welfare interests

Part IV of the Family Law Act 1996, which came into effect on October 1st 1997, provides the civil remedies of proceedings for non-molestation orders and for occupation orders for victims of domestic violence. This legislation builds on previous provisions, brings together some caselaw developments and broadly gives effect to the recommendations of the Law Commission.[60] As the victims, directly or otherwise, are always any children involved, there can be no doubting the importance of these provisions for their welfare interests.

The two orders available, as under previous legislation, are the non-molestation order and the occupation order. Before making either order the court must apply the 'balance of harm' test: the order must be made if it appears that the applicant or a relevant child is likely to suffer significant harm attributable to the respondent's conduct; unless either is likely to suffer greater harm if the order is not made.

Conclusion

The legislative intent, to replace the 'winners and losers' approach to issues concerning the future care arrangements for children arising in the context of matrimonial proceedings, with one which instead presumes that the parties should be able to make their own arrangements outside the court, has radically altered the welfare threshold. In practice the presumption now operates to re-privatise most welfare related decisions taken in this context. This in itself gives rise to questions about the logic and equity of treating contested as opposed to uncontested applications in private law proceedings differently, and treating both differently from public law proceedings, in relation to the common benchmark of the welfare principle. It is not evident that a causal relationship exists between parental agreement and satisfying the welfare test. Nor is it apparent that welfare interests in private proceedings would not equally benefit from the mandatory representation provided in public proceedings by solicitor and guardian *ad litem*.

The range of persons who may now appear as parties in private contested proceedings has greatly changed from the time when family law meant the law relating to the marital family unit. Now, the 'child of the family' who is the subject of the contest need not necessarily have a blood relationship with the contesting adults. The latter may include grandparents, foster-parents, uncles and aunts or any person who although unrelated has an established care relationship with the child in question. In fact the boundaries constituting 'family', the forum within which, or in reference to which, the law has always sought to determine the welfare of the child, have now become so wide and fluid as to defy definition. This generalised deconstruction is also apparent in the function of proceedings which are now more likely to address and adjust specific aspects of care arrangements, such as contact, rather than simply deal with long-term custody.

When proceedings come before the court the fact of contest establishes the welfare threshold and triggers the mandatory judicial scrutiny of proposed care arrangements. This will not necessarily lead to a rigorous examination and testing of the parties plans, nor definitely involve the children having their views represented before the court. It does, however, provide for the possibility of the child concerned being fully engaged as a party to proceedings, with attendant representation, which marks a significant advance for the role of welfare interests in private law. The mandatory application of the paramountcy principle to determine issues relating to upbringing is also an important safeguard for those interests in this context.

At point of disposal, the exercise of judicial powers is now both more restricted and yet more flexible than formerly. There is no longer any power to direct a local authority to accept care responsibility for a child, nor any opportunity to make orders in respect of uncontested proceedings and the discretion to interpret welfare interests is now subject to the welfare checklist. However, the s 8 orders together with the ability to attach conditions provide wide opportunities for tailoring a disposal option to match the needs profile of a particular child. These orders permit a real shift in the judicial role in contested private proceedings from an adjudicative to an adjustive function.

Notes

1 [1995] 3 FCR 543.

2 See *G v Kirklees Metropolitan Borough Council* [1993] 1 FLR 805 per Booth J.

3 See in particular, the House of Lords rulings in both *Re KD (A Minor)* [1988] AC 806 and in *S v M (Access Order)* [1997] 1 FLR 980.

4 See, for example, *Re O (A Minor) (Custody: Adoption)* [1992] 1 FLR 77.

5 See *Sanderson v McManus* [1997] SLT 6.

6 See s 2: (4) The rule of law that a father is the natural guardian of his legitimate child is abolished.

7 See *A v A (Family: Unborn Child)* [1974] Fam 6, [1974] 1 All ER 755.

8 SeeW *v W (Child of the Family)* [1984] FLR 796, CA.

9 See, for example, *A v A* [1994] 1 FLR 669 where a residence order was used to achieve a sharing of parental responsibilities.

10 See *Re AD (A Minor)* [1993] Fam Law 43.

11 [1994] 1 FLR 26. Also, see, *Re O (Minors) (Leave to seek Residence Order)* [1992] 1 FLR 172.

12 See *Re K (A Minor) (Removal from the Jurisdiction)* [1992] 2 FLR 98 and *M v M (Minors) (Removal from the Jurisdiction)* [1992] 2 FLR 303 CA.

13 See *H v H (Residence Order: Leave to Remove from the Jurisdiction)* [1995] 1 FLR 529.

14 See *M v A (Wardship: Removal from Jurisdiction)* [1993] 2 FLR 715.

15 See *Re B (Change of Surname)* [1996] 1 FLR 791 and *Re P (Change of Surname: Parent's Rights)* [1997] 2 FLR No 5.

16 [1997] 2 FLR 629 at p 635.

17 See, for example, *W v A (Minor: Surname)* [1981] 2 WLR 124 where the children were aged 12 and 10 and *Re B (Change of Surname)* [1996] 1 FLR 791 where they were aged 16, 14 and 12.

18 See, in particular, *A v A (Minors)(Shared Residence Order)* [1994] 1 FLR 669, also see *Re H (A Minor)(Shared Residence)* [1994] 1 FLR 717 and *G v G (Joint Residence Orders)* [1993] Fam Law 615.

19 See *Re A (A minor)(Contact Application: Grandparent)* (1995) The Times, March 6, CA.

20 See *Re O (A minor)(Contact: Imposition of Conditions)* [1995] 2 FLR 124 where the contact was in the form of school reports and *Re M (A Minor)(Contact: Conditions)* [1994] 1 FLR 272 where permission was given for contact by post between an unmarried father in prison and his two year old son.

21 [1973] 2 All ER 81.

22 This principle has been repeatedly asserted in such cases as *Re S (Minors: Access)* [1990] 2 FLR 166, *Re H (Minors)(Access)* [1992] 1 FLR 148 CA, *Re R (A Minor)(Contact)* [1993] 2 FLR 762 and *Re M (Contact: Welfare Test)* [1995] 1 FLR 274.

23 See *Re B (Minors: Access)* [1992] 1 FLR 142.

24 See *A v L (Contact)* [1998] 1 FLR.

25 See *Re M (Minors)(Access*) [1992] Fam Law 152.

26 See *Re D (Contact: Reasons for Refusal)* [1997] 2 FLR 48, *Re H (Contact: Domestic Violence)* [1998] 2 FLR and *Re A (Contact: Domestic Violence)* [1998] 2 FLR 171. Also, see, Hester and Radford, *Domestic Violence and Child Contact Arrangements*, Joseph Rowntree Foundation, 1996.

27 See *Churchard v Churchard* [1984] FLR 635 at 638 F - H.

28 See *Re D (A Minor)(Contact: Mother's Hostility)* [1993] 2 FLR 1.

29 As in *Re W (A Minor)(Contact)* [1994] 2 FLR 441 and *Re H (A Minor)(Contact)* [1994] 2 FLR 776.

30 See the judgment of the House of Lords in *Sanderson v McManus* [1997] SLT 629.

31 See *Re J (A Minor)(Contact*) [1994] 1 FLR No 6.

32 See *A v N (Committal: Refusal of Contact)* [1997] 1 FLR 533, where the Court of Appeal upheld a sentence of 6 weeks imposed on the parent concerned.

33 See *Re M (Contact: Welfare Test)* [1995] 1 FLR 274 CA.

34 See Bowlby et al.

35 As in *Re P (A Minor)(Education)* [1992] 1 FLR 316, CA.

36 As in *Re D (A Minor)(Removal from the Jurisdiction)* [1992] 1 All ER 892, CA.

37 [1993] Fam Law 577.

38 This in fact was the type of activity instanced as the rationale for such an order by the Law Commission in its paper No 172 at para 4.20.

39 As in *Croydon London Borough Council v A and Others* [1992] Fam 169.

40 See *Nottingham County Council v P* [1993] 3 All ER 815 at 825b, CA.

41 See *Re H (Prohibited Steps Order)* [1995] 1 FLR 638, CA.

42 See for example, in *Re X (A Minor)* [1975] Fam 47 where it was held that in the particular circumstances of the case the interests of the ward should not prevail over the interests of freedom of publication. Note, also, that the court's inherent powers are butressed by the Administration of Justice Act, s 12, which makes it a contempt of court to publish any report of a wardship hearing.

43 See *Re W (A Minor)(Medical Treatment: Court's Jurisdiction)* [1992] 3 WLR 785, [1992] 4 All ER 627.

44 See *Barking and Dagenham LBC v O and Another* [1993] 3 WLR 493.

45 See *Re X (A Minor)(Adoption Details: Disclosure)* [1994] 2 FLR 450.

46 See *Re CT (A Minor)(Wardship: Representation)* [1993] 2 FLR 278 and *Re R (A Minor): Blood Transfusion)* [1993] Fam Law 577 for judicial views on the effect of restrictions imposed by the 1989 Act on access to wardship in private and public law respectively.

47 See *Re CT (A Minor)(Wardship: Representation)* [1993] 2 FLR 278.

48 [1995] 1 FLR 1055.

49 [1998] 1 FLR 384.

50 [1993] 2 FLR 149. See, also, *Re R (A Minor)(Blood Transfusion)* [1993] 2 FLR 757.

51 See also *Re B (A Minor)(Wardship: Medical Treatment)* [1981] 1 WLR 1421, *Re R op cit* and *Re S (A Minor)(Medical Treatment)* [1993] 1 FLR 376. However, more recently

the practice has been to use specific issue orders to deal with less controversial issues such as blood transfusions.

52 [1997] 1 WLR 242. For an authorative dissection of the issues, see Michalowski, S., 'Is it in the best interests of a child to have a life-saving liver transplantation? *Re T (Wardship: Medical Treatment)*' in *Child and Family Law Quarterly*, Vol 9, No 2, 1997.

53 *Op cit*.

54 See Fortin, J., '*Re C (Medical Treatment)* A baby's right to die' in *Child and Family Law Quarterly*, Vol 10, No 4, 1998.

55 See, for example: *Re R (A Minor)(Wardship: Medical Treatment)* [1991] 4 All ER 177; *Re W (A Minor)(Medical Treatment)* [1992] 4 All ER 627; *Re K, W and H (Minors)(Medical Treatment)* [1993] 1 FLR 854; *A Metropolitan Borough Council v DB* [1997] 1 FLR 767; *Re C (Detention: Medical Treatment)* [1997] 2 FLR 180.

56 *Op cit*.

57 See Downie, A., '*A Metropolitan Borough Council v DB* and *Re C (Detention: Medical Treatment)* Extra-statutory confinement – detention and treatment under the inherent jurisdiction' in *Child and Family Law Quarterly*, Vol 10, No 1, 1998.

58 This was the case in *Re M and N (Minors)(Wardship: Publication of Information)* [1990] Fam 211 CA.

59 See *Re Z (A Minor)(Freedom of Publication)* [1996] 1 FLR 191.

60 See Law Commission Report No. 207 *Family Law, Domestic Violence and Occupation of the Family Home* 1992.

14 Adoption

Introduction

Adoption now serves an additional range of social functions very different from the one it was initially designed to meet. Its traditional legal function[1] of "providing homes for children who need them" with third-party applicants is dying out. As a consensual process for securing homes for indigenous healthy babies with unrelated applicants it most probably has no future.

Far from continuing as a fairly simple and essentially private family law process, adoption has in recent years become quite complicated with a growing public law dimension. It no longer sits comfortably in either public nor private law and its proceedings are now as likely as not to be contested. Adoption has become a pivotal sector for all of family law and one which has been functionally distorted by a legislative and judicial requirement that it respond to the pressures and changes characteristic of the family in modern society. To understand what is happening to adoption is a key to understanding much of what is happening to the whole body of family law. The role played by the welfare interests of the child is crucial to any such understanding.

This chapter examines the role of the welfare principle in the modern adoption process. This it does by considering both the legislative role assigned to the principle and the extent to which this has been broadened by the exercise of judicial discretion. It identifies and assesses the roles also of the main parties, officials and agencies in relation to the principle. It considers the nature and significance of changes which have occurred to the law and practice of adoption in recent years.

Welfare and the parties

Adoption traditionally bound the three sets of parties - child, natural parent/s and adopters - into a process characterised by secrecy and stigma and sealed permanently and exclusively. Of all orders affecting children, adoption was the most immutable in its legal consequences for all concerned. The future welfare of the child concerned was thus predicated on legally sanctioned denial. Only in recent years has adoption acquired characteristics of 'openness' and a more flexible legal relationship is now being shaped between the parties.

The child

The child is clearly the most important party in any adoption process. Both statutorily prescribed eligibility criteria and the rather more flexible availability criteria must be satisfied before a child can enter the process. To be eligible for adoption a child must first be born,[2] be more than 19 weeks old but less than 18 years of age and, if related to the applicant or placed by an adoption agency, have been in the care of that person for at least 13 consecutive weeks prior to the order being made. In all other third party applications (e.g. with foster parents) the child must be at least 12 months old and have been with the applicants for at least the 12 month period immediately preceding the order. The 1976 Act continues the traditional requirement that the child is not and never has been married. Further, the fact that the child has previously been adopted is not a bar to his or her subsequent adoption. To be available for adoption a child must also be resident within the jurisdiction, though neither domicile nor citizenship are necessary.[3]

Of the children now being adopted only a declining minority conform to the traditional stereotypical image of the healthy white caucasian baby lovingly relinquished by an unmarried British mother to adopters able to afford a standard of care she is unable to provide. Then the threshold of access to the adoption process was set not by adopters suitability but more by the child meeting eligibility criteria of 'adoptability'; the closer to the stereotype the greater the probability of adoption and *vice versa*. This approach to adoption served the welfare interests of only a small proportion of the children available, the remainder of whom had to settle for options such as long-term foster care, institutional care in children's homes or benign transportation overseas. Now the proportion of children entering the process have characteristics which do not conform to the traditional stereotype and they also constitute a much greater proportion of the total available than was previously the case. Professional experience indicates that although far few orders are now being made, they are being made in respect of children who are much more likely to be non-nationals, legitimate, abused, older and/or suffering from a disability than was the case formerly. Modern adoption practice has inverted the previous balance in the relationship between adopters and child; it is the adopters eligibility which must now be established, only a small proportion of whom will be successful, the remainder having to explore options such as surrogacy etc. Adoption, at least in its third party form, is now playing a key role in addressing the welfare interests of children who would otherwise remain in public care.

The natural parent/s

The parent or parents to whom the child is born are the parties with whom an adoption process begins. The natural mother of a non-marital child, who wished to relinquish that child to a voluntary adoption society, traditionally formed the primary set of needs around which adoption, as a legal process, was constructed. The consent of a natural mother is still most likely to trigger the start of an adoption process. Consenting natural mothers, wishing to freely relinquish their children for adoption, are a rapidly dwindling minority of all natural parents engaged in the adoption process. Consensual proceedings are now most likely to take the form of a natural mother making joint application with her husband to adopt her child, born of a previous relationship. The consent of the mother is now given for reasons precisely opposite to those which traditionally characterised her role in this process. Adoption is the chosen option of such a mother because it offers the opportunity to legally cement the child into her new marital family unit to the exclusion of any relationship claims which may be made by the child's father and/or any of his relatives. At the end of the twentieth century, most adoptions in England and Wales are step-adoptions and thus most children being adopted would not otherwise enter the adoption process. The role played by child welfare considerations is as difficult to objectively evaluate in the context of the modern natural mother who adopts, as in the more traditional circumstances when such a mother relinquished, her child.

Now such a mother is likely to want to continue carrying care responsibility for her child but parental fault or default will cause her reluctant involvement with the adoption process. When such circumstances occur the judiciary will place a heavy burden of proof upon her to prove that she has made the arrangements necessary to secure a stable home environment for her child. Many such mothers are very young, a factor which will not weigh in their favour as the standard of reasonableness required in relation to any proposed arrangements are those appropriate to a mature reflective parent able to give objective consideration to a child's best interests.[4]

The *locus standi* of a natural father in adoption proceedings, though statutorily strengthened, remains marginal affording him little direct opportunity to significantly affect the legal role of the welfare principle. As he does not have parental responsibility (though he may acquire it) he is not therefore accorded the same legal standing as a marital father. For example, in *Re C (Adoption: Parties)*[5] the court held that such a father did not even have to be made a respondent to an adoption or freeing application.

The adopters

The third set of interests represented in an adoption are those of the adopters. The eligibility of adoption applicants is statutorily prescribed (status criteria) and form threshold criteria for adoption proceedings. Their suitability is largely determined by permissive criteria set by the adoption agencies (including reference to religion, maximum age, quality of relationships and lifestyle). Suitability criteria are in theory more discretionary and can permit a degree of flexibility which permits the matching of an applicant's attributes to the particular welfare needs of a child. The bearing of such criteria on the standing of the applicants differs according to whether they are first or third party applicants. In relation to the latter, the criteria set by agencies has at times been such as to leave them open to accusations of 'fettering their discretion' by imposing quite rigid rules (e.g. in regard to age, race and lifestyles) which have the effect of erecting a further threshold. The informal suitability threshold, ostensibly constructed around welfare indicators, has proved to be at least as formidable a barrier for a prospective applicant in adoption proceedings as the formal statutory threshold. In recent years the courts have demonstrated an alertness to instances where agencies have sought to introduce such unjustified suitability criteria and have been at pains to emphasise that while matters such as sexual orientation, lifestyle, race, religion etc may be taken into account they cannot be permitted to prevail over the fundamental consideration of what is in a particular child's best interests (see, further, below).

Statutory law and welfare interests

Adoption in the UK is very much a creature of statute. The legislative intent is to prescribe the criteria to be met if the status of a child is to be so radically and irrevocably changed. Although the welfare of a child is of central importance, it is still only a factor in rather than the objective of adoption law. The welfare requirement is personal to the child and the adopters. It is positive and prognostic; that an order would merely be consistent with the child's welfare would not in itself provide sufficient grounds for adoption.

The principles governing the adoption process are as stated in s 6 of the 1976 Act:

> In reaching any decision in relation to the adoption of a child, a court or adoption agency shall regard to all the circumstances, first consideration being given to the need to safeguard and promote the welfare of the child throughout his childhood; and shall so far as practicable ascertain the wishes and feelings of the child regarding the decision and give due consideration to them, having regard to his age and understanding.

This statement of the welfare principle is of central importance to the 1976 Act. It does not, however, make the welfare interests of a child the paramount concern. The directive is binding on both the court and an adoption agency "in reaching any decision in relation to the adoption of a child". This has been interpreted in an important precedent[6] to mean that 'any decision' does not apply to the issue of dispensing with agreement. The welfare principle has, therefore, continued to be excluded from determining the issue of dispensing with parental agreement. Indeed, in relation to the role of the principle as a determinant of proceedings, it can be argued that satisfaction of the welfare requirement as part of the judicial function comes too late in the adoption process to be helpful to the child. Blom-Cooper once rightly observed that:

> the process of adoption is not essentially justiciable; the issues in adoption are hardly susceptible of solution by the application of legal concepts and rules of law.[7]

There is also something of a philosophical conflict between the exclusiveness of an adoption order with its presumption of severing all ties between a child and his or her family of origin and the sharing of parental responsibility ethos underpinning the orders introduced under the 1989 Act.[8] A distinction acknowledged by the comment of Wall J that it is:

> logical that a different test needs to be applied to the making of an order which extinguishes parental rights as opposed to one which regulates their operation.[9]

However, the conflict has existed largely on a philosophical level and adoption law remains relatively intact.[10] The fact that under the Children Act 1989, adoption proceedings are family proceedings does carry some specific implications for the adoption process. It means, for example, that the 'no order' presumption applies, though this may be open to a slightly different interpretation than the s 6 direction that "the order if made be for the welfare of the child concerned". The 'no delay' rule similarly applies.

The draft Adoption Bill issued in 1996 (now lapsed), following the White Paper of 1993, promised to introduce the paramountcy principle to adoption law.

Adoption placement

Arguably, because of its capacity to determine future welfare, the most critical decision in the adoption process is the placement decision. Such placements are of two distinct types: third party and 'family'.

In relation to third party placements, safeguards have now been provided by the statutory requirement, mandatory in most circumstances, that they be subject to prior professional assessment. Indeed, one objective of the 1976 Act was to end the possibility (as graphically expressed by the Houghton

Committee) of a parent, or someone acting on their behalf, giving a child to a casual acquaintance such as someone met in a launderette.[11] This objective is largely achieved by s 11 which prohibits a parent from either making a 'direct' adoption placement of their child with a 'stranger' or authorising a third party to do so. It does, however, permit a parent to place or make an arrangement to place a child with a proposed adopter who is a relative of that child. A third party adoption placement will now only be legal if made by a registered adoption agency, by authority of the High court, by freeing order or with a relative of the child; though a third party placement may arise from a foster care placement.[12]

A 'family' adoption most usually results from one natural parent simply retaining care and possession after a breakdown in joint parenting arrangements. The child is never actually 'placed' before an adoption application is made. The parent, who has retained care responsibility, then applies jointly with a new spouse to adopt that child. The welfare factor only becomes susceptible to professional scrutiny at a time chosen by the prospective adopters.

Both third party and family placements are statutorily required to be professionally scrutinised, specifically for welfare assurance purposes, prior to the hearing of an adoption application.

Placement by freeing order

The primary legislative intent behind the introduction of 'freeing' to the adoption process was to provide a mechanism for the consensual involvement of a natural mother whereby she could take an early decision to voluntarily relinquish her child for adoption and be spared any further legal role in that process. It was also thought that this would provide a means whereby the mother could be constructively involved, if thought appropriate, in the transfer phase until the child settled. Although only an adoption agency can apply for a freeing order, it was expected that applications would be made by agency and parent acting jointly. Initially, indeed, it was possible to make such an application in respect of a child in care on a voluntary basis,[13] but this is now prohibited. However, for various reasons, including changes made by the 1989 Act, freeing has now become very much a public law proceeding with applications being largely made on a non-consensual basis by adoption agencies in respect of children already the subject of care orders.

Freeing without parental consent occurs when an adoption agency as sole applicant makes what is almost always a contested application in respect of a child in local authority care and the subject of a care order. In such cases the child is seldom a baby but is usually under five years of age. However, before making application under ss 18-20 of the 1976 Act, an agency must be sure that it can meet certain basic requirements. A preliminary issue for the court will be whether the order if granted would satisfy the 'best interests' test of s 6.[14] There is also a clear expectation that the child concerned is either already placed with prospective adopters or is about to be so placed. In the absence of parental consent, the applicant must satisfy the court that evidence exists to prove that agreement to the making of an order should be dispensed with on a ground specified in s 18(2). Once made, the order operates to vest parental responsibility wholly in the adoption agency.

Where a freeing order is made an adoption process is then commenced which may or may not conclude in an adoption order. Unless the parent concerned has made a 'no further involvement' declaration, then twelve months later the agency must inform that parent whether the child has or has not been placed for adoption and/or been adopted. In the event of no declaration being made and the child being neither adopted nor placed for adoption, then the parent has the right to apply for a revocation of the freeing order. If granted, revocation has the effect of extinguishing the parental responsibility vested in the agency, returning that responsibility to the parents and reviving any previous parental responsibility agreement, order or appointment of guardian but not reviving any order made under the 1989 Act. This posed risks which were a disincentive for an agency looking to the freeing process as a means of effecting an early clean break.

The freeing process also presents risks for the welfare interests of the child concerned. The actual process itself can be as time consuming as an application for an adoption order, which raises questions as to whether a lengthy two-stage process with accompanying uncertainty is always justifiable. Once granted, a freeing order consigns the freed child to what the Adoption Law Review describes as 'a legal limbo'.[15] The uncertainty regarding the legal status of such a child extends to doubt as to his or her succession rights. Finally, in the event of an adoption placement never being made or an adoption application failing, then it seemed that all parental responsibilities vested by the freeing order in the agency remained so vested for the duration of the subject's childhood.

The welfare role of agencies and officials

Adoption legislation contains few objective criteria; control over the adoption process has effectively been delegated to adoption agencies. In recent years that process has both greatly contracted and at the same time become increasingly professionalised. The fewer children now being adopted, many in the course of contested proceedings and bringing with them complicated legal problems, receive attention from a new range of bodies and officials. Their bearing on the process differs according to whether an application is public or private.

A registered adoption agency is the key professional reference point in the adoption process. It has been defined as a "body of persons whose functions consist of, or include the making of, arrangements for the adoption of children".[16] Each agency is required to set up at least one Adoption Panel. This must take all referrals relating to whether: adoption is in the best interests of a particular child; a prospective adopter should be approved as an adoptive parent and; if the home of a particular approved prospective adopter would provide a suitable placement for a particular child. This Panel provides a vital and discretionary function by matching prospective adopters with available children. Although it makes recommendations rather than decisions for its agency, the latter is prevented from taking decisions in those areas without first inviting recommendations from the Panel.

The local authority also plays an important role in the adoption process. Under s 1 of the 1976 Act the adoption responsibilities of local authorities rest on four planks: their contribution to forming and maintaining a local adoption service; linking adoption to their other child care services; managing their own work as registered adoption agencies and; carrying out certain supervisory duties in relation to placements. The adoption service requirement, as stated in s 1(2), entails each local authority ensuring the provision within its area of services (including, for example, residential, assessment and counselling services) appropriate to the needs of all parties to an adoption. The 1976 Act also places supervisory duties on the local authorities in respect of 'protected' children.

Two officials, the guardian *ad litem* and to a lesser extent the reporting officer, are assigned vital roles under s 65 of the 1976 Act in ensuring the welfare interests of a child in the adoption and freeing processes. The GAL and RO are independent of the adoption agency involved in a particular application and are each appointed from panels established under the Children Act 1975. Once appointed, the GAL is required to carry out an exhaustive investigation into all the circumstances of the proposed adoption. The guardian must interview all applicants and respondents including, where feasible, the child and ensure that any factor having a bearing on the welfare of the child is brought to the attention of the court. The legal significance of the role of both officers in safeguarding the welfare of children entering the adoption process is considerable. The GAL represents a child's welfare interests before the court while the RO is the child's legal representative and advocate for his or her views. This functional separation of roles, combined with their independent status, allows a balanced picture of a child's particular needs to be brought before the court. This particular balance in professional representation, providing separately for a child's welfare interests and legal rights, is very much in keeping with public family law proceedings (notably child care cases) and very untypical of private family law proceedings.

The Registrar General is another official whose duties have a bearing on the adoption process, though in effect they are tied to a post-adoption role. This official is obliged, by s 50 of the 1976 Act, to maintain an Adopted Children Register, keep an index of this in the General Register Office and ensure that records are kept which provide a link between an entry in the Register of Births marked 'adopted' and the corresponding entry in the Adopted Children Register. This allows for the collection of information sufficient to identify child, adopters, the date and place in respect of every adoption order issued. Under Sched 10, para 21 of the 1989 Act the Registrar General is required to maintain an Adoption Contact Register which enables adopted persons and their natural parents who want to contact each other to do so.

The welfare test

Much of the discussion on the policy of adoption legislation has centred on the distinction between adoption and custody and the consequential functions of welfare in each process. Some of the most authoritative pronouncements to that effect may be found in the judgments given in the House of Lords in *J v C*.[17] Lord MacDermott argued that "....wardship orders as to custody and adoption orders are so different in concept, nature and legal consequences that one cannot validly argue from either of these jurisdictions to the other".[18] Lord Upjohn commented that "...an adoption order, if made, is the antithesis of an order made in wardship proceedings".[19] Lord Hailsham, in the debates on the Children Bill in 1975, argued that while the paramountcy principle applied to "care and control, custody and guardianship, it cannot be equally true of adoption". The debate continues. The position, however, remains that the welfare test in the context of adoption is that the child's interests should be treated as the first though not the only consideration. Welfare interests are not of paramount importance.

Welfare and adoptions of children in care

The flow of children from the public child care sector into the private law adoption process has been a relatively recent development. For many generations, when care in the family of origin failed, whether due to criminal abuse perpetrated by a culpable parent or neglect by a well meaning but inadequate parent, children have entered the public care system. However, the long-term residential care option in children's homes has proved damaging to the welfare interests of thousands of children placed in the care of local authorities by court orders. Consequently modern child care legislation has introduced and gradually broadened the grounds for freeing such children for adoption. This change of policy, introducing non-consensual adoption for older and often abused or impaired children, might not have been as successful if it had not coincided with both a dramatic decline in the availability of freely relinquished healthy babies and a continued increase in the number of childless couples wishing to adopt. It has resulted in very many children being given the opportunity of an upbringing in a normal family environment, where they are wanted, which they would not otherwise have had.

It is clearly a most difficult judgment as to whether the welfare interests of a child committed to long-term local authority care would be best furthered by plans to rehabilitate him or her with their family of origin or by plans for adoption. The principles and ethos of the 1989 Act now exercise an influence, not present in earlier legislation, towards a preference for the former option. It must be right that all prospects for safe rehabilitation are exhausted before preparations for adoption are commenced; the preferences for a partnership approach between parents and local authority and for care in the family of origin provide wholly appropriate guidance in that context. However, in many cases the prospects for rehabilitation can be assessed as unrealisable on the basis of the facts grounding the care order, the parent/s track record etc, or the number of years the child has been in care. In those circumstances the principles and ethos of the 1989 Act should not impede decisions to place for adoption.

Welfare and intercountry adoptions

Inter-country adoptions have given rise to eligibility issues. These most often occur in relation to the prohibition on unauthorised payments,[20] unauthorised placements and proof of consents. The first two represent the traditional legal abhorrence of 'trafficking' in children and are criminal offences under s 57 and s 11 respectively of the 1976 Act. Improper payments (e.g. direct or indirect payments to the child's mother) may, if proven, prevent the court from making an adoption order;[21] though much will depend on the circumstances and whether the child's welfare interests are otherwise impaired. Improper placements are viewed more seriously by the courts and are more likely to result in the refusal of an adoption order. The problems in relation to proof of consents refers to the difficulty in establishing, across geographical, cultural and language barriers, the legal status of parent and child and confirming that any consent given was done so freely and with full understanding of the consequences. Any one or combination of these issues may well complicate the court's ultimate application of the welfare test to a particular intercountry adoption application. However, as was illustrated most recently and graphically in *Re C (Adoption: Legality)*,[22] the fact that there have been irregularities - in adopter approval, payments, matching and introduction of adopter and child – will not be sufficient to outweigh the fact that once the placement is made the passing of time steadily dictates the making of an adoption order as the best option available to the court.

Applying the welfare test to the child subjects of intercountry adoptions does of course give rise to some fundamental questions. It must be accepted that the circumstances of war and natural disaster governing the availability of many children are such that their welfare interests can only be improved by this modern 'child rescue' approach of adopters. This rationale, perhaps, lay behind the decision of the court in *Re K (Adoption and Wardship)*[23] which concerned a five year old orphan who as a wounded baby had been removed from Bosnia and then 'adopted' by her English rescuers. The court, when faced with a petition from the child's relatives, set aside the defective adoption order but rather than direct her return to her extended family and her country of origin it ruled that she should remain with the English couple who had become her 'psychological parents'. However, for some children their availability is conditioned by the social economics of their country of origin and it may be that the dislocation to family and culture resulting from adoption may prove in the long-term not to be conducive to the promotion of their welfare interests. This line of reasoning was present in the decision of in the Court of Appeal in *Re M (Child's Upbringing)*[24] where it was held that preserving the Zulu identity of a ten year old boy, reared for seven years by white foster parents, was sufficiently important to order his return to natural parents in South Africa despite his strong wishes to the contrary. While it is admittedly difficult to reconcile the judicial rationale of both cases, it may be that intercountry adoption will only satisfy the welfare test where, as with other adoptions, rehabilitation in the family of origin has become impossible. The consent, or absence of dissent, of the child concerned must also be a factor in meeting that test.

Welfare and transracial adoptions

Some of the same tensions which prevail in intercountry adoptions exist also in this context. The media generated controversy surrounding transracial adoptions has tended to center on a practice by adoption agencies and local authorities to make and break placements on the basis of whether or not there was a racial match between child and prospective adopters. There have been a number of cases where the propriety of this practice has been examined[25] and the emerging consensus is that where possible placement arrangements should reflect a child's ethnic background and cultural identity insofar as such considerations are compatible with the welfare interests of that child which must always have priority. In particular, the courts have upheld the value of preserving established relationships as a key component of welfare interests in transracial as in all other kinds of placements; the duration of current care arrangements and age of the child being of crucial importance. In *Re N (A Minor)(Adoption)*[26] Bush J warned that:

> ...the emphasis on colour rather than on cultural upbringing can be mischievous and highly dangerous when you are dealing in practical terms with the welfare of children.

The practice was addressed most recently in the White Paper on adoption.[27] The view then expressed was to the effect that a child's ethnic background and cultural identity should always be factors to be considered by agency staff when making adoption placements but not necessarily to be given any greater consideration than other factors.

Welfare and family adoptions

An unmarried mother may adopt her own child.[28] An unmarried father may also do so.[29] However, it is the increasing recourse to adoption by mothers of illegitimate children applying jointly with their husbands to adopt her child, in order to legally seal the boundaries of their new family units, that is most contentious. The effect of an adoption order in such circumstances may be to marginalise not only the natural father but also his side of the family. The European Court of Human Rights in *Soderback v Sweden*[30] accepted that such an adoption amounted to interference with the natural father's right to respect for family life as it totally and permanently deprived him of the opportunity to enjoy family life with his child (see, further, Chap 15). But in this jurisdiction there has been little evidence of suitability criteria being applied by the judiciary to refer uncontested step-parent applications to marital proceedings, despite the warning in the Houghton Report that an adoption order in such circumstances might prejudice rather than benefit the welfare of the child.[31] However the Court of Appeal in a recent ruling,[32] which goes very much against the normal trend, allowed the appeal of a natural father against an adoption order made in respect of his child and in favour of the child's mother and husband on the grounds that the father had demonstrated the appropriate attachment, commitment and motive to be eligible for a parental responsibility order.

The Houghton Report also took the view that adoption by grandparents was not, as a rule, desirable.[33] This reservation rests on the significance of age differentials between adopter and adopted and echoes the warning given by Vaisey J that 'they should be regarded as exceptional and made with great caution.[34] There is little evidence that the availability of s 8 orders under the 1989 Act is serving to significantly raise the suitability threshold for step-parent applicants.

Applications or petitions by natural parents, grandparents, relatives, foster-parents and others with an established relationship with the child are apt to cause problems. A new and lesser legal relationship is being substituted for an existing legal and actual relationship. Purpose and motive become relevant. The use of adoption by family members is held to be unsatisfactory because it adds a veneer to an existing legal status in the relationship between child and adopter which may obscure that relationship. The possible obscuring of family relationships and potential loss of contact with significant relatives are among the reasons why family adoptions are not necessarily conducive to promoting the welfare interests of the children concerned.

Welfare and same sex adoptions

The 1976 Act is silent on the prospect of adoption by a same sex couple; it simply was not within the ambit of legislative intent. The possibility of adoption by a single person, however, was and is provided for; the earlier statutory prohibition on adoption of a female child by a single adult male having been removed. An adoption application by a single homosexual male or lesbian, where the applicant is living with a partner of the same gender, has therefore for some time been legally possible but not until recently has it become professionally and socially acceptable. Judicial notice has been taken of research findings indicating that child rearing by same sex couples has not had any deleterious effects on the children concerned. This has led to the current position where judgments emphasise that providing such applicants satisfy the s 6 welfare test then their sexual orientation is of little relevance. So, for example, in *AMT (Known as AC) (Petitioners for authority to adopt SR)*,[35] where the subject was a three year old boy and the applicant a male homosexual living with a long-term male partner, the court granted an adoption order. Again, in *Re W (Adoption: Homosexual Adopter)*[36] an application for a freeing order was unsuccessfully opposed by the natural mother who objected to the local authority placement of her child with two lesbian women who intended to adopt. This trend undoubtedly brings adoption practice more closely into line with the realities of modern family life.

The welfare test and an adoption order

Welfare is always the final threshold requirement to be met by applicants before an adoption order can be made. The principle is then given a 'first consideration' rather than a 'paramount' weighting. A distinction which has been explained by Lord Simon in the following words:

> In adoption proceedings the welfare of the child is not the paramount consideration (ie outweighing all others) as with custody or guardianship; but it is the first consideration (ie outweighing any other).[37]

At the hearing (or earlier in freeing order proceedings) welfare is also present as a component in the threshold requirements to be satisfied by an adoption agency. The agency is then faced with the statutorily prescribed duty that it provide evidence of the existence of either parental agreement or of grounds for dispensing with the necessity for it.

Parental agreement to adoption may only be dispensed with on the grounds stated in s 16 of the 1976 Act:

> (2) that the parent or guardian -
> (a) cannot be found or is incapable of giving agreement;
> (b) is withholding his consent unreasonably;
> (c) has persistently failed without reasonable cause to discharge his parental duties for the child;
> (d) has abandoned or neglected the child;
> (e) has persistently ill-treated the child; and
> (f) has seriously ill-treated the child but only where (because of the ill-treatment or for other reasons) the rehabilitation of the child within the household of the parent or guardian is unlikely.

The final two grounds are explicitly child care in nature. Despite the opportunity they provide to base the rationale for an adoption on evidence of parental abuse of a child's welfare interests, these grounds have been largely ignored. By far the majority of such cases proceed on the grounds of parental unreasonableness. The test then is whether a reasonable person in the parent's position, being mindful of the child's welfare interests, would be justified in withholding agreement. As Lord Hailsham said in *Re W (An Infant)*[38] "...welfare *per se* is not the test" or, as stated in the same case by Lord MacDermott:

> ...the mere fact that an adoption order will be for the welfare of the child does not itself necessarily show that a parent's refusal to consent to that adoption is unreasonable...(p 706).

The judicial role in adoption is essentially adjudicative. Adoption proceedings afford little scope for discretion and almost always end with a decision to either grant or not to grant the order sought. For an order to be made evidence is required that the above s 6 test can be satisfied. Judicial interpretation of the welfare principle, in relation to the particular circumstances of the child, is then of determining significance. The comparative material advantages[39] offered by the prospective adopters have been held not to satisfy the welfare principle, neither have reasons such as legitimation,[40] immigration[41] or simply the wish to change a child's name.[42] The granting of the proposed adoption order must, in the words of Davies LJ[43] demonstrably further the welfare interests of a child by offering

> ...material and financial prospects, education, general surroundings, happiness, stability of home and the like.

While welfare is an important factor to be taken into account in all adoption applications, it will be insufficient in itself to justify an order.

Welfare may be interpreted as benefit, but this is not necessarily confined to benefits of a material nature as removal of the stigma of illegitimacy has itself been considered a benefit. In the words of Josling[44] "the main benefit of adoption will be to give the child the social, legal and psychological benefits of belonging to a family". However, where an application would clearly safeguard and promote the welfare of the child the order sought may still be refused as when, for example, its purpose is to circumvent immigration policy[45] or is construed by the court as merely the means whereby the applicants could secure the benefits of education and a better standard of life for the child in question.[46] If a proposed adoption satisfies the welfare test in all other respects then the fact that the applicant is homosexual[47] or that the applicants and social worker have committed criminal offences in breach of ss 11 and 57 of the 1976 Act[48] will not necessarily provide grounds for rejecting the order sought. In *Re B*[49] Wall J commented that the interests of a child in being brought up in accordance with the religious beliefs of his natural parents would be displaced where his welfare interests required it. Under s 6 of the 1976 Act there is an explicit requirement to consider whether the adoption order, if made, would promote the welfare of the child "throughout his childhood". This adds a prospective dimension to the welfare test. So, for example, where the Court of Appeal upheld[50] an adoption order granted six days before the subject with a learning disability attained his 18th birthday, it was held that in such circumstances the welfare consideration should extend beyond childhood. The similar requirement in s 6 to take into account whether the applicants can offer "a stable and harmonious home" has the effect of raising a presumption in favour of adoption for long term care arrangements such as those provided by step-parents and foster-parents. This, perhaps, was the determining factor in *Re MW*[51] where the court dismissed a surrogate mother's opposition to an adoption application by commissioning parents, despite certain illegalities committed by the latter, as 'first consideration' had to be given to the welfare of the child who by then had been cared for by the applicants for two-and-a-half years.

Welfare and the views of the child

Under the second part of s 6 there is a requirement to "...ascertain the wishes and feelings of the child...having regard to his age and understanding". Following the *Gillick* ruling and the Children Act 1989, a certain amount of caselaw has built up around the weighting given to a child's views (see, also, Chaps 6 and 7). For example, the decision of a court[52] to dispense with parental agreement was significantly influenced by an 11 year old boy's views on adoption. This judicial approach has been endorsed by an official recommendation[53] that the court should not be allowed to make an adoption order in relation to a child aged 12 years or over unless that child's consent has either been obtained or has been dispensed with. In *Re I (Adoption Order: Nationality)*[54] the court attached considerable importance to the expressed consent of children aged 13 and 16 when approving their adoption despite opposition from the Home Secretary who submitted that the application was a sham intended to defeat immigration controls. The question of the importance of taking into account children's views has arisen also in the context of professional privilege. In *Re D (Adoption Reports: Confidentiality)* the House of Lords[55] considered a case concerning a contested adoption application in which the father and stepmother sought to dispense with the natural mother's consent, on the grounds that it was being unreasonably withheld. The GAL had a number of interviews with the mother and children, some of the content of which was entered in his report. The wishes and feelings of the children were recorded in two sections of the report and the issue facing the court was whether these sections could be disclosed to the mother in accordance with her request. The decision of the court at first instance to veto disclosure was endorsed by the Court of Appeal but the appeal was upheld by the House of Lords. In giving judgment, the House took into account: existing caselaw;[56] the differential in significance of disclosure in the context of proceedings in adoption, wardship and under the 1989 Act and; the lack of any similar differential in relation to the reports of a GAL, adoption agency or social services social worker. The ruling of the House, an important benchmark for welfare interests relative to professional privilege, was as follows:

> (1) It was a fundamental principle of fairness that a party was entitled to the disclosure of all materials which might be taken into account by a court when reaching a decision adverse to that party. That principle applied with particular force to adoption proceedings.
> (2) When deciding whether to direct that notwithstanding r 53(2) of the Adoption Rules 1984 a party referred to in a confidential report supplied by an adoption agency, a local authority, a reporting officer or a guardian *ad litem* should not be entitled to inspect that part of the report referring to him or her, the court should first consider whether disclosure of the material would involve a real possibility of harm to the child.
> (3) If it would, the court should next consider whether the overall interests of the child would benefit from non-disclosure, weighing the interests of the child in having the material properly tested against the magnitude of the risk that harm would occur and the gravity of that harm.
> (4) If the court was satisfied that the interests of the child pointed towards non-disclosure, the next and final step was for the court to weigh that consideration against the interests of the parent or other party in having an opportunity to see and respond to the material. In the latter regard the court should take into account the importance of the material to the issue in the case.

(5) Non-disclosure should be the exception and not the rule. The court should be rigorous in its examination of the risk and the gravity of the feared harm to the child, and should order non-disclosure only where the case for doing so was compelling.
(6) In the present case the judge had erred in approaching the question of disclosure in the manner of a pure discretion and in giving no weight to the strong presumption in favour of disclosure in adoption proceedings.

Welfare and conditional adoption orders

The future welfare interests of an adopted child may also be affected by the judicial power to issue an adoption order subject to a condition. Under s 12(6) of the 1976 Act, the court may attach such conditions as it thinks fit to an adoption order. For example, where a relationship already exists between the child and a natural parent or sibling, which may constitute a psychological bond and thus in itself be a determining factor of such welfare, then the courts may well see fit to attach a contact condition when making an adoption order. In the past the existence of such a meaningful bond has often been judicially viewed as vitiating the welfare ground for an adoption order: adoption and continued contact being seen as mutually exclusive. The two factors which have now come to determine whether a contact condition (or any other condition) should be attached to an adoption order are the welfare of the child and enforceability. Both factors arose for consideration in a leading case[57] where the condition sought and granted was for sibling access. It was then held that a distinction could be meaningfully drawn between the legal standing of a parent and a sibling as regards the legitimacy of their respective claims that an access condition would be to the benefit of the child concerned. While the former would have had every opportunity to bring their claim before the court at the time the substantive issue of consent was being determined, the latter would not. However, once an adoption order has been made then the court will take a different view. In *Re S (Contact: Application by Sibling)*[58] the court refused an adopted nine year old child leave to apply for a contact order enabling her to resume her relationship with a seven year old half brother with special needs who had been adopted into a different family. The application was resisted by the boy's adoptive parents on the grounds that it would disrupt his life. The court held that the making of an adoption order was intended to be permanent and final and issues such as contact should not be considered after that event; except in the most unusual circumstances. Generally, however, in recent years the new flexibility permitted by the introduction of contact orders under the Children Act 1989, together with the tacit encouragement offered in a subsequent White Paper[59] to the practice of facilitating more 'open' adoptions and the concern expressed about step-adoptions, has led to a proliferation of adoption orders being made subject to a contact condition.

Adoption proceedings are now defined as family proceedings (See, s 8(4)(d) of the Children Act 1989). The court is therefore entitled, instead of granting an adoption order, to make any of the orders available under s 8 (e.g. residence order etc) which may be more appropriate where the prospective adopter already has, in relation to the child, the status of step-parent, relative or foster-parent. For example, in a recent case[60] an unmarried couple wished to adopt a 5 year old child whom they had been fostering for three years. An adoption order was granted to the father, despite opposition from the child's mother, and a shared residence order was granted to both foster parents. The adoption order was considered appropriate as it placed the child on the same legal footing as the couple's other two children, and gave the adopted child the same surname as them. The residence order gave the foster parent, who was the primary carer, a secure legal relationship with the child.

Conclusion

Adoption is the most radical of all family law orders. No other order so fundamentally changes the legal status of its subject on a lifetime basis. Its effect is to re-write the relationships between three sets of legal interests with implications for the wider family circles of those involved, the consequences of which will be felt by subsequent generations. Perhaps for these reasons, the law has traditionally focussed on status requirements as the threshold of entry of all parties to an adoption process. The judicial role has been largely confined to a simple, and usually very brief, adjudication on the issues relating to availability of child, consent of parent/s and entitlement of applicants. There has been little need for exercises of judicial discretion. The welfare factor has tended to be treated negatively, the court confining its considerations to ensuring that no consequences adverse to the child's welfare were likely to ensue as a result of it making an adoption order. The paramountcy principle has never had any bearing on the outcome of the process. Overall, this approach was not inappropriate when adoption was almost exclusively a private family law proceeding in which, typically, the care of a voluntarily relinquished child had been assumed by unrelated, agency approved and supervised, adoption applicants. Then, the three sets of needs and legal interests neatly dovetailed.

Adoption, however, has greatly changed in the years since the introduction of the current governing legislation. Adoptions are now complicated by issues arising from either the public law or step-parent contexts which together generate the availability of by far the largest proportion of all children entering the adoption process. The role of consent as a threshold requirement has become fraught; its determining effect in the context of testing the rights of a natural parent can be as difficult to judge when withheld in the context of abuse as when freely given in the context of step-parent applications.

Many children are now of an age, and/or have needs complicated by varying forms of disability or by their foreign origin, to require an in depth professional and judicial examination of their welfare interests. The legislative role ascribed to the welfare principle, however, continues to exclude a paramountcy weighting and to be essentially negative, serving as the final and routine test of outcome when all formal status criteria have been satisfied. The judicial role in relation to this principle has been broadened by the exercise of discretion to allow for the more frequent involvement of expert witnesses and for the attachment of conditions to adoption orders. But exercises of judicial discretion to provide for welfare adjustments in determining the final outcome of adoption processes have not been matched by similar exercises of discretion in relation to the interpretation of threshold requirements at point of entry. Little use has been made of discretionary opportunities to employ the welfare principle to deal with the appropriateness of step-parent applications or to hold that agreement has been unreasonably withheld. The courts have preferred to decide the issues almost exclusively in terms of the threshold requirements. Welfare continues to be more a factor in than the objective of the adoption process.

Notes

1 See, the Houghton Committee *Report of the Departmental Committee on the Adoption of Children* (1972) where the view is expressed that "The child is the focal point in adoption; providing homes for children who need them is its primary purpose".

2 It is not possible to adopt a foetus. However, as was apparent in *Re Adoption Application (Adoption: Payment)* [1987] 2 FLR 291, it is possible to contract in respect of a foetus to be carried to full-term by a surrogate mother on behalf of a sperm donor in order that she may eventually be in a position to commence adoption proceedings.

3 Subject to the limitations imposed by the Adoption (Hague Convention) Act (NI) 1969.

4 See, the Court of Appeal decisions in both *Re V (A Minor)(Adoption: Consent)* [1987] 2 FLR 89 and *Re R (A Minor)(Adoption: Parental Agreement)* [1987] 1 FLR 391 where the court held that young mothers were being unreasonable in withholding consent when their conduct was viewed objectively.

5 [1995] 2 FLR 483. But, see also, *Re O (A Minor)(Custody: Adoption)* [1992] 1 FLR 77 where the court ruled that the custody of a child, aged15 months and placed at birth by mother with an adoption agency, should be granted to a natural father. It appears that the court took the view that neither the welfare interests of the child nor the marital status of the father should be determinative. See, further, Bainham A., *Children: The Modern Law* (2nd ed) 1998, pp 167-8 for evidence that the court will give weight to an application from a natural father where the contest lies between him and a third party rather than directly with the natural mother.

6 See, the ruling of the House of Lords in *Re M (A Minor)* [1980] CYLB 1801 endorsing the judicial approach in *Re P (An Infant)(Adoption: Parental Consent)* [1977] Fam 25.

7 See, *Parental Rights in Adoption cases: a New Approach to the Law of Adoption*, 1958 54 Child Adoption 19.

8 See, *Re T and E* [1995] 1 FLR 581 for a case where the conflict was more than philosophical.

9 See, *Re D (An Infant)(Adoption: Parent's Consent)* [1995] 1 FLR 895 at p 898. A view endorsed in para 7.1. of the 1992 Review.

10 In due course the findings of the *Review of Adoption Law: Report to Ministers of an Interdepartmental Working Group* (DoH, 1992) and the subsequent White Paper *Adoption: the Future* (Cmnd 2288) should result in changes to adoption law which will address the problem of harmonising the role of the welfare principle in child care and adoption.

11 See, Report of the Houghton Committee, para 81, (1972).

12 A foster care placement made on the traditional basis of 'long-term with a view to adoption' is now prohibited; see, *Gatehouse v Robinson* [1986] 1 WLR 18.

13 Research in England and Wales had shown that a high proportion of freeing orders (approx 33% in one study) were made in relation to children in care with parental consent. The Adoption Act 1976, s 18(2), (2A) as amended by the 1989 Act, Sched 10, para 6, has had the effect of ending any possibility of the freeing process being used in respect of any child who is not the subject of a statutory care order.

14 See, *Re D (A Minor)(Adoption: Freeing Order)* [1991] 1 FLR 48, CA.

15 See, *Adoption Law Review*, Discussion Paper No 2, 1990, para 134.

16 Josling and Levy *Adoption of Children* 10th ed., London, Longman 1985, p 23.

17 [1970] AC 668, [1969] 2 WLR 540, [1969] 1 All ER 788, HL.

18 *Op cit*, p 714.

19 *Op cit*, p 719.

20 See, *Re An Adoption Application* [1992] 1 FLR 341, *Re AW (Adoption Application)* [1992] Fam Law 539 and *Re C (A Minor)(Adoption Application)* [1992] Fam Law 538.

21 The court may, however, retrospectively authorise payments; see, for example, *Re WM (Adoption: Non-Patrial)* [1997] 1 FLR 132.

22 [1998] 1 FLR.

23 [1997] 2 FLR 230.

24 [1996] 2 FLR 441. See, also, *Re B (Adoption: Child's Welfare)* [1995] 1 FLR 895 which concerned an adoption application arising from the informal foster care arrangement made for a Gambian child. In refusing the application, Wall J placed considerable importance upon the child's cultural inheritance as an integral aspect of its welfare.

25 See, for example: *Re P (A Minor)(Adoption)* [1990] 1 FLR 96; *R v Lancashire County Council , ex parte M* [1992] 1 FLR 109; and *Re JK (Adoption: Transracial Placement)* [1991] 2 FLR 340.

26 [1990] 1 FLR 58 at p 63. Also, see, *Re O (Transracial Adoption: Contact)* [1995] 2 FLR 597.

27 See, *Adoption: The Future*, (Cmnd 2288) HMSO, 1993, para 4.32.

28 See, *Re D (An Infant)* [1959] 1 QB 229 [1958] 3 All ER 716.

29 See, *F v S* [1973] Fam 203 at 207, [1973] 1 All ER 722 at 725 CA.

30 [1999] 1 FLR 250.
31 paras 97 and 103.
32 See, *Re G (Adoption Order)* [1999] 1 FLR 400.
33 Paras 111-114.
34 See, *In re DX (An Infant)* [1949] 1 Ch 320 at p 321.
35 [1997] *AMT (Known as AC) (Petitioners for authority to adopt SR)* [1997] FAM Law 8 and 225
36 [1997] 2 FLR 406. See, also, *Re E (Adoption: Freeing Order)* [1995] 1 FLR 382.
37 See, *Re D (An Infant)(Adoption: Parent's Consent)* [1977] AC 602, at p 638.
38 [1971] AC 682 at p 699.
39 See, *Re D (No 2)* [1959] 1 QB 229.
40 See, *CD Petitioners* [1963] SLT (Sh Ct) 7.
41 See, *In re A (An Infant)* [1963] 1 WLR 34. Also see, *In re H (A Minor)(Adoption: Non-Patrial)* [1982] Fam Law 121 where an adoption order was granted in respect of an immigrant despite contrary advice from the Secretary of State.
42 See, for example, *In re D (Minors)* [1973] Fam 209.
43 See, *In re P* [1977] Fam 25, CA.
44 Josling and Levy, *Adoption of Children* (10th Ed), London: Longman (1985) p 5.
45 See, *Re A (An Infant)* [1963] 1 All ER 531, [1963] 1 WLR 231; *Re R (Adoption)* [1963] 3 All ER 613, [1967] 1 WLR 34. However, see also, *Re H (Adoption: Non-patrial)* [1966] 1 FLR 717 and also *Re J (Adoption: Non-Patrial)* [1998] 1 FLR 225 where adoptions were allowed despite breach of immigration rules. This factor was outweighed in importance by the welfare interests of the children concerned which would be appropriately safeguarded by adoption.
46 See, *Re B (Adoption Order: Nationality)* [1998] 1 FLR 965.
47 See, *AMT (Known as AC) (Petitioners for authority to adopt SR)* [1997], *Re W (Adoption: Homosexual Adopter)* [1997] 2 FLR 406 and *Re E (Adoption: Freeing Order)* [1995] 1 FLR 382.
48 See, *Re C (Adoption: Legality)* [1999] 1 FLR.
49 [1995] 1 FLR 895.
50 See, *In Re D (A Minor)(Adoption Order: Validity)* [1991] 2 FLR 66.
51 [1995] 2 FLR 759.
52 See, *Re B (Minor)(Adoption: Parental Agreement)* [1990] 2 FLR 383. See, also, *Re G (TJ)(An Infant)* [1963] 1 All ER 20 CA; *Re D (Minors)(Adoption by Step-Parent)* [1980] 2 FLR 103, and; *Re B (A Minor)(Adoption)* [1988] 18 Fam Law 172.
53 See, Interdepartmental Group, DoH, *Review of Adoption Law*, para 3, (1992).
54 [1998] 2 FLR.
55 See, [1995] 2 FLR 687.
56 In particular: *Official Solicitor v K* [1965] AC 201; *Re B (A Minor)(Disclosure of Evidence)* [1993] Fam 142, [1993] 1 FLR 191 and *McMichael v United Kingdom* [1995] Fam Law 478.
57 See, *Re C (A Minor)* [1988]1 AER 712h.
58 [1998] 2 FLR.
59 See, *Adoption: The Future*, (Cmnd 2288).
60 See, *Re AB (Adoption: Shared Residence Order*) [1996] 1 FLR No 1. For a judicial appraisal of the relative merits of a residence order and adoption order see the Court of Appeal judgment in *Re M (Adoption or Residence Order)* [1998] 1 FLR 570.

Part 5: The Future Role of the Welfare Principle: An International Perspective

Introduction to Part 5

The role and functions of the welfare principle in the family law of the UK have for some time been affected by legal initiatives emanating from outside the jurisdiction, particularly from the United Nations and the Court of Human Rights. Influences from such sources can only become more frequent and directive in future years. There is now a discernible convergence, at least across western nations, in the interpretations given to the welfare principle. There is also a trend towards re-interpreting some welfare interests as children's rights. Identifying and evaluating the effect of particular provisions, directives, judicial rulings and academic publications - which, despite originating outside the UK jurisdiction, contribute to shaping the law relating to children within it – provides an important final theme.

This Part draws from the indigenous and extraneous influences on the shaping of the welfare principle in contemporary UK family law to identify those aspects of the principle which have been verified over time and internationally as the essential core constituents of children's welfare interests. In addition to interests confirmed by their pervasiveness and durability, this Part evaluates those rights which have more recently gained currency by being incorporated in and applied through UN Conventions. The balance now struck between the welfare interests and the rights of children, and their inter-relationship with other principles and considerations, in the family law of the UK are explored. Some resulting implications for the legal system are discussed.

Having identified and considered the separate strands constituting the "golden thread", the legal machinery for use in respect of them and the conditioning effect of contemporary social and other pressures, it then becomes possible to estimate the future significance of the welfare principle in the family law of the UK. One possibility is that it may provide a means for binding together both sectors of family law and other related areas insofar as they deal with matters affecting the welfare of children. This would necessitate far-reaching changes to the present legal system. Considering the principle's potential as providing the rationale for a family court - around which the future of the law relating to children in the UK may be re-structured - is a major and concluding theme of this book.

15 International Influences and the Shaping of the Modern Welfare Principle in the UK

Introduction

International convergence in the recognition of key family law principles is gathering momentum. The strategy of facilitating the harmonisation of principles and procedures between the nations of the European Union has been underway now for some decades. Countries sharing common and relatively 'open' borders, such as the United States of America and Canada, the two jurisdictions on the island of Ireland and those comprising Scandinavia have also had to at least explore areas of commonality and difference. There are now many international treaties, conventions and protocols in place designed explicitly to promote a common recognition of principles, to co-ordinate procedures and to effect agreed joint action. Such developments are best viewed as intended to facilitate communication between different legal systems rather than as incremental steps towards merger.

This is no longer a process driven solely by pragmatic necessity. A body of academic enquiry directed towards exploring the legacy of empire, in terms of legal principles and practices, is steadily accumulating. In the law of modern independent states can be found resonances from a time of subjugation when the legal template of a foreign nation constrained an indigenous culture. The receding tide of empire has left the residual legal architecture of Islam, Spain, France, Britain etc to challenge modern planners of legislative development in nations far removed in time, geography and culture from their imperial progenitors. In the resulting blend of indigenous and imperial the latter can play a vigorous role, producing examples of modern practice which, by emphasising its origins, carries implications for contemporary law in the post-imperial nation. The common law, exported with the expansion of the British empire, is such a residual legacy embedded in the legal structures of many nations. Some of these produce legal developments which manifestly demonstrate their common heritage and now resonate with modern UK law.

This chapter examines the source, nature and effect of modern international influences upon the role of the welfare principle in the civil law as it relates to children in the UK. Rather than attempt an exhaustive survey and assessment, which would be wholly beyond the scope of this study, it aims only to select the material necessary to demonstrate the fact of such influence and, though to a lesser extent, to illustrate the range of sources and their effects. The chapter is in two parts. The first chronicles the history of the formal European instruments which have impinged on this role. Reference is also made to the contribution from sources which share a common law heritage with the UK. The second part considers the effect of these influences. It does so by identifying and examining key caselaw developments in both Europe, under the various Conventions, and in countries with common law foundations. It considers the relevance of such caselaw for this jurisdiction in relation to public and private family law. The exercise undertaken in the second part rests to some degree on conjecture. This is most obviously so in relation to the caselaw of countries such as the USA, which clearly has no precedent value for UK judiciary but may nevertheless on occasion influence an approach taken by the latter and may also be taken into account by UK legislators. A reluctance to cede jurisdiction has also characterised the UK's relationship with the UN and the ECHR. Much of the history of this relationship reveals a UK resistance to prompt and full ratification of international Conventions and to opportunities for incorporating the results of related judgments.

Historical background

In the international arena, as in the local, the development of the law relating to the welfare interests of children has not been determined exclusively by either judicial or legislative initiative nor, in the latter case, solely by changes implemented through provisions specific to children. Changes directed towards improving the legal position of children are the most conspicuous, the legislative intent is more clearly discernible and the effects are usually readily identified. Changes directed more generally towards improving the rights, health and living conditions, institutions, and access to services infrastructure, of all persons are often more difficult to identify, trace and measure in terms of their implications for children. In the present context it is customary to distinguish between the effect of international influence when directed specifically towards child welfare considerations and when directed towards all persons but also affecting children. It is also necessary to bear in mind that while international influence has been and is exercised most directly from Europe, it has also been generated from other sources.

The influence from Europe

The Geneva Convention of 1924 is the accepted starting point for any history of international influence on the development of national law relating specifically to the welfare of children. The fifth Assembly of the League of Nations then adopted a declaration emphasising children's material needs. Responding to the deprivations which followed the first world war, it proclaimed that children 'must have' means requisite for their normal development - including food for the hungry, nursing for the sick, help for the handicapped and shelter and succour for the orphan and waif. Essentially this was an aspirational document.

In 1948 the General Assembly of the United Nations unanimously adopted the European Convention for the Protection of Human Rights and Fundamental Freedoms. This addressed the fundamental rights of all persons and declared that an infringement by court or by tribunal[1] would be actionable. A procedure for enforcement was eventually established in 1959 when the European Court of Human Rights was set up. The Convention made no specific reference to children but, in its preamble, referred instead to 'the inherent dignity and...equal and inalienable rights of all members of the human family'. The rights pronounced did eventually come to be viewed as applicable also to children.[2] In the UK, its relevance to their welfare interests and legal rights began in 1966 when this country declared its recognition of the Commission's jurisdiction. It acquired a more direct immediacy when it became incorporated into UK law with the introduction of the Human Rights Act 1998. This has 'gifted' UK jurisprudence with the body of caselaw accumulated by the ECHR; requiring existing domestic precedents to be revised to ensure conformity with standards set by the ECHR. Until then it had been necessary for a litigant, having first exhausted all domestic appeal procedures, to petition the European Commission for leave to appeal to the ECHR. Now, instead of seeking redress in the ECHR, a UK litigant can have 'Convention rights' directly enforced by the UK courts. It remains to be seen what priority the UK courts will accord a ECHR judgment where it conflicts with a domestic precedent.

Because this Convention is so emphatically focussed on rights, it has great potential for exercising leverage on behalf of children's independent legal interests as opposed to their welfare interests; the former requiring a firmness of differentiation between adult and child interests not necessarily required in the latter. It positively represents rights, does so in a prescriptive manner, provides an adversarial forum for adjudication and is now directly and wholly embedded in the UK body of law by the 1998 Act. This may well come to distinguish its influence on domestic law from such others as the 1989 Convention which represents welfare interests in a negative manner, is somewhat ambivalent in the balance it strikes between rights and welfare, has not been wholly and directly incorporated by statute and does not have a formal enforcement capacity (see, further, below).

The UN Declaration of the Rights of the Child was issued in 1959. This was based on the premise that 'mankind owes to children the best it has to give' and addressed the needs of children particularly for service provision in the areas of health, housing and education. It contained an implicit emphasis on duties to children. However, although going further than protection to recognise an entitlement to some rights, it succeeded in little more than proclaiming 10 general principles.

Both the 1924 League of Nations Declaration and the 1959 UN Declaration emphasised child protection, particularly from discrimination, rather than rights. Each declaration called for assistance in the child's normal development,[3] protection from exploitation,[4] and abandonment[5] and to receive relief in times of disaster.[6] Of the two, the 1959 Declaration was more comprehensive and covered standards for play and recreation,[7] parental care,[8] name and nationality,[9] social security,[10] education,[11] and care of the handicapped.[12]

The significance of the 1959 Declaration lies in the fact that it traced out the foundations of principle and subject upon which the 1989 Convention was later to build. Of particular importance was that it articulated, for the first time, the paramountcy principle:

> Principle 1 -
> The child shall enjoy special protection, and shall be given opportunities and facilities, by law and by other means, to enable him to develop physically, mentally, morally, spiritually and socially in a healthy and normal manner and in conditions of freedom and dignity. In the enactment of laws for this purpose, the best interests of the child shall be the paramount consideration.

This resolute statement of the standard to be set in relation to specified aspects of a child's development provided an important international benchmark for reliance on the prescriptive legislative approach rather than on judicial discretion. However, as Bainham, has pointed out,[13] the standing of the 1959 provisions is now somewhat uncertain as they may be taken to be superseded by those of the 1989 UN Convention on the Rights of the Child.[14]

The work of the Council of Europe has been overshadowed, particularly by the UN Declaration of the Rights of the Child in 1959 and by the 1989 Convention. The Council was responsible for producing some influential Conventions including the European Convention on the Legal Status of Children Born Out of Wedlock which was ratified by the UK in 1981. It also issued the European Convention on the Adoption of Children 1967, the European Convention on Recognition and Enforcement of Decisions Concerning Custody of Children and on Restoration of Custody of Children 1980.

The International Year of the Child in 1979, being the twentieth anniversary of the 1959 Declaration, provided an important child oriented landmark.[15] To mark the occasion, a draft update of the Declaration was drawn up by the government of Poland as a proposed template for a new international law on the rights of children. This was found to be inadequate and was superseded by preparations for the UN Convention on the Rights of the Child which was formally adopted by the General Assembly of the UN in 1989, on the thirtieth anniversary of the 1959 Declaration.

The UN Standard Minimum Rules for the Administration of Juvenile Justice (or 'the Beijing Rules') dealt exclusively with juvenile justice and was adopted by the General Assembly in 1985. It outlined a framework for relating the needs of juveniles to the requirements of the legal system.

The UN Convention on the Rights of the Child in 1989, ratified by the UK[16] on 16th December 1991 and applicable to all children below the age of 18, provided the first positive assertion of entitlement to rights. In so doing, it purports to represent a change of approach from the concern with 'special protection' of children which characterised the 1959 Declaration. Of its 38 articles devoted to substantive rights, at least 10 had never been recognised as rights for children in any other international instrument.[17] They all relate to the child's 'individual personality': the right to be heard (Article 12), freedom of expression and information (Article 13), freedom of thought, conscience and religion (Article 14), freedom of association and assembly (Article 15) and the right to privacy (Article 16). The emphasis on rights was, however, balanced by reference to the more familiar need to assure protection of welfare interests. This ideological compromise is well illustrated in the wording of the two key provisions. In Article 12 states were required to:

> ...assure to the child who is capable of forming his or her own views the right to express those views freely, on all matters affecting the child, the views of the child being given due consideration in accordance with the age and maturity of the child. ...For this purpose, the child shall in particular be provided the opportunity to be heard in any judicial and administrative proceedings affecting the child.

Although giving a child the opportunity to participate in proceedings and the right to express views and for those views to be taken into account, it stopped short of giving a right to separate representation. Again in Article 3, para 1, this tendency to favour welfare rather than rights when faced with a choice between the two is evident in the directive that:

> In all actions concerning children, whether undertaken by public or private social welfare institutions, courts of law, administrative authorities or legislative bodies, the best interests of the child shall be a primary consideration.

The compromises embodied in this Convention are not restricted to the welfare/rights dilemma. It also equivocates on the separation of parental and child interests. In its Preamble, it states:

> ...that the family, as the fundamental group of society and the natural environment for the growth and well-being of all its members and particularly children, should be afforded the necessary protection and assistance so that it can fully assume its responsibilities within the community.

So, the family is given full recognition as a vehicle for achieving the well-being of children and state interference can be a violation both of it and of the child's right to a secure and private family life.

The fact that a majority of countries have now subscribed to the 1989 Convention means that the welfare principle as expressed in this provision has, for the first time, become elevated to the status of a truly international legal standard in 'all actions concerning children'. However, the corollary is that it has also thereby made it internationally permissible for a welfare rather than a rights approach to be sufficient in such actions. Then there is the question of the precise weighting to be attached to the welfare standard. The wording used clearly avoids any suggestion that a child's welfare is to be treated as the matter of paramount importance but it also infers that it may be only one of a number of primary considerations.

Article 3, para 1, gives rise to three distinct implications for the present role and functions of the welfare principle in UK law. Firstly, the uniform application of the 'primary consideration' standard, across the range of legal and administrative decision making bodies, is a most significant extension of its role. Instead of being confined by the 1989 Act to judicial decisions taken in the context of matters concerning upbringing, welfare interests are required to be a primary consideration for social workers, social security officers and for just about everyone involved in the formal decision making processes of an agency on any matter which concerns a child. It is difficult to see what limits might be set on the principle's application. A matter may, presumably, be quite tangential to the main business but if it concerns a child then the welfare principle will have to come into play. The business of very many agencies may well have to be routinely 'welfare proofed'; not only those with a statutory child care, health or education remit but perhaps also agencies such as planning bodies, leisure centres, housing and libraries. Secondly, the fact that the international requirement is for a welfare weighting less than that already demanded under the 1989 Act raises questions as to which is more appropriate. While there can be no question as to whether welfare in this jurisdiction is 'the paramount' or 'a primary' consideration (the first is correct in law in the UK), for judicial determination of upbringing issues, it may be queried whether this weighting is appropriate. Arguably, by imposing relative disadvantages on the interests of others, most notably parents, the 1989 Act does not conform with the balance between the interests of family members required by the 1989 Convention. Thirdly, and paradoxically, this provision stamps a welfare rather than a rights ethos on the decision making *modus operandi* of all relevant bodies. Just when the 1989 Act and the *Gillick* line of precedents had made room for a distinct children's rights focus in UK law, the Convention has brought a requirement that all relevant judicial and administrative forums should be infused with a welfare orientation. Given the title of the 1989 Convention and the fact that it does address so many rights, it is striking that this particular provision is so unequivocal in its welfare focus. The 1989 Convention, like the public law provisions of the 1989 Act, juggles the two different approaches of legal rights and welfare interests.

If its implications for family law in the UK are to be of more than academic interest then the provisions of the 1989 Convention must meet an enforceability test. It has sought to provide for this and consolidate its impact on domestic law by establishing, under Article 43, a Committee on the Rights of the Child. This enables the progress of member states to be monitored and periodically reviewed to assess the extent which each has complied with the provisions of the Convention. The Committee reviewed and reported on UK progress in 1995 when, as Bainham notes,[18] it recorded its concern about matters such as 'the extent of child poverty, the law permitting corporal punishment, the low age of criminal responsibility and the lack of children's rights in the educational sphere'.[19] While some progress has been made, due largely to pressure from the ECHR, in relation to corporal punishment the remaining matters have not improved; indeed legislative change regarding criminal responsibility will increase the number of younger children being drawn into the criminal justice system. When we remember that it was ratified by the UK in 1991 the question must be asked - Why is there not more evidence of internally induced legislative and administrative change to comply with Convention provisions?

In addition to the broad sweep of the 1989 Convention there have been a number of Hague Conventions focussed on particular aspects of children's welfare interests.

Abduction was the first in what was to become a series of specific issue child welfare matters addressed at The Hague. The need to end the practice of 'forum shopping' and restore some semblance of comity between nations in private family law disputes had become increasingly urgent by 1980. This prompted the making of both the Hague Convention on the Civil Aspects of International Child Abduction and the European Convention on Recognition and Enforcement of Decisions Concerning Custody of Children. These were incorporated into UK law by the Child Care and Custody Act 1985 and now provide the basis for regulating the wrongful removal of children to or from the UK. Both in effect place considerations of comity before those of welfare by directing the prompt return of any wrongfully removed child to the country with jurisdiction where all matters, including those affecting welfare interests, must be addressed. Both also make concessions to the welfare principle. Article 13 of the Hague Convention allows a court to refuse to order a child's return in circumstances:

> ...where the child objects to being returned and has attained an age and degree of maturity at which it is appropriate to take account of its views.

Usually the court has declined to accord a child's views sufficient weight to prevent his or her return, holding that to do so would be to defeat the central purpose of the Convention. Article 10 of the European Convention provides the basis for a similar court refusal in circumstances:

> ...where it is found by reason of a change of circumstances including the passage of time but not including a mere change in the residence of the child after an improper removal, the effects of the original decision are manifestly no longer in accordance with the welfare of the child.

This provision submits attainment of the central purpose of the European Convention to a frank application of the welfare test; more so than Article 13 does in relation to that of the Hague Convention.

Inter-country adoption was the next specific issue addressed at The Hague, by the standing Hague Conference on Private International Law, drawing from the principles established in Article 21 of the 1989 Convention. In 1993 the Hague Convention on Intercountry Adoption was issued and although the UK subsequently became a signatory it has yet to proceed to full ratification. This Convention declares in Article 1 its intent to influence the welfare interests of children by establishing:

> ...safeguards to ensure that intercountry adoptions take place in the best interests of the child and with respect for his or her fundamental rights as recognised in international law.

This it endeavours to do, in the first instance, by promoting the development of professional adoption services in 'donor' countries i.e. countries which for reasons of poverty and/or social instability are allowing children to be adopted by non-nationals. This is a significant moral stand with long-term implications for the future international role of the welfare principle. The 'child rescue' approach, with its attendant dislocation for human relationships and cultural identity, is not the preferred means of safeguarding welfare interests either locally or internationally. Giving priority to retaining a child in need within his or her family and social context of origin is an interpretation of the welfare principle common to both the 1993 Convention and the Children Act 1989. The convergence between the two is evident also in circumstances where consensually based retention is not feasible. Both then favour the provision of foster care services which would permit a child to be placed as close as possible, in terms of geography and relationships, to his or her family/culture/community of origin. Only when these options are not possible do both facilitate adoption and then again preference is given to maintaining the child within the cultural norms of his or her family of origin. The Convention views intercountry adoption as the final step in a continuum, to be taken when all others have been tried, and only then if all the professional filters are in place and the adoption process regulated to ensure that welfare interests are safeguarded.

The protection of children was the specific issue addressed by the Hague Child Protection Convention 1996. This was based on its predecessor the Hague Convention on the Protection of Minors 1961 and dealt with matters of jurisdictional conflict arising in relation to child protection proceedings. It outlined the inter-jurisdictional rules and procedures for taking protective measures in relation to a child's property and physical integrity. It established that the primary jurisdiction for dealing with issues relating to such matters was the child's country of habitual residence. It remains to be ratified and implemented by the UK.

In the European Convention on the Exercise of Children's Rights 1996, the Council of Europe sought to strengthen the mechanisms for enforcing the provisions of the 1989 Convention. In keeping with the latter, it continues the equivocal balance between legal rights and welfare interests. Its central objective being, as stated in Article 1(2):

> ...in the best interests of children, to promote their rights, to grant them procedural rights and to facilitate the exercise of these rights by ensuring that children are, themselves or through other persons or bodies, informed and allowed to participate in the proceedings affecting them before a judicial authority.

A statement which would seem to make the exercise of legal rights conditional upon this being compatible with the welfare interests of the child concerned while also confining the assurance of participatory rights to judicial proceedings. Article 3 of the Convention requires signatory states to ensure that a child 'considered by internal law as having sufficient understanding' has the right:

(a) to receive all relevant information;
(b) to be consulted and express his or her views; and
(c) to be informed of the possible consequences of his or her wishes and the possible consequences of any decision.

Article 4 requires that separate representation be provided for a child in cases where a conflict of interest arises between him or her and a party with parental responsibility. Article 7 imposes a 'no-delay' principle.

The influence from other common law jurisdictions

Common law principles are to be found in the foundations of many modern legal systems, particularly those of the Commonwealth nations but also and most notably in that of the USA. There are some distinctive characteristics of the common law which have modern implications for welfare interests.

One such characteristic is the focus on wrongs and related remedies. This, together with the welfare principle as developed by the Court of Chancery, having been transplanted to countries such as New Zealand and north America, then generated legislation and caselaw which has had an indirect influence upon the law relating to children in the UK. In the USA, the Constitution and Bill of Rights provided both a legal framework for articulating the 'wrongs' of minority groups, such as those disadvantaged by race or disability, and a basis for 'class actions' to remedy those legal inequities. The anti-discriminatory and equal opportunities jurisprudence, assembled in the context of campaigns to gain leverage for the socially disadvantaged, when applied to the legal interests of children, began to yield caselaw with a relevance for the UK from the 1960s.

Another characteristic of the common law is the emphasis on legal status. This is accompanied by the corollary that the formal authority of court proceedings is necessary when any question of change to that status arises. In circumstances where the UK courts have jurisdiction over issues affecting the welfare of children of foreign cultures then conflict can arise concerning the necessity to impose common law formal procedures on arrangements entered into by the parties. For example, some countries issue adoption orders which do not irrevocably extinguish the rights of natural parents. Once in England, however, such orders are likely to be automatically transformed into orders as defined - the 1976 Act which will have that effect. This may produce a result contrary to that intended by the parties and perhaps adverse to the welfare interests of the child.

In New Zealand, the experiments with open adoptions and foster care arrangements and, more recently, arguments that the common law did not present a bar to same sex marriages have also attracted the attention of legislators and judiciary in the UK.

The reason why these foreign initiatives influenced developments in this jurisdiction was partly due to timing. Coincidentally, the law relating to children in the UK was undergoing its most intense period of review since its common law origins when reports were being published of challenging new developments in other common law jurisdictions. One initiative, successfully developed in such common law jurisdictions as Australia, New Zealand, parts of Canada and in many states in the USA, but to which this jurisdiction has remained impervious, has been the forming of unified family courts (see, further, Chap 16).

Private family law, welfare interests and international influences

The welfare principle has become a potent force for leveraging the interests of children relative to those of parents and others. The correlation between the rise of the principle and the decline of the traditional nuclear marital family unit is clearly not coincidental. This dynamic became a characteristic of all affluent western societies at much the same time. The incidences of decline were also similar and contemporaneous: fall in numbers of marital families; rise in serial parenting; developments in artificial methods of human reproduction; increase in forms of substitute parenthood and in a reliance on a range of third party carer arrangements etc. It would have been most surprising if the UK had managed to insulate its domestic legislative and judicial response to this international pattern of change from the similar experiences of other western societies; particularly given the increase in volume of international travel. The evidence is that changes in UK private family law were heavily influenced by formal international instruments, not just those to which it was a party, and also by the example of legislators and judiciary in other countries as they responded to the same problems.

Private law in general

The boundaries of private family law in the UK have been redrawn in recent years, most notably by the Children Act 1989. While it is certain that seminal international academic publications contributed towards forming the domestic legislative intent to restrict state interference in family affairs, it is more difficult to estimate the significance of that contribution. In particular the work of the American partnership Goldstein, Freud and Solnit[20] gained wide circulation and credibility among UK academics and professionals. Their powerfully argued case that the welfare interests of children would be enhanced if the state increased its respect for the legal integrity, autonomy and privacy of the family found general acceptance on this side of the Atlantic. This fitted well with the general privatisation objectives of the Thatcher government and its particular concern to restrict state intervention in family affairs. Their work may well have influenced the legislative intent which formulated the no-order, parental responsibility and family based care principles underpinning the 1989 Act. It may also have contributed towards the preference placed on family based care, parental responsibility and non-interference by the state in Article 5 of the Convention:

> State parties shall respect the responsibilities, rights and duties of parents or, where applicable, the members of the extended family or community as provided for by the local custom, legal guardians or other persons legally responsible for the child, to provide, in a manner consistent with the evolving capacities of the child, appropriate direction and guidance in the exercise by the child of the rights recognised in the present Convention.

This Article and the provisions of the 1989 Act are too close in time and substance to each other and to the approach advocated by the American writing team for the legislative initiative in this jurisdiction not to have been heavily influenced by both.

Rights and duties of parents

The 1989 Convention, despite its focus on children's rights, makes several clear statements about the need for states to protect the standing of the family and respect the rights and responsibilities of parents when attending to the interests of children.[21] This need to balance the welfare interests of children against the rights of parents, and to weigh any conflict between them against the threat this presents to the sustainability of the family unit, has been more evident in the caselaw than in the legislation of the UK in recent years.[22] To that extent, the ambivalence in the 1989 Convention between giving priority to rights or welfare, children or parents, family unity or unilateral action by its members, has influenced domestic law by confirming the appropriateness of the judicial approach. The most significant point of difference being, that whereas the 1989 Act firmly assigns a paramountcy weighting to a child's welfare interests the 1989 Convention does not.

The common law right of a UK parent to administer or authorise reasonable chastisement to their child has been scrutinised by the EHRR. In two significant rulings the court, while declining to remove it from private family law, held that the right was personal to parents and should not be available to public bodies. This led directly to the abolition of corporal punishment in UK state schools.[23] An initiative strengthened by further legislation following a case concerning the administration of corporal punishment to a seven year old boy in preparatory school.[24] Recognition of this parental right has been further narrowed by the ruling of the European Court of Human Rights in *A v United Kingdom (Human Rights: Punishment of Child)*[25] where it was held that the acquittal by an English court of a stepfather who had beaten a nine year old boy with a stick did not comply with Convention requirements to respect the human rights. However, in the long run, the greater influence on the defensibility of this UK practice may be the knowledge that it is being prohibited in an increasing number of European countries.[26]

Rights and duties of children

The principles forged during the course of the 'social movement' litigation in the USA during the 1960s, began to form a platform for children's rights jurisprudence by the end of that decade. Civil liberties for minors as much as for minority groups and the positioning of the children's rights debate in the context of the civil rights campaign, was directly attributable to writers such as Foster and Freed.[27] This ethos generated a certain amount of caselaw and related publications which aroused interest and stimulated controversy in this jurisdiction. The US judiciary recognised that children possessed rights under the 14th Amendment and under the Bill of Rights,[28] that prohibitions on the sale of obscene materials to minors could be constitutional but that they may be unconstitutional if imposed on adults,[29] that a child had a right to freedom of speech[30] and a right to a hearing in school discipline cases where suspension was threatened.[31] More recently, the cases concerning children purporting to 'divorce their parents',[32] attracted considerable UK media attention.

The welfare interests of a child are clearly contingent upon a basic right to life. Perhaps because it is so basic it has never been stated as such in UK domestic law; it has been left to the criminal law to frame penalties for breach of an implied right to life and to the civil law of tort to identify the circumstances and liability for endangering life. This negative approach was evident also in Article 6(2) of the 1989 Convention (see, below). Not until the incorporation of the European Convention for the Protection of Human Rights and Fundamental Freedoms into domestic law, with the passing of the Human Rights Act 1998, did Article 2 finally establish a child's positive right to life. It is too early to judge what difference, if any, this will make to future decision-making in the Jamee Bowen and *Re T* type cases (see, Chaps 12 and 13). But, as J Fortin points out, Article 2 will force UK courts "to justify the merit of decisions to withhold life-saving treatment".[33]

Under Article 12 of the 1989 Convention (see, above), children of an age to do so are given the right to express their views freely in all matters affecting them and the right to have those views taken into account. These very significant rights are made applicable to any relevant judicial or administrative proceedings. However, the influence of this particular provision will not always be felt in private family law in the UK where statute law does not necessitate that the views of a child should be heard by the court; its influence can, nonetheless, be detected in judicial rulings. Articles 3, 4, 13 and 17 supplement this provision by giving a child the right to access relevant information and to be represented independently from any adult where there may be a conflict of interests.

Articles 7 and 8 of the 1989 Convention recognise the rights of a child 'to know and be cared for by their parents' and 'to preserve his or her identity', respectively. However, the UK laws relating to assisted or substitute parenthood whether taking the form of artificial insemination by donor (AID), in vitro fertilisation (IVF), gamete intra-fallopian transfer (GIFT), surrogacy or adoption, fail to satisfy Convention provisions. There is no right, exercisable during childhood, enabling a child: to access information regarding the identity of their genetic parents (should such information exist); to be brought up by genetic parents; or to have an identity other than that provided by the legal rather than the genetic parent. These are difficult matters to resolve to the satisfaction of the parties concerned but the Convention provisions require that they be addressed by the UK. The role played by the welfare principle, as defined by Article 3 of the 1989 Convention, will be crucial in determining the parameters for the exercise of the parties rights in this context.[34] That the UK judiciary recognise, and are prepared to act to rectify, legislative omission has become apparent in recent caselaw. In two cases the requirements of Article 7 were cited to justify overturning previous decisions in support of a parental veto and to instead direct that blood tests be conducted so as to ensure that children had access to accurate information regarding their parentage.[35]

The recognition of a child's independent rights is constrained by Article 5 of the 1989 Convention (see above) which requires states to respect the parental right to give 'appropriate direction and guidance in the exercise by the child of the rights recognised in the present Convention'. A child's exercise of a particular right may also be constrained by the court's ruling that this would be detrimental to the child's welfare interests.

Uncontested proceedings

The influence of European instruments has challenged, and ultimately contributed significantly towards broadening, the traditional definition of 'family' in the UK. For example, an incentive to eliminate the remaining differential between the legal position of marital and non-marital families has been provided by judgments given under the European Convention on Human Rights against other European countries. As Bainham noted:[36]

> Belgium[37] and the Republic of Ireland[38] have, for example, both fallen foul of the Convention in failing to give adequate recognition to the principle that 'family life' can be constituted outside marriage, can arise from the moment of a child's birth and can give rise to positive obligations on the part of States to foster it, as well as the more obvious negative obligations not to interfere with it.

These rulings of the EHRR, to the effect that the definition of 'family' was not to be determined by marital status, led directly to the reform of the UK relating to 'illegitimacy'.[39] The legislation in this jurisdiction continues, however, to overtly discriminate against the legal standing of unmarried fathers.[40] Article 18(1) of the 1989 Convention, with its emphasis on 'the principle that both parents have common responsibilities for the upbringing and development of the child', provides a clear challenge to the inequitable UK approach towards unmarried fathers. Again, the orthodox model of UK family relationships has been challenged by rulings upholding the rights of transsexuals.[41] The fact that UK law prevented a marriage involving a transsexual did not mean that the law should deny the capacity of such a person, their partner and child to enjoy 'family life'. These discrepancies between UK and Convention interpretations of legally constituted family units are important. They disclose the extent to which legal status in this jurisdiction endures as the test of defensible parental relationships. Endorsing the validity of forms of family life and parental relationships other than those based on marital union, gives legal and social security to the children involved and confirms the need to safeguard their welfare interests in that context.

There is also a significant discrepancy between the provisions of the Family Law Act 1996 and the 1989 Convention in relation to the legal standing of a child in the context of divorce proceedings; a problem which is particularly acute when the proceedings are uncontested. The requirement in Article 9(1) that 'a child shall not be parted from his or her parents against their will' is not provided for within the 1996 Act. In the majority of divorce proceedings there is little possibility of the court taking into account the will of the child concerned and every probability, should it do so, that the will of such a child is not allowed to determine his or her future care arrangements. Parental decisions and procedural requirements effectively nullify opportunities for a child's exercise of the right promised under Article 9(1).

The influence from New Zealand has also been challenging.[42] The Court of Appeal in *Quilter v Attorney-General*[43] accepted the argument of the plaintiffs, three lesbian couples seeking marriage licences, that:[44]

> ...the traditional common law does not actually address the question of same-sex marriages and it may be that it does not reflect current social realities and values...Community attitudes in 1996 are much more relaxed to lesbian and gay couples as a result of social change...

The eventual ruling against the plaintiffs was based on a finding that legislation, if not specifically the common law, operated on an assumption that only heterosexual partnerships met the definition of 'marriage'.

Contested proceedings

In the UK the paramountcy principle must be applied in the context of contested proceedings. This places domestic law at variance with the lesser demands made under the 1989 Convention. By so doing UK legislation imposes a corresponding disadvantage on other parties and ascribes a lesser weighting to other considerations, relative to the balance struck in the Convention. In the future the influence of the 1989 Convention may be brought to bear to challenge this overriding advantage conferred on UK children's welfare interests.

Divorce, nullity and separation

There is no statutory provision for children to be independently represented in such contested proceedings. The amendment to s 41 of the Matrimonial Causes Act 1973 by the 1989 Act, now leaves UK divorce law at variance with the requirements of Articles 9(2) and 12 of the 1989 Convention; the latter in particular requires that a child be given 'the opportunity to be heard in any judicial and administrative proceedings affecting the child'.

Contact

Most contested private family law procedures concern rights of access or contact between a child and other adults after family breakdown; proceedings being instigated by parents after their divorce, by unmarried parents after their relationship has broken down, by grandparents or foster parents etc. Articles 7, 8 and 9(3) of the 1989 Convention may be invoked to lend weight to any claim that a UK child's right to contact with a parent or significant other should be restored but are unlikely to be needed given the substantial body of domestic statutory and caselaw material already available to support such a claim. In this context, the ruling of the ECHR in *Hokkanen v Finland* [45] is significant because, while acknowledging the justice of the father's custody claim, the court ruled that the removal of a 10 year old child from grandparents who had provided care for the previous eight years was not an option when this would be against the child's express wishes.

Abduction

The Hague Convention on the Civil Aspects of International Child Abduction and the European Convention on Recognition and Enforcement of Decisions Concerning Custody of Children 1983 governs the problem of international child abductions. Article 10 submits attainment of the Convention's central purpose to a frank application of the welfare test.[46] Article 13 provides for judicial discretion to endorse the decision of a child who is of an age and maturity to refuse to return. In recent years there have been indications of a growing judicial willingness to permit the views of children to have the effect of vetoing a return to jurisdiction of habitual residence.[47] The UK judiciary have often sought and given a determining weighting to the opinions of quite young children[48] but not always.[49] In circumstances where neither Convention applies then the UK courts continue to have no hesitation in applying the welfare test to determine this particular issue.[50]

Adoption

The main significance of the Hague Convention on Intercountry Adoption for welfare interests lies in the stand it takes for preserving the 'identity' of children, within the broad meaning of Article 8 of the 1989 Convention. By placing an emphasis on the expectation that 'donor' countries will provide the professional supports necessary to retain children within their countries of origin, wherever possible, the numbers of children becoming available for intercountry adoption has been considerably reduced. By encouraging the good practice in some 'receiving' nations, such as the UK, of ensuring that adopted children are provided with information about their culture of origin, the Convention gives such children the opportunity to maintain a sense of cultural identity.

There are instances when the influence of an international initiative is to turn a spotlight upon an aspect of UK law and reveal the extent of its incompatibility with a required welfare standard. For example, the provision in the 1993 Convention that intercountry adoption requires the consent of the child serves to remind us that there is no comparable consent requirement in UK adoption law, nor in most of its family law proceedings. The setting of this requirement as an international standard places considerable pressure on the UK to review its position in relation to proceedings which require the views rather than the consent of the child concerned. Also, the provision in Article 2 of the same Convention gives equal and separate recognition to two forms of adoption: 'full' which permanently ends legal ties between child and parent/s of origin; and 'simple' which allows for retention of some level of legal relationship. UK legislation, however, has always provided for the most absolute or 'full' model of adoption with the result that it is now proposed that intercountry adoptions arranged in 'donor' countries on a 'simple' adoption basis should, on entering the UK, be converted automatically to 'full' status; with parental agreement. If, on entry, that agreement proves to be unavailable this could have serious implications for the child's welfare interests. Even if available, it will be contrary to initial parental intentions which may have been formed to give best effect to those interests.[51] Again, the ruling of the Court of Human Rights in *Soderback v Sweden*[52] has set a benchmark against which UK judicial practice of accommodating step-parent adoption applications can be measured. These are all instances where the setting of an international standard calls into question established UK practice.

Another source of influence on UK adoption practice has been the development of the 'open' model of adoption in New Zealand during the past two decades. The widespread media and academic attention given to the positive experience in New Zealand of this more relaxed approach to the legal boundaries of adopting families has served to challenge the orthodox view in the UK that a 'closed', unconditional and permanent model was necessary to secure a child' welfare interests.[53]

Public family law, welfare interests and international influences

While the future impact of the Human Rights Convention on UK law remains speculative, other than the certainty of a speedier judicial response to litigation, the record of its past contribution towards improving the position of children within the public family law of this jurisdiction is considerable. The UN Convention on the Rights of the Child 1989 is having a growing influence upon the law relating to local authority child care practice while caselaw and academic publications produced within other jurisdictions have also proved influential.

Public law in general

The requirement in Article 12 of the 1989 Convention that the views of a child shall be heard 'in any judicial and administrative proceedings affecting the child' has yet to be fully addressed by local authorities. Involvement of children in case conferences, for example, is patchy; a child may be present at the beginning or end or not at all, there is no uniformity of practice. Again, children have virtually no rights in relation to education and there would not appear to be any plans for a legislative initiative to give them a place on administrative forums.

The balance struck between the interests of parents and children in the public law provisions of the 1989 Act is also different from that required by the Convention; children's interests in the UK are accorded a paramount weighting not required by the Convention.

Consensual state intervention

There is a considerable emphasis in the 1989 Convention on the need for states to provide support services for vulnerable families. The influence of this approach may be seen in certain provisions in the 1989 Act such as those relating to children in need, family based care and partnership with parents. Article 6(2) of the 1989 Convention requires states to 'ensure to the maximum extent possible the survival and development of the child'. Article 18(2) and (3) require states to assist parents to provide for their children.

Prevention and promotion

J Fortin draws attention to the preventative emphasis in the 1989 Convention. As she observes:

> ...children must also be provided with the resources to develop their full potential.[54] The Convention acknowledges that a child cannot do so without a standard of living adequate for her 'physical, mental, spiritual, moral and social development,[55] social security benefits,[56] and the right to the 'highest attainable standard of health and to facilities for the treatment of illness and rehabilitation of health.[57]

But, it is not enough to provide protection for a child's welfare interests. States are also required to go further and, as noted by J Fortin, 'promote positively children's civil, economic, social and cultural rights in order to enjoy a full life, with the ability to mature into healthy adulthood'.[58]

Coercive state intervention

Again, the example from New Zealand has had its influence on broadening an established UK approach to welfare interests. In addition to innovation in foster care practice, New Zealand pioneered the 'family group conference' which has operated on a statutory basis since 1989. Convening a meeting of relevant family members, together with the professionals concerned, is the preferred means of planning an appropriate response to the needs and deeds of children who have become the subject of coercive intervention in either a care or an offence context. This approach of shared responsibility between family and state and making room in decision making for family members can be seen in the principles of the Children Act 1989 and in the more recent juvenile justice legislation.

The balance to be struck between private and public family law has been the central issue for UK legislators in recent years and arose for consideration by the European Court of Human Rights in *Johansen v Norway*.[59] The court then considered the extent to which a state's coercive intervention powers, enabling a child to be taken into care, were 'necessary in a democratic society' as required by Article 8(2) of the European Convention on Human Rights. It determined that the appropriate balance could not be prescribed by the court but must be left to individual states, provided they took into account the crucial importance of children's welfare interests.

Care

The capacity of the Human Rights Convention to influence the welfare interests of UK children was perhaps most clearly demonstrated in cases[60] where the EHRR ruled that the power of local authorities, to coercively assume full parental responsibilities in respect of children consensually placed in care, contravened the Convention. This led directly to the abolition of that power. Subsequently, the rights of UK children, or more specifically those subject to proceedings under the Scottish hearing system, were found to be inadequately protected by the proceedings for lodging preliminary documents in care proceedings.[61] The welfare interests of children were the incidental beneficiaries of EHRR rulings that the procedural rights of parents in relation to public child care proceedings were unsatisfactory[62] and that disclosure should be made of confidential records relating to children in care.[63] The influence of these rulings has been noted by Bainham.[64] Most often the role of the EHRR has been to clarify and adjudicate upon the rights of adults, the welfare interests of children being incidental to the main issues.

J Fortin draws attention to a recent trend she has detected in the approach taken by the EHRR in relation to cases where the rights infringed concern children.[65] Instead of simply ruling on whether or not a state party is in breach of a duty owed to a child, or in respect of a child, the court would seem to be developing a more flexible and discretionary approach in its interpretation of the weighting to be given to the welfare interests of a child relative to other considerations. She sees the court adopting an approach which is more mediatory than adjudicatory; demonstrating a concern to reach a balanced resolution between parental rights and child welfare; and taking into account the value system of the society in question when doing so. This approach is very similar to that adopted by the UK courts, serves to reinforce its appropriateness and illustrates the extent of the convergence between the rulings of the EHRR, the provisions of the 1989 Convention and those of the 1989 Act.

Control

The current legislative trend in the UK towards accentuating punitive and custodial measures instead of emphasising diversion and rehabilitation, is distancing the domestic response to juvenile crime from that advocated in the 1989 Convention[66] and in the Beijing Rules.[67] The influence of the 1989 Convention may be seen in the establishing of youth courts which comply with the requirement in Article 37 that states ensure the separation of juvenile and adult detainees and keep deprivation of liberty to a minimum. However, the application of Crown court procedures to children as young as 10 is clearly not compatible with Article 40 of the 1989 Convention nor is the practice of remanding children to prisons while awaiting trial.[68] Article 39 requires that they promote the rehabilitation of offenders in the community. The fact that the welfare interests of UK children are disadvantaged relative to those of children elsewhere in Europe, because the age of criminal responsibility is so much lower in this jurisdiction, has attracted criticism from the United Nations. In the report of the UN Committee on the Rights of the Child it was recommended that 'serious consideration be given to raising the age of criminal responsibility throughout the areas of the United Kingdom'.[69]

The severity of court directed restrictions on the liberty of UK children have also given rise to concern in Europe. For example, the indeterminate nature of sentences to be served 'during Her Majesty's pleasure' have been challenged for being in breach of Article 5(4) of the European Convention on Human Rights[70] as has the introduction of a penal 'tariff' to be determined at the discretion of the Home Secretary before the Parole Board can consider setting a date for release.[71] It is unlikely that this practice, whereby sentence duration is determined by government rather than court, can survive further exposure to the European Court. Again, because the secure accommodation provisions fail to provide opportunities for representation for a child or for independent review, after the order is made, it is probable that they also would be in breach of Article 5.

Protection

Article 19(1) of the 1989 Convention requires states to provide the necessary coercive intervention powers to ensure that children are protected from all forms of neglect and abuse while in the care of parents, guardian or other authorised carer. The fact that local authorities may exercise a discretion available under the 1989 Act not to do so calls into question whether the statutory definition of their duties is wholly in compliance with Convention requirements. This may possibly arise for clarification in the future. In the meantime there is every probability that such an exercise of discretion, resulting in avoidable harm to a child, may fall foul of the recent ruling in *Osman v UK*.[72] The European Court of Human Rights then held that a public body (the police) was not immune from challenge for negligence in its duty to afford protection to the plaintiff. The claim to immunity on the grounds of public policy was held to be in breach of Article 6. It is highly likely that in future a local authority claim not to be judicially accountable for negligence in respect of an exercise or non-exercise of its statutory powers would leave it open to a similar challenge; one which could be immediately made in domestic courts following implementation of the 1998 Act. The *Osman* ruling challenges not only the discretionary power provided by s 47(8) of the 1989 Act and the precedent value of related recent cases (see, further, Chap 10) but it even raises a question about the status of *A v Liverpool City Council*.[73]

Conclusion

The extent to which the law relating to the welfare interests of children in the UK has been influenced by international instruments and by principles developed in the caselaw and academic publications of other jurisdictions is difficult to judge. The process has only become explicit and systematised in recent years with the ratifying of Conventions and the judgments of the ECHR. Certainly the many and frequent judicial references made in the course of everyday family proceedings cases to the provisions of international instruments testifies to an increased awareness of the relevance of this additional tier of law. But it is highly probable that UK legislators and judiciary have for many decades been conducting low profile adjustments to the law relating to children in order to take account of principles developed elsewhere.

The fact that a majority of countries have now subscribed to the 1989 Convention means that the welfare principle has, for the first time, become elevated to the status of a truly international legal standard in 'all actions concerning children'. This provides endorsement for the principle's role and functions which for many centuries have been developed by the judiciary and ascribed by statute within the family law of the UK. There is, however, an argument that the Convention poses a challenge to the paramountcy weighting given to the principle when applied to matters affecting a child's upbringing in this jurisdiction. It clearly does not sit comfortably with the emphasis on sustaining family unity which pervades the 1989 Convention as it is relatively disadvantageous to the interests of others, most notably parents. It could be argued that such a weighting, applied in any context other than following judicially confirmed family breakdown, would be contrary to the spirit of the Convention. On the other hand, 'family' has now become such an uncertain social and legal entity in the UK (see, further Chap 13) that giving a priority weighting to its most vulnerable members on all issues relating to their upbringing is perhaps an appropriate and culturally relevant interpretation of 'welfare'.

The influence of the 1989 Convention is evident in the language of rights which now envelops much of the debate concerning welfare interests. Convention rights now underpin many but not all welfare interests. Those which have attained rights status often have a negative or defensive function: rights to life, to privacy, to protection from abuse etc. Some, however, have a definite positive or promotional function: rights to representation, to information, to an identity and to express views on all matters concerning them etc. The former, representing a minimum international baseline of rights, have often been refined through successive legislation and are no longer culturally relevant to the UK (with some notable exceptions such as the right not to serve in the nation's armed forces). The latter frequently have not been fully addressed by UK legislation, a fact which also discloses cultural dissonance. If the law of this jurisdiction is to become more Convention compliant then it will have to move further away from the paternalistic model which has hitherto conditioned the role and functions of welfare interests and move towards recognising children as competent participants in decision-making on matters affecting their welfare. The implementation of the Human Rights Act 1998 is likely to force the pace of change for such a move.

Notes

1 See Clause 6.

2 In the period 1984-89, 14 judgments concerning its application to minors were passed at the European Court of Human Rights in Strasbourg; 5 in period 1976-84.

3 The League of Nations Declaration 1924: para 1. The UN Declaration of the Rights of the Child 1959: principle 2.

4 1924: para 4. 1959: principle 9.

5 1924: para 2. 1959: principle 6.

6 1924: para 3. 1959: principle 8.

7 1959: principle 7.

8 1959: principle 6.

9 1959: principle 3.

10 1959: principle 4.

11 1959: principle 7.

12 1959: principle 5.

13 See Bainham A., *Children: The Modern Law*, (2nd ed) 1998, p 58.

14 See *Re A (Children: 1959 UN Declaration)* [1998] 1 FLR 354 where the Court of Appeal questioned the current relevance of the 1959 Declaration.

15 The provisions of the International Covenant on Civil and Political Rights and the International Covenant on Economic, Social and Cultural Rights, both ratified by the UK in 1976, were essentially assimilated into the 1989 Convention.

16 Currently ratified by 191 nations. Only two nations have failed to become parties to the Convention; the USA and Somalia. For an analysis of the former's reasons for non-ratification see, 'The wayward Americans – why the USA has not ratified the UN Convention on the Rights of the Child' in *Child and Family Law Quarterly*, Vol 10, No 3, 1998.

17 Articles 8, 10, 12, 13, 14, 15, 16, 25, 37 and 40 among others.

18 *Op cit*, p 59.

19 See *Concluding Observations of the Committee on the Rights of the Child: United Kingdom of Great Britain and Northern Ireland* C RC/C 15Add34 (1995).

20 See Goldstein, J., Freud, A., Solnit, A. *Before the Best Interests of the Child*, New York, Free Press, 1979.

21 See, for example, the Preamble, Articles 3(2), 5, 14(2) and 29.

22 See in particular, the Children Act 1989 and cases such as *Re C (A Minor)(Leave to Seek Section 8 Orders)* [1994] 1 FLR 26.

23 See *Campbell and Cozans v United Kingdom* (1982) 4 EHRR 293. See, also, *Tyrer v United Kingdom* (1979-80) 2 EHRR 1.

24 See, *Costello-Roberts v United Kingdom* [1994] ELR 1.

25 [1998] 2 FLR 959.

26 Currently prohibited in Sweden, Finland, Denmark, Norway, Austria and Cyprus.

27 See Foster and Freed, *A Bill of Rights for Children*, 6 Family Law Quarterly 343, 1972.

28 See *Re Gault* 387 US 1, 13 (1967).
29 See *Ginsberg v New York* 390 US 629 (1968).
30 See *Tinker v Des Moines Independent Community School District* 393 US 503 (1969).
31 See *Goss v Lopez* 419 US 565 (1975).
32 See *Kingsley v Kingsley* 623 So. 2d 780 (Fla. Dist. Ct. App. 1993) and *Polovchak v Meese* 774 F. 2d 731 (1985). Note, also, that by 1986 some 20 states had in place legislation which permitted children to petition the courts for a declaration of independence.
33 See Fortin, J., 'Re C (Medical Treatment) A baby's right to die', in *Child and Family Law Quarterly*, Vol 10, No 4, 1998, p 413.
34 See *Gaskin v UK* (1980) 12 EHRR 36 where a person who had been in care sought identity information.
35 See *Re H (Paternity: Blood Test)* [1996] 2 FLR 65 and *Re G (Parentage: Blood Sample)* [1997] 1 FLR 360.
36 *See Bainham A.,* Children: The Modern Law, *(2nd ed)* 1998, p 598.
37 *Marckx v Belgium (1979) 2 EHRR 330.*
38 *Johnston v Ireland (1986) 9 EHRR 203 and Keegan v Ireland (1994) 18 EHRR 342.*
39 See Law Commission No 118, *Family Law Report on Illegitimacy* HMSO 1982. The recommendations of which led to the Family Law Reform Act 1987.
40 See ss 2, 4, and 12(1) of the Children Act 1989.
41 See, for example, *X, Y and Z v United Kingdom* Application No. 21830/93. European Commission of Human Rights, and *B v France* Series A, No 232 (1993); 16 EHRR 1. However, the decisions in *J v ST* [1997] 1 FLR 402 and *Sheffield and Horsham v UK* [1998] 2 FLR 928 demonstrate continued UK resistance to recognising the legal validity of a marriage where one partner is a transsexual.
42 See Atkin, B., 'New Zealand: Challenging Conventional Understandings' in *The International Survey of Family Law, 1996*, Martinus Nijhoff Publishers, 1998.
43 [1996] NZFLR 481.
44 *Ibid* at 491 and 494.
45 [1996] 1 FLR 289
46 See for example, *F v F (Minors)(Custody: Foreign Order)* [1989] Fam 1; *Re G (A Minor)(Child Abduction: Enforcement)* [1990] 2 FLR 325; and *Re R (Abduction: Hague and European Conventions)*[1997] 1 FLR 663.
47 See for example, *The Ontario Court v M and M (Abduction: Children's Objections)* [1997] 1 FLR 475 and *Re B (Abduction: Children's Objections)* [1998] 1 FLR 667.
48 Non-return, in compliance with the objections of the children concerned, was ordered in: *S v S (Child Abduction: Child's Views)* [1992] 2 FLR 492, where the child was aged 9; *B v B (Child Abduction)* [1993] 1 FCR 382, where they were aged 9 and 7; and *Re R (A Minor: Abduction)* [1992] 1 FLR 105, in respect of a 14 year old child.
49 See *Re HB (Abduction: Children's Objections)* [1997] 1 FLR 392, where Hale J held that in the absence of firm evidence that the Hague Convention requirements could not be met the children, aged 13 and 11, should be returned not withstanding their objections.
50 See for example, *Re P (A Minor)(Child Abduction: Non-Convention Country)* [1997] 1 FLR 780 and *Re JA (Child Abduction: Non-Convention Country)* [1998] 1 FLR 231.
51 See further, Duncan W, 'Children's Rights, Cultural Diversity and Private International Law' in *Children's Rights and Traditional Values* op cit.

52 [1999] 1 FLR 250.
53 See, for example, Dominick, *Early Contact in Adoption*. Research series No 10 (Wellington, New Zealand, 1988).
54 Article 6(2).
55 Article 27.
56 Article 26.
57 Article 24.
58 See Fortin, J., *Children's Rights and the Developing Law, Butterworths*, 1998, p 38.
59 See (1997) 23 EHRR 33.
60 See *W, O, B and R v United Kingdom* (1987) 10 EHRR 29, ECHR and *R v United Kingdom* [1988] 2 FLR 445.
61 *McMichael v United Kingdom* (1995) Series A, No 307 which concerned procedures under the Scottish 'children's hearings' system.
62 Influenced in part by *W, O, B and R v United Kingdom* (1987) 10 EHRR 29 and *R v United Kingdom* [1988] 2 FLR 445.
63 See *Gaskin v United Kingdom* (1989) 12 EHRR 36.
64 See A Bainham, *Children – The Modern Law*, (2nd ed), Family Law, 1998, p 600.
65 See for example, *Johansen v Norway* (1997) 23 EHRR 33, *Olsson v Sweden (No 2)* (1994) 17 EHRR 134 and *Hokkanen v Finland* [1996] 1 FLR 289.
66 See Article 40(3)(b) of the UN Convention on the Rights of the Child 1989.
67 See Rules 11.1 – 11.4 of the UN Standard Minimum Rules for the Administration of Juvenile Justice 1985.
68 See the criticism of this practice in 'Children, Crime and Society: Perspectives of the UN Convention on the Rights of the Child' in *Child Offenders: UK and International Practice*, the Howard League, 1995, p 20.
69 See *Concluding Observations of the Committee on the Rights of the Child: United Kingdom of Great Britain and Northern Ireland*, United Nations, 1995, para 36.
70 See *Hussain v United Kingdom* (1996) 22 EHRR 1.
71 See, *Thynne, Wilson and Gunnell v UK* (1990) 13 EHRR 666.
72 [1999] 1 FLR 193.
73 *Op cit*.

16 Family Law and the Welfare Principle: Some Implications for the Future

Introduction

Family law is dynamic law. In the space of a few decades the pace and scale of legislative change, the volume of litigation, the range of professionals involved and the plethora of published material have transformed it from a marginal to a mainstream area of practice for lawyers, academics and others. Keeping up is a problem, remembering where we've come from is a luxury.

This book has provided an opportunity to stand back and take the long view of developments through a lens provided by the welfare principle. A longitudinal study of this nature offers a chance to appreciate the changes that have occurred over time in the legislative framework, in the volume and type of cases and in the parties, professionals and processes utilised by the legal system. It allows us to note the reference points which have remained constant, recognise the characteristic tensions underpinning the internal dynamics of family law and the source of external pressures to which it must respond. By providing us with information regarding past, present and emerging trends it also places us in a position to take a considered view about their future nature and direction. We are thereby better placed to shape a more appropriate role for the future of the welfare principle in family law.

Looking ahead is the business of this concluding chapter. It can be readily accepted that welfare is a relative term, that it is defined and given effect within a legal framework which is itself constantly evolving and that the United Kingdom at the approach of Y2K is a vastly more complex society than when Chancery first applied the welfare principle. Yet some basic questions arise. Firstly, are there some strands in this 'golden thread' which have remained constant and are likely to continue to weave a recognisable welfare motif into the future of our law as it relates to children? Secondly, what new welfare indicators have emerged and how are they likely to contribute to such law? Finally, what adjustments if any should be made to the legal system if it is to more appropriately accommodate and more effectively apply the welfare principle in the future? These and other issues are explored below under the headings: the content, role, weight and context of the welfare principle; the welfare principle in relation to other principles; rights and welfare interests; and the legal system and a family court.

The content, role, weight and context of the welfare principle

The comment that 'this case turns on its own particular facts...' is one which we have become accustomed to finding ritually added as a rider to explain the outcome of cases where the welfare principle has played a part. The inference being that the welfare component will so distort the interpretation of facts and choice of disposal option that we should not expect a similarity of outcome in cases of the same type. But is the inference justified? Is it necessarily so that there is a lack of consistency in the use of welfare indicators resulting in unpredictable decisions?

Content

An historical perspective discloses certain immutable benchmarks for the content of a child's welfare interests. The most obvious of these are concerned with safeguarding physical integrity. This book has detailed the record of legislative and judicial attention to matters such as care, protection, health, safety, control and maintenance of children. Importance has also been given to preserving the 'psychological bond' which allows a child to develop and sustain a relationship with at least one nurturing adult; the younger the child the more important the bond and the more probable that this is best supplied by a mother or maternal figure. Centuries of caselaw provide testimony to the issue of upbringing being addressed in this way. Distinct, but often in practice closely related, is the judicial significance attached to the 'blood-tie'. The preference shown for care arrangements which permit a child to have his or her home with a parent or member of their family of origin has always been evident, for example, in contests between first and third parties. It can also be seen playing a part in step-parent adoptions where the order made favours the caring parent in a position to provide the child concerned with continuity of home environment. An extension of the respect for such attachments can be seen in the judicial attention now given to maintaining for a child those reference points which are demonstrably important to his or her psychological development, such as contact with members of nuclear and extended family, friends, neighbours and neighbourhood.

The content of welfare, as judicially interpreted over the centuries, reflects an acknowledgement that the law relates to children in a different way than it does to adults. A child's inherent immaturity and consequent dependency (physical, emotional and financial) on an adult or adults has fixed a set agenda for determining how the law recognises and addresses their welfare interests. This approach will prevent the position of children from being swept along in the wake of social movements campaigning for rights for minority groups.

Role

In the civil law of this jurisdiction children have always been treated as dependent and others have therefore been required to take decisions on their behalf. The law identifies the welfare related areas in which decisions may need to be taken, sets the parameters and processes for decision-making and identifies or authorises those who may make the decisions. The traditional exclusion of children from participation in decisions concerning their welfare is weakening. One particular judicial approach to the application of the welfare principle which is gradually gaining ground is an age based differentiation in the degree of influence a child can exercise on decisions concerning his or her welfare. This is grounded on or closely bound up with the capacity of a child to give meaningful consent. Although hedged around with caveats such as the child's understanding relative to the complexity or gravity of the issues, there is every indication that the future role of welfare will make room for subject involvement somewhere on a spectrum of passive participation to determination depending on age and understanding.

For judicial decision-makers the welfare principle plays its most critical role at the end of legal processes by licensing varying degrees of discretion (from maximum latitude in wardship to a minimum in criminal proceedings) in the choice of disposal option relative to the needs and deeds of the child concerned.

From the earliest times, the law has given priority attention to those areas with negative connotations for children because of the possible consequences for their physical welfare. This is still the case. Public law legislation proscribes things, circumstances and behaviour held to be detrimental to welfare and sets the threshold for intervening in family affairs on behalf of any child whose welfare has been impaired. State intervention on welfare grounds occurs after the event, justified by the fact of harm caused. Orders are then made to remove legal authority from those found to have defaulted on their responsibilities to a child and to vest it elsewhere so as to best afford protection from future abuse or neglect. In the process, precedence may well be given to protecting the welfare interests of the child concerned and inhibiting the principle of the freedom of the press, by a direction restricting the publication of material which may be harmful to that child.

The negative role played by the welfare principle in public law will undoubtedly continue in its traditional form within a modernised, highly structured, densely professionalised and tightly calibrated system for balancing public and private interests in the needs of children. It will remain largely focussed on determining entry to and exit from child protection proceedings where judicial decision-makers will determine where authority will thereafter lie in respect of children whose welfare has been impaired. Although its range of application has been restricted by the removal of offence based proceedings, judicial discretion has been broadened by the 1989 Act. That phase of decision-making is now highly resourced. The next phase, where the child is either accommodated by local authority or placed with family, remains under-resourced.

In relatively recent times the law has also developed a positive approach to welfare interests. This is evident to some degree in public law where legislation requires preventative state intervention, makes provision for support services to vulnerable children and families and regulates general child care facilities. Consensual state intervention in family affairs, to prevent further weakening of adequate but vulnerable child care standards and maintain family based care arrangements, is a very significant development in the role of the welfare principle. The legislative emphasis on promoting the welfare interests of children in the care of the state is perhaps more aspirational than realisable in the short-term but it also indicates an awareness of a need to improve rather than to just monitor existing rudimentary care standards.

But, it is in the context of private law that, in recent times, the role of the welfare principle has undergone its most significant legislative adjustment. The scale of state withdrawal from decision-making in relation to the future care arrangements of children, following the breakdown of their parents' marriage, amounts to a watershed in the triangular legal relationship between state, children and parents. The incremental extension to carers of opportunities to acquire the rights and duties previously restricted to parents has served to accelerate the general trend in relation to decision-making regarding care responsibility for children: a retraction in state involvement accompanied by a broadening range of possible private decision-makers. In no branch of family law is the re-balancing of public and private interests more concentrated and apparent than in adoption.

In both public and private law the opportunities provided by the welfare principle for judicial exercises of discretionary power have been increased by the menu of orders introduced by the 1989 Act. However, the scope for judicial flexibility in interpreting welfare relative to the needs of a particular child have been curbed by new legislative requirements for greater specificity in the interpretation of welfare interests. The introduction of checklist criteria has the effect of restraining judicial discretion previously exercised in a paternalistic and protectionist fashion.

Weight

The weighting attached to the child's welfare interests has threatened to destabilise family law in the UK. The directive that when deciding any issue concerning a child's upbringing the court should treat the welfare of the child as the matter of paramount importance correspondingly reduced the relative significance of all other factors. In particular this served to devalue the rights of parents and undermine from within the fundamental premise of family law that the integrity of the family unit was entitled to protection in law (see further below). The welfare principle had come to assume the position of a new reference point; not like 'fault' in matrimonial proceedings or 'reasonableness' in adoption but more akin to the governing and centrifugal influence once exercised by 'paternal authority'.

Arguably, there has been a steady withdrawal from this position. The application of the paramountcy principle is being judicially reined in as the number of exempted circumstances increase (see, further, below).

Context

The intrinsic relativeness of 'welfare' is thrown into sharp relief when the particular needs of the child concerned are not representative of the social context within which they are being measured. This contrast is most obvious where welfare issues arise in a UK court concerning a child from a third world country. This may also occur when the child is a UK citizen but part of a discrete minority as where he or she is disabled, a member of a religious sect or of a family caught in the 'poverty trap'. In the cultural pluralism of contemporary Britain the upbringing of many children conform to the values of their immediate social group and are not representative of the broad mainstream of our society. Michael Freeman has written lucidly and with passion about the consequences of such cultural disparity and has drawn attention to cases[1] which graphically illustrate the scale of the problem. In contrast, the words of Wilson J in *Re D (Care: Threshold Criteria: Significant Harm)*[2] offer evidence of a different approach which would seem to promise a more uniform application of the welfare test; at least as far as the threshold of significant harm is concerned.

> Today in England and Wales we are not a collection of ghettoes, but one society enjoying the benefit of the composition of very many racial and cultural groups

> and one society governed by one set of laws. It would concern me if the same event could give rise in one case to a finding of significant harm and in another to a finding to the contrary.

This approach cannot be faulted if the principles of non-discrimination and equal opportunities are to prevail.

The anomaly, contradicting the logic of the paramountcy principle, whereby welfare is viewed by the law in its context rather than separated out from it, is evident in other areas. The tendency to merge the welfare of a child with that of the mother or parents increases in proportion to the dependency of the child. Whether the dependency is due to being a foetus, suffering from a serious but treatable disability, or being so severely incapacitated as to be on a life support machine, there are many examples in this book of a judicial willingness to impute the welfare interests of the child to the parent. In such circumstances a decision compatible with the interests of a parent, unaccompanied by any evidence of willfulness or recklessness on the part of the latter, will quite often be held as synonymous with the welfare interests of the child. Somewhat tangentially, this tendency to contexturalise welfare is also evident in the poverty debate. For those who support the argument that a high proportion of child care problems are a consequence of parental poverty then the current government aspirations to eradicate poverty offers hope that it will thereby also substantially reduce those problems, on the 'rising tide lifts all boats' principle.

The movement against the contexturalising of welfare has been assisted by the Conventions which have now gained widespread ratification, being incorporated wholly or partially in the constitutions of some countries. This has raised the importance of children's welfare nationally and internationally. It has also brought a degree of specificity to inform understanding of what constitutes 'welfare interests' and to allow a more uniform acceptance of the standards by which they may be defined and measured. To a large extent, there are now legal forums and frameworks for holding national governments accountable for a failure to measure up to recognised welfare benchmarks. The international dissemination of national welfare audits provides a mechanism for encouraging national compliance with set, uniformly applicable, international standards.

Welfare interests in relation to other interests

Reference to the 'welfare interests of a child' carries two implications. Firstly, that a child has interests additional to those of 'welfare'. Secondly, that there is a need to make room for a child's interests in the context of interests other than those of children. Essentially it points to the fact that a child's welfare interests cannot be considered in total isolation: other factors have to be taken into account; it reveals that balances must be struck. Where welfare interests are governed by legislative priority setting, usually by a direction that they be treated as the matter of first consideration or of paramount importance, then it might appear that the balance to be struck is self-evident and pre-set. But, in some circumstances, judicial creativity has blurred the distinction between welfare and other interests by judgments which assert that only by ruling in favour of the latter can effect best be given to the former.

Interests of a child other than those of welfare

The court is only required to give paramount importance to welfare interests when considering issues relating to a child's upbringing. Outside 'courts of law' there is a vast range of tribunals dealing with matters affecting children which are not bound by the welfare principle; for example, immigration tribunals, social security, housing, schools and health care. It is sufficient for each that they give precedence to performing their respective statutory functions. In so doing they may take into account welfare interests insofar as this does not deflect from giving effect to their functions; these are ancillary to but distinct from welfare interests. Schools, because of their prolonged influence on all children, are particularly important. They manifestly focus on addressing children's educational interests and make virtually no provision for the representation of their welfare interests.

In public law there is no legislative obligation on a local authority to give priority to a child's welfare interests. This, in conjunction with the directive to 'promote the upbringing of such children by their families' and the 'no-order' presumption of the 1989 Act, allows it to give precedence to other interests; for example, preserving family unity or the partnership basis of its relationship with parents. It may well take the view that maintaining a marriage or keeping siblings together would be more important in the long-term for all parties concerned than giving priority to a particular child's immediate welfare interests. A local authority may also, of course, simply choose to allocate its resources for purposes other than addressing the welfare needs of a particular child.[3]

In private law the tension between welfare and other interests is growing steadily more pronounced. Because paramountcy is restricted to matters affecting 'upbringing' it therefore has no bearing on other issues. In matters relating to a child's finances, property or maintenance other interests will be given priority. As demonstrated in a number of cases in recent years, the presumption favouring the preservation of life must give way to the welfare principle. In effect, the courts may and frequently do find that the welfare interests of a child with complex health needs who is reliant upon medical intervention are best addressed by measures designed to result in death. Also, the welfare interests of a child who is not the primary subject of proceedings will remain subordinate to those of the child who is.

Interests other than those of children

The courts are steadily extending the list of exceptions to the legislative requirement that welfare interests should be given priority.

Public law proceedings provide numerous examples of areas where other interests take priority over those of children. Most obviously in an offence context the welfare interests of a child are now clearly subordinate to the interests of justice; judicial attention focuses on accountability, punishment, proportionality, reparation and social rehabilitation rather than on the indicators of welfare listed above. In applications for secure accommodation orders matters other than welfare, such as public safety, govern the outcome. Similarly in the context of immigration issues, priority is given to upholding the government's immigration laws rather than to welfare. The courts have even adjusted the balance between the weighting given to welfare interests and to the standard of proof required in civil cases. In *Re H and R*[4] where the House of Lords, confirming that the standard of proof required was the normal balance of probabilities, went on to state a new rule that the more serious the allegation the more substantial the evidence should be. The welfare interests of a child are not even a necessary priority for a local authority; as it has a discretion not to initiate proceedings. The ruling of the House of Lords in *X v Bedfordshire CC*[5] confirmed that a local authority cannot be liable for a breach of statutory duty, for negligence nor even for a breach of the common duty of care. This judgment was a significant setback for welfare interests but its standing is now open to question in the light of the decision of the ECHR in *Osman v UK*[6](see, Chap 15).

In private law there would now seem to be a general retreat from judicial intrusion into parenting matters, unless clear notice is served of circumstances in which welfare interests may be compromised. There has been no development carrying as much significance for the welfare interests of children, in terms of reducing the proportion of judicial decisions affecting those interests, than the removal of the welfare test in uncontested matrimonial proceedings. In this context welfare interests are now subordinate to the right of parents not to have their privacy invaded. In contested private proceedings the legislative decision not to provide parity with public proceedings, by standardising arrangements for the representation of welfare interests, indicates an intent to respect those interests as being presumptively private and therefore not necessarily requiring equivalent resources. In adoption, the law continues to place greater importance on the availability of parental consent than on welfare interests when determining whether the legal criteria for an order are satisfied. Welfare interests now give way to property rights in applications for ouster orders and to principles and laws regulating comity between nations in the context of applications made under the Hague Convention.

The courts in recent years have given much attention to balancing welfare interests against the rule that all parties should make a full disclosure of information known to them and having a bearing on the proceedings.[7] For example, in *Re D (Minors)(Adoption Reports: Confidentiality)*[8] the House of Lords ruled that welfare interests could not prevail against the fundamental principle of fairness that a party was entitled to the disclosure of all materials which might be taken into account by a court when reaching a decision adverse to that party; the principle applied with particular force to adoption proceedings. This increasing tendency to treat children like any other parties has also been evident in cases such as *Oxfordshire County Council v M*[9] and *Re L (Police Investigation: Privilege)*[10] where the court ordered disclosure of documents and other material relevant to the future of the child concerned.

The rights and welfare interests of children

The tide is threatening to turn decisively against 'welfare interests'. The discretionary scope for interpretation, decision making and time scales that the term permits sat comfortably within the tight framework of rights and duties that traditionally comprised family law when the latter was grounded on the benchmark of monogamous marital union for life. The proportion of families in which a breakdown in the relationship between spouses or in standards of parental care brought the question of future care arrangements before the courts was then relatively small. When this occurred children were incidental to the main issues, namely the rights and duties of their parents towards each other. Matters affecting upbringing could be accommodated flexibly and with a discernment which sought to protect the child's home with his or her primary carer. But the goal posts have shifted in family law.

From upholding the legal coherence, inviolability and autonomy of the marital family unit, where the whole was so much more than the sum of its parts, the law has evolved to a point where it now recognises and facilitates the freedom of individual family members to form, leave and re-form family units more or less at will. This upheaval in private law, and the acceptance of a more flexible, fluid interpretation of what constitutes 'family' and 'home', has been accompanied by a greater awareness and more effective detection of child abuse in a public law context. From both sectors of family law, the numbers of litigants presenting the courts with issues relating to the long-term care arrangements of children have multiplied in recent years. The resulting pressure from the volume, the range and the complexity of these issues has led to a move in the law away from the traditional rather generalised protective regard for welfare interests towards a more assertive and sharply focussed approach.

Rights

The concept of 'children's rights' is virtually without any history in this jurisdiction. It has its genesis in welfare interests. Having mutated from an earlier role played by welfare, in the experience of family breakdown as a significant social phenomenon in such common law jurisdictions as the US and from an evolving series of European Conventions, it is now becoming an increasingly powerful presence within and outside the law of this jurisdiction. The step from welfare interests to rights is one which has been made in order to equip children to take their place in an adversarial court system where the numbers of adult litigants, the costs and the shortage of court time might otherwise cause their interests to be treated in a cursory, subservient and paternalistic fashion. But, as Fortin J has commented "showing a greater regard for a child's welfare is not the same as showing a greater regard for their rights".[11]

Regard for rights rather than for welfare interests, necessitates attentiveness to a more extensive set of legal machinery. The fact of party status, entitlement to legal aid, access to a range of professional support and representation and full exposure to the dynamics of adversarial family law proceedings are among the more prominent accompaniments of a rights approach. Inescapably, it also brings with it a sharp focus on adjudication rather than mediation as the preferred means of resolving disputes; a 'winners and losers' outcome is the fully intended objective of the process.

Following the judgment of the European Court of Human Rights in *Osman*,[12] and given the imminent introduction of the Human Rights Act 1998, there can be little doubt that UK law is going to have to make room for a new and more positive rights enforcement approach to children's interests. Until then, the challenging observation of Fortin J, remains to be disproved:

> There is the real danger that the language of rights is becoming a form of political correctness used to mask claims made on behalf of children which might not otherwise escape legal analysis.[13]

Rights, consent and welfare interests

There is no greater indicator of respect for the individual in civil law than the extent to which it requires or permits the consent of that individual in the determination of issues affecting him or her. In family proceedings, issues affecting children can be located on a spectrum from welfare interests to rights according to whether or not they meet that test. Applying the test brings into play two important factors: the competence of the child as determined by his or her age and understanding; and the gravity or complexity of the issue.

The argument that the viability of consent is subject to the variables of the age and understanding of the child in question is not wholly convincing; effective and independent representation should enable the child's voice to be heard. Clearly consent is unassailably authentic and authoritative if given directly and with full understanding by the child concerned. Of those instances where this is not possible, there are only a small proportion where skilled professionals could not determine the child's wishes; which, admittedly, may be quite different from his or her welfare interests. This approach is already being developed to some degree in public law proceedings under the 1989 Act.

The argument that the gravity or complexity of an issue is such that a child should be protected from bearing responsibility for the decisions to be made in respect of it, is more difficult to overcome but can be met in the same way. It may be accepted that complex facts or a complex interplay of facts cannot necessarily be simplified to a point where the child concerned can have sufficient grasp of them to give a reasoned consent. Arguably, the capacity to take a dispassionate view of matters intimately concerning the subject, identify and weigh possible options and their respective short and long-term implications for all concerned and then make a choice, requires a high level of maturity. No matter how 'mature for their age' a child is manifestly not able to be wholly objective about themselves nor to fully understand and be objective about individuals upon whom he or she is psychologically dependent. Maturity is also a necessary precondition for appreciating the full gravity of some matters. To be objective about issues concerning the subject's life or death or, for example, to take decisions relating to urgent and acute treatment the outcome of which presents the prospect of multiple disability, requires a level of knowledge and perhaps some experience of matters which a child will not have acquired. But the proportion of such cases is small and some will be sufficiently susceptible to professional exploration and interpretation to enable the child concerned to give an authentic decision.

So, the traditional view that children are debarred from being decision-makers, or from giving or withholding a binding consent to the decisions of others, because they lack competence due to their age and understanding or to the gravity or complexity of the issues and their consequences, is no longer sustainable given the range of professional skills now available. However, in a small proportion of cases, that combination of variables will be such as to prevent consent and/or indicate that the child concerned should be protected from having to bear decision-making responsibility. In this latter category it seems wholly appropriate that the law should continue to take a welfare oriented approach. In all other cases it should be possible to facilitate an appropriate level of decision-making by the child concerned balanced by such regard for his or her welfare interests as required by the particular facts of a case. There seems no good reason why such an approach should be confined to family proceedings or indeed to courts of law.

The legal system and family courts

The changes over the last decade, to the content, weighting and scope of the welfare principle have yet to be wholly reflected in adjustments to that part of the legal system charged with giving effect to it. Changes in administrative and procedural law have not kept pace with those in the substantive law relating to children. The current appropriateness of the legal system, in terms of court structures, proceedings and administrative systems, as a facilitative medium for determining matters affecting the rights and welfare interests of children must be questioned. The comparative advantages of a family court must be re-examined.

Disadvantages of current legal system for welfare interests

Access to the court, followed by representation in proceedings, are the most basic prerequisites for operationalising the role of the welfare principle. But in juvenile justice cases, the availability of legal aid and representation by a solicitor are by no means automatic. In private law cases, acquiring party status and legal representation are equally uncertain. In neither is a guardian *ad litem*, from the GAL panel, available. Only in public law proceedings initiated under the 1989 Act are full party status, legal aid and representation by both a solicitor and a guardian *ad litem* definitely available, if not always deemed appropriate. Once commenced a number of other factors further infringe upon the welfare of the child concerned. These include, for example, the delay until hearing, the proliferation of officials, the formality and obscurity of proceedings and the lack of in-court, user friendly, child support services. Access, from the perspective of the children concerned, is as much about taking away psychological barriers caused by anxiety, lack of information and an absence of caring support as it is about legal aid.

The welfare interests of children are not confinable to those matters which are currently dealt with under the umbrella of family proceedings. Family proceedings courts are now shorn of virtually all responsibilities for child support and juvenile justice and are unable to scrutinise local authority performance of their child care duties. This prevents judicial application of the welfare principle in contexts which are crucial to the upbringing of the children concerned. In those matters where this court does have jurisdiction its capacity to give full effect to the welfare principle is inhibited by the structurally embedded adversarial approach to family law. Cases are, for example: commenced by petitioner/applicant/complainant; defended by respondent; solicitors and expert witnesses are partisan; and the child, whose welfare is the focus of the court's concern, may be required to appear as a witness and be subjected to all the stress that this role entails. One characteristic of this traditional approach, particularly inimical to the welfare principle, is the reliance on precedent. The value of applying the paramountcy principle and the welfare checklist to establish an individualised profile of a child's present welfare is largely undone if this is subjected to a standardised rule.

While the legacy of an adversarial structure impedes the implementation of a welfare ethos this has no bearing on another pervasive problem; the welfare principle is applied with an inconsistency which though confusing for legal practitioners must be more so for the children concerned. It should be hastily added that even greater reliance on the value of precedents is not the answer! The 1989 Act has clearly done much to simplify what was previously a wider spread of inconsistency in the role and weighting accorded to welfare, but the problem persists. Currently, the principle is applied differentially according to type of proceedings (family proceedings, adoption, justice) with further differences between proceedings and applications for leave to commence proceedings, and according to whether the child whose welfare is of concern is the child who is the actual subject of proceedings. There are some differences between its role in private as opposed to public proceedings commenced under the 1989 Act. Increasingly, differences are also surfacing in the application of such welfare indicators as 'consent'. A child's right to consent to treatment, for example, does not extend to a right to refuse it. There is no provision requiring the consent of a child the subject of adoption proceedings, nor in respect of planned major changes to home or family life. Where the consent of children aged 16, 14 and 12 is available for a proposed change of surname, it may still be overruled by the court.[14] Age is also proving to be an unreliable predictor of judicial respect for the consent of abducted children the subject of Hague Convention proceedings.

Family court

The arguments for and against a family court are lengthy and have been well rehearsed over the years. Having now travelled a considerable distance down this road, with the introduction of family proceedings under the 1989 Act, it may be appropriate to consider how those arguments have been affected by that experience. Arguably, some new factors have recently come into play and other longstanding ones have become more apparent which suggest that the time is rapidly approaching when it will be difficult to continue denying the considerable advantages that a family court would provide for deciding and managing the application of the law to matters affecting the welfare of children.

Integrated system

The need for a more fully integrated and coherent system, for example, is becoming more pressing as the number and range of associated professionals increase. Organising and timetabling court business is made more difficult by the fact that other agency agendas control the availability of staff needed for court hearings. Assigning welfare staff (from the GAL panel, the court welfare service and local authority) to management by a centralised court administrative system would simplify the organisational tasks, ensure consistency in professional staff input to proceedings as well as permitting inter-disciplinary teamwork and training. Given the nature of problems presenting before the court and the increased reliance on expert witnesses, an intake team which included provision of a psycho-social assessment service would be appropriate. A more fully rounded system would be possible if the central core consisted of legal staff, from judiciary and solicitors to court clerks, who were similarly trained and assigned to work exclusively as specialists in the law relating to children. However, it has to be acknowledged that such a 'one-stop shop' model, the aspiration of many administrators in service provision sectors, may not be welcomed in an area of work where the independent contribution of the professionals concerned is so highly valued.

Holistic approach to legal proceedings

Children are children first and the subjects of proceedings second. The manner in which very young children are currently processed by the criminal justice system is certainly incompatible with their welfare interests and, given the accompanying incomprehension, probably incompatible with the requirements of justice. The present distinction between justice and care proceedings, between public and private and between courts and tribunals is not very logical when the issues directly relate to welfare interests. The developmental needs of children provide the common denominator and the basic argument for treating them within our legal system both differently from adults and similarly in respect of their peers. While the outcome of offence based and care based proceedings will inevitably have to be different, the process or processes whereby children pass through the legal system must be benchmarked to the same welfare standards which guarantee respect for age related developmental needs. Regardless of the reason for their appearance, every child should be assured of the same sympathetic reception before a specially designed court imbued with a welfare ethos, which facilitates their comprehension and meaningful participation, is staffed by personnel with child care training and has other specialist professional support services readily available.

A family court would be integrated horizontally as well as vertically. It would have jurisdiction to deal with all matters affecting the welfare interests of a child; not just the present family proceedings but also criminal matters, child support, housing and such other issues where there is a significant welfare component. It would provide uniform rights to full party status, access to legal aid, direct participation and to professional representation. It would be able to co-ordinate the legal and therapeutic response to welfare issues. It would rely more upon mediation and orders which adjust than on adjudication and orders which create winners and losers. It should have some authority to contribute to the on-going planning, management and review processes of all children who appear before it.

Welfare consistency

Processing all welfare related matters through the same court and by the same team of specialists would promote greater consistency in the recognition of welfare indices and in the use of welfare related disposal options. While accepting that the same objective conduct or circumstance will be experienced subjectively by each child with a correspondingly individualised impact on their welfare interests, it should still be possible to achieve a greater degree of harmonisation in judicial practice than prevails at present. It should, for example, facilitate a more consistent judicial response in relation to matters such as the age-related consents of children. Such concentrated expertise should also assist in differentiating between welfare interests, other interests and the rights of children.

Conclusion

It is not the intention that this book should make a case for establishing a family court. The objective has been no more than to put on record the history of the welfare principle as this has affected the law relating to children in the UK. However, it is difficult to avoid concluding that the complexities now surrounding the role, functions and weighting of the principle, its differential application in certain types of proceedings, coupled with the influence from outside the jurisdiction and the uncertain line currently drawn between interests and rights point towards a family court as being a best option for the future management of welfare related proceedings. It would provide an opportunity for a new synthesis of principle, the co-ordination of professional expertise and the promotion of coherence within the family law and related legal system of the UK.

Notes

1 See, *Alhaji Mohamed v Knott* [1969] 1 QB 1 involving a married couple who were Nigerian Muslims; he in his mid-twenties, she perhaps 13, maybe 11 and suffering from venereal disease contracted as a consequence of her husband's promiscuity. An application for a care order in respect of the girl was rejected, the court explaining that the couple were validly married and within the context of their culture the girl would not be considered to be sufficiently at risk to warrant coercive state intervention.

Also, see, *R v Derrivierre* (1969) 53 Cr. App.Rep. 637 where a West Indian father, charged with assaulting his 12 year old disobedient son by punching him in the face, was found not guilty on the grounds that within his culture this would constitute acceptable chastisement.

2 [1998]

3 Protected by the ruling in *J v C* [1969] 1 All ER 788, which prohibits judicial scrutiny of discretionary exercises of local authority statutory powers.

4 [1996] 1 FLR 80.

5 [1995] 2 FLR 276.

6 [1999] 1 FLR 193.

7 [1995] 2 FLR 687.

8 [1995] 4 All ER 385. See, also, *Re G (A Minor)(Social Worker: Disclosure)* [1996] 2 All ER 65.

9 [1994] 2 FLR 175.

10 [1996] 2 WLR 1235.

11 Fortin, J., *Children's Rights and the Developing Law*, London, Butterworths, p 226.

12 *Op cit*.

13 *Op cit*, p 31.

14 See, *Re B (Change of Surname)* [1996] 1 FLR 791.

Bibliography

Books and Articles

Alston, P., (ed), *The Best Interests of the Child*, Clarendon, 1994.

Archard, D., *Children: Rights and Childhood*, London, Routledge, 1993.

Bainham, A., *Children: The Modern Law*, 2nd ed., Family Law, 1998.

Bainham, A., *Children, Parents and the State*, Sweet & Maxwell, 1988.

Bean, P., and Melville, J., *Lost Children of the Empire*, London, Unwin Hyman, 1989.

Bedingfield, D., *The Child in Need*, London, Family Law, 1998.

Blackstone, W., *Commentaries on the Laws of England*, vol. 1, 7th ed, Clarendon, 1775.

Bowlby, J., *Attachment*, London, Penguin, 1969.

Bowlby, J., *Child Care and the Growth of Love*, London, Penguin, 1972.

Bromley, P.M., *Bromley's Family Law*, 8th ed., Butterworths, 1992.

Cavadino, P., (ed), *Children Who Kill*, Waterside Press, 1996.

Cretney, S.M., *Family Law*, 3rd ed., Sweet & Maxwell, 1997.

Cromack, V., 'Welfare of the Child – Conflicting Interests and Conflicting Principles; Re T and E (Proceedings: Conflicting Interests)', in *Child and Family Law Quarterly*, Vol 8, No 1 1996.

Dingwall, R., Eekelaar, J., and Murray, T, *The Protection of Children: State Intervention and Family Life*, Blackwell, 1983.

Douglas, G., & Sebba L., (eds.), *Children's Rights and Traditional Values* , Ashgate, 1998.

Downie, A., '*A Metropolitan Borough Council v DB* and *Re C (Detention: Medical Treatment)* Extra-statutory confinement – detention and treatment under the inherent jurisdiction' in *Child and Family Law Quarterly*, Vol 10, N0 1, 1998.

Eekelaar, J., *The Emergence of Children's Rights*, 6 Oxford Journal of Legal Studies 161, 1986.

Eekelaar, J., 'The Eclipse of Parents Rights' in *Law Quarterly Review*, Vol 102, No 4, 1986.

Eekelaar, J., *The Importance of Thinking that Children have Rights* (1992) 6 IJLF 221.

Eekelaar, J., and Dingwall, R., *The Reform of Child Care Law – A Practical Guide to the Children Act 1989*, London, Routledge, 1990.

Eekelaar, J., and Thandabantu, N.,*The Changing Family*, Hart Publishing, Oxford, 1998.

Farrington, D., *Understanding and Preventing Youth Crime*, Joseph Rowntree Foundation, 1996.

Farson, R., *Birthrights*, Penguin, 1974.

Fisher, D., *The Concept of the Welfare of the Child*, Edinburgh University (unpublished Ph.D.), 1978.

Flekkoy, M., *A Voice for Children*, London, Jessica Kingsley, 1991.
Fortin, J., *Children's Rights and the Developing Law*, Butterworths, 1998.
Foster, H., and Freed, D., *A Bill of Rights for Children*, 6 Family Law Quarterly 343, 1972.
Fox Harding, L., *Perspectives in Child Care Policy*, Longman, 1997.
Freeman, M., *State, Law and the Family*, London, Sweet & Maxwell, 1984.
Freeman, M., *The Moral Status of Children*, Martinus Nijhoff, Kluwer Law, 1997.
Freeman, M., *Children, Their Families and The Law*, Macmillan, 1998.
Freeman, M., 'Cultural Pluralism and the Rights of the Child', in *The Changing Family*, 1998.
Freeman, M., & Veerman P., *The Ideologies of Children's Rights*, Martinus Nijhoff, Kluwer Law, 1992.
Freestone, D., *Children and the Law*, Hull University Press, 1990.
Goldstein, J., Freud, A & Solnit, A.H., *Beyond the Best Interests of the Child*, Collier Macmillan, 1973.
Goldstein, J., Freud, A & Solnit, A.H., *In the Best Interests of the Child*, Free Press, Collier Macmillan, 1986.
Hafen, 'Puberty, Privacy and Protection: the Risks of Children's Rights' *American Bar Association Journal* 63, 1383, 1977.
Hodgson, D., *The Historical Development and 'Internationalisation' of the Chidren's Rights Movement*, Fam Law 252, August, 1992.
Hoggett, B., *Parents and Children*, 4th ed, Sweet and Maxwell, 1993.
Holt, J., *Escape from Childhood: the Needs and Rights of Children*, E.P. Dutton and Co., 1974.
Kellmer-Pringle, M., *The Needs of Children*, London, Hutchinson, 1980.
Kilkelly, 'The UN Committee on the Rights of the Child – an evaluation in the light of recent UK experience', in *Child and Family Law Quarterly*, 1996.
King, M., (ed.),*Childhood, Welfare & Justice*, Batsford Academic and Educational Ltd, 1981.
King, M., and Trowell J., *Children's Welfare and the Law: The Limits of Legal Intervention*, Sage, 1992.
Lansdown, G., *Taking Part: Children's Participation in Decision Making*, IPPR, London, 1995.
Lansdown, G., 'Implementing the UN Convention on the Rights of the Child in the UK', in *Child and Family Law Quarterly*, 1995.
Lowe, N., and White, R., *Wards of Court*, London, Butterworths, 1979.
Maidment, S., *Child Custody and Divorce*, London, Croom Helm, 1985.
Manton, J., *Mary Carpenter and the Children of the Streets*, Heinemann, 1976.
Mnookin, R.H., *Child, Family and State*, Little, Brown & Company, 1978.
Mnookin, R.H., *In the Interests of Children*, London, Chatto & Windus, 1985.
Mnookin, R.H. & Coons, J.E., 'Towards a Theory of Children's Rights', *Harvard Law Bulletin*, vol. 28, No. 3, 1977, pp. 18-22.
Morris, A., & Giller, H., Szwed, E & Geach, H., *Justice for Children*, Macmillan, 1980.
Pinchbeck, I. & Hewitt, M., *Children in English Society*, vol. 2, Routledge & Kegan Paul, 1973.
Platt, A., *The Child Savers*, Chicago, University of Chicago Press, 1969.
Purdy, L., *In Their Best Interests? The Case Against Equal Rights for Children*, Cornell University Press, 1992.

Rodham, H., *Children Under the Law*, Harvard Educational Review 43, 487, 1973.
Rosenbaum, M., and Newell, P., *Taking Children Seriously: A Proposal for a Children's Rights Commissioner*, Calouste Gulbenkian Foundation, 1991.
Rutter, M., *Maternal Deprivation Reassessed*, Penguin, 1972.
Spencer and Flin, *The Evidence of Children*, (2nd ed), Blackstone Press, 1993.
Thorpe, J., 'Independent Representation for Children' in *Family Law*, Vol 20, 1994.
Tizard, B., *Adoption: A Second Chance*, Open Books, London, 1977.
Veerman, P.E., *The Rights of the Child and the Changing Images of Childhood*, Martinus Nijhoff, Kluwer Law, 1991.
White, R., Carr, P., and Lowe, N., *The Children Act in Practice*, Butterworths, 1995.

Reports

Adoption: The Future, (Cmnd 2288) HMSO, 1993.
A Child in Trust: The Report of the Panel of Inquiry into the Circumstances surrounding the death of Jasmine Beckford , London Borough of Brent, 1985.
Children in Trouble, Home Office, Cmnd 3601, HMSO, 1968.
Child Protection: Messages from Research, HMSO, 1995.
Concluding Observations of the Committee on the Rights of the Child: United Kingdom of Great Britain and Northern Ireland, United Nations, 1995.
Crime, Justice and Protecting the Public, Home Office, White Paper Cmnd 965, HMSO, 1990.
Law Commission Report No. 15, *Arrangements for the Care and Upbringing of Children*, No 15, HMSO, 1968.
Law Commission Report No. 91 *Review of Child Law: Guardianship*, HMSO, 1985.
Law Commission Report No. 96 *Custody*, HMSO, 1986.
Law Commission Working Paper No. 100 *Review of Child Law: Care, Supervision and Interim Orders in Custody Proceedings*, HMSO, 1987.
Law Commission Working Paper No. 101 *Review of Child Law: Wards of Court* HMSO, 1987.
Law Commission Report No. 172 *Review of Child Law: Guardianship and Custody* HMSO, 1988.
Law Commission Report No. 207 *Family Law, Domestic Violence and Occupation of the Family Home*, HMSO, 1992.
Levy, A., and Kahan, B., *The Pindown Experience and the Protection of Children*, Stafford, Staffs C.C., 1991.
Looking to the Future, HMSO, 1993.
Report of the Advisory Group on Video Evidence , (the Pigot Report), Home Office, 1989.
Report of the Care of Children Committee, (the Curtis Report), HMSO, 1946.
Report of the Committee of Inquiry into the Care and Supervision Provided for Maria Colwell, Dept of Social Security, HMSO, London, 1974.
Report of the Committee on Children and Young Persons, (the Ingleby Report) Home Office, Cmnd 1191, HMSO, 1960.
Report of the Inquiry into Child Abuse in Cleveland 1987 (1988) (Cmnd 412).
Report of the Royal Commission on Marriage and Divorce, (the Morton Report), Cmnd 9678, 1956.
Rights Brought Home: The Human Rights Bill, Home Office, White Paper Cmnd 3782, HMSO, 1997.

The Child, the Family and the Young Offender, Home Office, Cmnd 2742, HMSO, 1965.
The UK'S First Report to the U.N. Committee on the Rights of the Child, The UN Convention on the Rights of the Child, HMSO, 1994.
UK Agenda for Children, the Children's Rights Development Unit, 1994.
Utting, W., *Children in the Public Care: A Review of Residential Child Care*, London, HMSO, 1991.
Working Together Under the Children Act 1989: A guide to arrangements for inter-agency co-operation for the protection of children from abuse, HMSO, 1991.

Index